MANDATORY COOPERATION UNDER INTERNATIONAL LAW

Humanity in the twenty-first century faces serious global challenges and crises, including pandemics, nuclear proliferation, violent extremism, refugee migration, and climate change. None of these calamities can be averted without robust international cooperation. Yet, national leaders often assume that because their states are sovereign under international law, they are free to opt in or out of international cooperation as they see fit. This book challenges conventional wisdom by showing that international law requires states to cooperate with one another to address matters of international concern – even in the absence of treaty-based obligations. Within the past several decades, requirements to cooperate have become firmly embedded in the international legal regimes governing oceans, transboundary rivers, disputed territories, pollution, international security, and human rights, among other topics. Whenever states address matters of common concern, international law requires that they work together as good neighbors for their mutual benefit. This title is also available as Open Access on Cambridge Core.

EVAN J. CRIDDLE is the Ernest W. Goodrich Professor, Associate Dean for Research and Faculty Development, and Director of the Center for International Law and Policy at William & Mary Law School. His scholarship has appeared in the *American Journal of International Law*, *European Journal of International Law*, and *Yale Journal of International Law*.

EVAN FOX-DECENT is Professor, Canada Research Chair in Cosmopolitan Law and Justice, and President of the Association of McGill Professors of Law at McGill University, Faculty of Law. Other titles include *Sovereignty's Promise: The State as Fiduciary* (2012) and *Fiduciaries of Humanity: How International Law Constitutes Authority* (2016) (with Evan J. Criddle).

MANDATORY COOPERATION UNDER INTERNATIONAL LAW

EVAN J. CRIDDLE
William & Mary Law School
EVAN FOX-DECENT
McGill University

CAMBRIDGE
UNIVERSITY PRESS

CAMBRIDGE
UNIVERSITY PRESS

Shaftesbury Road, Cambridge CB2 8EA, United Kingdom

One Liberty Plaza, 20th Floor, New York, NY 10006, USA

477 Williamstown Road, Port Melbourne, VIC 3207, Australia

314–321, 3rd Floor, Plot 3, Splendor Forum, Jasola District Centre,
New Delhi – 110025, India

Cambridge University Press is part of Cambridge University Press & Assessment,
a department of the University of Cambridge.

We share the University's mission to contribute to society through the pursuit of
education, learning and research at the highest international levels of excellence.

www.cambridge.org
Information on this title: www.cambridge.org/9781009305020

DOI: 10.1017/9781009304993

First published 2026

Cover image: Aerial view on the colorful old town of Guanajuato, Mexico, © Marco Bottigelli

A catalogue record for this publication is available from the British Library

A Cataloging-in-Publication data record for this book is available from the Library of Congress

ISBN 978-1-009-30502-0 Hardback

We are at an inflection point in history . . . Humanity's welfare – and, indeed, humanity's very future – depend on solidarity and working together as a global family to achieve common goals.

For people, for the planet, for prosperity and for peace.

UN Secretary-General António Guterres
Our Common Agenda – Report of the Secretary General (2021)

For Elin, our peacemaker
EJC

For my colleagues
EFD

CONTENTS

CONTENTS

PREFACE

Existential threats are powerful motivators for international cooperation. In the twentieth century, two calamitous world wars and the advent of nuclear weapons persuaded states to embrace cooperation as humanity's last, best chance for survival. Through the Charter of the United Nations, states pledged to resolve their disputes through peaceful means and work together to suppress threats to international peace and security. Although the international community has not always honored these commitments, cooperation through the United Nations has been the principal institutional means for affirming sovereign equality and pursuing lasting peace.

The threats humanity faces today are no less dire and, in some respects, even more complex than those that catalyzed the establishment of the United Nations. Great power rivalries, violent extremism, and nuclear weapons continue to jeopardize international peace and human security. Accelerating technological innovation and a globally networked digital economy have spawned new dangers. Computer viruses, political disinformation, and financial contagion now traverse national borders at lightning speed. Scientific advances that deliver miraculous cures for disease can also be abused to create terrifying bioweapons. And looming over these challenges is the great existential crisis of our time: global climate change, which threatens to inflict catastrophic environmental harm on a planetary scale. None of these calamities can be averted without robust international cooperation.

A substantial obstacle to progress in countering these threats is the conventional wisdom that states are free to decide for themselves whether to embrace international cooperation. National leaders often assume that because their states enjoy sovereignty under international law, they may sit on the sidelines while other states pursue solutions to global challenges. Within the past several years, for example, some states have refused to contribute meaningfully to international efforts to combat climate change, protect refugees, suppress cyberattacks, prevent global pandemics, and prosecute international crimes. While these policies have attracted criticism, few question the prevailing wisdom that international law permits states to opt out of international cooperation if they so choose.

In this book, we argue that the prevailing wisdom is mistaken: international law requires states to cooperate with one another to address matters of transnational or global concern – even in the absence of treaty-based obligations. Obligations of international cooperation are now firmly embedded in the international legal regimes that govern transboundary rivers, oceans, disputed territories, landlocked states, pollution, international peace and security, and human rights, among other topics. We describe these regimes as cases of *mandatory cooperation.*

A recent advisory opinion from the International Tribunal for the Law of the Sea (ITLOS) illustrates the power and promise of mandatory cooperation. In December 2022, a consortium of small-island nations threatened by sea level rise asked ITLOS to clarify states' legal obligations with respect to the impacts of atmospheric pollution on the global marine environment. The tribunal delivered its opinion in May 2024.[1] Citing the UN Convention on the Law of the Sea (UNCLOS), the tribunal declared that international law requires states to cooperate with one another to protect the oceans from warming temperatures, acidification, and other harm from greenhouse gas emissions.[2] This obligation to cooperate applies to all states under "general international law," the tribunal asserted, regardless of whether states have joined UNCLOS,[3] and it is not limited to states' voluntarily determined contributions under the 2016 Paris Climate Agreement.[4] Thus, the tribunal concluded that states must participate as full and active partners in the fight against climate change, accepting their fair share of global greenhouse gas reductions, even if they have not voluntarily undertaken this legal obligation.[5]

1 Request for an Advisory Opinion Submitted by the Commission of Small Island States on Climate Change and International Law, Advisory Opinion, 21 May 2024, ITLOS (quoting UNCLOS article 197).

2 Ibid. para. 321 (quoting UNCLOS article 197).

3 Ibid. para. 296 (citing MOX Plant (Ireland/U.K.), Provisional Measures, Order of 3 Dec. 2001, ITLOS Reports 2001, p. 95, at p. 110, para. 82).

4 Ibid. para. 311.

5 Following the ITLOS tribunal's advisory opinion, the International Court of Justice and the Inter-American Court of Human Rights both issued advisory opinions concurring that customary international law obligates states to cooperate in suppressing and mitigating the adverse effects of climate change. See Obligations of States in Respect of Climate Change, Advisory Opinion, 2025 ICJ Rep., paras. 140–42, 301–15 (23 July); Climate Emergency and

Setting aside the advisory opinion's far-reaching implications for climate change law and policy, the tribunal's assertion that states must cooperate to fight climate change raises important questions about the role of international cooperation within the international legal order. For example, if states are obligated to cooperate with one another to prevent and suppress climate change, what is the basis for that obligation? When must states pursue international cooperation, and when are they free to chart their own independent course? And which kinds of requirements – substantive or procedural – are entailed in mandatory cooperation?

In this book, we develop an account of mandatory cooperation that answers these questions. Our account defends three theses. First, we argue that *mandatory cooperation is based on, and responsive to, the principle of sovereign equality*. As enshrined in the UN Charter and other instruments, the principle of sovereign equality requires states to respect one another as formal equals, possessing equivalent sovereign rights and authority, regardless of the disparities in resources, power, and influence that otherwise inform their relations. The sovereign equality of states reflects the equal rights and self-determination of their peoples. International courts and tribunals also bear special responsibilities to affirm states' equality before the law. An important application of the principle of sovereign equality, we argue, is that a state may not hold itself out as judge and party to the same cause (*nemo iudex in causa sua*) with respect to matters that touch and concern other states' rights and authority. Whenever a state cannot exercise its sovereign powers without impacting matters subject to another state's competency, there is a risk that it will undermine the principle of sovereign equality. The only way to resolve this potential conflict, consistent with the principle of sovereign equality, is for the states concerned to negotiate or otherwise reach a peaceful settlement through international cooperation. Respect for sovereign equality implies that states must work together to address common concerns. This is the basis for mandatory cooperation under international law, we argue.

Our account of the legal basis for mandatory cooperation leads to a second thesis: *mandatory cooperation applies whenever states lack exclusive sovereign rights or authority with respect to a matter of international concern*. An important function of international law is to distribute authority among states, establishing spheres within which states possess mutually exclusive sovereign jurisdiction. These spheres of

Human Rights, Inter-Am. Ct. H.R, Advisory Opinion OC-32/25, 29 May 2025, paras. 247–65.

mutually exclusive jurisdiction make it possible for peoples around the world to practice self-determination free from foreign domination.

In some settings, however, states do not have mutually exclusive rights or authority under international law, raising the possibility that the exercise of power by one state might have the effect of subordinating other states. When this is the case, respect for sovereign equality mandates international cooperation. These insights allow us to identify four categories of cases in which mandatory cooperation applies: (1) unsettled jurisdiction, (2) concurrent jurisdiction, (3) jointly shared jurisdiction, and (4) rights conflicts. These four categories account for all of the diverse settings in which international law currently recognizes obligations of mandatory cooperation. As we shall see, these categories also draw attention to other sectors of international law where the international community has been slow to recognize mandatory cooperation thus far, but where respect for sovereign equality arguably requires states to cooperate (e.g., refugee protection, regulating international cartels, and so on).

Our third thesis is that *mandatory cooperation imposes a common set of substantive and procedural requirements whenever it applies*. Substantively, states must endeavor to resolve their disputes in accordance with equitable principles, paying due regard to other states' sovereign rights and authority. Procedurally, states must investigate, consult, and negotiate with one another in good faith. If negotiations fail, states must pursue mediation, arbitration, adjudication, or other third-party dispute resolution. These requirements ensure that when states lack exclusive rights or authority, they can nonetheless resolve their disputes in a manner that affirms their equal sovereignty.

Significantly, our account of mandatory cooperation is firmly grounded in state practice and the judgments of international courts and tribunals. Rather than reason from first principles toward an ideal theory that might be only dimly realized in legal practice, we provide a "rational reconstruction" of mandatory cooperation:[6] we take the actual practice and self-understanding of states and international institutions seriously as the object of our analysis, and we seek to distill a principled justification that best explains this practice and self-understanding. Across the thirteen chapters that follow, we make the case that mandatory cooperation is a set of substantive and procedural requirements common to the distinct contexts addressed in those chapters. Taken together, these requirements

[6] Jürgen Habermas, *Between Facts and Norms: Contributions to a Discourse Theory of Law and Democracy* (William Rehg transl., Cambridge: MIT Press, 1996), p. 82.

are a feature of general international law that it is best explained and justified by reference to the principle of sovereign equality.

This book construes sovereign equality as a constitutional norm of international law. By invoking constitutionalism, we do not mean to claim that international law has a written constitution akin to those that govern some domestic legal systems.[7] Instead, following the usage of most scholars who study international constitutionalism, we employ the term to emphasize how certain international norms perform constitutional functions, facilitating international law's development as a coherent normative system.[8] We argue that the principle of sovereign equality operates as an organizing idea of international legal order by governing a number of international law's constitutional aspects, including: international law's allocation of equal sovereign authority to states; international law's framework for the production and validity of international customary and treaty norms; and international law's framework for the peaceful resolution of conflicts, including through mandatory cooperation. By requiring states to cooperate with one another to resolve disputes, the principle of sovereign equality restricts the unilateral exercise of sovereign power, spurs states to address common concerns based on shared interests and values, and promotes the growing conformity of the international system with an appropriately international rule of law.

A major theme of this book is that mandatory cooperation's promise has been only partially realized at the quarter mark of the twenty-first century. This should come as no surprise. Legal scholars have recognized that constitutionalization is a process that tends to unfold haltingly, and rarely in a linear fashion.[9] Over the past century, international law has followed a halting and uneven path of constitutionalization, evolving from a thin "law of coexistence" into a more robust "law of cooperation"

[7] For an argument that the UN Charter is a constitution for the international legal system, see Bardo Fassbender, 'The United Nations Charter as Constitution of the International Community' (1998) 36 CJTL 529.

[8] See, e.g., Erika de Wet, 'The International Constitutional Order' (2006) 55 ICLQ 51; Jeffrey L. Dunoff and Joel P. Trachtman, 'A Functional Approach to International Constitutionalization' in Jeffrey L. Dunoff and Joel P. Trachtman (eds.), *Ruling the World? Constitutionalism, International Law, and Global Governance* (New York: Cambridge University Press, 2012) 3; Andreas Paulus, 'International Legal System as a Constitution' in Dunoff and Trachtman (eds.), *Ruling the World?*, at 69; Anne Peters, 'Compensatory Constitutionalism: The Function and Potential of Fundamental International Norms and Structures' (2006) 19 LJIL 579.

[9] Aoife O'Donoghue, *Constitutionalism in Global Constitutionalisation* (Cambridge: Cambridge University Press, 2014), pp. 15–16.

which requires states to work together to address common concerns.[10] The chapters that follow highlight various "constitutional moments"[11] when subfields of international law have shifted decisively to embrace mandatory cooperation. However, the broader historical narrative developed in this book suggests that international law's turn to mandatory cooperation has been a gradual and partial process, reflecting an ongoing paradigm shift in the self-understanding of international law by its practitioners toward a "constitutional mindset."[12]

In recounting the rise of mandatory cooperation, this book illuminates many positive contributions that international law has made in safeguarding humanity from serious threats and promoting the peaceful settlement of disputes. It also highlights the need for further international cooperation to address the new perils of the twenty-first century. As the ITLOS tribunal recognized, international cooperation will be essential in the years to come to prevent and mitigate the adverse environmental impacts of global climate change, including devastating storms, droughts, fires, and sea level rise. Without international cooperation, states will also struggle to protect their people from pandemics, cyberattacks, terrorist violence, and economic upheavals produced by the introduction of artificial intelligence and other new technologies. Mandatory cooperation offers a budding and promising legal framework for facilitating multilateral solutions to these global challenges. Most ambitiously, we hope to persuade the reader that our constitutionalist interpretation of mandatory cooperation offers a plausible explanatory and normative account of the practice as it has developed over the past century. Less ambitiously, the book is a plea for recognizing mandatory cooperation as an organizing idea of international legal order that no credible account of contemporary international law can ignore.

These features of international law could not be more timely or important today. As this book goes to press, resurgent nationalism in some countries has catalyzed an "anti-globalization backlash," unsettling the legal norms and institutions that have sustained international cooperation since World War II.[13] Emboldened by Brexit, the United Kingdom's

[10] Wolfgang Friedmann, *The Changing Structure of International Law* (New Haven, CT: Columbia University Press, 1964), pp. 61–62.

[11] Bruce Ackerman, *We the People: Foundations* (Cambridge, MA: Harvard University Press 1991), pp. 3, 5.

[12] Martti Koskenniemi, 'Constitutionalism as Mindset: Reflection on Kantian Themes About International Law and Globalization' (2007) 8 *Theoretical Inquiries L.* 9.

[13] Eric Posner, 'What Happened to International Law?', Project Syndicate, 16 January 2025.

controversial departure from the European Union, anti-globalists have pressured their governments to abandon multilateral treaties and withdraw from the compulsory jurisdiction of international courts. The United States has exited the World Health Organization, disavowed the Paris Agreement on climate change, and sidelined the World Trade Organization by avoiding its dispute-resolution mechanism and blocking appointments to its Appellate Body. Afghanistan, Burundi, and the Philippines have pulled out of the International Criminal Court. Several states in Latin America and the Caribbean have withdrawn from the compulsory jurisdiction of the Inter-American Court of Human Rights. Meanwhile, some powerful states have taken aggressive measures to expand their spheres of influence in violation of international law, including Russia's military aggression against Ukraine and China's efforts to establish de facto sovereign control over the South China Sea. Since returning to the White House in January 2025, US President Donald Trump has expressed similar imperialistic ambitions, threatening to annex Canada, Gaza, Greenland, and the Panama Canal. These developments have undermined the international legal order established under the UN Charter, which envisions states working together to affirm "the equal rights . . . of nations large and small," to suppress "the scourge of war," and "to establish conditions under which justice and respect for . . . international law can be maintained."[14]

Time will tell whether the current anti-globalization backlash is merely a temporary setback or a more enduring obstacle to international cooperation and the rule of law. As UN Secretary-General António Guterres cautions in the epigraph to this book, humanity has reached a crucial "inflection point in history" beyond which it will no longer be possible for societies to survive and thrive while retreating into isolation within their national borders.[15] International cooperation will be necessary not only to address existential threats, such as nuclear proliferation, deadly pandemics, and climate change, but also to secure humanity's future as a global community governed by the rule of law, and not the unilateral will of powerful states. Mandatory cooperation explains how all states, large and small, can coexist and interact with one another within a legal framework that makes sovereign equality and global justice possible. At a time when national authorities around the world are revisiting their

[14] UN Charter pmbl.

[15] UN Secretary-General António Guterrez, *Our Common Agenda – Report of the Secretary General* (New York: United Nations 2021), p. 3, available at www.un.org/en/content/common-agenda-report/assets/pdf/Common_Agenda_Report_English.pdf.

commitments to international norms and institutions, this book illuminates what is at stake in the choice between cooperation and unilateralism – what humanity stands to gain when states honor their legal obligations to work together as good neighbors, and what humanity will lose if they do not.

ACKNOWLEDGMENTS

No scholar is an island. Many wonderful colleagues and friends have encouraged our work on this project and have offered feedback on portions of this manuscript and a related article, including Payam Akhavan, Thomas Burelli, Jay Butler, Mikael Cleverley, Anthony Colangelo, Nancy Combs, John Coyle, François Crépeau, Jonathan Crock, Kristina Daugirdas, M.J. Durkee, Andreas Føllesdal, Fergus Green, Nienke Grossman, Andrea Harrington, Thomas Hochmann, Richard Janda, Silje Aambø Langvatn, David Lefkowitz, David Luban, Patrick Macklem, Frédéric Mégret, Nathan Oman, Marcus Patberg, Carmen Pavel, Steven Ratner, Darryl Robinson, Clara Lopez Rodriguez, Leila Sadat, Theresa Squatrito, Paul Stephan, Oisin Suttle, Cora True-Frost, Ozlem Ulgen, Samantha Velluti, Johan Wibye, and Peer Zumbansen; several anonymous reviewers for the *American Journal of International Law* and Cambridge University Press; and workshop participants at Cumberland Lodge, McGill University, the University of Oslo, the University of Richmond, and William & Mary Law School. We are fortunate to have worked on this project with a bevy of talented research assistants, including Justin Apperson, Giusto Amadeo Boccheni, Kathy Bacuta, Brittany Besser, Dorronda Bordley, Boaz Campbell, Oliver Chan, Peter Cox, Jenna Daley, Marie-Laure Dufour, Luke Foley, Erin Gaide, Matthew Griffin, Steven Haig, Gabriel Ibrahim, Michael Jordan, Brooke Lowell, Joanne Murray, Janhvi Patel, Elizabeth Raymakers, Jeyle Sanchez, Sun Shen, Celine Song, Grant Toler, Ryan Walkenhorst, Mark Wilson, and Lexi Zerillo. We also gratefully acknowledge that this book would not have been possible without the sustaining support of our home institutions, the McGill University Faculty of Law and William & Mary Law School. We thank colleagues at McGill's Faculty of Law for their solidarity and support as the Faculty unionized–and led further unionization across McGill–while this book was taking form. As always, we express love and appreciation to our families: Anika, Isaac, Andrew, Elin, Claire, and Lucie (for Evan Criddle) and Adriana, Maya, and Ronin (for Evan Fox-Decent).

The authors thank the Canada Research Chair in Cosmopolitan Law and Justice and the Social Science and Humanities Research Council of Canada for funding that made open access possible.

ABBREVIATIONS

AJIL –	*American Journal of International Law*
AJIL Supp. –	*American Journal of International Law Supplement*
AYBIL –	*Australian Yearbook of International Law*
BJIL –	*Berkeley Journal of International Law*
BYBIL –	*British Yearbook of International Law*
CJTL –	*Columbia Journal of Transnational Law*
EJIL –	*European Journal of International Law*
ETS –	*European Treaty Series*
GLJ –	*Georgetown Law Journal*
HILJ –	*Harvard International Law Journal*
HLR –	*Harvard Law Review*
HRQ –	*Human Rights Quarterly*
ICJ Rep. –	*Reports of the International Court of Justice*
ICLQ –	*International and Comparative Law Quarterly*
ILM –	*International Legal Materials*
ILR –	*International Law Reports*
ITLOS Rep. –	*Reports of the International Tribunal for the Law of the Sea*
LJIL –	*Leiden Journal of International Law*
LNTS –	*League of Nations Treaty Series*
PCA –	*Permanent Court of Arbitration*
PCIJ –	*Reports of the Permanent Court of International Justice*
RIAA –	*Reports of International Arbitral Awards*
SJIL –	*Stanford Journal of International Law*
TIAS –	*Treaties and Other International Acts Series*
TLCP –	*Transnational Law and Contemporary Problems*
UNTS –	*United Nations Treaty Series*
US –	*United States Reports*
UST –	*United States Treaties*
VJIL –	*Virginia Journal of International Law*
YBILC –	*Yearbook of the International Law Commission*
YJIL –	*Yale Journal of International Law*
YLJ –	*Yale Law Journal*

1

Introduction: From Sovereign Equality to Mandatory Cooperation

Unilateralism or Cooperation?

On February 24, 2022, Russian President Vladimir Putin stunned the world by announcing in a televised address that Russia would conduct a "special military operation" against Ukraine. According to Putin, Russia would not stand idly by while "far-right nationalists and neo-Nazis in Ukraine" committed "genocide" against pro-Russian separatists. Military intervention was also a necessary exercise of self-defense, Putin argued, because Ukraine's warming relations with the North Atlantic Treaty Organization (NATO) could eventually bring advanced western weaponry to Russia's doorstep. "Russia cannot feel safe, develop, and exist while facing a permanent threat from the territory of today's Ukraine," Putin asserted.[1] Moments later, Russian tank columns pierced Ukraine's borders from multiple directions as missiles rained down on Kyiv.[2]

While Ukraine was resisting Russia on the battlefield, it also mounted a vigorous legal defense. Just two days after Russia launched its invasion, Ukraine instituted proceedings against Russia in the International Court of Justice (ICJ), a tribunal established under the United Nations (UN) Charter to adjudicate disputes between states.[3] Ukraine urged the Court to adjudge and declare that Russia's accusations of genocide against separatists in eastern Ukraine were unfounded, having no basis in fact or international law. Ukraine also asked the ICJ to grant provisional

[1] 'Transcript: Vladimir Putin's Televised Address on Ukraine', Bloomberg News, 24 February 2022. NATO countries denied the accusation that they planned to invite Ukraine to join the alliance.

[2] Jessie Yueng et al., 'Russia Attacks Ukraine', CNN, 24 February 2022.

[3] Allegations of Genocide Under the Convention on the Prevention and Punishment of the Crime of Genocide (Ukr./Russ.), Provisional Measures Order, 16 March 2022. The ICJ also occasionally issues advisory opinions at the request of UN bodies.

measures requiring Russia to suspend its invasion while legal proceedings continued before the Court.[4] Russia declined to appear for oral argument but contested Ukraine's application, asserting that the ICJ lacked jurisdiction over the case.[5]

While Ukraine's application was pending before the ICJ, the international community rebuked Russia in the strongest possible terms. On March 2, 2022, the UN General Assembly met in emergency session and voted overwhelmingly in favor of a resolution condemning Putin's televised speech, deploring Russia's invasion, and demanding that Russia "immediately, completely and unconditionally withdraw all of its military forces from the territory of Ukraine within its internationally recognized borders."[6] Two weeks later, the ICJ took note of the General Assembly's resolution in an order granting Ukraine's request for provisional measures and directed Russia to suspend its military operations in Ukraine.[7] The European Court of Human Rights (ECtHR) also granted interim measures at Ukraine's request, instructing Russia "to refrain from military attacks against civilians and civilian objects, including residential premises, emergency vehicles and other specially protected civilian objects, such as schools and hospitals."[8]

Russia refused to change course. Shrugging off the interim orders from the ICJ and the ECtHR, Russia continued to pound Ukrainian cities with missiles, artillery, and aerial attacks. In his annual Victory Day speech from Red Square, Putin repeated his grievances against Ukraine and defended Russia's "pre-emptive strike" as "forced, timely, and the only correct decision. A decision by a sovereign, strong, and independent country."[9] According to Putin, Russia's status as an independent

[4] Ibid. pp. 2–3.

[5] Ibid. p. 5. On February 2, 2024, the ICJ concluded that it possessed jurisdiction over the dispute pursuant to the Genocide Convention. Allegations of Genocide Under the Convention on the Prevention and Punishment of Genocide (Ukr./Russ.), 2 Feb. 2024, pp. 36, 56–59, paras. 58, 149, 151.

[6] GA Res. A/RES/ES-11/1, paras. 1–4 (2 March 2022). The final vote was 141–5, with 35 abstaining. 'General Assembly Resolution Demands End to Russian Offensive in Ukraine', UN News, 2 March 2022, https://news.un.org/en/story/2022/03/1113152. The five votes against were cast by Russia, Belarus, North Korea, Syria, and Eritrea. The United States voted in favor.

[7] Ibid. p. 15, para. 76 and p. 17, para. 81.

[8] 'The European Court Grants Urgent Interim Measures in Application Concerning Russian Military Operations on Ukrainian Territory', Press Release, Eur. Ct. Hum. Rts., 1 March 2022.

[9] 'Transcript of President Vladimir Putin's Victory Parade Speech on Red Square', 9 May 2022, http://en.kremlin.ru/events/president/transcripts/68366.

sovereign meant that it was entitled to decide for itself whether its attacks against Ukraine were legally justified – without regard to other states' views or the considered judgments of international courts.

On February 24, 2025, the third anniversary of the invasion, the UN General Assembly met in emergency session and passed two further resolutions. The first resolution reaffirmed the General Assembly's earlier condemnation of the invasion and reiterated "its demand that the Russian Federation immediately, completely and unconditionally withdraw all of its military forces from the territory of Ukraine."[10] The resolution likewise called for a peaceful resolution to the conflict "consistent with the [UN] Charter, including its principles of sovereign equality and territorial integrity of States."[11]

Mariana Betsa, Ukraine's Deputy Foreign Minister, introduced this resolution on behalf of fifty-three state cosponsors. She accused Russia of aiming to replace "the world based on international law" with a "world based on the rule of force."[12] She characterized Ukraine's struggle as seeking a world in which states are not segregated into "predators and prey."[13] Denouncing the Great Power politics that preceded the United Nations, she said that Ukraine was "fighting for a world which cannot be divided by another Molotov-Ribbentrop Pact ... where a future of a nation cannot be determined [by foreign powers] at another Yalta Conference."[14] In other words, Betsa presented Ukraine as defending the world order envisioned in the UN Charter under which all sovereign states are entitled to equal recognition and respect under the rule of international law.

A second General Assembly resolution adopted the same day originated in a proposal from the United States. One week earlier, the United States had held talks with Russia in Saudi Arabia to discuss resolution of the Russia–Ukraine war, without inviting participation from Ukraine or other European nations.[15] At the subsequent General Assembly emergency session, the United States introduced a draft resolution that

[10] GA Res. A/RES/ES-11/7 (25 Feb. 2025), paras 1–4.

[11] Ibid. para. 2.

[12] 'Statement by Deputy Minister for Foreign Affairs of Ukraine H.E. Mariana Betsa at the 11th Emergency Special Session of the UN General Assembly', 24 Feb. 2025, https://un.mfa.gov.ua/en/news/statement-deputy-minister-foreign-affairs-ukraine-he-mariana-betsa-11th-emergency-special-session-un-general-assembly.

[13] Ibid.

[14] Ibid.

[15] 'US and Russia Agree to Explore Mutual Opportunities of End to Ukraine War', The Guardian (18 Feb. 2025).

mourned the loss of life in Ukraine and reiterated the United Nations' mandate "to maintain international peace and security and to peacefully settle disputes," but declined to condemn Russia, demand Russian withdrawal, or affirm the core UN principles of sovereign equality and territorial integrity.[16] The US draft called for a "swift end to the conflict" and "a lasting peace," but without specifying anything about how this was to happen or the nature of the peace envisioned.[17] Ultimately, European states amended the draft to reaffirm the General Assembly's commitment to "the sovereignty, independence, unity and territorial integrity of Ukraine," with a further stipulation that the "swift end to the conflict" must take the form of a "just, lasting and comprehensive peace . . . in line with the Charter of the United Nations and the principles of sovereign equality and territorial integrity of States."[18]

The content of the two February 24, 2025, General Assembly resolutions was hardly groundbreaking; they essentially echoed previous resolutions. What made the resolutions remarkable was that the United States declined to support them, despite having voted for a resolution with near-identical content two years prior.[19] The United States stunned the world by joining Russia, Belarus, Hungary, Israel, North Korea, Sudan, and eleven other states in voting against the first resolution. Ninety-three states voted in favor while 65 abstained, marking a sharp overall decline from the 2023 resolution, which garnered 141 votes for, 7 against, and 32 abstentions.[20] When called to vote on the second resolution, the United States abstained. That resolution passed with ninety-three in favor, eight against, and seventy-three abstentions.[21]

The United States' votes on these resolutions reveal a dramatic shift under the Trump Administration toward an attitude of tolerance, if not outright support, for an international regime of Great Power dominance. The United States' policy shift also seems to have persuaded many other states to back away from expressly defending the UN Charter's vision of a world that is not divided into "predators and prey." By declining to support resolutions affirming the principles of sovereign equality and the

16 A/ES-11/L.11 (21 Feb. 2025).

17 Ibid.

18 The Path to Peace, GA Res. A/RES/ES-11/8 (24 Feb. 2025).

19 See Principles of the Charter of the United Nations Underlying a Comprehensive, Just and Lasting Peace in Ukraine, GA Res. A/RES/ES-11/6 (23 Feb. 2023). There were 141 in favor to 7 opposed, with 32 abstentions.

20 Ibid.; GA Res. A/ES-11/7 (voting record).

21 GA Res. A/ES-11/8 (voting record).

territorial integrity of states, the United States breathed new life into a conception of state sovereignty that had fallen into disrepute during the twentieth century. According to that conception, espoused in Putin's public statements defending Russia's invasion of Ukraine, sovereigns as "uncommanded commanders" are not subject to any superior authority.[22] They therefore are free to choose whether to undertake international obligations, as well as to interpret those obligations for themselves. On this understanding, sovereigns have unqualified discretion to decide whether to cooperate with other states on matters of common concern or adopt a recalcitrant or even belligerent approach. In recognition of its salient features, throughout this book we refer to this conception of state sovereignty as *unilateralist*, *absolutist*, or *voluntarist*. A distinguishing feature of this conception is the idea that states are entitled to exercise their sovereign rights and authority however they wish, subject only to those limitations that they voluntarily embrace.

Ukraine's appeal to international institutions in response to Russia's invasion reflects a different conception of state sovereignty. International institutions like the General Assembly, the ICJ, and the ECtHR are predicated on understanding sovereigns as legal equals interacting within an international legal system that imposes certain obligations on all states. Under this conception of international legal order, the principle that states are equally sovereign means that they are not entitled to exercise authority over one another unilaterally, including by asserting the prerogative to act as final arbiters for the international legality of their own actions (*nemo iudex in causa sua*). Instead, to respect sovereign equality under international law, states sometimes *must* engage cooperatively with others. That is, they must engage in what we will call *mandatory cooperation*. This means that states must pursue peaceful dispute resolution and may resort to force only for limited reasons, such as self-defense, and then only in a limited manner. We generally refer to this conception of international legal order as *constitutional*, although we also sometimes describe it as *equitable*.

The argument of this book is that when states disagree over matters of mutual or common concern, the constitutional model now undergirds and constitutes international law's dominant framework for interstate dispute resolution, establishing requirements of mandatory

[22] H. L. A. Hart, 'Positivism and the Separation of Law and Morals' (1958) 71 HLR 593, 603 (critiquing John Austin's command theory of law according to which law consists in commands backed by force of an uncommanded commander).

cooperation. Procedurally, mandatory cooperation imposes an obligation to consult and investigate, negotiate in good faith, and seek third-party dispute resolution if negotiation fails to yield an amicable outcome. Substantively, mandatory cooperation looks to equitable principles to limit the exercise of sovereign rights in order to take account of the legitimate interests of other states and foreign peoples. For instance, we shall see that mandatory cooperation limits how upstream states may use a waterway on which foreign nationals in a downstream state depend. Mandatory cooperation also limits states' authority to apportion migratory fisheries, conduct maritime delimitation, and regulate transit through their territory. Exploring these and other topics, we will show that mandatory cooperation reflects an equitable conception of sovereignty. Conceptualizing sovereignty in this manner not only clarifies international law's current requirements (*lex lata*) but also offers legal principles to guide the law's progressive development in areas where mandatory cooperation has yet to take firm hold (*lex ferenda*).

To illustrate the continuing tensions between the voluntarist and constitutional conceptions of sovereignty, this chapter further explores how these dueling approaches have been expressed throughout the blood-soaked history of Russia's efforts to establish sovereignty over Ukraine. We then flesh out what we mean by a "constitutional" conception of sovereignty, and we explain how this conception supports the equitable requirements of mandatory cooperation under contemporary international law. The chapter concludes with a brief roadmap for the remainder of the book.

Into the Valley of Death

With territory extending into the Black Sea from southern Ukraine, the Crimean Peninsula has been a theatre of frequent and brutal wars for centuries. Catherine the Great of Russia annexed Crimea in 1783 after several decades of territorial conflict with the Ottoman Empire.[23] Seventy years later, the Crimean War (1853–1856) pitted Russia against the combined might of the Ottoman Empire, France, Britain, and Sardinia, with devastating results. Russia lost 400,000 soldiers in the conflict, and the verdant peninsula was laid waste as "[w]ar devoured every vine, tree,

[23] Kelly O'Neal, *Claiming Crimea: A History of Catherine the Great's Southern Empire* (New Haven: Yale University Press, 2017), pp. 1–2, 16–18.

or blade of grass in its path."[24] The brute ferocity of the conflict inspired Lord Tennyson's iconic 1854 poem, *The Charge of the Light Brigade*, which begins:

Half a league, half a league,
Half a league onward,
All in the valley of Death
Rode the six hundred.
"Forward, the Light Brigade!
Charge for the guns!" he said.
Into the valley of Death
Rode the six hundred.
"Forward, the Light Brigade!"
Was there a man dismayed?
Not though the soldier knew
Someone had blundered.
Theirs not to make reply,
Theirs not to reason why,
Theirs but to do and die.
Into the valley of Death
Rode the six hundred.[25]

To Tennyson, the errant charge of the Light Brigade into withering cannon fire captured the heroism of individual soldiers caught up in a seemingly senseless international conflict marked by savage violence, extreme misery, and frequent mishaps. Reflecting on his service as a Russian captain in Sevastopol during this period, Leo Tolstoy offered a similarly bleak assessment of the prospects for enduring peace, observing that a dispute that had "not been solved by diplomacy will still less be solved by powder and blood."[26]

The subsequent history of Russian involvement in Crimea confirmed Tolstoy's fears. In the Treaty of Paris, which ended the Crimean War, Russia agreed to refrain from establishing military bases on the Black Sea in exchange for retaining sovereignty over much of Crimea, but the promised demilitarization did not last. In 1870, Russia unilaterally repudiated the Treaty's Black Sea clauses and proceeded to rebuild its

[24] Mara Kozelsky, *Crimea in War and Transformation* (New York: Oxford University Press, 2018), pp. 2–3.

[25] Alfred, Lord Tennyson, 'The Charge of the Light Brigade'.

[26] Leo Tolstoy, 'Sevastopol in May 1855', *Sevastopol (Stories)*, translated by Isabel F. Hapgood (London: Walter Scott Publishing Co., 1888), p. 38.

navy, reigniting regional tensions.[27] Decades later, in 1954, the Soviet Union incorporated Crimea into what was then the Ukrainian Soviet Socialist Republic. When the Soviet Union collapsed in 1991, Crimea became part of the newly independent Ukraine as an autonomous republic. The 1997 Treaty of Friendship, Cooperation and Partnership between Russia and Ukraine officially recognized Ukraine's sovereignty over Crimea.[28] As with the Treaty of Paris, however, this agreement proved to be fragile.

On February 22, 2014, the Euromaidan protests in Ukraine prompted pro-Kremlin President Viktor Yanukovych and many of his ministers to flee Kyiv. An interim government in favor of integration with the European Union replaced the Yanukovych regime and repealed the official status of the Russian language, sparking pro-Russian demonstrations in the south and east of Ukraine, including in Crimea.[29] On February 27, armed soldiers operating without identifying markings on their fatigues seized control of the Crimean legislature and other government buildings, raising the Russian flag. Although Putin described these "little green men" as self-defense units created by residents of Crimea,[30] they were later identified as Russian special forces.[31]

Already hostile to the pro-EU government in Kyiv, and with yet-unidentified soldiers arriving in greater numbers daily to occupy airfields, ports, and other public venues, the Crimean provincial legislature organized a referendum on independence. The reported vote on March 16, 2014, was 95.5 percent in favor of seceding from Ukraine and joining Russia, with 83 percent turnout, though the process and its results were widely condemned.[32] On March 17, the provincial legislature declared the Republic of Crimea an independent nation, and on that

[27] W. E. Mosse, 'The End of the Crimean System: England, Russia and the Neutrality of the Black Sea 1870–71' (1961) IV *Hist. J.* 164, 167.

[28] Treaty of Friendship, Cooperation and Partnership between the Russian Federation and Ukraine, Kyiv, 31 May 1997, Rus.-Ukr., ceased to operate from 1 April 2019 onward ("Treaty of Friendship").

[29] Michael Kofman et al., 'Lessons from Russia's Operations in Crimea and Eastern Ukraine', *Santa Monica: RAND Corporation* (2017), p. 33.

[30] 'Vladimir Putin Answered Journalists' Questions on the Situation in Ukraine', Presidential Press Service, 4 March 2014, http://en.kremlin.ru/events/president/news/20366.

[31] Alexey Nikolsky, 'Little, Green and Polite: the Creation of Russian Special Operations Forces', in Colby Howard and Ruslan Pukhov (eds.), *Brothers Armed: Military Aspects of the Crisis in Ukraine* (Minneapolis: East View Press, 2014), pp. 124–125.

[32] Ilya Somin, 'Russian Government Agency Reveals Fraudulent Nature of the Crimean Referendum Results', Washington Post, 6 May 2014.

same day renounced its independence and applied to join the Russian Federation.[33] Putin immediately granted the request, purporting to annex Crimea into the Russian Federation.[34]

The next day, the European Union denounced Russia's aggression and the Crimean referendum, declaring that "the sovereignty, territorial integrity and independence of Ukraine must be respected. The European Union does neither recognize the illegal and illegitimate referendum in Crimea nor its outcome. The European Union does not and will not recognize the annexation of Crimea and Sevastopol to the Russian Federation."[35]

Russia was subsequently ousted from the Group of Eight, and both the Russian state and key national leaders faced economic sanctions.[36] The UN General Assembly also rejected the referendum and affirmed "the sovereignty, political independence, unity and territorial integrity of Ukraine within its internationally recognized borders."[37]

Russia's aggression against Ukraine extended that same year to the eastern Donetsk and Luhansk provinces, known collectively as the Donbas. In March 2014, ethnic Russians in the Donbas launched protests in response to the Euromaidan protests and the ousting of Yanukovych. Armed separatist groups supported by Russia seized provincial legislatures and government buildings across the Donbas.[38] Separatists in Donetsk proclaimed the Donetsk People's Republic on April 7, 2014. Other insurgents in Luhansk declared the Luhansk People's Republic on April 27.[39] Ukraine replied with an "Anti-Terrorist Operation" that would eventually retake much of the territory that had been lost in the preceding months.[40] Russian support for the separatists escalated. Russia

33 Luke Harding and Shaun Walker, 'Crimea Applies to Be Part of Russian Federation After Vote to Leave Ukraine', Guardian, 17 March 2014.

34 'Ukraine Crisis: Putin Signs Russia-Crimea Treaty', BBC, 18 March 2014.

35 Herman Van Rompuy and José Manuel Barroso, 'Joint Statement on Crimea', European Union Delegation to the United Nations, 18 March 2014.

36 European Commission, 'The Hague Declaration Following the G7 Meeting' 24 March 2014; 'Council Implementing Regulation (EU) No 477/2014' Official Journal of the European Union 137, no. 3. 5 December 2014; 'Treasury Sanctions Russian Officials, Members of the Russian Leadership's Inner Circle, and an Entity for Involvement in the Situation in Ukraine', US Treasury Department, 20 March 2014.

37 GA Res. A/Res/68/262, Territorial Integrity of Ukraine, art. 1 (27 March 2014).

38 Oksana Grytsenko, 'Armed Pro-Russian Insurgents in Luhansk Say They Are Ready for Police Raid', Kyiv Post, 12 April 2014.

39 'Ukraine Crisis: Protesters Declare Donetsk "Republic"', BBC News, 7 April 2014.

40 'Lessons from Russia's Operations in Crimea and Eastern Ukraine', p. 44.

deployed some 4,000 regular troops across the border, where they defeated Ukrainian forces in the Battle of Ilovaisk.[41]

Shortly thereafter, the Organization for Security and Cooperation in Europe organized peace talks in Minsk, Belarus, leading to the two sides concluding the Minsk Protocol ceasefire agreement on September 5, 2014.[42] The agreement drew a demarcation line across roughly the eastern third of the Donbas, leaving control of the ceasefire territory (and the Ukraine–Russian border within it) with separatists and Russia.[43] The agreement soon collapsed when Donbas separatists began a fresh offensive in January 2015.[44] A subsequent and more comprehensive ceasefire agreement (Minsk II) was concluded on February 12, 2015, but sporadic fighting continued in the Donbas.[45]

Five years later, the twenty-ninth attempt at a "full ceasefire" came into effect on July 27, 2020.[46] A period of relative calm followed the truce, with Ukraine reporting just twenty-five soldiers killed in the conflict zone in the first three months of 2021, compared with fifty the year before.[47] This brief lull would prove to be the calm before the storm. The following year, Putin's February 24 speech launched Russia's full-scale invasion of Ukraine.

At the time of writing, the conflict in Ukraine has ground on for nearly three years with no end in sight. Although Ukraine managed to repulse Russia's initial drive to take Kyiv,[48] Russia has continued its offensive operations in Ukraine's eastern and southern regions, seeking to extend its control from the Donbas to Crimea and beyond.[49] The war has taken a heavy human toll. By May 2022, the UN High Commissioner for Refugees reported that more than six million people had fled Ukraine

41 'Serving Russian Soldiers on Leave Fighting Ukrainian Troops Alongside Rebels, Pro-Russian Separatist Leader Says', Telegraph, 28 August 2014.

42 Protocol on the outcome of consultations of the Trilateral Contact Group on joint steps aimed at the implementation of the Peace Plan of the President of Ukraine, P. Poroshenko, and the initiatives of the President of the Russian Federation, V. Putin, S/2015/135.

43 'Ukraine Deal with Pro-Russian Rebels at Minsk Talks', BBC News, 20 September 2014.

44 Shaun Walker and Oksana Grytsenko, 'Ukraine Forces Admit Loss of Donetsk Airport to Rebels', Guardian, 21 January 2015.

45 'Ukraine Crisis: Leaders Agree Peace Roadmap', BBC News, 12 February 2015.

46 'Deal Reached for East Ukraine Ceasefire from July 27', Reuters, 22 July 2020.

47 'Ukraine Conflict: Moscow Could "Defend" Russia-backed Rebels', BBC News, 9 April 2021.

48 'What's Happened in the 100 Days Since Russia Invaded Ukraine', CBC News, 3 June 2022.

49 'Ukraine War in Maps: Tracking the Russian Invasion', BBC News, 19 November 2024.

and a total of eight million had been displaced.[50] The numbers of dead and wounded are contested, but on all accounts reach into the hundreds of thousands.[51] Scores of Ukraine's cities, or large parts of them, have been reduced to rubble.

Two Models of Sovereignty

We have spent some time recounting Russia's tumultuous history in Ukraine because it illuminates vividly two models of state sovereignty under international law. Russia's annexation of Crimea under Catherine the Great and the subsequent prosecution of the Crimean War took place under what Oona Hathaway and Scott Shapiro have called the rules of the "Old World Order."[52] The Old World Order accepted war as a permissible means for redressing wrongs and accorded sovereigns absolute and unreviewable authority to determine whether there was just cause for war.[53] Hence, when Catherine first annexed Crimea, and when Nicholas I later battled the Ottomans and their allies in the Crimean War, the sovereigns involved had exclusive and absolute power to go to war, annex foreign lands, or sue for peace. Cooperation with allies was based on good will and a common purpose, while cooperation with the counterparties to a peace treaty was based on assent to the treaty and its terms. Properly understood, then, the legal permissibility of war and conquest under the Old World Order was not its foundational or organizing principle, but rather a consequence of the absolute, exclusive, and unilaterally enforceable sovereign power held by states.

Russia's purported annexation of Crimea in 2014 suggests a commitment on Russia's part to the same unilateralist understanding of its sovereign power.[54] Russia intervened solely and unilaterally – amid widespread international condemnation – seizing control of public institutions to stage a faux referendum and annex Crimea to the Russian Federation. As noted above, however, both the UN General Assembly and the European Union have refused to recognize Russia's attempted

[50] 'Ukraine, Other Conflicts Push Forcibly Displaced Total over 100 Million for First Time', UNHCR, 23 May 2022, www.unhcr.org/us/news/news-releases/unhcr-ukraine-other-conflicts-push-forcibly-displaced-total-over-100-million.

[51] 'Troop Deaths, Injuries in Ukraine War Nearing 500,000—NYT Citing US Officials', Reuters, 18 August 2023.

[52] Oona A. Hathaway and Scott J. Shapiro, *The Internationalists: How a Radical Plan to Outlaw War Remade the World* (New York: Simon & Schuster, 2017) pt. I.

[53] Ibid. p. 47.

[54] See ibid. pp. 309–311, 328 (emphasizing this point).

annexation. Moreover, the prevailing international legal context was one in which decisions over Crimea and access to her ports had to be decided by treaty between Ukraine and Russia, as they had been, for a time, with the 1997 Treaty of Friendship.[55] It is noteworthy that Russia and her allies in Crimea went ahead with a referendum in 2014 which, even if in reality just a sham, suggests that Russia did not believe it could simply raise its flag over Crimea and expect the world to recognize its annexation. Although decision-makers in Moscow might have subscribed to a unilateralist understanding of sovereignty, they plainly knew that the international community did not. To receive broader international recognition, any settlement of the Crimean crisis would have to be achieved through free negotiation or third-party dispute settlement rather than military conquest or other unilateral coercion.

Much the same can be said of the Russian intervention in the Donbas between 2014 and 2022. Although fighting in the Donbas continued sporadically from 2014 onward, the parties negotiated and agreed to a host of admittedly short-lived ceasefire agreements. In other words, there was available all along an international legal framework to support a pacific end to the conflict. It is revealing that despite the outright wartime violence and the frequent collapse of ceasefires, the parties nonetheless continued to engage in regular negotiations. Such steady participation in peace talks during a time of active fighting reflected the parties' recognition that the international community now regards negotiation and mediation – not armed conflict – as the preferred means to resolve even entrenched territorial disputes. With international law requiring peaceful dispute settlement, both Russia and Ukraine appreciated that they would suffer reputational harm if they refused to participate in peace negotiations, whatever their views of their sovereign prerogatives.

The 2022 invasion of Ukraine essentially enlarged and extended Russian operations that began in the Donbas and Crimea in 2014. Here, too, Russia's invasion was undertaken as a unilateral exercise of force, reflecting Putin's ostensible commitment to an absolutist and exclusive sovereign entitlement to go to war. Nonetheless, Russia has gone to great lengths to attempt to justify its invasion based on settled rules of international law. As noted, Putin claims that Russia is acting in self-defense under Article 51 of the UN Charter,[56] alleging NATO

[55] See Treaty of Friendship, above, n. 28.

[56] UN Charter art. 51 (recognizing "the inherent right of individual or collective self-defence if an armed attack occurs against a Member of the United Nations").

encroachment and danger to Russia from Ukraine. He also justifies Russia's action as humanitarian intervention on behalf of ethnic Russians in the Donbas. While Russia has reserved to itself the prerogative to interpret and apply international norms to its case (e.g., self-defense, humanitarian intervention), it at least pays lip service to those norms as general principles of international law. Russia thus implicitly acknowledges that there is an international legal order that requires states to justify the use of force on limited terms, and it seeks to justify its actions in accordance with those limited terms – including in the United Nations, where it continues to participate alongside other states. Additionally, Russia continues to engage in sponsored talks with Ukraine, discussing matters such as humanitarian corridors and prisoner exchanges. This too suggests a recognition on Russia's part that the international community takes international legal order seriously, and that good faith dialogue and negotiation during times of crisis is part of what it means to be a state in good standing within that order. Thus, even as Russia's invasion reflects a unilateralist assertion of power, flouting the UN Charter's strict prohibition against aggression,[57] its rhetoric demonstrates that in the public forum, at least, it accepts the prevalent international legal framework on the use of force, as well as the expectation that it must cooperate with other states to resolve the conflict in Ukraine by participating in UN meetings and peace talks.

The tension between Russia's unilateral actions and its rhetorical commitment to multilateral norms and institutions reflects two competing understandings of sovereignty. Under one account, sovereignty confers exclusive authority on states to determine their own legal rights and obligations and entitles them to decide for themselves whether those rights and obligations have been violated. This voluntarist conception of sovereignty was a central organizing principle of the Old World Order, which authorized territorial conquest and enabled colonial rule. Some contemporary international legal materials – treaty law, customary law, judicial decisions, and scholarship – continue to presuppose a voluntarist account of sovereign equality. In contrast, the second account of sovereignty envisions states as equal participants within an international legal system that imposes limits on their exercise of sovereign rights and powers. According to this constitutionalist account, states are subject to certain positive

[57] See ibid. art. 2(4) ("All Members shall refrain in their international relations from the threat or use of force against the territorial integrity or political independence of any State").

obligations simply in virtue of their membership and participation in the international legal system, including obligations to resolve their disputes peacefully through good faith negotiation or third-party dispute resolution. Over the past century, the constitutionalist account of sovereignty has emerged as a serious rival to – and, in many respects, has eclipsed – the voluntarist account. Although both accounts endorse sovereign equality as a foundational and organizing principle of international law, they conceptualize the principle differently and draw different implications from it. This is because the two accounts are premised upon fundamentally different visions of international legal order, as we shall now explain.

Voluntarism

Hugo Grotius, the great Dutch international lawyer and diplomat, laid the groundwork for the voluntarist theory of sovereign equality in the early seventeenth century. For Grotius, states on the international stage are akin to individuals in the state of nature; in both contexts, there is no common public authority to offer protection and vindicate rights. However, Grotius did not think that the state of nature was a condition bereft of moral rights and duties. In the state of nature, Grotius claimed, individuals possessed natural rights and powers under the law of nature, including rights to life and bodily integrity.[58] The law of nature likewise recognized in individuals a capacity to possess things rightfully, eventually as property, and to enter binding agreements.[59] In addition to these substantive rights, individuals in the state of nature enjoyed enforcement powers to seek redress for wrongs and act in self-defense.[60] Importantly, individuals under Grotius's law of nature possessed these kinds of natural rights and powers *equally*.[61] They could also transfer these rights and powers to states through "collective agreement."[62]

By analogizing states in international affairs to individuals in the state of nature, Grotius was well placed to model the law of nations on the law of nature.[63] According to Grotius's account, states enjoy sovereign

58 Hugo Grotius, *The Rights of War and Peace* (Richard Tuck ed., Indianapolis: Liberty Fund, 2005) (1625) 1.2.3.

59 Ibid. 1.1.10.1–7; 2.11.1.1.

60 Ibid. 2.20.8.1–5.

61 Ibid. 2.20.9.1–6.

62 Hugo Grotius, *Commentary on the Law of Prize and Booty* (Indianapolis: Liberty Fund, 2006) (1603), p. 87.

63 Grotius, *The Rights of War and Peace*, 1.2.4.

equality in the limited sense that they have equal rights to territorial integrity and equal capacity to enter treaties with other states. They also possess equal enforcement rights exercisable through war to pursue redress for wrongs committed against them or their subjects (including unpaid debts and treaty breaches), self-defense, and punishment of transgressors of the law of nations (sometimes called "punitive war").[64] Crucially, under Grotius's theory states alone were the arbiters of whether they had been wronged, imperiled, or whether the law of nations had been violated; that is, states were entitled to decide unilaterally whether there was just cause to go to war. Furthermore, when states went to war and a victor annexed territory or took spoils, Grotius's solution to the legality of conquest or taking of booty was that might makes right; battlefield success determined and secured title.[65] The main justification Grotius offered was that title to territory and goods taken by the victor had to be settled conclusively so as not "to lay a Foundation for a new War" to recover lost lands and chattels, potentially *ad infinitum*.[66] In the absence of courts or other institutions capable of governing international affairs, Grotius filled the void with the equal sovereign powers of states to assess unilaterally the fitness of their causes, go to war as they deemed justified, and acquire good title to any territory they conquered or prizes they seized. Sovereign equality on Grotius's model was thus fully consistent with an absolutist, voluntarist, and unilateralist understanding of state sovereignty under international law.

For centuries after Grotius, international publicists continued to analogize states in international relations to individuals in the state of nature.[67] Reasoning from this premise, Emmerich de Vattel offered a classic statement of sovereign equality:

> Since men are by nature equal, and their individual rights and obligations the same, as equally coming from nature, Nations, which are composed of men and may be regarded as so many free persons living together in a state of nature, are by nature equal and hold from nature the same obligations and the same rights. Strength or weakness, in this case, counts for nothing.

64 Ibid. 2.1.2.2.

65 Ibid. 3.6.2.1.

66 Ibid. 3.9.4.3.

67 See Richard Tuck, *Natural Rights Theories: Their Origins and Development* (Cambridge: Cambridge University Press, 1979); Richard Tuck, *The Rights of War and Peace: Political Thought and the International Order from Grotius to Kant* (Oxford: Oxford University Press, 1999).

> A dwarf is as much a man as a giant is; a small Republic is no less a sovereign State than the most powerful Kingdom.[68]

Significantly, Vattel disputed Grotius's assertion that might makes right – "Strength or weakness . . . counts for nothing" – insisting that "a small Republic is no less a sovereign state than the most powerful Kingdom."[69] On Vattel's view, therefore, no state was entitled to impose legal obligations on another state unilaterally.[70] Nonetheless, Vattel agreed that because there were no international institutions in a position of authority to establish legal order among states, when disputes arose concerning the interpretation and application of international legal norms, states remained the ultimate arbiters of the legality of their actions.[71] This voluntarist conception of sovereign equality, which Vattel bequeathed to subsequent generations of international lawyers, gives pride of place to the thought that sovereigns exercise power without being subject to the authority of any other sovereign. As the Permanent Court of International Justice (PCIJ) put it in the 1923 *Status of Eastern Carelia* case, "[i]t is well-established in international law that no State can, without its consent, be compelled to submit its disputes with other States either to mediation or arbitration, or any other kind of pacific settlement."[72] On this view, sovereigns are supreme within their jurisdiction and independent in their relations to other sovereigns. The voluntarist view captures some of modern international law's prohibition on unilateralism in that no sovereign state is entitled to dictate terms to another, for such an entitlement would compromise the formal principle of sovereign equality. However, for voluntarists the independence of states also implies that "States have the right to be the judge in their own case" and that without their assent "they are subject to no court or tribunal for the interpretation of the rights conferred upon them by international law."[73] Thus, voluntarists view state consent as the *sine*

[68] Emmerich de Vattel, *The Law of Nations, Or The Principles Of Natural Law Applied to the Conduct and Affairs of Nations and Sovereigns* (Charles D. Fenwick trans., Dobbs Ferry, New York: Oceana Publications, 1964) (1758), Preliminaries, § 18.

[69] Ibid.

[70] Ibid. § 15.

[71] Ibid. §§ 16, 20 (asserting that because states were free, independent, and equal, each possesses the "right of judging" its own actions).

[72] Status of Eastern Carelia, Advisory Opinion, 1923 PCIJ (Ser B) No. 5, p. 27 (23 July).

[73] P. J. Baker, 'The Doctrine of Legal Equality of States' (1923–1924) 4 BYBIL 1, 11 (quoting Sir Frederick Pollock).

qua non – the necessary and sufficient normative condition – of all international obligations.[74]

Voluntarists often invoke *The Lotus*, a 1927 judgment of the PCIJ, as their doctrinal touchstone.[75] In a passage of the judgment that has been endlessly debated, a narrow majority of the Court opined that all "rules of law binding upon States . . . emanate from their own free will as expressed in conventions or by usages generally accepted as expressing principles of law . . . Restrictions upon the independence of States cannot therefore be presumed."[76] According to the Court, states enjoy "a wide measure of discretion, which is only limited in certain cases by prohibitive rules; as regards other cases, every State remains free to adopt the principles which it regards as best and most suitable."[77] From these broad pronouncements, voluntarists have extrapolated a general principle that "whatever is not explicitly prohibited by international law is permitted."[78] Thus, Prosper Weil celebrates *The Lotus* for endorsing a "voluntarist conception of international law" under which states "are bound by a rule of law only because, and to the extent that, they have consented to it. Freedom to act remains the basic principle."[79]

There are significant conceptual problems with this account of international legal order.[80] Recall that an attraction of the theory is that it purports to subscribe to international law's prohibition on unilateralism under which no state can impose terms on another. However, because states are subject only to legal rules or norms to which they consent, it follows that consent is the only means of establishing a rule or norm under international law. Recalcitrant and nonconsenting states therefore

[74] What we characterize as "voluntarism" has also described elsewhere as "consensualism" or "classical international legal positivism," i.e., the idea that "consent is the (pre-legal) criterion giving law its binding force and legitimacy." Jean d'Aspremont and Jörg Kammerhofer, 'Introduction: The Future of International Legal Positivism', in Jean d'Aspremont and Jörg Kammerhofer (eds.), *International Legal Positivism in a Post-Modern World* (Cambridge: Cambridge University Press, 2014), p. 3.

[75] Some more radical political voluntarists are sceptics regarding international law, arguing that treaties and customary law are not really law but rather expressions of, at most, political or moral obligations. See, e.g., John R. Bolton, 'Is There Really "Law" in International Affairs?' (2000) 10 TLCP 1, 4–7.

[76] The Lotus, 1927 PCIJ (Ser. A) No. 10 (7 September), at p. 18.

[77] Ibid. p. 19.

[78] Prosper Weil, "'The Court Cannot Conclude Definitively' . . . Non Liquet Revisited', (1998) 36 CJTL 109, 112.

[79] Weil, "The Court Cannot Decide," p. 113.

[80] Samantha Besson, 'State Consent and Disagreement in International Law-Making: Dissolving the Paradox' (2016) 29 LJIL 289; Allain Pellet, 'The Normative Dilemma: Will and Consent in International Law-Making' (1988–1989) 12 AYBIL 22.

would find themselves subject to few, if any, international legal obligations. They would find themselves effectively outside international legal order, and with a virtually unlimited liberty-right of action – the absolute discretion of the uncommanded commander. Yet, by ceding to nonconsenting states a potentially unlimited liberty-right of action, voluntarism gives these states the liberty-right to decide for themselves the terms on which they will interact with others, regardless of whether the counterparty consents. If a recalcitrant state refuses to agree to fair and equal terms, voluntarism lacks the resources to censure that state from a legal point of view. Under voluntarism, the intractable state will have breached no legal rule to which it was subject.

Our point is not to equate voluntarism with unilateralism, but rather to explain why voluntarism, taken seriously, may permit or collapse into unilateralism within the conception of international legal order it endorses. During the colonial era, voluntarism emboldened states from the Global North to exploit and dominate other political communities for their own gain. In the absence of "prohibitive rules" affirmatively outlawing territorial conquest and colonialism, states used war as an instrument of national policy and built overseas empires on the backs of foreign peoples.[81] While international law no longer permits territorial conquest and colonialism, the voluntarist thinking that enabled those practices continues to drive the idea that states are subject only to legal requirements they have affirmatively endorsed. Voluntarism also lends credence to the idea that states are entitled to judge for themselves whether their conduct is consistent with their obligations under international law. Rather than resolve disputes over the meaning or application of international law through dialogue, negotiation, or third-party dispute resolution, voluntarism suggests that if states have not actively opted in to international cooperation, they are free to go it alone. It is this aspect of voluntarism – the notion that states are entitled to judge the legality of their own actions – that Putin has brandished as both sword and shield to rationalize Russia's aggression against Ukraine and deflect international criticism.

Whatever merit the voluntarist approach may have had in the age of Grotius and Vattel, it no longer accurately describes international legal order in the twenty-first century. Voluntarism stands in tension with international law's contemporary understanding of sovereign equality

[81] Antony Anghie argues that European states and their legal advisers "improvised" the doctrine of sovereignty to deal with "problems relating to colonial order." Antony Anghie, *Imperialism, Sovereignty and the Making of International Law* (Cambridge: Cambridge University Press, 2004), pp. 6–7.

because sovereign equality, we explain now, denotes equal sovereign authority and a formal right to independence from foreign intervention and domination. As formal equals under international law, states are subject to reciprocal duties that safeguard their equal independence. These duties apply to all states, regardless of whether they have affirmatively accepted them via treaty or customary international law.

Constitutionalism

During the same period when the PCIJ was endorsing voluntarism in *The Lotus*, an alternative account of sovereignty was emerging based on the idea that states are members of an international legal order that constrains how they may exercise their rights and powers. In an influential 1920 monograph titled *The Equality of States in International Law*, Professor Edwin DeWitt Dickinson derived sovereign equality from the formal international legal personality of states.[82] Dickinson's conception of sovereign equality was formal, rather than substantive, in that it focused on states' legal status and standing rather than, say, the allocation of military power or material resources. This formal account of sovereign equality had important substantive implications. Like Grotius and Vattel, Dickinson accepted that states were entitled to participate as equals in establishing international law by concluding treaties and contributing to the formation of customary international law. But Dickinson disagreed that each state was entitled to decide for itself whether its conduct satisfied international law. "International persons are equal before the law when they are equally protected in the enjoyment of their rights and equally compelled to fulfill their obligations," Dickinson observed.[83] To respect the principle of sovereign equality, in other words, states must exercise their rights and powers in a way that respects the rights and powers of other states. And when disputes arise, states are entitled to be treated by their peers as formal equals under the rule of law. Accordingly, no state is entitled to hold itself out as the final arbiter of the international legality of its own actions.[84]

82 Edwin DeWitt Dickinson, *The Equality of States in International Law* (Cambridge: Harvard University Press, 1920), pp. 3, 102; see also American Institute of International Law, 'Declaration of the Rights and Duties of Nations' (1916) 10 AJIL 124, 125 ("Every nation is in law and before law the equal of every other nation belonging to the society of nations").

83 Edwin DeWitt Dickinson, *The Equality of States in International Law* (Cambridge: Harvard University Press, 1920), p. 3.

84 Dickinson was not the first international lawyer to frame sovereign equality as a formal legal constraint against great power domination. For decades, Latin American international lawyers had urged great powers of the Global North to take seriously the formal

Implicit in this formal account of sovereign equality is the idea that states interact with one another within an international legal system, not a state of nature. Dickinson observed that "equality before the law is essential to any legal system," and this principle held special significance for international legal order as "the necessary consequence of the denial [to states] of universal empire, and of the claim of separate states to live together in an international society controlled by law."[85] The alternatives to equality before the law for separate states, Dickinson warned, were "universal empire or universal anarchy."[86] Whereas Grotius and Vattel believed that states could judge the legality of their own actions for themselves, Dickinson anticipated that the legitimacy of international legal order would depend on international institutions playing an active role in interpreting international law and resolving international disputes.

The idea that states could look to international institutions for assistance in resolving their disputes had become plausible by the 1920s, when Dickinson published his monograph. A generation earlier, during the Hague Peace Conference of 1899, the international community had established the first Permanent Court of Arbitration (PCA) to handle interstate disputes. Argentina's delegate to the Conference celebrated this development as ensuring "that the political equality of states has ceased to be a fiction and that it abides, established as an obvious reality."[87] The PCA would be followed by the creation of the League of Nations in 1920, and the establishment of the PCIJ, which held its inaugural sitting in 1922. Hence, by the time the PCIJ decided *The Lotus* five years later, the majority's vision of international relations as a state of nature wherein states could generally do as they please was rapidly falling out of favor. The following year witnessed the signing of the Kellogg-Briand Pact, also known as the Pact of Paris, which outlawed "recourse to war for the solution of international controversies" and committed states to settle their disputes exclusively "by pacific means."[88] With the obligation to resolve disputes peacefully and the establishment of international courts and

equality of states when designing international institutions. Robert A. Klein, *Sovereign Equality Among States: The History of an Idea* (Toronto: University of Toronto Press, 1974), pp. 54–85.

85 Ibid.

86 Ibid. p. 335.

87 Ibid. p. 181.

88 Treaty for Renunciation of War arts. I & II, 27 August 1928, 46 Stat. 2343, 94 LNTS 57.

tribunals like the PCA and the PCIJ, states became equal members of an international legal system in which they were no longer free to rely solely on their own independent judgment to determine what international law required of them. By the end of World War II, Dickinson's account of sovereign equality had become the prevailing wisdom among international publicists.[89]

Some members of the *Lotus* Court anticipated and embraced this paradigm shift. The dissenting opinion of Judge Bernard Loder offers an especially clear account. Judge Loder held that states, as equal participants in the international legal system, relate to each other on terms of "mutual independence."[90] For states to be sovereign, they must be independent, and for them all to be independent, they must be independent *mutually* or *equally*. At the heart of Loder's opinion, then, is the constitutional insight that universal independence in a community of formally equal states implies mutual or equal independence. If independence is a necessary condition of sovereignty, then sovereign equality must secure states' independence on equal terms. One sense in which all sovereigns are *equal* is that none are entitled to dictate terms to others unilaterally, and conversely, none can be made to suffer such terms. Under international law, sovereign states are *independent* within their respective spheres of exclusive jurisdiction: none depends on the permission of another to exercise domestic or international public functions.[91] Thus, as Judge Charles Andre Weiss observed in a separate dissenting opinion, international law serves "to harmonize and reconcile the different sovereignties over which it exercises sway."[92]

On this constitutional reading of sovereign equality, international law both empowers states as international legal actors and constrains them in their dealings with other states and nonstate actors. There is now a considerable literature on the constitutionalization of international law, much of which emphasizes how international law

[89] See Lassa Oppenheim, *International Law: A Treatise* (Hersch Lauterpacht ed., London: Longmans, Green & Co., 6th ed., 1947) vol. 1, p. 238, § 115 ("The equality before International Law of all member-States of the Family of Nations is an invariable quality derived from their international personality.").

[90] The Case of the S.S. Lotus, 1927 PCIJ (Ser. A) No. 10, p. 35, para. 106 (7 September) [hereinafter Lotus].

[91] See Schooner Exchange v. McFaddon, 11 US 116, 136–37 (1812) (reasoning based on the "perfect equality and absolute independence of sovereigns" that "[t]he jurisdiction of the nation within its own territory is necessarily exclusive and absolute").

[92] Lotus, above, pp. 40, 44 (Weiss, J., dissenting, but not on this point).

shares with national law certain core commitments to human rights, self-determination, and the rule of law.[93] The constitutional perspective offers a congenial framework within which international law empowers states by recognizing them as the de jure governors of their people at the domestic level and as the de jure representatives of their people in international affairs. International recognition empowers states to establish political and legal order nationally, as well as to enter binding treaties and otherwise represent their people internationally. Crucially, the constitutional perspective foregrounds international legal norms that are constitutive of international legal order as a legal system. In *The Lotus*, Judge Weiss observed that among "these rules there is one which is paramount and which does not even require to be embodied in a treaty: that is the rule sanctioning the *sovereignty of States*," without which "no international law would be possible."[94] This "paramount" rule of state sovereignty is defined, in part, by the principle of sovereign equality, as affirmed in the UN Charter and other authoritative instruments.[95] Thus, the principle of sovereign equality has become a constitutional norm of international law, subjecting states to reciprocal limits that reflect their equal status and secure their mutual independence vis-à-vis one another.

Two Threats to Sovereign Equality

The mutual independence that states enjoy under international law constitutes a form of freedom or liberty. On our view, the liberty of independence has two constitutive elements: a principle of noninterference and

[93] See, e.g., Jan Klabbers, Anne Peters and Geir Ulfstein, *The Constitutionalization of International Law* (Oxford: Oxford University Press 2009); Stephen Gardbaum, 'Human Rights and International Constitutionalism', in Jeffrey L. Dunoff and Joel Trachtman (eds.), *Ruling the World? Constitutionalism, International Law, and Global Governance* (Cambridge: Cambridge University Press, 2012); Anne Peters, 'Compensatory Constitutionalism: The Function and Potential of Fundamental International Norms and Structures' (2006) 19 LJIL 579.

[94] Lotus, above, pp. 40, 44 (italics original).

[95] See, e.g., UN Charter art. 2(1) (stipulating that the United Nations "is based on the principle of the sovereignty equality of all its Members"); UN General Assembly, 'Declaration on Principles of International Law concerning Friendly Relations and Co-operation among States in Accordance with the Charter of the United Nations', UN Doc. A/RES/25/2625 (24 October 1970) [hereinafter Friendly Relations Declaration] (affirming that all states are "judicially equal" and that each "enjoys the rights inherent in full sovereignty").

a principle of nondomination.[96] The principle of noninterference prohibits states from wrongfully interfering with each other through any unilateral act that infringes another state's legal interests or authority. International law's principle of nonintervention can be seen as a salient legal expression of the normative principle of noninterference. The most general formulation of this legal principle in the UN Declaration on Non-Interference provides that "[n]o state has the right to intervene, directly or indirectly, for any reason whatever, in the internal or external affairs of any other State."[97] Consistent with the UN Charter,[98] the Declaration specifically decries "armed intervention" as a prohibited form of conduct, as well as "the use of force to deprive peoples of their national identity" and efforts "directed towards the violent overthrow of the regime of another State."[99] Military aggression, such as Russia's invasion of Ukraine, is an especially striking example of wrongful interference, since one state violates the territorial integrity of another through the unilateral use of force.

The Declaration makes clear, however, that the principle of nonintervention is broader than the principle of noninterference. Specifically, the Declaration avows that *threats* of unilateral acts – and not just unilateral acts themselves – are legally wrongful. The Declaration stipulates that "attempted threats against the personality of the State or against its political, economic and cultural elements are condemned."[100] States may not "use or encourage the use of economic, political or any other type of measures to coerce another State in order to obtain from it the subordination of the exercise of its sovereign rights or to secure from it advantages of any kind."[101] Because the principle of noninterference only explains how actual and wrongful unilateral acts compromise freedom, it cannot explain how unrealized *threats* of those acts compromise

[96] We discuss this conception of freedom as independence as it pertains to human rights bearers in Evan Fox-Decent and Evan J. Criddle, 'The Fiduciary Constitution of Human Rights' (2009) 15 *Legal Theory* 301, 310–311.

[97] UN General Assembly, 'Declaration on the Inadmissibility of Intervention in the Domestic Affairs of States and the Protection of Their Independence and Sovereignty', UN Doc. A/RES/2131(XX) (21 December 1965), para. 1 [hereinafter Declaration on Non-Intervention].

[98] UN Charter art. 2(4) ("All Members shall refrain in their international relations from the threat or use of force against the territorial integrity or political independence of any state, or in any other manner inconsistent with the Purposes of the United Nations.").

[99] Declaration on Non-Intervention, paras. 1–3.

[100] Ibid. para. 1.

[101] Ibid. para. 2. References to "subordination" and securing "advantages" suggest that the coercion referred to in this provision relates more to the threat than the use of force.

freedom.[102] For an account of the wrongfulness of threats and their infringement of liberty, we need the principle of nondomination.

For republicans, domination consists in subjection to the arbitrary will of another and is the chief cause of unfreedom.[103] In the classic example of the enslaved person and the benevolent master, republicanism invites us to imagine a master who wishes only the best for the person enslaved. She treats him like family, supports his hopes and aspirations, encourages his projects, and so on. In short, the master does not interfere with, but rather supports, the enslaved person and his choices. Nonetheless, the individual enslaved is still unfree, republicans assert, because the master is entitled to crack the whip at any time, for any reason (including malicious or spiteful reasons), and to do so with impunity. Republicans point out that this asymmetrical power structure ordinarily leads to bowing, scraping, and a constant sense of unease (if not terror) on the part of the dominated party.[104] But the distinct evil of domination – the evil and unfreedom suffered by the enslaved person of the benevolent master – is simply subjection to the looming threat of arbitrary force against which there is no recourse.

When the Declaration on Non-Intervention prohibits "threats" against a state's "personality" or against its "political, economic, and cultural elements," the Declaration puts into positive legal form the principle of nondomination. A state's personality is the law-created artificial entity to which the words and actions of the state's representatives are attributed when they act in the name of the state.[105] Consequently, certain threats against the state's personality may constitute existential threats. The threat of military aggression and occupation is this kind of threat. And

[102] One can attack the unilateral-act/threat-of-unilateral-act distinction by saying that a threat to act unilaterally is itself a unilateral act. See Matthew H. Kramer, *The Quality of Freedom* (Oxford: Oxford University Press, 2003), ch. 2. The distinction we are making, however, is substantive rather than linguistic or semantic, and could be recast as "actual unilateralism" versus "promised-and-realizable-but-as-yet-unrealized unilateralism." For simplicity, we will stick with "act" and "threat" to mark these categories.

[103] See, e.g., Philip Pettit, *Republicanism: A Theory of Freedom and Government* (Oxford: Oxford University Press,1999) ; Quentin Skinner, *Liberty Before Liberalism* (Cambridge: Cambridge University Press, 1998).

[104] Ibid.

[105] See Thomas Hobbes, *Leviathan with Selected Variants from the Latin Edition of 1668* (Cambridge: Hackett Publishing, Edwin Curely ed., 1994) (1651) ch. 16. Compare Quentin Skinner, 'Hobbes and the Purely Artificial Person of the State' (1999) 7 J. *Pol. Phil.* 1, with David Runciman, 'What Kind of Person Is Hobbes's State? A Reply to Skinner' (2000) 8 *J. Pol. Phil.* 268.

threats against a state's "political, economic, and cultural elements" are likewise threats of wrongful unilateralism. A powerful state may threaten valued public goods in order to impose terms on a weaker state – for example, by threatening to cut off the weaker state's access to fresh water or natural gas if the weaker state does not capitulate to its demands. Notably, Russia used these tactics in 2022, seeking to deter European countries from opposing its aggression against Ukraine.[106] Such threats are arbitrary in the sense that they aim to secure through a unilateral assertion of will the "subordination" of another state or the gaining of "advantages" to which the dominating state has no entitlement.

These features of the Declaration on Non-Intervention reflect a paradigm shift that reshaped international legal order during the middle decades of the twentieth century, one driven in large part by global pressures for decolonization. Throughout the colonial era, international publicists offered pious tributes to the principle of sovereign equality as all the while European nations declined to recognize other peoples around the world as equal sovereigns. As Edward Keene has observed, this approach led to a bifurcated international legal order:

> The European order of toleration [among recognized states] was predicated on the principle that states should respect each other's territorial sovereignty, and hence their equality and independence. By contrast, the extra-European order was based on the principle that sovereignty should be divided across national and territorial boundaries, creating hierarchical institutions through which colonial and imperial powers transmitted the supposed benefits of their civilization to the rest of the world.[107]

By the early twentieth century, this division of the world into fully sovereign states, on the one hand, and "semi-sovereign" states and colonial possessions, on the other, had become conventional wisdom among Western legal scholars, cementing as a formal legal hierarchy the practical subordination of non-Western peoples.[108]

[106] See Emily Rauhala et al., 'Russia Cuts Off Gas to Poland, Bulgaria, Stoking Tensions with EU', Washington Post, 27 April 2022.

[107] Edward Keene, *Beyond the Anarchical State: Grotius, Colonialism and Order in World Politics* (Cambridge: Cambridge University Press, 2002) xi.

[108] See, e.g., John Westlake, *International Law*, in Lassa Oppenhaim (ed.), *The Collected Papers of John Westlake on Public International Law* (Cambridge: Cambridge University Press, 1914), pp. 86–101 (distinguishing equal and independent states from "semi-sovereign states"); Baker, 'The Doctrine of Legal Equality of States', pp. 8–10 (arguing for this reason that "the doctrine of equality has never been consistent with the facts of the international system to which the rules of international law are supposed to apply").

The decolonization movement sought to dismantle these features of the colonial era – not only by extending formally equal statehood to former colonies but also by outlawing foreign intervention and domination wherever and however they might manifest in international relations.[109] In the celebrated 1960 Declaration on the Granting of Independence to Colonial Countries and Peoples (Declaration on Colonial Independence), the UN General Assembly solemnly declared that "[t]he subjection of peoples to alien subjugation, domination, and exploitation constitutes a denial of fundamental human rights, is contrary to the Charter of the United Nations and is an impediment to the promotion of world peace and co-operation."[110] Hence, states must "observe faithfully and strictly" their obligations under the UN Charter to respect the principles of self-determination and nonintervention "on the basis of equality, non-interference in the internal affairs of all States, and respect for the sovereign rights of all peoples and their territorial integrity."[111] A decade later, the General Assembly reaffirmed these principles in its unanimous Declaration on Principles of International Law concerning Friendly Relations and Cooperation among States in accordance with the Charter of the United Nations (Friendly Relations Declaration):

> By virtue of the principle of equal rights and self-determination of peoples enshrined in the Charter of the United Nations, all peoples have the right freely to determine, without external interference, their political status and to pursue their economic, social and cultural development, and every State has the duty to respect this right in accordance with the provisions of the Charter.
>
> Every State has the duty to promote, through joint and separate action, realization of the principle of equal rights and self-determination of peoples, in accordance with the provisions of the Charter, and to render assistance to the United Nations in carrying out the responsibilities entrusted to it by the Charter regarding the implementation of the principle, in order:

(a) To promote friendly relations and co-operation among States; and
(b) To bring a speedy end to colonialism, having due regard to the freely expressed will of the peoples concerned; and bearing in mind

109 See Adom Getachew, *Worldmaking After Empire* (Princeton: Princeton University Press, 2019), p. 2 (arguing "that decolonization was a project of reordering the world . . . to create a domination free and egalitarian international order").

110 Declaration on the Granting of Independence to Colonial Countries and Peoples para. 1, GA Res. 1514(XV), UN Doc A/4684 (14 December 1960) [hereinafter Declaration on Colonial Independence].

111 Ibid. para. 7.

> that subjection of peoples to alien subjugation, domination and exploitation constitutes a violation of the principle, as well as a denial of fundamental human rights, and is contrary to the Charter.[112]

The Declaration on Colonial Independence and the Friendly Relations Declaration underscore that international intervention and domination violate two bedrock norms of contemporary international law. First, intervention and domination are incompatible with the principle of sovereign equality because they subordinate a state's sovereign authority to another's unilateral will. A state that is subject to foreign coercion does not enjoy the mutual independence of sovereign equality. Second, intervention and domination violate the right to self-determination – a people's exclusive privilege to choose the laws and institutions by which it is governed.[113] Whenever a state intervenes unilaterally in another state's exclusive territorial jurisdiction, or threatens to do so, it denies a foreign people their legal privilege to decide for themselves how they will arrange their internal affairs. It consigns them to live under "alien subjugation, domination and exploitation."[114] By prohibiting foreign intervention and domination, contemporary international law prohibits powerful states from reviving territorial conquest and other features of colonial-era unilateralism. Thus, sovereign equality and self-determination complement one another as constitutional foundations for a postcolonial international legal order.

[112] Friendly Relations Declaration; see also Declaration on the Occasion of the Fiftieth Anniversary of the United Nations ¶ 1, GA Res. 50/6, UN GAOR, 50th Sess., Supp. No. 49, UN Doc. A/50/49 (1995) [hereinafter 50th Anniversary Declaration] (declaring that states "reaffirm the right of self-determination of all peoples, taking into account the particular situation of peoples under colonial or other forms of alien domination").

[113] Common Article 1 of the International Covenant on Civil and Political Rights and the International Covenant on Economic, Social and Cultural Rights provide that self-determination is a "right" that belongs to "[a]ll peoples." International Covenant on Civil and Political Rights art. 1, 16 December 1966, S. Exec. Doc. E, 95-2 (1978), 999 UNTS 171, 174; International Covenant on Economic, Social and Cultural Rights art. 1, 3 January 1976, 993 UNTS 3. While international lawyers have debated which peoples may claim the right to self-determination, it is uncontroversial that the right can be claimed (at a minimum) by national polities within their territorial jurisdiction vis-à-vis foreign states. See Tom Sparks, *Self-Determination in the International System: Whose Claim, to What Right?* (Oxford: Hart Publishing, 2023), pp. 4, 19, 22 (explaining how this national polity-based formulation has become firmly established in international law).

[114] Friendly Relations Declaration.

Mandatory Cooperation

By preserving domains within which states are mutually independent, international law aims to safeguard sovereign equality and facilitate national self-determination.[115] During the colonial era, the close connection between independence and sovereign equality led some voluntarists to conflate the two concepts, suggesting that they were synonymous.[116] However, in some contexts, mutual independence is not enough to support a constitutional approach to sovereign equality. The ideal of mutual independence presupposes that state jurisdiction is settled and mutually exclusive, but this premise does not always hold true. Sometimes, state jurisdiction is unsettled, concurrent, or shared jointly. At other times, states hold rights and powers that are in tension with one another, raising the possibility that the exercise of a right or power by one state would adversely impact another state's legal entitlements. In these cases, a state cannot act unilaterally without violating the principle of sovereign equality because any steps it takes on its own with respect to such matters would effectively subordinate another state's legal rights or authority to its policy choices and decisions.

Consider the following scenarios:

- *Unsettled Jurisdiction* – Two neighboring states disagree in good faith over the location of their common border. An important function of international borders is to define the territories within which states are entitled to claim mutual independence. Nonetheless, as long as the location of a border remains unsettled, it may be unclear which state has jurisdiction over the disputed territory. Both states may view the other's territorial claim as wrongful interference with their sovereignty. Without an international legal framework in place to address the dispute, each state may plausibly claim to suffer domination and interference from the other's unilateral assertion of sovereign power.

[115] See Andrew Hurrell, *On Global Order: Power, Values, and the Constitution of International Society* (Oxford: Oxford University Press, 2009), p. 49 (observing that under "a view of international law as the law of a society of states or a 'Family of Nations', . . . each state enjoy[s] a measure of independence from other states and the powers of supreme government over its territory and its people").

[116] See, e.g., Lassa Oppenheim, *International Law: A Treatise*, vol. 1 (London: Longman, Green & Co., 1905), p. 101 (defining sovereignty as "an authority which is independent of any other earthly authority . . . [and] includes therefore independence all around, within and without the borders of the country"); Westlake, *International Law*, pt. I, ch. 87 p. 87 (asserting that "the independence and the full sovereignty of a state are identical").

- *Concurrent Jurisdiction* – A large oil field straddles the maritime boundary between two states. Each state in the exercise of its territorial jurisdiction is entitled to determine how much oil it will extract from the field. However, due to the unitary nature of the field, any oil extracted on one side of the boundary will reduce the volume available on the other side. In this scenario, the sovereign interests of the neighboring states are inextricably connected. Neither can drill for oil without adversely affecting the other's sovereign interests, and either could dominate the other simply by threatening to drill unilaterally.
- *Jointly Shared Jurisdiction* – An international river flows through multiple states on route to the sea. The states concerned conclude a treaty designating the river as a shared resource subject to their joint stewardship and collective administration. Having placed the river under their joint jurisdiction in this manner, any unilateral regulation, use, diversion, or adulteration of the river by a single state would undermine the other states' equal rights and authority under the collective regime.
- *Rights Conflicts* – An organized crime group in State A counterfeits the national currency of State B. International law obligates State A to exercise due diligence to suppress counterfeiting.[117] However, State A is unable to eradicate the counterfeiting operation without foreign assistance due to the organized crime group's power. If State B offered to dispatch police to State A to disrupt the counterfeiting operation, State A might object, invoking its territorial sovereignty as a basis for withholding consent to foreign intervention. However, by exercising its sovereign right to exclude in this way, State A would undermine State B's sovereign authority over its own currency.

At first glance, these scenarios might seem like exceptional cases at the periphery of international legal order. Yet nothing could be further from the truth. As we show in subsequent chapters, states frequently encounter circumstances where their sovereign rights and powers are unsettled, concurrent, shared jointly, or in tension with one another. States rely on international law "to harmonize and reconcile" their "different sovereignties" in these cases of sovereign interdependence, just as in settings where their sovereignties are mutually independent.[118] International law performs this service, for example, when international disputes arise over

[117] United States v. Arjona, 120 US 479, 484 (1887) (citing Vattel).
[118] Lotus, above, pp. 40, 44 (Weiss, J., dissenting).

transboundary rivers, oceanic fisheries, and maritime delimitation. Other relevant disputes include controversies about transboundary pollution, global cartels, transnational terrorism, piracy, cybercrime, and atrocity crimes. The jurisprudence of international courts and tribunals is replete with cases in which states have tangled over unsettled jurisdiction, concurrent jurisdiction, jointly shared jurisdiction, or conflicting legal entitlements. An inventory of these cases reads like a "greatest hits" collection of international case law, including the *Alabama Arbitration*,[119] the *Trail Smelter Case*,[120] the *River Oder Case*,[121] the *Lake Lanoux Arbitration*,[122] the *Corfu Channel Case*,[123] the *Fisheries Jurisdiction Cases*,[124] the *North Sea Continental Shelf Cases*,[125] and the *Bosnian Genocide Case*.[126] Far from being outlier exceptions to the general rule of mutually independent sovereignty, these cases involving unsettled jurisdiction, concurrent jurisdiction, jointly shared jurisdiction, and conflicting rights are ubiquitous in international legal practice. Thus, addressing the challenges these cases pose to sovereign equality has become a major preoccupation of international law.

The voluntarist and constitutionalist conceptions of sovereign equality respond to these challenges in different ways. Under the voluntarist approach, states are free to avoid the norms of mandatory cooperation arising from nonexclusive forms of jurisdiction and rights conflicts, even at the expense of dominating their neighbors' sovereign interests. In practice, this gives great powers like China, the European Union, Russia, and the United States license to exercise their sovereign rights and powers as they see fit, subject only to international law's limited set of prohibitive rules. By allowing more powerful states to dictate the terms of their relationships with foreign nations in this manner, voluntarism exposes foreign peoples to "alien subjugation, domination and exploitation," arguably in violation of

[119] Thomas Willing Balch, *The Alabama Arbitration* (Philadelphia: Allen, Lane & Scott 1900), p. 135 (reprinting the *Alabama* Decision and Award).

[120] Trail Smelter Case (US v. Can.), 3 RIAA 1905, 1917 (Trail Smelter Arb. Trib. 1941).

[121] River Oder Case, 1929 PCIJ (ser. A) No. 23, p. 27.

[122] Lake Lanoux Arbitration (Fr./Sp.), 24 ILR 101 (1957).

[123] Corfu Channel Case (U.K. v. Alb.), 1949 ICJ Rep. 4 (9 Apr.).

[124] Fisheries Jurisdiction Case (UK/Iceland), Merits, 1974 ICJ Rep. 3 (25 July).

[125] North Sea Continental Shelf Case (FRG/Den., FRG/Neth.), 1969 ICJ Rep. 3 (20 February).

[126] Application of the Convention on the Prevention and Punishment of the Crime of Genocide (Bosn. & Herz. v. Serbia & Montenegro), 2007 ICJ Rep. 43, 49, para. 1 (26 February).

the right to self-determination.[127] In this respect, the voluntarist account of sovereign equality is a recipe for great power domination.

The constitutionalist approach, in contrast, holds that when sovereign rights and powers clash or the equitable use of a sovereign entitlement is otherwise in question, no state may claim the prerogative to resolve the matter on its own because doing so would dominate other states by threatening to subject them to its unilateral will. Even if a state acted in perfectly good faith, imposing a solution that favored its neighbors, its unilateral decision-making would undermine sovereign equality by arrogating to itself a prerogative and standing that is not held by others. The constitutional approach to sovereign equality therefore requires that states refrain from dictating the terms of their interactions with other states unilaterally. Instead, they must resolve international disputes cooperatively through dialogue, negotiation, or third-party dispute resolution. A simple refusal to negotiate with other states on a matter that calls for multilateral cooperation would undermine sovereign equality because it would frustrate the authority of other states to negotiate fair terms of cooperation jointly for all concerned.[128] Hence, states must cooperate with one another to resolve disagreements about, among other things, the location of shared land borders[129] and the coordinated exploitation of border-straddling oil fields.[130] The tensions inherent in unsettled jurisdiction, concurrent jurisdiction, jointly shared jurisdiction, and conflicting rights can be resolved only through international cooperation. Constitutionalism thus embraces mandatory cooperation as the institutional framework for safeguarding sovereign equality when states operate outside their exclusive jurisdiction or when the equity of an otherwise ordinary use of sovereign power is in question.

[127] Friendly Relations Declaration.

[128] By "fair terms of cooperation" we have in mind something like the reciprocal terms on which free and equal persons might interact under Rawls's conception of justice as fairness. See, e.g., John Rawls, *Justice as Fairness* (Cambridge: Harvard University Press, 2001), p. 6 (distinguishing social coordination from social cooperation).

[129] See PCA Case No. 2012-04, Arbitration Between the Republic of Croatia and the Republic of Slovenia, Final Award, 29 June 2017, at 108, para. 334 (describing mutual state consent as "the fundamental principle applicable to the establishment of land boundaries between sovereign States").

[130] See Charter of Economic Rights and Duties of States, GA Res. 3281 (XXIX), UN Doc. A/9631, 29 UN GAOR Supp. (No. 31), art. 3 (1974) ("In the exploitation of natural resources shared by two or more countries, each State must co-operate on the basis of a system of information and prior consultations in order to achieve optimum use of such resources without causing damage to the legitimate interest of others.").

Substantive Obligations – Mandatory cooperation requires states to pursue equitable solutions to international controversies with an eye to balancing their own legal rights and authority, on the one hand, with the legal rights and authority of other individual states and the international community collectively, on the other. International treaties and judicial decisions refer to this as an equitable requirement that states accord "due regard" to other states' sovereign rights and authority.[131] Due regard does not demand "total or maximum regard" for foreign interests, but rather "reasonable, appropriate, optimal regard."[132] States must pursue "an objectively positive interaction with another [state]'s interests and with those of the international community"[133] for the purpose "of reconciling them in as equitable a manner as possible."[134] Mandatory cooperation thus aims to harmonize conflicting sovereign rights and powers through a proportionality analysis that equitably balances contending national interests.[135]

The due regard standard is often linked to other legal concepts, such as "abuse of right," signaling that states must avoid exercising their rights in a manner that causes arbitrary or disproportionate injury to others' rights.[136] An abuse of right is acting within the scope of a right but in

[131] See, e.g., UN Convention on the Law of the Sea arts. 56, 58, 60, 66, 87, 142, UN Doc. A/CONF. 62/122(1982); Request for an Advisory Opinion Submitted by the Sub-Regional Fisheries Commission (SRFC), Advisory Opinion of 2 April 2015, ITLOS Rep. 2015, para. 219; *Chagos Marine Protected Area Arbitration (Mauritius/U.K.)*, Case No. 2011-03, Award, para. 534 (Perm. Ct. Arb. 2015); *Fisheries-Germany*, 1974 ICJ Rep. p. 198, para. 60.

[132] Jonathan B. Wiener, 'Disregard and Due Regard' (2021) 29 *NYU Envt'l L.J.* 437, 461.

[133] Julia Gaunce, 'On the Interpretation of the General Duty of "Due Regard"' (2018) 32 *Ocean Y.B.* 27.

[134] Fisheries Jurisdiction Case, p. 30, para. 70; see also Lake Lanoux Arbitration (Sp./Fr.), 124 I.L.R. 101, 139, para. 22, XII UNRIAA 281 (French), at 315 (explaining that states must "take into consideration the various interests involved, . . . seek to give [other states] every satisfaction compatible with the pursuit of its own interest, and . . . show that it is genuinely concerned to reconcile the interests of the other . . . State with its own.").

[135] See Chagos, para. 534 (observing that the duty of "due regard" for another state's interests "entails, at least, both consultation and a balancing exercise with its own rights and interests").

[136] See, e.g., World Trade Organization, United States—Import Prohibition of Certain Shrimp and Shrimp Products, Report of the Appellate Body, paras. 158, 160, AB-1998-4, WT/DS58/AB/R (Oct. 12, 1998); WTO, United States—Import Prohibition of Certain Shrimp and Shrimp Products, Recourse to Art. 21.5 by Malaysia, Report of the Panel, paras. 5.51–.60, WT/DS58/RW (June 15, 2001) [hereinafter Shrimp/Turtle Panel Report II]; see generally Robert Kolb, *Good Faith in International Law* (Oxford: Hart Publishing, 2017), pp. 142–145 (discussing international "abuse of right" as including "manifest disproportion of interests" and "arbitrary action").

a way that produces manifest inequity.[137] Accordingly, in contexts where states' rights and powers are unsettled or enmeshed, the constitutional approach suggests that these rights and powers must be porous to equitable principles and peaceful dispute resolution to prevent an abuse of right. Thus, mandatory cooperation ensures that ordinary exercises of sovereign power and assertions of sovereign rights are equitable rather than abusive.

Procedural Obligations – Mandatory cooperation also imposes procedural obligations. Within mandatory cooperation's domain, states must investigate,[138] consult,[139] and negotiate with one another in good faith.[140] The duty of good faith negotiation demands initiative and sustained commitment.[141] Good faith negotiation "entail[s] more than the plain opposition of legal views or interests between two parties, or the existence of a series of accusations and rebuttals, or even the exchange of claims and directly opposed counter-claims."[142] Instead, negotiations must be "meaningful" in the sense that each side demonstrates a willingness to pursue agreement, not merely to go through the motions.[143] Good faith negotiation also requires openness to "compromise, even if that mean[s]

137 Typically, the inequity is only made possible by the generality of the right. For example, building owners are sometimes enjoined from stopping cranes from passing over their property even though, strictly speaking, they own the airspace above their property and possess a right to exclude. *Woollerton & Wilson, Ltd. v. Richard Costain, Ltd* [1970] 1 WLR 411 (Eng.); see generally Larissa Katz, 'Spite and Extortion: A Jurisdictional Principle of Abuse of Property Right' (2013) 122 YLJ 100 (arguing that owners abuse property rights if they exercise them solely for the sake of spite or extortion).

138 See Fisheries-Iceland, p. 31, para. 72 (emphasizing the parties' obligation "to keep under review the fishery resources in [a maritime zone where they have conflicting rights] and to examine together, in the light of scientific and other available information, the measures required for the conservation and development, and equitable exploitation, of those resources").

139 See Chagos Case, para. 519 ("In the majority of cases, [due regard for other states' rights] will necessarily involve at least some consultation with the rights-holding State.").

140 See North Sea Continental Shelf (Germ./Den.; Germ./Neth.), 1969 ICJ Rep. 3, 47, para. 86 (20 February) (characterizing the duty to negotiate as "a special application of a principle which underlies all international relations").

141 See WTO, United States—Import Prohibition of Certain Shrimp and Shrimp Products, Recourse to Art. 21.5 of the DSU by Malaysia [Shrimp-Turtle Dispute], Report of the Appellate Body, para. 133, AB-2001-4, WT/DS58/RW, Oct. 22, 2001 [Shrimp-Turtle Appellate Body II] (concluding that the duty of negotiation requires "serious, good faith efforts").

142 Case Concerning Application of the International Convention on the Elimination of all Forms of Racial Discrimination (Georgia/Russ.), Prelim. Objections, 2011 ICJ Rep. 70, 132, para. 157 (1 April).

143 Application of the Interim Accord Case (FYROM/Gr.), Judgment, 2011 ICJ Rep. 644, 685, para. 132 (Dec. 5) [hereinafter Interim Accord Case], p. 685, para. 132 (internal citation and quotation marks omitted).

the relinquishment of strongly held positions earlier taken. It implies a willingness for the purpose of negotiation to abandon earlier positions and to meet the other side part way."[144] Hence, the idea that one side would "insist upon the complete capitulation of the other side" is "inconsistent with ... 'negotiation.'"[145] States must undertake a "persevering quest for an acceptable compromise,"[146] demonstrating that they are "internally concerned with balancing the [relevant] rights and interests," rather than simply going through the motions.[147]

In the end, however, the requirement of good faith negotiation does not obligate states to actually conclude an agreement resolving their disputes.[148] Mandatory cooperation imposes obligations of conduct, not result.[149] Sometimes states disagree in perfectly good faith about the terms of an equitable solution. To require states to accept an agreement that they genuinely believe is inequitable would subject them to the unilateral will of the other side, which is inconsistent with sovereign equality and joint stewardship. Accordingly, mandatory cooperation does not require states to conclude agreements, provided they persevere in pursuing an equitable resolution in good faith.[150]

International courts and tribunals have been reluctant to find bad faith absent "clear and convincing evidence" that a state seeks "to prevent any reasonable agreement."[151] Bad faith might be established if a state arbitrarily breaks off or delays negotiations, declines to follow established procedures for negotiation, or refuses to consider counter-proposals or relevant equitable considerations.[152] Under any of these circumstances,

144 German External Debts Case (Greece/Germ.), 19 RIAA 27 (1972), p. 56, para. 62.

145 Ibid.

146 Kuwait v. AMINOIL, 66 ILR 578, 1017, para. 70(i) (1982) (emphasis added).

147 See Chagos, para. 528.

148 See Pulp Mills on the River Uruguay (Arg./Ur.), Judgment, 2010 ICJ Rep. 14, 68, para. 150 (20 April) (observing that the duty of good faith negotiation "does not imply an obligation to reach an agreement" (internal citation and quotation marks omitted).

149 Rüdiger Wolfrum, 'Obligations of Result Versus Obligations of Conduct: Some Thoughts About the Implementation of International Obligations', in Mahnoush H. Arsanjani, Jacob Cogan, Robert Sloane, and Siegfried Wiessner (eds.), *Looking to the Future: Essays in Honor of W. Michael Reisman* (Leiden: Martinus Nijhoff Publishers, 2011), p. 363.

150 Cf. Tacna-Arica Arbitration (Chile/Peru), 2 RIAA 921, 929 (1925) (observing that where two states have entered an agreement to negotiate a maritime delimitation, neither state is "bound to make an agreement unsatisfactory to itself provided it did not act in bad faith").

151 Ibid. p. 929; see also Interim Accord Case, p. 685, para. 132 (endorsing these requirements).

152 See Interim Accord Case, p. 685, para. 132 (emphasizing these considerations).

a state's intransigent behavior would reflect unilateralism through covert means, which in turn would infringe sovereign equality.

If negotiations stall, states must pursue mediation, arbitration, adjudication, or some other form of third-party dispute resolution. Support for this principle can be found in Article 33 of the UN Charter, which charges states with resolving their disputes through peaceful means.[153] The General Assembly's Friendly Relations Declaration likewise describes the pursuit of peaceful third-party dispute resolution as an obligation incumbent upon all states.[154] Third-party dispute resolution promotes sovereign equality under the constitutional approach by ensuring that states do not appoint themselves judge and party to the same cause. In cases where states are unable to agree on a negotiated solution or a forum for arbitration, they must maintain a continuous dialogue and refrain from taking steps that would prejudice the outcome of negotiations.

These procedural duties are explained by international law's commitment to sovereign equality: in settings where states are not mutually independent, they can harmonize and reconcile their respective rights and powers only through negotiations, mediation, democratic procedures (e.g., fair voting), or by submitting to third-party dispute resolution. Mandatory cooperation ensures that states have an opportunity to participate and have their preferences taken into account in decisions that impact their legal interests.[155] It also attends to the collective right to self-determination by ensuring that states resolve their disputes in a manner that reflects the collective will of the peoples concerned.[156]

Mandatory cooperation suggests that international legal order is not concerned merely with establishing minimal terms of co-existence among independent states.[157] Instead, international law requires states to embrace international cooperation, pooling their sovereign authority

[153] See UN Charter art. 33.

[154] See Friendly Relations Declaration (declaring that "[e]very State shall settle its international disputes with other States by peaceful means," such as mediation, arbitration, and judicial settlement, and that if these mechanisms fail to yield a solution, "[t]he parties to a dispute have the duty ... to continue to seek a settlement of the dispute by other peaceful means agreed upon by them").

[155] See Wiener, 'Disregard and Due Regard', p. 463 (explaining that due regard aims "[t]o remedy omitted voice, to see those who are invisible, to listen to those who were unheard" by enabling participation in decision-making).

[156] See ICCPR art. 1; ICESCR art. 1.

[157] Pace Hurrell, *On Global Order*; and Hedley Bull, *The Anarchical Society: A Study of Order in World Politics* (London: Palgrave Macmillan Press, 1977).

to develop common norms and institutions, in settings where their respective sovereign rights and authority are unsettled or otherwise entangled. These features of the constitutional approach to sovereign equality are well-suited to our current era of global interconnectivity and interdependence, when activities occurring in one country routinely reverberate across national borders to affect people, markets, ecosystems, and legal and political systems around the world.[158]

Roadmap

In subsequent chapters, we explore how mandatory cooperation has been incorporated into a wide range of fields of international law. We shall see that mandatory cooperation finds expression in numerous international treaties and norms of customary international law. It also features prominently in dozens of decisions from national and international courts, including judgments of the ICJ and arbitral tribunals convened under the PCA. Our methodology throughout the book is mostly descriptive, inasmuch as it begins with the existing practice and self-understanding of international law. But our method is also interpretive, since we use the organizing principle of sovereign equality to explain the extant legal norms of mandatory cooperation. Collectively, the case studies we develop in this book chronicle how the constitutional approach to sovereign equality is gradually eclipsing (but has not yet fully eclipsed) the older voluntarist approach.

The remainder of this book is divided into three parts. The first two parts use case studies to characterize and assess international law's deployment of mandatory cooperation in contexts where the practice is reasonably well entrenched, while the last part will explore contexts where mandatory cooperation is less well developed.

In Part I – *Conflicting Sovereignties* – we consider cases of overlapping rights, shared sovereign powers, or unsettled jurisdiction to explain why sovereign equality requires states to resolve disputes through international cooperation. In Chapter 2, we begin by examining how

158 See Eyal Benvenisti, "Sovereign as Trustees of Humanity: On the Accountability of States to Foreign Stakeholders" (2013) 107 AJIL 295 (observing that while international lawyers in the past viewed sovereignty as "akin to owning a large estate separated from other properties by rivers or deserts" – in other words, conditions of mutual independence – "today's reality is more analogous to owning a small apartment in one densely packed high-rise," where each owner's rights and interests are inextricably bound up with others' rights and interests).

international law governing rivers has established a requirement that upstream and downstream sovereigns must consult and negotiate in good faith to determine mutually satisfactory solutions for the shared use of rivers. Chapter 3 shows how the international law of the sea moved away from state unilateralism in favor of the equitable model of sovereignty by requiring states to resolve disputes over international fisheries and maritime boundaries through cooperation in accordance with equitable principles. Chapter 4 considers how duties of international cooperation safeguard sovereign equality by reconciling the territorial sovereignty of coastal states with landlocked states' rights to access the oceans through negotiation or binding arbitration. Chapter 5 demonstrates that states have accepted obligations of mandatory cooperation with respect to a variety of other transboundary harms, including piracy, terrorism, and at least some cyberattacks. Chapter 6 shows that international environmental law embraces an equitable approach whereby states must cooperate to suppress transboundary pollution. In both Chapter 5 and Chapter 6, we argue that states where transboundary harms originate bear legal obligations to cooperate with injured states to suppress threats from nonstate actors by taking effective measures to prevent or suppress those threats.

In Part II – *Collective Stewardship* – we show that cooperation is required when international law commits authority to groups of states for the collective stewardship of the international community as a whole or a matter of common concern. In Chapter 7, we examine climate change as a transnational and existential threat to humanity generally, and to certain smaller and vulnerable states most dramatically. Since it poses an existential threat to low-lying coastal states and raises the frequency and intensity of extreme weather events, we make the case that climate change should be understood to trigger duties of international cooperation. Chapter 8 considers international territorial administration through multilateral governance structures, devoting special attention to Antarctica as a global *res communis* for peaceful exploration and scientific study. In Chapter 9, we explain how mandatory cooperation applies to the international community's collective responsibility to safeguard international peace, security, and human rights. With the establishment of the United Nations, the Grotian paradigm of states deciding when to use force for themselves shifted to a collective stewardship model whereby states must cooperate with one another to avoid armed conflict, punish atrocity crimes, and combat global poverty, including through collective consultation, negotiation, and peaceful dispute resolution.

Part III – *Future Directions* – begins with Chapter 10, where we examine whether states bear duties of international cooperation with respect to forced migration, including the mass displacement caused by Myanmar's campaign of ethnic cleansing against its Rohingya Muslim minority. We make the case that the international community has accepted the protection of forced migrants as a common concern of humanity under the community's joint stewardship. Although states have not come close to satisfying this collective responsibility, the system of national pledges established under the 2018 Global Compact for Safe, Orderly and Regular Migration[159] and the Global Compact on Refugees[160] represent substantial (albeit nonbinding) measures in the direction of fulfilling states' nascent duties of mandatory cooperation. Chapter 11 uses antitrust law as a case study to explore the phenomenon of extraterritorial regulation. Over the past several decades, many states have extended their domestic competition laws extraterritorially, subjecting foreign actors outside their borders to the concurrent regulation of multiple states. We argue in Chapter 11 that the principle of sovereign equality requires states to resolve disputes involving fields of concurrent prescriptive jurisdiction through mandatory cooperation. Chapter 12 offers a provocative and jurisprudentially ambitious argument: that sovereign equality requires states to submit to international adjudication or arbitration even in ordinary legal disputes that do not involve overlapping sovereign rights or powers. Drawing on the ICJ's groundbreaking judgment in the Case Concerning Military and Paramilitary Activities in and Against Nicaragua,[161] we argue that even if international law permits states to opt out of the jurisdiction of a particular court, in practice the ICJ interprets that entitlement restrictively, and the principle of sovereign equality prohibits states from abandoning third-party dispute resolution entirely. Finally, Chapter 13 concludes by recapping the book's key themes, considering potential obstacles to mandatory cooperation, and identifying other matters of international concern, such as pandemics, that are good candidates for mandatory cooperation under the equitable conception of sovereign equality.

[159] Global Compact on Safe, Orderly, and Regular Migration (GCM), New York, 19 December 2018, A/RES/73/195.

[160] Global Compact on Refugees, New York, 2 August 2018, A/73/12 (Part II).

[161] Case Concerning Military and Paramilitary Activities in and Against Nicaragua (Nicar./US), Merits, 1986 ICJ Rep. 14 (27 June).

While this chapter began with a story of international cooperation in retreat – the ongoing calamity in Ukraine, where the failure of cooperation is being paid in blood – we shall see that in many other contexts states' obligations of mandatory cooperation are taken seriously and have attained the status of customary international law, even where their initial source is treaty-based (e.g., international watercourses, maritime delimitation, the duty to resolve disputes using peaceful means). Even in an era when multilateralism faces serious setbacks under assault from nationalist movements, fueling pessimism about the future of international cooperation, the fact remains that international law continues to thrive across many fields. International treaties and the judgments of international courts and tribunals continue to affirm that states must cooperate to address a host of common challenges. Mandatory cooperation is the legal framework that enables states to make policy together as equals, as joint stewards of both their people and humanity.

PART I

Conflicting Sovereignties

2

Rivers

A Regal River Runs Dry

Rising from the snow-capped San Juan Range of Colorado's Rocky Mountains, the Rio Grande River descends through New Mexico, nips the western tip of Texas, then snakes eastward, marking the Mexico–US border for hundreds of miles before finally emptying into the Gulf of Mexico. In the sixteenth century, Spanish explorers christened the Rio Grande "the Fierce River of the North" (*El Rio Bravo del Norte*) out of respect for the turbulent cataracts in its upper reaches. These days, however, the once-regal river has been dethroned by a confluence of forces. Explosive population growth, increasing demand for irrigation and industrial uses, a decades-long "mega-drought," and rising temperatures attributed to climate change have conspired to dramatically diminish the river's flow. In June 2021, observers watched with horror as New Mexico's Elephant Butte Reservoir, which had brimmed over during the 1980s and 1990s, dropped to a paltry 5 percent of its full capacity. Other reservoirs that feed the Rio Grande have experienced similar distress due to rising temperatures and growing demand, forcing regulators in Mexico and the United States to adopt extreme rationing policies that restrict the lower basin to about 2 percent of its historic annual flow. Residents of Albuquerque, El Paso, and Ciudad Juarez have seen the Rio Grande run dry for longer periods each year, its mirrored surface replaced with a parched sandbar.[1]

Dwindling fresh water threatens vital interests on both sides of the Mexico–US border. Over six million people rely on the Rio Grande and its tributaries for agriculture, industry, and municipal uses, and

[1] See Di Minardi, 'A River Used to Run Through It: How New Mexico Handles a Dwindling Rio Grande', The Guardian, 12 January 2021; Danielle Prokop, 'Western Rivers and the Binational Climate Challenge', El Paso Matters, 7 September 2021.

population centers in the region continue to expand. In the past, farmers in southern New Mexico and El Paso County could count on forty inches of water to irrigate their onions, corn, and green peppers; by 2021, some received as little as four inches. Across the border, Mexican pecan growers have complained likewise that water rationing is imperiling their groves.[2] Less water to go around means fewer acres of arable farmland, shorter growing seasons, and mounting pressure to transition to more drought-resistant (but generally less lucrative) crops – all of which equates to fewer jobs and diminishing profits. Meanwhile, ecologists have expressed concern that hydroelectric dams are imperiling the basin's flora and fauna. Hundreds of native plants and animals have been decimated by the region's changing ecology, including the endangered silvery minnow and cottonwood trees that have evolved to rely on the basin's natural hydrological cycle.[3] To make matters worse, scientists predict that current drought conditions are likely to get worse over time, as climate change continues to dry out the Rio Grande basin while inundating other regions with floods and hurricanes.[4] As the fresh water crisis in the Rio Grande Basin has dragged on, regulators on both sides of the border have confronted difficult tradeoffs regarding the competing interests of farmers, industrialists, and ordinary residents, as well as the moral imperative to practice prudent stewardship of the natural environment.

If these domestic policy dilemmas were not daunting enough, the crisis at the Rio Grande also poses a serious diplomatic challenge. Because the river passes through and collects tributary water from both Mexico and the United States, both states have legitimate claims to the river's limited flow. This clash of national interests might appear to be a recipe for intractable conflict or hegemonic domination. Yet, remarkably, the opposite is true: for well over a century, the Rio Grande has emerged as a success story for international cooperation. Even as climate change has depleted reservoirs, raising the political and economic stakes on both

2 Lauren Villagran, 'Gov. Abbott: Mexico Owes Texas a Year's Worth of Rio Grande Water', El Paso Times, 21 September 2020.

3 Minardi, 'A River Used to Run Through It'; Erick S. Albarran, 'A Drying River', Medium, 22 March 2021.

4 See Itzchak E. Kornfeld, *Transboundary Water Disputes: State Conflict and the Assessment of their Adjudication* (Cambridge: Cambridge University Press, 2019), p. 10; Edith Brown Weiss, *International Law for a Water-Scarce World* (Leiden: Martinus Nijhoff Publishers, 2013), p. 2.

sides of the border, thus far a spirit of cooperation and compromise has sustained the bilateral partnership.[5]

This chapter tells the story of how cooperation has flourished at the Rio Grande in the face of formidable challenges. International law plays a central role in this history. By the middle of the twentieth century, international courts and tribunals were promoting cooperation in disputes over transboundary rivers by decisively rejecting the absolutist conception of national sovereignty. They declared that general principles of equity required riparian states to cooperate with one another to reconcile conflicts between their sovereign rights. These developments in international law greased the wheels for international cooperation over transboundary rivers, helping to avert and defuse conflicts during an era when demand for fresh water was increasing exponentially.

Abandoning Absolute Sovereignty

The Rio Grande is one of 276 transboundary rivers that collectively serve 2.8 billion people – approximately 40 percent of the world's population. Transboundary river basins, also known as "international watercourses,"[6] occupy nearly half of the earth's land surface and account for roughly 60 percent of global river flow.[7] The fresh water that flows through these rivers is vital to human survival and economic development, facilitating agriculture, industry, transportation, electricity generation, and other uses.

Transboundary rivers have been at the center of international disputes for millennia. The earliest recorded international treaty addresses tensions between two Ancient Sumerian city-states over the Euphrates River

[5] Whether Mexico and the United States will be able to sustain this partnership remains to be seen, as climate change-induced water scarcity has strained their ability to satisfy their respective commitments. See Scott Dance, 'A Water War Is Brewing Between the United States and Mexico. Here's Why', Washington Post, 16 May 2024.

[6] The UN Watercourses Convention defines a "watercourse" as "a system of surface waters and groundwaters constituting by virtue of their physical relationship a unitary whole and normally flowing into a common terminus." Convention on the Law of the Non-navigational Uses of International Watercourses, New York, 21 May 1997, in force 17 August 2014, art. 2(a), GA Res. 51/229, UN GAOR, 51st Sess., UN Doc. A/RES/51/229 [hereinafter UN Watercourses Convention].

[7] See Laurance Boisson de Chazournes, *Fresh Water in International Law* (Oxford: Oxford University Press, 2021), p. 3; Bjørn-Oliver Magsig, *International Water Law and the Quest for Common Security* (New York: Routledge, 2015); Stephen C. McCaffrey, Christina Leb and Riley T. Denoon (eds.), 'Introduction', in *Research Handbook on International Water Law* (Cheltenham Edward Elgar Publishing, 2019), p. 1 [hereinafter *Research Handbook*].

in approximately 2,500 BCE. Since then, political communities have concluded thousands of agreements on the use and management of transboundary rivers.[8] Disputes over these agreements have also led to international arbitration and adjudication, including an advisory opinion and two judgments in contentious cases from the Permanent Court of International Justice (PCIJ), the first international tribunal with general jurisdiction (i.e., authority to hear any kind of case brought before it that is amenable to international adjudication).[9]

Notwithstanding the importance of transboundary rivers to human flourishing, the international legal norms governing them were unsettled at the turn of the twentieth century. This uncertainty was attributable in part to a paradox at the heart of the then-prevailing theory of absolute sovereignty. Recall from Chapter 1 that Grotius conceptualized states as possessing exclusive authority and proprietary interests over their own sovereign territory, as well as the prerogative to judge the legality of their own actions for themselves. In disputes over transboundary rivers, upstream states invoked the absolutist conception of territorial sovereignty to support their position that they could use transboundary rivers however they pleased, including by diverting water for domestic irrigation. But downstream states also relied on territorial sovereignty to defend their national interests. In their view, sovereignty entailed the right to absolute territorial integrity, including the unimpaired natural flow of fresh water from upstream sources. How to choose between these dueling theories of sovereign rights – known today as "absolute territorial sovereignty" and "absolute territorial integrity" – was by no means obvious under the prevailing Grotian theory of sovereignty. Consequently, upstream and downstream riparians could each plausibly claim that international law authorized them to dictate how a transboundary river running through their borders should be utilized.

A nineteenth-century dispute between Mexico and the United States over the Rio Grande illustrates this dilemma.[10] In July 1848, the United States and Mexico concluded the Mexican-American war by signing the

8 Alistair Rieu-Clarke, 'From Treaty Practice to the UN Watercourses Convention', in *Research Handbook*, pp. 11–12.

9 Jurisdiction of the European Commission of the Danube, 1927 PCIJ (ser. B) No. 14, p. 64 (advisory); River Oder Case, 1929 PCIJ (ser. A) No. 23, p. 27 (contentious); Oscar Chinn Case, PCIJ (ser. A/B) No. 63 (1934) (contentious).

10 The discussion of the Harmon episode that follows draws on Stephen C. McCaffrey's excellent account in *The Law of International Watercourses* (Oxford: Oxford University Press, 2007), pp. 76–102.

Treaty of Guadalupe Hidalgo.[11] The treaty designated the deepest channel of the Rio Grande as the boundary line between the two countries for 1,255 miles, and it prohibited both parties from constructing "any work that may impede or interrupt" navigation along this section of the river without the other party's consent.[12] As time wore on, diversions of the river by American farmers depleted the Rio Grande to the point that Mexico felt constrained to file a formal diplomatic protest. In October 1894, Mexico's chief representative to the United States, Matías Romero, sent a note to US Secretary of State Walter Q. Gresham asserting the "urgent necessity" to address the United States' "taking of water from the Rio Bravo (Rio Grande) del Norte, which has so seriously affected the existence of the frontier communities for several miles below [Ciudad Juárez]" that they "may be annihilated." Romero argued that further discussions between the countries should focus on maintaining "the equitable division of the waters of the river."[13]

Responding two weeks later, Gresham disputed Romero's factual assertion that American irrigation – rather than natural drought – had diminished the Rio Grande's flow.[14] At Gresham's request, US Attorney General Judson Harmon provided a legal opinion that vigorously defended the United States' sovereign right to use the Rio Grande as it saw fit, without regard to Mexico's rights and interests. Harmon explained that the Treaty of Guadalupe Hidalgo did not prohibit the United States from diverting water for irrigation, as long as these diversions did not impede navigation. Turning next to principles of general international law, Harmon emphasized that the "fundamental principle of international law is the absolute sovereignty of every nation, as against all others, within its own territory."[15] He then quoted a passage from Chief Justice John Marshall's opinion for the US Supreme Court in *Schooner Exchange v. McFaddon*:

[11] Treaty of Peace, Friendship, Limits, and Settlement with the Republic of Mexico, 2 February 1848, US-Mex., 9 Stat. 922.

[12] Treaty of Peace, Friendship, Limits, and Settlement with the Republic of Mexico, arts. V, VII.

[13] 'Minister Romero to Secretary Gresham, 12 October 1894', in *Papers Relating to the Foreign Relations of the United States* (Washington: U.S. Government Printing Office 1894), p. 386.

[14] 'Secretary Gresham to Minister Romero, 1 November 1894', in *Papers Relating to the Foreign Relations of the United States* (Washington: U.S. Government Printing Office 1894), p. 387.

[15] Treaty of Guadalupe Hidalgo – International Law, 21 Op. Attorney Gen. 274, 281 (12 December 1895).

> The jurisdiction of the nation within its own territory is necessarily exclusive and absolute. It is susceptible of no limitation not imposed by itself. Any restriction upon it, deriving validity from an external source, would imply a diminution of its sovereignty to the extent of the restriction, and an investment of that sovereignty to the same extent in that power which could impose such restriction.
>
> All exceptions, therefore, to the full and complete power of a nation within its own territories must be traced up to the consent of the nation itself. They can flow from no other legitimate source.[16]

In Harmon's view, the United States' prerogative to use as much of the Rio Grande as it wished reflected two basic principles of international law: (1) the "necessarily exclusive and absolute" nature of its territorial sovereignty, and (2) the voluntarist principle (later associated with *The Lotus Case*) that any limitations on state sovereignty must be attributable to state consent. Thus, because the United States had not consented to limit its use of the Rio Grande for irrigation, it was not violating international law.

Harmon's defense of absolute territorial sovereignty – the so-called "Harmon Doctrine" – supplied legal cover at a moment when the United States was anxious to preserve existing irrigation works and parry Mexican claims for monetary reparations. The opinion might have advanced these objectives, but its legal analysis was highly problematic from the start. If every state had "exclusive and absolute" jurisdiction over its own territory, as Harmon supposed, then what about Mexico's territorial sovereignty? Surely Mexico could also claim "full and complete" authority to ensure its own self-preservation by guaranteeing the Rio Grande's uninterrupted flow through its territory? Allowing the United States to divert the river without Mexico's consent would, in the Chief Justice's words, "imply a diminution of [Mexico's] sovereignty to the extent of that restriction, and an investment of that sovereignty to the same extent in [the United States]" – a result antithetical to Mexico's sovereignty. Yet, how could Mexico and the United States *both* exercise "exclusive and absolute" jurisdiction over the Rio Grande's flow? The only way to resolve this dilemma without violating the territorial sovereignty of either state would be for Mexico and the United States to either negotiate an agreement or submit to international arbitration.

In fact, this is precisely what happened. Well before Harmon weighed in with his now-infamous opinion, the US State Department pursued

[16] Treaty of Guadalupe Hidalgo, 281–82 (quoting Schooner Exchange v. McFaddon, 11 US (7 Cranch) 116, 136 (1812)).

negotiations with Mexico.[17] US President Grover Cleveland delivered an address to Congress in which he argued that tensions over "the storage and use of the waters of the Rio Grande for irrigation should be solved by appropriate concurrent action of the two interested countries."[18] Congress apparently agreed. Expressing concern that US irrigation practices were "rendering the lands [downstream] arid and unproductive, to the great detriment of the citizens of the two countries who live along its course," Congress adopted a joint resolution in 1890 urging the President to pursue negotiations with Mexico to resolve the issue.[19] Thus, in stark contrast to Harmon's legal opinion, US foreign policy throughout this period demonstrated respect for Mexico's sovereign rights and interests and a commitment to resolve the issue through bilateral cooperation.

Rather than proceed unilaterally, the two governments asked the International Boundary Commission, which they had established in 1889, to evaluate the facts on the ground and help them determine "the best and most feasible mode" of regulating the Rio Grande "so as to secure to each country concerned and to its inhabitants their legal and equitable rights in said waters."[20] Guided by the Commission's recommendations, Mexico and the United States concluded a treaty in 1906 "to provide for the equitable distribution of the waters of the Rio Grande for irrigation purposes, and to remove all causes of controversy between them in respect thereto."[21] Under the treaty, the United States committed to deliver 60,000 acre-feet of water from the Elephant Butte Dam annually, and Mexico agreed to waive legal claims arising from the United States' diversions.[22]

Mexico and the United States have continued this cooperative relationship into the present. In 1944, the two states concluded a new treaty in which the United States expressly recognized Mexico's sovereign

[17] Minister Romero to Secretary Olney, 28 December 1985, US Appendix, pp. 211–12.

[18] President G. Cleveland, Annual Message, 3 December 1894, quoted in John Basset Moore, 'A Digest of International Law' (1906) 1 AJIL 764.

[19] Concurrent Resolution of 29 April 1890, Con. Rec. – Senate, 29 April 1890, p. 3963, Con. Rec. – House, 29 April 1890, p. 3977; US Appendix, p. 145.

[20] Protocol contained in note from Minister Romero to Secretary Olney, 6 May 1896, US Appendix, p. 226.

[21] Convention Between the United States and Mexico Providing for the Equitable Distribution of the Waters of the Rio Grande for Irrigation Purposes, Washington, D.C., 21 May 1906, US-Mexico, 34 Stat. 2953, UNTS No. 455.

[22] Convention Between the United States and Mexico Providing for the Equitable Distribution of the Waters of the Rio Grande for Irrigation Purposes, art. I.

interest in utilization of the Rio Grande.[23] Each of the states committed to contribute a defined volume of water to the Rio Grande from tributaries within their respective jurisdictions.[24] The treaty established an International Boundary and Waters Commission (IBWC) to coordinate the planning, construction, and operation of works along boundary waters, including hydropower dams, storage and diversion structures, and flood control measures.[25] It also contemplated that the parties would work through the IBWC to develop additional bilateral agreements – described as "minutes" – to facilitate continued cooperation and resolve future disagreements related to their transboundary waters.[26] In the 1960s and 1970s, as demand for water accelerated and both countries struggled to meet their contribution commitments, the IBWC's minutes focused largely on issues of equitable apportionment. By the 1990s, drought management and ecological preservation became more salient.[27] Thus, cooperation between Mexico and the United States evolved over time in response to the states' shifting priorities.

A dispute between Mexico and the United States illustrates the resiliency of this cooperative framework. In September 2020, Texas Governor Greg Abbott delivered a letter to US Secretary of State Mike Pompeo formally complaining that Mexico was close to defaulting on its obligations under the 1944 treaty. At the time, Mexico owed the United States "almost a year's worth of water" – over 300,000 acre-feet – with only six months remaining until the deadline. When Mexico announced that it would honor its treaty obligation, thousands of pecan farmers converged on the Bolaquilla Dam in northern Mexico. Brandishing sticks and stones, the protesters seized control of the dam and closed its valves in an attempt to preserve the dam's scarce water for their own parched orchards. Rather than appease the farmers, the Mexican government directed its National Guard to reclaim the dam by force and reopen the valves, leading to violent clashes that claimed the life of a protestor,

23 Treaty Between the United States of America and Mexico on Utilization of the Waters of the Colorado and Tijuana Rivers and of the Rio Grande, Washington, D.C., 3 February 1944, in force 8 November 1945, and Protocol, 14 November 1944, 59 Stat. 1219.

24 Treaty Between the United States of America and Mexico on Utilization of the Waters of the Colorado and Tijuana Rivers and of the Rio Grande, art. 4.

25 Treaty Between the United States of America and Mexico on Utilization of the Waters of the Colorado and Tijuana Rivers and of the Rio Grande, arts. 2, 5–9, 12, 24.

26 Treaty Between the United States of America and Mexico on Utilization of the Waters of the Colorado and Tijuana Rivers and of the Rio Grande, arts. 24–25.

27 Weiss, *International Law for a Water-Scarce World*, p. 164.

Yesica Silva.[28] In the end, despite intense regional resistance, the cooperative relationship between Mexico and the United States prevailed, allowing water to continue to flow to the lower Rio Grande. Although Mexico has since fallen further behind in its obligations under the 1944 treaty and political tensions between communities on either side of the river continue to run high, thus far the two sides have managed to prevent the situation from escalating into further violence.[29]

Reconciling Conflicting Rights

The robust Mexico–US partnership at the Rio Grande demonstrates that international cooperation is possible even when states have divergent interests with respect to scarce resources. It does not yet show, however, that international law affirmatively *requires* such cooperation, much less what the grounds of such a requirement would be. Beginning early in the twentieth century, however, national courts and international courts and tribunals began to recognize that general principles of law do, in fact, obligate states to cooperate with one another to resolve disputes over transboundary rivers. Through these decisions and supportive state practice, mandatory cooperation became firmly enshrined in the customary international law of transboundary rivers.

In the early twentieth century, the US Supreme Court decided a series of cases supportive of mandatory cooperation involving disputes between states of the United States.[30] In 1907, Kansas sued Colorado for diverting water from the Arkansas River, allegedly depriving Kansas and its inhabitants of the full volume of water to which they were accustomed.[31] The Court observed that "because Kansas and Colorado are states sovereign and independent in local matters, the relations between them [arguably] depend . . . upon principles of international law."[32] The Court then proceeded to identify the applicable legal principles:

[28] Eoin Wilson, 'Mexico's Water Crisis Heats Up as Transfer to US Looms', Al Jazeera, 8 October 2020.

[29] Dance, 'A Water War Is Brewing'; 'US, Mexico Reach Agreement on Rio Grande Water Deliveries Amid Drought, Shortages', Reuters, 9 November 2024.

[30] See, e.g., Kansas v. Colorado, 185 US 125 (1902); Kansas v. Colorado, 206 US 46 (1907); New Jersey v. New York, 283 US 336 (1931).

[31] Kansas v. Colorado, 205 US 46, 47 (1907).

[32] Ibid. p. 97.

> One cardinal rule, underlying all the relations of the states to each other, is that of equality of right. Each state stands on the same level with all the rest. It can impose its own legislation on no one of the others, and is bound to yield its own views to none. Yet, whenever … the action of one state reaches, through the agency of natural laws, into the territory of another state, the question of the extent and the limitations of the rights of the two states becomes a matter of justiciable dispute between them, and this court is called upon to settle that dispute in such a way as will recognize the equal rights of both and at the same time establish justice between them.[33]

In light of these principles, the Court held that the equal rights of Colorado and Kansas required an "equitable division" of water between the two states.[34]

Similarly, in a 1931 case, *New Jersey v. New York*,[35] the Court considered New Jersey's request for an injunction to prevent New York from channeling water away from the Delaware River and its tributaries toward New York City. In an opinion authored by Justice Oliver Wendell Holmes, the Court acknowledged that

> New York has the physical power to cut off all the water within its jurisdiction. But clearly the exercise of such a power to the destruction of the interest of lower States could not be tolerated. And on the other hand equally little could New Jersey be permitted to require New York to give up its power altogether in order that the river might come down to it undiminished. Both States have real and substantial interests in the River that must be reconciled as best they may.[36]

According to Justice Holmes, the goal of reconciling sovereign rights in this manner "always is to secure an equitable apportionment without quibbling over formulas."[37]

Eight years later, the Italian Court of Cassation confirmed that equitable principles also apply to states under international law. In the Convention of December 17, 1914, France and Italy had established a joint framework for utilization of the transboundary Roya River. France later objected to an Italian firm's plan to construct a power station on the Italian side of the border.[38] In deciding in favor of the Italian firm, the Court described the applicable law as follows:

33 Ibid. pp. 97–98.
34 Ibid. p. 104.
35 283 US 336 (1931).
36 Ibid. at 342–343.
37 Ibid. at 343.
38 See Victor Petaccio, 'Water Pollution and the Future Law of the Sea' (1972) 21 ICLQ 15, 22.

> International law recognizes the right on the part of every riparian State to enjoy, as a participant of a kind of partnership created by the river, all the advantages deriving from it for the purpose of securing the welfare and the economic and civil progress of the nation ... However, although a State, in the exercise of its right of sovereignty, may subject public rivers to whatever regime it deems best, it cannot disregard the international duty, derived from that principle, not to impede or to destroy, as a result of this regime, the opportunity of other States to avail themselves of the flow of water for their own national needs. In order to settle this conflict between the exercise of the right of sovereignty and the fulfilment of the duty imposed by the *comitas gentium*, regulations have been laid down by international conventions. By these treaties riparian States impose upon themselves those self-limitations in the exercise of their own sovereign prerogatives which are regarded as necessary to exclude reciprocal noxious interference with the concurrent utilisation of the common course of the river.[39]

Applying these principles, the Court concluded that international cooperation was required under international law to reconcile the states' conflicting sovereign rights relative to the Roya.

An arbitral tribunal eventually delivered the most influential statement on mandatory cooperation in the 1957 *Lake Lanoux Arbitration*.[40] The dispute concerned the rights of France and Spain respectively to waters flowing from Lake Lanoux in the Pyrenees.[41] Lake Lanoux is situated entirely in France, but its waters flow into the Carol River, which enters Spanish territory after traveling roughly twenty-five kilometers through France.[42] The Treaty of Bayonne of 1866 established the Franco-Spanish border and contained provisions regulating the use of transboundary watercourses like the Carol River.[43] Article 8 of the Treaty affirmed that "standing and flowing waters ... are subject to the sovereignty of the State in which they are located."[44] Anticipating that situations could arise in which works in one country might affect waters in the other, Article 11 provided that any proposal "to construct works or to grant concessions which might change the course of the volume of a [transboundary] watercourse" could proceed only after "prior notice" to the other state.

[39] Société Energie Electrique du Littoral Miditerranéen v. Compagnia Imprese Elettriche Liguri, Italian Court of Cassation, 13 February 1939, (1938–1940) Annual Digest of Public International Law Cases (Lauterpacht) 120–122 (No. 47).

[40] Lake Lanoux Arbitration (Fr. v. Sp.), 24 ILR 101 (1957).

[41] Ibid. p. 101.

[42] Ibid. p. 101–102.

[43] Ibid. p. 102–105.

[44] Ibid. p. 102–103.

The purpose of this requirement was to enable aggrieved states to raise timely objections, thus ensuring that "the interests that may be involved on both sides will be safeguarded."[45]

In 1950, France announced that it would divert some of the waters from Lake Lanoux to develop a hydroelectric project on its own soil. France proposed to return the diverted waters to the Carol River (the natural destination of those waters) through an engineered tunnel.[46] Spain objected to the proposed project, arguing that Article 11 of the Treaty of Bayonne required France to obtain Spain's consent before proceeding.[47] In response, France invoked Article 8, which affirmed the parties' sovereign jurisdiction over "standing and flowing waters" within their borders. France argued that in any event Spain would suffer no harm from the project because all of the diverted water would return to the Carol River before it crossed into Spain.[48]

The Tribunal emphatically rejected the suggestion that France must obtain Spain's consent before diverting water from Lake Lanoux. The Tribunal expressed concern that if Spain had the right to veto such works in French territory, Spain could dominate its neighbor, suppressing France's "exercise of territorial jurisdiction" through "unconditional and arbitrary opposition" to new development projects.[49] Spain's argument would exalt territorial integrity to the detriment of territorial sovereignty, subjecting upstream riparians to the unilateral power of downstream riparians. This would place the sovereign rights of France and Spain on an unequal footing in violation of the principle of sovereign equality.

Although the Tribunal rejected Spain's argument, it confirmed that France was legally obligated to cooperate with Spain to provide equitable utilization of the disputed waters. Accordingly, France could not treat Spanish interests with indifference; rather, it must consult and negotiate

[45] Ibid. p. 103.
[46] Ibid. p. 105.
[47] Ibid. p. 120.
[48] Ibid. pp. 117–119. Throughout the dispute, the states' respective obligations "to negotiate the apportionment of the waters of [the] international watercourse was uncontested, and was acknowledged by France not merely by reason of the terms of the Treaty of Bayonne and its Additional Act, but as a principle to be derived from the authorities." 'The Law of the Non-Navigational Uses of International Watercourses', art. 3, *in* Report of the International Law Commission on the Work of Its Thirty-Second Session (1980) 2 YBILC 117, UN Doc. A/CN.4/SER.A/1980/Add.1.
[49] Lake Lanoux Arbitration, p. 128.

with its downstream neighbor in good faith.[50] In this context, "the reality of the obligations thus undertaken is incontestable and sanctions can be applied in the event, for example, of an unjustified breaking off of the discussions, abnormal delay, disregard of the agreed procedures, systematic refusals to take into consideration adverse proposals or interests, and, more generally – in cases of violation of the rules of good faith."[51] In particular, the Tribunal stressed the "necessity to reconcile [conflicting interests] by mutual concessions,"[52] and that to this end "there would thus appear to be an obligation to accept in good faith all communications and contracts which could, by a broad comparison of interests and by reciprocal good will, provide States with the best conditions for concluding agreements."[53]

More specifically, the Tribunal held that it would not be enough for France, the upstream state, to engage in a mere box-ticking exercise "such as taking note of complaints, protests or representations made by the downstream State."[54] Instead, "the upstream State is under the obligation to take into consideration the various interests involved, to seek to give them every satisfaction compatible with the pursuit of its own interests, and to show that in this regard it is genuinely concerned to reconcile the interests of the other riparian State with its own."[55] France had satisfied these obligations by negotiating with Spain in good faith and giving reasonable consideration to Spanish interests by agreeing to restore waters diverted to the Carol River in a manner that would best accommodate Spanish agriculture.[56]

Because France's efforts to cooperate with Spain were carried out within a mandatory legal framework, Spain was not subject to unilateralism on the part of France, notwithstanding the fact that France was exercising sovereign rights over the waterway. Although Spain did not obtain a veto over France's hydroelectric project, the Tribunal concluded that Spain was entitled to meaningful consultation and equitable accommodation, thus providing a legal bulwark against French unilateralism. In particular, the Tribunal emphasized that French sovereignty over the upstream waterway must not be used to interfere arbitrarily with Spanish

[50] Ibid.
[51] Ibid.
[52] Ibid. p. 129.
[53] Ibid. p. 130.
[54] Ibid. p. 139.
[55] Ibid.
[56] Ibid. p. 142.

interests or to threaten such interference.[57] Spain had argued that diverting water into a hydroelectric project was wrongful because it would make Spain dependent on France for the continued delivery of water from Lake Lanoux.[58] The Tribunal did not reject this argument on principle, but on the grounds that the facts did not bear it out: because France could not shut off the flow of water without causing serious injury to its own interests, any threat to interfere with Spain's access to water from Lake Lanoux would be an empty one.[59] Accordingly, there was no genuine prospect of France using the proposed hydroelectric project to dominate Spain or interfere with Spain's territorial integrity. The Tribunal concluded that France had adequately respected Spain's sovereign interests by notifying Spain of the proposed project, engaging in extensive consultation and negotiation, submitting to arbitration, and giving due regard to Spain's sovereign interests in the shared watercourse.

Legal scholars today often characterize *Lake Lanoux* as affirming a doctrine of "limited sovereign rights" over international watercourses, but this characterization requires qualification.[60] As noted previously, the Treaty of Bayonne expressly preserved the states-parties' sovereign authority over their respective territories.[61] The Tribunal did not question this proposition. Accordingly, the Tribunal left the parties' sovereign rights undisturbed but held that each of the parties must exercise their rights in accordance with equitable principles that respect the other's equal sovereignty.

This approach to reconciling conflicts of sovereign rights resonates with equity's operation in national legal systems. As Henry Smith has observed, equity constitutes a form of "second-order law" or "meta-law" that formally preserves legal rights but conditions how those rights may be exercised in some contexts.[62] Equitable principles characteristically apply to disputes involving conflicting rights, where the exercise of a right

[57] Ibid. pp. 138–142.
[58] Ibid. p. 113.
[59] Ibid. pp. 125–126.
[60] See, e.g., Kornfeld, *Transboundary Water Disputes*, p. 62 (observing that a doctrine of limited territorial sovereignty "has received wide-scale acceptance within [the] transboundary water law community"); McCaffrey, *The Law of International Watercourses*, p. 135 (describing "the doctrine of 'limited territorial sovereignty'" as "probably the prevailing theory of international watercourse rights and obligations today").
[61] Treaty of Bayonne, art. 8.
[62] Henry Smith, 'Equity as Meta-Law' (2021) 130 YLJ 1050.

by one party could prejudice others' rights.[63] Equity's response to conflicting rights is to impose second-order "*in personam*" obligations that "leave the presumptive rights in place and to reconcile them ex post based on an equitable, context-sensitive style of reasoning."[64] Equity accommodates conflicting rights by constraining how parties may exercise rights to prevent what the civilian legal tradition calls an "abuse of right." Hence, a state may not abuse its sovereign authority over a transboundary river by unilaterally imposing regulations that effectively subordinate another riparian state's sovereign authority. Nor may a state divert water from a transboundary river in a manner that would disproportionately impact another state's sovereign rights to the same resource. Consistent with the dominant proportionality-based approach to adjudicating conflicts of rights,[65] international law calls for apportioning water between riparian states in a manner that accounts for the states' respective equitable interests.[66] This distinctively equitable approach to conflicts of rights has become "the cornerstone of customary international law" governing the use of transboundary rivers.[67]

By placing equitable principles at the heart of its regime governing transboundary rivers, international law aims to mitigate practical inequities generated by its allocation of territory among states. If equitable principles did not apply, upstream states (e.g., France, the United States) might invoke their own territorial sovereignty as a trump justifying the unilateral diversion of water that would otherwise flow to downstream states (e.g., Mexico, Spain). Or economically and militarily powerful downstream states (e.g., Egypt) might cite territorial integrity as a justification for coercing upstream states to refrain from using an equitable portion of transboundary waters (e.g., Burundi, Ethiopia, Uganda). By

[63] Ibid. pp. 1055–1056. The polycentricity of transboundary river disputes also supports recourse to equitable principles. *See* Kornfeld, *Transboundary Water Disputes*, pp. 30–41.

[64] Smith, 'Equity as Meta-Law', pp. 1068, 1073.

[65] *See* Alec Stone Sweet and Jud Mathews, 'Proportionality Balancing and Global Constitutionalism' (2008) 47 CJTL 72, 73, 87–88 (contrasting hierarchy-based approaches to conflicts of rights with proportionality-based approaches, and characterizing proportionality analysis as "the preferred procedure for managing disputes involving an alleged conflict between two rights claims").

[66] See UN Watercourses Convention, art. 5 ("Watercourse States shall participate in the use, development and protection of an international watercourse in an equitable and reasonable manner.").

[67] Boisson de Chazournes, *Fresh Water in International Law*, p. 26; see also Christina Leb, *Cooperation in the Law of Transboundary Water Resources* (Cambridge: Cambridge University Press, 2013), p. 80; Stephen C. McCaffrey, 'Intertwined General Principles', in *Research Handbook*, pp. 83, 88.

affirming that equitable principles apply to international rivers, international law bars states from dominating their neighbors by unilaterally dictating the terms upon which these shared resources will be governed and apportioned.[68]

Establishing a Community of Interest

Recognizing the uncertainty that surrounded the international law of international watercourses at the dawn of the twentieth century, the eminent Swiss jurist Max Huber identified four possible legal paradigms: absolute territorial sovereignty, absolute territorial integrity, limited territorial sovereignty, and community of interest. The last option – community of interest – would treat an international watercourse (including the primary river and all tributaries) holistically as a unitary common resource.[69] Proponents of the community interest paradigm tend to link the idea to concepts of "internationalization" or "denationalization," suggesting that transboundary rivers are subject to the joint-stewardship of the entire community of riparian states.[70] Under this approach, no member of the community could claim unilateral jurisdiction over a transboundary river, but each would have an equal right to use the river, and each would have equal voice in collective governance.

In its first case on the merits, the PCIJ applied the community of interest paradigm to the Oder, a river that presently traverses the territory of the Czech Republic, Germany, and Poland. Under the Treaty of Versailles, an international commission was responsible for regulating navigation on the Oder.[71] The question presented in *The River Oder Case* was whether the commission's jurisdiction extended to certain tributaries of the Oder in Polish territory. Purporting to summarize "the principles governing international fluvial law in general," the Court indicated that

[68] Much depends on how states' equitable interests are identified and assessed. See Valentina Okaru-Bisant, 'Institutional and Legal Frameworks of Preventing and Resolving Disputes Concerning the Development and Management of Africa's Shared River Basins' (1998) 9 *Colo. J. Int'l Envt'l L. & Pol'y* 331, 354 (expressing concern that applying equitable principles may "reward the countries ... that are first to develop a shared river," thereby systematically disadvantaging poorer countries that are behind the development curve).

[69] Max Huber, 'Ein Beitrag zur Lehre von der Gebietshoheit an Grenzflüssen', in *Zeitschrift für Völkerrecht und Bundesstaatsrecht* (Breslau: J. Kern, 1907), pp. 161–162.

[70] See McCaffrey, *The Law of International Watercourses*, p. 60; Weiss, *International Law for a Water-Scarce World*, p. 21.

[71] River Oder Case, p. 13.

> a solution of the problem has been sought not in the idea of a right of passage in favour of upstream States, but in that of a community of interest of riparian States. This community of interest in a navigable river becomes the basis of a common legal right, the essential features of which are the perfect equality of all riparian States in the use of the whole course of the river and the exclusion of any preferential privilege of any one riparian State in relation to the others.[72]

Decades later, the International Court of Justice (ICJ) would cite this passage from *The River Oder Case* with approval in *Gabčikovo-Nagymaros v. Hungary*, asserting that the subsequent "development of international law has strengthened this [community of interest] principle for non-navigational uses of international watercourses as well."[73]

The community of interest paradigm aptly describes some treaty regimes, like the Mexico–US partnership at the Rio Grande, which establish international commissions to govern watercourses holistically for the shared benefit of riparian states. It also helps to make sense of watercourse treaties (or provisions thereof) that are designed to promote environmental conservation, sustainability, and intergenerational equity. The purpose of these agreements is to remove matters of common concern from the unilateral jurisdiction of individual states and commit those matters instead to the joint stewardship of a community of riparian states.[74] Within a community of interest regime, each state must cooperate with the rest of the community to achieve the regime's objectives, while sharing equitably in the associated benefits and burdens. Significantly, because community of interest regimes are premised on sovereign equality, they are subject to the same equitable principles that apply in conflict of rights cases like Lake Lanoux. In both contexts, states must share relevant information, seek consensus through consultation and negotiation, and, if all else fails, resort to peaceful third-party dispute resolution.

Most transboundary rivers have not been fully internationalized through treaties that establish a community of interest.[75] The reason

[72] Ibid. p. 27.

[73] Case Concerning the Gabčikovo-Nagymaros Project (Hungary/Slovakia), 1997 ICJ Rep. 7, 85 (25 September).

[74] Cf. Cara Nine, 'When Affected Interests Demand Joint Self-determination: Learning From Rivers' (2014) 6 *Int'l Theory* 157, 163 (arguing that "rivers should be sites of joint political structures, because without them groups are in jeopardy of losing their capacity to be self-determining").

[75] See Rémy Kinna and Alistair Rieu-Clarke, *The Governance Regime of the Mekong River Basin: Can the Global Water Conventions Strengthen the 1995 Mekong Agreement?*

why states have not concluded more treaties is not hard to imagine. States are often reluctant to relinquish their territorial sovereignty. They do not necessarily trust neighboring states as prospective partners. They might hesitate to conclude agreements that could lock in long-term disadvantages or strengthen a competitor. When states decline to establish a community of interest regime for these or other reasons, *Lake Lanoux*'s customary default rule applies: each state retains its sovereign rights but must exercise those rights in a manner that satisfies equitable principles.

Codifying Mandatory Cooperation

International watercourse treaties often codify aspects of *Lake Lanoux*'s customary default rules. In some instances, these agreements have sustained productive international partnerships even among otherwise bitter regional rivals. A striking example is the Indus Waters Treaty of 1960.[76] Originating on the Tibetan plateau, the Indus River travels 1800 miles through India and Pakistan, sustaining the lives and livelihoods of approximately 215 million people throughout its basin. Following the 1947 partition of India and Pakistan, the World Bank averted possible hostilities between the two states by brokering an agreement that has held firm for over sixty years.[77] Rather than treat the Indus River Basin as a unitary system under a community of interest regime, India and Pakistan elected to divide the basin's waters equitably, with India taking the three eastern rivers (the Ravi, Beas, and Sutlej) and Pakistan the three western rivers (the Indus, Jhelum, and Chenab), subject to India's right to use some water for irrigation, hydropower generation, and other purposes before the western rivers enter Pakistan.[78] The two states also agreed to develop dams, canals, and other works (bankrolled largely by the World Bank) to increase the total volume of water available for agriculture, electricity generation, and other uses.[79] The treaty establishes an orderly process for information-sharing, consultation, and dispute

(Leiden: Brill, 2017), p. 4 ("Only approximately 40 percent of the world's 263 international watercourses are now covered by a basin-specific agreement, which suggests that a significant number of basins are reliant upon customary international law.").

76 Indus Waters Treaty, Karachi, 19 September 1960, 419 UNTS 6032.

77 For discussion of the World Bank's role, see Salman M. A. Salman and Kishor Uprety, *Conflict and Cooperation on South Asia's International Rivers* (New York: Kluwer Law International, 2002), pp. 45–58.

78 Indus Waters Treaty, arts. II–III.

79 Ibid. art. IV.

resolution through a Permanent Indus Commission.[80] If the commissioners fail to reach agreement, the parties may jointly submit unresolved "differences" either to a neutral expert who is a highly qualified engineer or to the Permanent Court of Arbitration (PCA).[81] Against all odds, this cooperative framework between India and Pakistan has survived three wars (1965, 1971, 1999), a nuclear arms race, intensifying nationalism, and a host of other challenges,[82] though its future remains fragile in light of enduring tensions between the two historic rivals.[83]

Another important codification of mandatory cooperation is the UN Economic Commission for Europe's 1992 Convention on the Protection and Use of Transboundary Watercourses and International Lakes, also known as the "Helsinki Convention."[84] Following the devastating 1986 Sandoz chemical spill, which dyed the Rhine River blood red, wiping out flora and fauna for hundreds of miles, European countries cooperated to establish an "ecosystem-oriented, holistic approach to the sustainable use and integrated management of freshwater resources in Europe."[85] The keystone of this effort is the Helsinki Convention, which requires state-parties to "prevent, control, and reduce pollution of waters causing or likely to cause transboundary impact"; "ensure that transboundary waters are used with the aim of ecologically sound and rational water management, conservation of water resources and environmental protection"; "ensure that transboundary waters are used in a reasonable and equitable way"; and "ensure conservation and, where necessary, restoration of ecosystems."[86] The Convention also obligates states-parties to "cooperate in the conduct of research into and development of effective

[80] Ibid. arts. VI–VII.

[81] Ibid. art. IX; see also In re. Indus Waters Kishenganga Arbitration (Pak. v. India), Partial Award (Arb. Trib 18 February 2013); In re. Indus Waters Kishenganga Arbitration (Pak. v. India), Final Award (Arb. Trib. 20 December 2013).

[82] See Magsig, *International Water Law and the Quest for Common Security*, p. 185.

[83] See Betsy Joles, 'With Indus Water Treaty in the Balance, Pakistan Braces for More Water Woes', NPR, 8 July 2025 (discussing India's suspension of the Indus Water Treaty in response to an April 2025 "attack in which militants killed 26 people in Indian-administered Kashmir").

[84] UN Economic Commission for Europe, Convention on the Protection and Use of Transboundary Watercourses and International Lakes, Helsinki, 17 March 1992, in force 6 October 1996, 31 ILM 1312 [hereinafter Helsinki Convention].

[85] Götz Reichert, 'Europe: International Water Law and the EU Water Framework Directive', in *Research Handbook*, pp. 397, 397–398. Since 2016, the Helsinki Convention has been open for ratification by non-European states. UNECE, *Introduction*, https://unece.org/environment-policy/water/about-the-convention/introduction.

[86] Helsinki Convention, art. 2(2).

techniques for the prevention, control and reduction of transboundary impact,"[87] and to practice the "widest exchange of information, as early as possible, on issues covered by the provisions of this Convention."[88] The Helsinki Convention makes international cooperation mandatory by declaring that states-parties "shall on the basis of equality and reciprocity enter into bilateral or multilateral agreements or other arrangements" on a wide range of issues "in order to define their mutual relations and conduct regarding the prevention, control and reduction of transboundary impact."[89] Each of these features of the Helsinki Convention affirms states' joint stewardship over the sustainable use and environmental protection of transboundary rivers.

Perhaps the most important codification of mandatory cooperation for transboundary rivers is the landmark 1997 Convention on the Law of Non-Navigational Uses of International Watercourses (the UN Watercourses Convention).[90] Article 5 endorses the principle of equitable and reasonable utilization by providing that states-parties "shall in their respective territories utilize an international watercourse in an equitable manner . . . taking into account the interests of the watercourse States concerned, consistent with adequate protection of the watercourse."[91] Factors relevant to the equitable apportionment of water include a river's natural characteristics, the social and economic needs of riparian states, how usage affects other states, and the need for conservation and efficient use of water resources.[92] The Convention also obligates states "when utilizing an international watercourse in their territories, [to] take all appropriate measures to prevent the causing of significant harm to other watercourse States."[93]

To foster international equity and prevent avoidable harm, the UN Watercourses Convention obligates states to "cooperate on the basis of

[87] Helsinki Convention, art. 5.

[88] Helsinki Convention, art. 6.

[89] Helsinki Convention, art 9; see also art. 10 ("Consultations shall be held between the Riparian Parties on the basis of reciprocity, good faith and goodneighbourliness, at the request of any such Party. Such consultations shall aim at cooperation regarding the issues covered by the provisions of this Convention.").

[90] UN Watercourses Convention.

[91] UN Watercourses Convention, art. 5(1).

[92] UN Watercourses Convention, art. 6(1).

[93] UN Watercourses Convention art. 7(1); see also Jutta Brunnée and Stephen J. Toope, 'The Changing Nile Basin Regime: Does Law Matter?' (2002) 43 HILJ 105, 149 (noting tensions between the equitable and reasonable utilization principle and the no significant harm requirement).

sovereign equality, territorial integrity, mutual benefit and good faith in order to attain optimal utilization and adequate protection of an international watercourse."[94] This general obligation entails specific duties to exchange data and information on the conditions of a watercourse,[95] including planned works that might adversely affect other riparian states.[96] In addition, the Convention requires states-parties to consult and negotiate with one another "in good faith," respecting the principle of sovereign equality by "pay[ing] reasonable regard to [others'] rights and legitimate interests."[97] If consultation and negotiation do not produce agreement, states-parties must "seek a settlement of the dispute by peaceful means." Options for peaceful dispute resolution include recourse to an impartial factfinder; the good offices, mediation or conciliation of a third party; submission to a joint watercourse institution; international arbitration; or adjudication in the ICJ.[98] These features of the UN Watercourses Convention codify the customary duties of mandatory cooperation.[99]

Managing Entrenched Disputes

When states fail to agree on mutually acceptable terms of cooperation for a transboundary river, this can lead to a protracted stalemate. Entrenched disputes over transboundary rivers are not necessarily the product of bad faith. In some cases, neighboring states may disagree in good faith about the ingredients of an equitable solution. They may prefer different dispute-resolution mechanisms (e.g., mediation, arbitration, adjudication) or institutions (e.g., ICJ, PCA, regional courts). While international dialogue can help to resolve discord between states, in some instances it can harden points of disagreement.[100] When this occurs, transboundary river disputes can easily drag on without the expectation of an immediate resolution.

Some of the world's most important watercourses have become mired in entrenched disputes. The iconic Nile River Basin, which covers over

94 UN Watercourses Convention, art. 8(1).
95 UN Watercourses Convention, art. 9.
96 UN Watercourses Convention, arts. 11–12.
97 UN Watercourses Convention, art. 17.
98 UN Watercourses Convention, art. 33.
99 The Convention entered force in August 2014. As of February 5, 2025, only forty states have joined the Convention. *See* UN Treaty Collection, https://treaties.un.org/Pages/ViewDetails.aspx?src=IND&mtdsg_no=XXVII-12&chapter=27&clang=_en.
100 See Monica Hakimi, 'The Work of International Law' (2017) 58 HILJ 1.

three million square miles and feeds 250 million people, illustrates this problem.[101] By 2050, the combined population of Nile Basin riparian states is expected to reach one billion, straining the basin's capacity to meet the population's basic needs for fresh water.[102] For generations, the eleven states within the Nile River Basin have debated how to apportion its finite waters. Citing historical practice, colonial-era treaties, and its continuing needs, Egypt has asserted the right to use over 55 percent of the Nile's annual flow. Sudan has also claimed preferential rights to Nile Basin waters.[103] However, as upstream riparians have grown in population, political influence, and the ability to attract foreign investment for hydropower and irrigation projects, the reaching claims of Egypt and Sudan have encountered increasingly stiff resistance.

In 2010, multilateral discussions among Nile Basin states produced the Nile Basin Cooperative Framework Agreement (CFA), a treaty that seeks to "promote integrated management, sustainable development, and harmonious utilization of the water resources of the Basin, as well as their conservation and protection for the benefit of present and future generations."[104] Modeled after the UN Watercourses Convention, the CFA embraces the general principles of equitable and reasonable utilization, avoiding significant harm, the preservation of endangered ecosystems, good faith consultation and cooperation, and mandatory dispute resolution.[105] The CFA specifically affirms "[t]he principle of cooperation between States of the Nile River Basin on the basis of sovereign equality, territorial integrity, mutual benefit and good faith in order to attain optimal utilization and adequate protection and conservation of the Nile River Basin and to promote joint efforts to achieve social and economic development."[106] Notably, the CFA also invokes the "community of interest" concept as a guiding principle, calling into question the

[101] Salman M. A. Salman, 'Mediation of International Water Disputes: The Indus, the Jordan, and the Nile Basins Interventions', in Laurence Boisson de Chazournes, Christina Leb, and Mara Tignino (eds.), *International Law and Freshwater: The Multiple Challenges* (Cheltenham: Edward Elgar, 2013), pp. 360, 387; Nile Basin Initiative, 'A Long River Journey: 20 Years of Cooperation Under the NBI' (2019) [hereinafter NBI].

[102] NBI, p. 13.

[103] Salman, 'Mediation', p. 390.

[104] Agreement on the Nile River Basin Cooperative Framework, 14 May 2010, www.internationalwaterlaw.org/documents/regionaldocs/Nile_River_Basin_Cooperative_Framework_2010.pdf [hereinafter Agreement on the Nile River Basin Cooperative Framework].

[105] Agreement on the Nile River Basin Cooperative Framework, arts. 3–11.

[106] Agreement on the Nile River Basin Cooperative Framework, art. 3(1).

sovereignty-based claims of Egypt and Sudan.[107] To date, only seven states have signed on to the CFA (Burundi, Ethiopia, Kenya, Rwanda, South Sudan, Tanzania, Uganda), leaving four holdouts (Democratic Republic of the Congo, Egypt, Eritrea, and Sudan).[108] The fact that so many downstream states have declined to endorse the CFA leaves the Nile's future in limbo, despite growing acceptance on both sides that equitable principles constitute the applicable international law[109] and despite burgeoning cooperation with respect to some issues of common concern, such as flood control and environmental conservation.[110]

Another well-known example of an entrenched dispute is the *Gabčikovo-Nagymaros Case.*[111] In 1993, Hungary and Slovakia sought the ICJ's assistance in resolving a dispute over Hungary's unilateral suspension of a joint-venture between the two countries to develop a system of locks and hydroelectric power plants on the Danube River.[112] Hungary argued that the project negatively impacted its legal interest and the international community's collective interest in preserving the river's ecological health.[113] Slovakia contended, in turn, that Hungary's actions violated a treaty between the two countries.[114] After concluding that both parties had violated their international legal obligations, the ICJ sent the dispute back to the parties with the instruction to "find an agreed solution" through "good faith" negotiation.[115] Although Slovakia eventually agreed to discontinue proceedings in the ICJ, for nearly two decades the two sides made little progress in negotiations, raising the specter of perpetual deadlock.[116]

107 Agreement on the Nile River Basin Cooperative Framework, art. 3(9).
108 Nile Basin Initiative, 'Cooperative Framework Agreement', https://nilebasin.org/about-us/cooperative-framework-agreement.
109 See Agreement on Declaration of Principles between the Arab Republic of Egypt, the Federal Democratic Republic of Ethiopia and the Republic of the Sudan on the Grand Ethiopian Renaissance Dam Project (GERDP), 23 March 2015, www.internationalwaterlaw.org/documents/regionaldocs/Final_Nile_Agreement_23_March_2015.pdf (endorsing principles of cooperation and equitable and reasonable utilization).
110 See NBI, p. 35 (outlining the 2017–2027 Nile Basin Strategy).
111 Gabčikovo-Nagymaros Project, 1997 ICJ Rep. 7.
112 Ibid. pp. 10–17, paras. 1–14.
113 Ibid. pp. 35–36, para. 40.
114 Ibid. p. 16, para. 13.
115 Ibid. pp. 78, 82 paras. 142, 155(2)(B).
116 In June 2017, Hungary resumed construction and Slovakia agreed to discontinue proceedings in the ICJ. Gabčikovo-Nagymaros Project (Hung./Slov.), Press Release (21 July 2017), www.icj-cij.org/files/case-related/92/092-20170721-PRE-01-00-EN.pdf.

International law responds to entrenched disputes like these by imposing special requirements of mandatory cooperation. First, as long as disputes remain unresolved, states must continue to explore dispute resolution mechanisms in good faith until they find a successful avenue for achieving an equitable resolution.[117] Second, although states may take provisional steps to secure their legal interests once it becomes clear that an impasse has been reached,[118] they must notify other interested parties of such measures,[119] maintain a continuous process of dialogue to ensure that their provisional measures do not foreclose a multilateral solution,[120] and avoid any actions that would "establish a fait accompli capable of prejudicing the outcome of negotiations."[121] The last requirement is especially critical as applied to transboundary rivers: states must refrain from constructing dams, diverting tributaries, and engaging in other invasive works that could cause permanent and irreversible harm to other riparian states' interests and the natural environment.[122] These obligations are necessary to reconcile sovereign equality and joint stewardship with the often-slow pace of international dispute resolution.

[117] See UN General Assembly, 'Declaration on Principles of International Law Concerning Friendly Relations and Co-operation Among States in Accordance with the Charter of the United Nations', 24 October 1970, UN Doc. A/RES/25/2625, p. 123 ("The parties to a dispute have the duty, in the event of failure to reach a solution by any one of the above peaceful means, to continue to seek a settlement of the dispute by other peaceful means agreed upon by them.").

[118] See WTO, United States—Import Prohibition of Certain Shrimp and Shrimp Products, Recourse to Art. 21.5 by Malaysia, Report of the Panel, 15 June 2001, WT/DS58/RW [hereinafter Shrimp/Turtle AB II] (noting that provisional measures are permissible under international law because otherwise "any country party to ... negotiations ... would have, in effect, a veto over [other states]," which "would not be reasonable").

[119] Dispute Regarding Navigational and Related Rights (Costa Rica/Nicaragua), Judgment, 2009 ICJ Rep. 213, 252 para. 95 (13 July) (explaining that a duty to provide notice arises when one state regulates a resource over which another state also has rights).

[120] See Shrimp/Turtle AB II, para. 153(b) (concluding that regulatory standards imposed unilaterally by the United States were permissible on a provisional basis, provided that the parties continued to pursue "ongoing serious good faith efforts to reach a multilateral agreement").

[121] Hugh Thirlway, *The Law and Procedure of the International Court of Justice: Fifty Years of Jurisprudence* (Oxford: Oxford University Press, 2013), p. 22.

[122] See Delimitation of the Maritime Boundary Case (Guy./Surin.), PCA 2004–04, para. 470 (17 September 2007) ("It should not be permissible for a party to a dispute to undertake any unilateral activity that might affect the other party's rights in a permanent manner.").

The Promise and Perils of Mandatory Cooperation

As the twenty-first century rolls onward, fresh water might be insufficient in some regions to meet the needs of swelling populations during an era of climate change and rapid economic development. Experts anticipate that by mid-century, 3.1 billion people will live in urban areas with seasonal water shortages.[123] International cooperation will be essential in this perilous new world of freshwater scarcity to respect, protect, and fulfill human rights, while safeguarding international peace and security.

Regrettably, international cooperation can also aggravate some of the very problems it aspires to solve. Consider the majestic Mekong River, which rises in China and traverses Laos, Myanmar, Thailand, and Cambodia before draining into the South China Sea through Vietnam's sprawling "Nine Dragon" river delta. Since the early 1990s, a spirit of robust regional cooperation[124] and an influx of foreign investment have enabled states to construct over three hundred hydroelectric dams along the Mekong.[125] This cooperative ethos has quickened the pace of development and enriched elites throughout the river basin, but at a terrible human and environmental cost. Dams have cut off the natural flow of nutrient-rich silt from China, endangering rice production and inland fisheries along the river's course. Eighty percent of the inhabitants of the Mekong River Basin – over sixty million people – depend upon these dietary staples for survival. Meanwhile, the basin's vibrant biodiversity, with over 20,000 types of plant and nearly 2,500 animal species, including freshwater dolphins and giant catfish, is tilting rapidly toward ecological collapse. Thus, national authorities in Mekong states have harnessed international cooperation to achieve economic development at the expense of fragile ecosystems and the most vulnerable members of their societies.[126]

123 Weiss, *International Law for a Water-Scarce World*, p. 1.

124 This so-called "Mekong Spirit" finds expression, inter alia, in the 1995 Agreement on the Cooperation for the Sustainable Development of the Mekong River Basin, 5 April 1995, 34 ILM 864 (1995).

125 McCaffrey, *The Law of International Watercourses*, pp. 285–286; Kinna and Rieu-Clarke, *The Governance Regime of the Mekong River Basin*, pp. 27–28.

126 Hannah Beech, '"Our River Was Like a God": How Dams and China's Might Imperil the Mekong', NY Times, 12 October 2019; Kay Johnson and Panu Wongcha-um, 'Water Wars: Mekong River Another Front in U.S.-China Rivalry', Reuters, 24 July 2020; 'Requiem for a River: Can One of the World's Great Waterways Survive Its Development?', Economist, www.economist.com/news/essays/21689225-can-one-world-s-great-waterways-survive-its-development [hereinafter Requiem].

Given that international cooperation has caused the Mekong's ecological crisis, it might seem counterintuitive to recommend more international cooperation as a solution. But multilateral engagement is the only plausible and potentially legitimate path to save the Mekong. The environmental harm wrought by proliferating dams cannot be reversed by any single state unilaterally; it requires collective action by the entire community of riparian states – including China, which has invested heavily in dam construction throughout the region.[127] Mekong states will have to share the costs and benefits of environmental conservation. To determine what equity and environmental stewardship require in this context, they must collect and share information regarding relevant factors such as their respective dependence on hydropower, the ecological health of the river, and the impact of dams and other works on their domestic agriculture and fishing. They will have to negotiate in good faith or agree to resolve their differences through third-party dispute resolution. In short, they will have to jointly embrace mandatory cooperation.

[127] Requiem.

3

Oceans

A Fighting Chance

On June 19, 2023, national delegates from nearly 200 countries gathered under the soaring rotunda of the UN's General Assembly Hall in New York City to approve, by consensus, a landmark agreement for the conservation and sustainable use of marine life.[1] Commonly known as the "High Seas Treaty" or the "Biodiversity Beyond National Jurisdiction (BBNJ) Agreement," the treaty represents the culmination of over a decade of multilateral negotiations.[2] At its heart is an ambitious framework for establishing large marine protected areas in the high seas – a critical step toward achieving the United Nations' goal of effectively conserving and managing 30 percent of the earth's oceans by 2030.[3]

This diplomatic breakthrough arrived not a moment too soon. As UN Secretary-General António Guterres reminded the assembled delegates, marine species in the twenty-first century face a harrowing number of existential threats, including warming oceans, shifting weather patterns, ocean acidification, and the disruption of coastal ecosystems. To make matters worse, human population growth and the rise of modern industrial fishing technologies have generated

1 Agreement Under the United Nations Convention on the Law of the Sea on the Conservation and Sustainable Use of Maritime Biological Diversity of Areas Beyond National Jurisdiction, 19 June 2023, A/CONF.232/2023/4*; see generally 'An Historic Achievement: Treaty of the High Seas Is Adopted', European Commission Directorate-General for Maritime Affairs and Fisheries, 19 June 2023, https://oceans-and-fisheries.ec.europa.eu/news/historic-achievement-treaty-high-seas-adopted-2023-06-19_en.

2 'An Historic Achievement'.

3 'An Historic Achievement'; see also 'Kunming-Montreal Global Biodiversity Framework', CBD/COP/15/L.25, 15 December 2022, www.cbd.int/doc/c/e6d3/cd1d/daf663719a03902a9b116c34/cop-15-l-25-en.pdf (establishing the 30 percent goal).

overfishing on an unprecedented scale, with over a third of global fish stocks subject to unsustainable harvesting.[4]

While acknowledging the daunting challenges ahead, Guterres praised the delegates for having "pumped new life and hope to give the ocean a fighting chance":

> By acting to counter threats to our planet that go beyond national boundaries, you are demonstrating that global threats deserve global action.
>
> That countries can come together, in unity, for the common good.
>
> That the spirit of multilateral cooperation that infuses this chamber is alive and well.[5]

In celebrating the "spirit of multilateral cooperation" that produced the High Seas Treaty, however, the Secretary-General glossed over an important point: international cooperation in this case was not merely good policy, it was also a legal obligation. For decades leading up to the High Seas Treaty, international courts and tribunals had affirmed that the law of the sea required states to cooperate with one another to ensure the conservation and sustainable use of marine resources.[6] Aided by the UN International Law Commission (ILC), states had also codified this requirement to cooperate in a multilateral convention with near-universal membership.[7] Thus, by working together to develop the High Seas Treaty, members of the General Assembly were not writing on a blank slate; rather, they were taking steps to fulfill a longstanding legal obligation to cooperate for the conservation and management of oceanic resources.

International law did not always require states to cooperate in this way. Prior to the middle of the twentieth century, the conventional wisdom among international lawyers was that states were free to use and exploit oceanic resources however they wished, without regard to the rights or

4 'Secretary-General's Remarks at the Intergov. Conference on an Int'l Legally Binding Instrument Under the Convention on the Law of the Sea on the Conservation and Sustainable Use of Marine Biological Diversity of Areas Beyond National Jurisdiction', 19 June 2023, www.un.org/sg/en/content/sg/statement/2023-06-19/secretary-generals-remarks-the-intergov-conference-intl-legally-binding-instrument-under-the-un-convention-the-law-of-the-sea-the-conservation-and-sustainable-use-of.

5 Ibid.

6 See, e.g., Fisheries Jurisdiction Case (Fed. Rep. Germ./Iceland), Merits, 1974 ICJ Rep. 175 (25 July); Fisheries Jurisdiction Case (UK/Iceland), Merits, 1974 ICJ Rep. 3 (25 July); North Sea Continental Shelf Cases (Fed. Rep. Germ./Den; Fed. Rep. Germ./Neth.), Merits, 1969 ICJ Rep. 3 (20 February).

7 UN Convention on the Law of the Sea art. 125(1), UN Doc. A/CONF. 62/122 (1982) [hereinafter UNCLOS].

interests of other states or the natural environment. The rise of mandatory cooperation during the twentieth century therefore marked a sharp break with centuries of precedent – a startling revolution in the law of the sea. As the law of the sea is one of the oldest and most important fields of international law, the historical developments recounted in this chapter serve as a bellwether for mandatory cooperation's emergence in international law more generally.

The Battle of the Books

On February 25, 1603, a violent episode in the Straits of Singapore sent shock waves around the world, rattling the capitols of Europe. In a stunning challenge to Portuguese naval supremacy in the Far East, three Dutch ships ambushed a massive Portuguese treasure ship, the *Santa Catarina*, capturing a cargo worth 3.5 million guilders – "more than 60 percent of the average annual expenditures of the English government at the time."[8] When the *Santa Catarina* eventually reached Amsterdam, the local admiralty board declared the seizure "good prize" and sent the ship with its lavish cargo of gold, silks, and spices to auction for the benefit of the Dutch East India Company.[9]

Seeking to bolster the legal case for the *Santa Catarina*'s capture, the Dutch East India Company enlisted Hugo Grotius to prepare a supportive legal opinion. Just twenty-one years old at the time, Grotius had already achieved fame as "the Miracle of Holland" for his formidable intellect, dazzling erudition, and literary flair.[10] Applying these prodigious talents to the Dutch East India Company's legal defense, Grotius argued that the laws of war permitted the *Santa Catarina*'s seizure in response to Portugal's illegal efforts to prevent Dutch ships from transiting through the East Indies.[11] Grotius asserted that Portugal could not claim exclusive dominion over the seas surrounding the Straits of Singapore because the sea, by its nature and according to the custom of nations, was not amenable to possession.[12] The ocean was not subject to possession in the same manner as land, because its constant motion

[8] Oona A. Hathaway and Scott J. Shapiro, *The Internationalists: How a Radical Plan to Outlaw War Remade the World* (New York: Simon & Schuster, 2017), pp. 3–4, 6.

[9] Verdict of the Amsterdam Admiralty Board Sept. 9, 1604, in Hugo Grotius, *Commentary on the Law of Prize and Booty* (Martine Julia van Ittersum ed., 1603), pp. 306–309.

[10] Hathaway and Shapiro, *The Internationalists*, pp. 6–8.

[11] Grotius, *Commentary on the Law of Prize and Booty*, ch. XII.

[12] Ibid.

prevented states from demarcating clear maritime boundaries.[13] Moreover, the abundant and apparently inexhaustible character of oceanic resources meant that no state could justly exclude others from sharing in the oceans' bounty.[14] To prevent any nation from sailing and fishing on the sea, when those activities pose no threat to the state's own interests, would reflect a "brainsick covetousness" incompatible with natural law and state practice since antiquity, Grotius claimed.[15] The sea therefore constituted a global commons (*res communis*) outside the scope of national jurisdiction and immune from claims to national appropriation. Portugal's defiance of these principles amounted to a just cause of war.

In 1609, Grotius published a slim pamphlet advancing these arguments against national appropriation of the seas under the title *Mare Liberum* (*The Free Sea*).[16] The pamphlet sparked a political firestorm. The Vatican placed *Mare Liberum* on its list of banned books, perceiving the tract (accurately) as an assault on the Papal Bull of Pope Alexander VI, which had partitioned the globe into two spheres – one for Portuguese expansion to the east and the other for Spanish conquest to the west.[17] Iberian scholars rushed to defend their nations' claims to dominion over the high seas.[18] British publicists also sparred with Grotius, seeking to defend their crown's claims to exclusive dominion over the English Channel and the North Sea.[19] As clashes between Grotius's supporters and opponents dragged on over the course of the seventeenth century, the debate came to be known as "the battle of the books" (*la bataille des livres*).[20]

Among those who opposed Grotius's vision of the free sea, his most influential and forceful critic was John Selden, the great English lawyer

[13] Ibid.

[14] Ibid.

[15] Ibid.

[16] Hugo Grotius, *The Free Sea* (Indianapolis: Liberty Fund, David Armitage ed., Richard Hakluyt transl., 2004) (1609).

[17] David Armitage, 'Introduction', in Grotius, *The Free Sea*, p. xvii; Donald R. Rothwell and Tim Stephens, *The International Law of the Sea* (Oxford: Hart Publishing, 2010), p. 2. Portugal and Spain incorporated this division of the earth in the 1494 Treaty of Tordesillas.

[18] Justo Seraphim de Freitas, *Do Justo Império Asiático dos Portugueses (De Justo Imperio Luistanorum Asiatico)* (1625); Juan Solózarno Pereira, *De Indiarum Jure* (1629).

[19] See, e.g., John Selden, *Mare Clausum* (London: Kembe & Thomas, G. H. Gent transl. 1663); 'William Welwod's Critique', in Grotius, *The Free Sea*, p. 62.

[20] Tullio Scovazzi, *The Origin of the Theory of Sovereignty of the Sea, in Law of the Sea, From Grotius to the International Tribunal for the Law of the Sea: Liber Americorum Judge Hugo Caminos* (Lilian del Castillo ed., Brill Nijhoff, 2015), pp. 48–49.

whom John Milton hailed as "the chief of learned men reputed in this land."[21] In a provocatively titled 1636 treatise, *Mare Clausum* (*The Closed Sea*), Selden dismantled Grotius's historical and empirical claims. He argued persuasively that maritime powers since antiquity had often claimed certain maritime zones as their exclusive possession, including the seas surrounding the British Isles.[22] He also observed that some maritime resources, such as coastal fisheries and gems and pearls in the seabed, were clearly finite and exhaustible. Accordingly, he argued that states could justifiably claim dominion over regions of the sea where such resources were located.[23]

Under pressure from his critics, Grotius eventually conceded that states could acquire sovereign rights over certain maritime zones, such as bays and straits, where they had established effective control through a sustained naval presence.[24] By the eighteenth century, this principle of possession through effective control produced the "cannon shot rule" whereby coastal states were allowed to claim sovereign rights over a "territorial sea" extending three miles from their shore.[25] Beyond this three-mile zone, however, Grotius's free sea became the undisputed customary norm. Although Selden arguably advanced the stronger argument from historical practice, Grotius's vision of the high seas as a global commons held greater appeal for subsequent generations who viewed blue water as the indispensable gateway to international commerce and domestic prosperity.[26]

The Tragedy of the Free Sea

Given the sharp divisions between Grotius and Selden, it is easy to overlook that their dueling accounts of the law of the sea shared a basic assumption about the juridical character of state rights and powers. Both accounts assumed that a state may exercise its rights and powers under the law of the sea however it liked, without regard to the competing rights

[21] Ofer Haivry, *John Selden and the Western Political Tradition* (Cambridge: Cambridge University Press, 2017), p. 1.

[22] Selden, *Mare Clausum*.

[23] Ibid. bk. I, ch. 22.

[24] Hugo Grotius, *On the Law of War and Peace* (Indianapolis: Liberty Fund, Richard Tuck ed., 2005) (1626), 2.3.8.

[25] Tullio Treves, 'Historical Development of the Law of the Sea', in Donald R. Rockwell, Alex G. Oude Elferink, Karen N. Scott and Tim Stephens (eds.), *The Oxford Handbook of the Law of the Sea* (Oxford: Oxford University Press, 2017), pp. 1, 5.

[26] Ibid. p. 62.

or interests of foreign states, indigenous peoples, and the global environment. According to Selden, a state that established dominion over a closed sea could exclude foreign vessels from fishing or traversing its waters for any reason or no reason at all. Treating the sea as a global commons, as Grotius advocated, invited unilateralism of a different kind: all states were free to exploit oceanic resources to their hearts' content – even if this endangered fish stocks, jeopardized fragile ecosystems, and undermined other peoples' economic and humanitarian interests. Although Grotius and Selden disagreed about the extent to which states could assert proprietary interests over the sea, they both assumed that if states held any rights and powers under the law of the sea, then the exercise of those rights and powers would be left to the states' absolute discretion. For Grotius, Selden, and their contemporaries, this prerogative to exercise rights and powers unilaterally defined what it meant to be sovereign.[27] Conceptualizing sovereign rights and powers in this manner facilitated European colonialism by empowering the great naval powers of the day to travel, fish, and dominate international commerce without regard to local needs elsewhere in the world.

The drawbacks of this unilateralist model of state sovereignty came into sharper relief over time as states confronted a dynamic that the twentieth-century ecologist Garrett Hardin famously described as "the tragedy of the commons."[28] Hardin's key insight was that in a world with an expanding human population and finite natural resources, resources held in common will inevitably trend toward depletion as individuals pursue their own rational self-interest.[29] "Ruin is the destination toward which all men rush, each pursuing his own best interest in a society that believes in the freedom of the commons," Hardin lamented. "Freedom in a commons brings ruin to all."[30]

By the end of the nineteenth century, the tragedy of the commons had begun to take a serious toll on global fisheries, prompting some national authorities to reconsider their commitment to the Grotian free sea. An early case involved a dispute between Canada and the United States over resources in the Bering Sea. Hundreds of miles east of Anchorage lie the Pribilof Islands, an inhospitable cluster of volcanic outcroppings which the

[27] Cf. Lassa Oppenheim, *International Law* (New York: Longmans, Green & Co., 8th ed. 1955) vol. I, pp. 118–119 ("Sovereignty in the strict and narrowest sense of the term implies . . . independence all round, within and without the borders of the country.").

[28] Garrett Hardin, 'The Tragedy of the Commons' (1968) 162 *Science* 1243.

[29] Ibid. p. 1244.

[30] Ibid.

United States acquired from Russia when it purchased Alaska in 1867.[31] The Pribilof Islands are noteworthy as the breeding ground of the North Pacific fur seal, the largest fur seal group in the world.[32] Throughout the nineteenth and early twentieth centuries, the fur seal's sleek brown coat was highly prized as a decorative element in aristocratic fashion, adorning the "jackets of Gilded Age heiresses" in the United States and "Belle Epoque aristocrats" in Europe, as well as appearing "draped over elegant shoulders in cities like Melbourne, Cape Town, or Canton."[33] During the summer mating season, North Pacific fur seals congregated on the islands' rocky shores. Hunters on shore could cull uncoupled males from the herd without materially impacting the population's overall birth rates.[34] As soon as the seals began their southward winter migration in search of warmer havens, however, they entered the high seas – a global commons where tragedy awaited. By the 1880s, a fleet of eighteen British Columbian schooners shadowed fur seals along their migration route, using shotguns and explosives to decimate the herd, driving the North Pacific fur seal to the edge of extinction.

The United States responded to this threat aggressively, in the process testing the limits of its authority under international law. In 1881, the US Treasury Department declared the entire Bering Sea a *mare clausum* over which the United States claimed exclusive dominion. American revenue cutters then began seizing Canadian schooners outside the three-mile territorial sea though inside the Bering Sea.[35] Relations between the two countries grew increasingly fractious, with the Canadian press and sealing industry calling on the powerful Royal Navy to intervene to protect its fishing rights under international law.[36]

Seeking to defuse escalating tensions, the United Kingdom (representing Canada) and the United States submitted the North Pacific fur seal dispute to international arbitration. The arbitrators who gathered at the Quai d'Orsay in Paris to resolve the dispute reflected the high political

31 M. I. H. Macallister, 'Seals, Empires and Mass Politics: The 1893 Fur Seal Arbitration' (2020) 42 *Int'l Hist. Rev.* 1192, 1994–1995.

32 James Thomas Gay, *American Fur Seal Diplomacy: The Alaskan Fur Seal Controversy* (New York: Peter Lang, 1987), p. 3.

33 Macallister, *Seals, Empires and Mass Politics*, pp. 1192–1193.

34 Ibid.

35 Macallister, *Seals, Empires and Mass Politics*, p. 1195; Gerald O. Williams, *The Bering Fur Seal Dispute: A Monograph on the Maritime History of Alaska* (Eugene: Alaska Maritime Publications, 1984), pp. 15–16.

36 Russell Duane, 'The Decision of the Behring Sea Arbitrators' (1893) *Am. L. Reg.* 901, 901; Macallister, *Seals, Empires, and Mass Politics*, p. 1198.

stakes: they included the newly elected Prime Minister of Canada Sir John Thompson, British Judge Lord Hannen, US Supreme Court Justice John Marshall Harlan, and Alabama Senator John Morgan.[37] The legal issues essentially boiled down to a single core question: did international law authorize the United States to regulate sealing outside its three-mile territorial sea?[38] Under the prevailing Grotian consensus, the answer to this question was clear: centuries of state practice and *opinio juris* dictated that waters beyond the territorial sea constituted a *res communis* that was not susceptible to state appropriation or regulation. The tribunal therefore concluded that the United States "has not any right of protection or property in the fur-seals frequenting the islands of the United States in [the] Behring Sea, when such seals are found outside the ordinary three-mile limit."[39] Under international law, British Columbian sealers were free to pursue their rational self-interest by hunting the endangered North Pacific fur seals in the Bering Sea whenever and however they wished.

Ecological disaster was averted only by a second feature of the parties' *compromis*: anticipating that the United States' argument for a *mare clausum* would fail, the parties also empowered the arbitral tribunal to establish binding regulations to promote sustainable sealing practices.[40] Here the arbitration proved its value. The arbitrators prohibited both states from killing or capturing North Pacific fur seals in waters located within sixty miles of the Pribilof Islands, where female fur seals sought food for their young. They also outlawed hunting on the high seas anywhere in the Pacific Ocean, including the Bering Sea, during the early summer when the fur seal herd migrated to their island rookeries.[41] Within the seasons and maritime zones where fur seal hunting was permitted, the arbitrators' regulations authorized hunting only by licensed sailing vessels,[42] and they prohibited sealers from deploying nets, fire arms, or explosives.[43] By accepting and implementing these regulations in a spirit of

[37] Macallister, *Seals, Empires, and Mass Politics*, p. 1202.

[38] Award between the United States and the United Kingdom relating to the rights of jurisdiction of United States in the Bering Sea and the preservation of fur seal (Great Britain v. United States), Moore's International Arbitrations (15 Aug 1893), 28 R.I.A.A. 263, 267 (listing five questions presented in the *compromis*).

[39] Ibid. p. 269. The panel decided this point by a vote of 5–2, with the two American panelists dissenting. Ibid.

[40] Ibid. pp. 269–270.

[41] Ibid. p. 270 (arts. 1–2).

[42] Ibid. (arts. 3–4).

[43] Ibid. (art. 6). Indigenous peoples were exempted from these requirements. Ibid. (art. 8).

cooperation, the parties prevented the North Pacific fur seal from being hunted out of existence.

Significantly, the parties to the *North Pacific Fur Seal Case* averted disaster not by relying on the international law of the sea, but instead by voluntarily embracing bilateral regulatory cooperation. Consistent with Hardin's theory of the tragedy of the commons, Grotius's free sea led the two states to the brink of ecological catastrophe and the near-collapse of their sealing industries. This outcome was the predictable consequence of treating wildlife in the Bering Sea as a *res communis* subject to unilateral state exploitation. Had the British Columbian fleet continued to hunt fur seals indiscriminately along their migration routes through the Bering Sea, as they were entitled to do under international law, the North Pacific fur seal might well have gone extinct. Only by setting aside the rights granted to them under international law and voluntarily submitting to binding arbitration were the parties able to chart a course toward sustainable management of the North Pacific fur seal population.

The Tide Turns

Following the *North Pacific Fur Seals Case*, an American commentator confidently declared:

> [T]his is probably the last occasion in the history of the world upon which any nation will claim to be the exclusive owner of any portion of the open sea . . . It is safe to assume that the ancient doctrine that the high seas are susceptible of ownership . . . has now passed away, and that this decision will stand as an insurmountable barrier to its ever being revived. It is the last mile-stone in the progress of international law from the medieval idea of marine property to the modern theory that the high seas are free.[44]

This prediction could not have been more wrong.

On September 28, 1945, US President Harry Truman issued two proclamations that shattered the Grotian consensus. The first proclamation claimed the natural resources of the seabed and subsoil of the continental shelf alongside the United States' coastline as being subject to the United States' exclusive territorial jurisdiction and control.[45] The second proclamation asserted regulatory jurisdiction, but not an

[44] Duane, *The Decision of the Bering Sea Arbitrators*, p. 909.

[45] Proclamation No. 2667, Policy of the United States with Respect to the Natural Resources of the Subsoil and Seabed of the Continental Shelf, 10 Fed. Reg. 12, 303 (29 Sept. 1945), reproduced in (1946) 40 AJIL Supp. 45.

exclusive proprietary interest, over certain living resources located in waters above the claimed continental shelf.[46] These unilateral measures catalyzed a global chain reaction, prompting other coastal states to issue their own proclamations asserting sovereign rights to maritime resources beyond their territorial seas. In 1947, Chile and Peru each claimed sovereignty not only over the seabed and subsoil of their appurtenant continental shelf, but also over the super-adjacent waters and associated living resources out to 200 miles beyond their coastlines.[47] Other states followed suit. The Truman proclamations thus set in motion a cascade of unilateral state actions and reactions that collectively unsettled the Grotian consensus regarding the sea's legal status as a global commons.

This dramatic shift in state practice and *opinio juris* was motivated, at least in part, by sustainability concerns similar to those that spurred the United States a half-century earlier to declare the Bering Sea a *mare clausum*. The United States feared that without immediate regulatory intervention, Japanese fishing fleets would destroy salmon fisheries in the Pacific Northwest.[48] Chile and Peru likewise hoped to protect dwindling whale pods along their coasts from predatory foreign fleets.[49] By the 1940s these concerns were widely shared by coastal states. However, the uncoordinated issuance of unilateral proclamations established a patchwork of inconsistent national standards that sat uncomfortably with the customary international law of the sea.[50]

The United Nations responded to this jural discord by organizing an international initiative to codify the law of the sea. In 1958, the ILC convened a Conference on the Law of the Sea that produced a set of treaties, known collectively as the Geneva Conventions on the Law of the Seas (GCLS).[51] The GCLS formulated new legal standards for the territorial sea and contiguous zone, the high seas, fishing and conservation of the

46 Proclamation No. 2668, The Policy of the United States with Respect to Coastal Fisheries in Certain Areas of the High Seas, 10 Fed. Reg. 12304 (28 Sept. 1945).

47 Treves, *Historical Development of the Law of the Seas*, p. 11.

48 Burke, *New International Law of Fisheries*, p. 6.

49 Francisco Orrego Vicuña, *The Changing International Law of High Seas Fisheries* (Cambridge: Cambridge University Press, 1999), p. 37.

50 Hersch Lauterpacht, 'Sovereignty Over Submarine Areas' (1950) 27 BYBIL 376, 382 (identifying inconsistencies among these national proclamations).

51 The GLCS consisted of four conventions and an optional protocol: the Convention on the Territorial Sea and the Contiguous Zone, 29 April1958, 15 UST 1606, 516 UNTS 206; the Convention on the High Seas, 29 April 1958, 13 UST 2312, 450 UNTS 82; the Convention on Fishing and Conservation of the Living Resources of the High Seas, 29 April 1958, 17 UST 138, 559 UNTS 286 [hereinafter CHS]; the Convention on the Continental Shelf, 29 April1958, 15 UST 471, 499 UNTS 312 [hereinafter CCS]; and the Optional Protocol of

living resources of the high seas, and the continental shelf.[52] Some important coastal states declined to join the GCLS, however, raising questions about whether the Conventions' provisions had sufficient support in state practice and *opinio juris* to reflect customary international law.[53]

Two years later, the ILC convened a second Conference on the Law of the Sea at the request of the UN General Assembly. The Conference considered a variety of topics that were not addressed in the GCLS, including the breadth of the territorial sea and the limits of state regulatory jurisdiction over coastal fisheries. The Conference was widely perceived as a failure when the two resolutions adopted at its conclusion left a host of key issues unresolved.[54]

Cod Wars

At this crucial transitional moment, a controversy arose in the North Atlantic that profoundly shaped the subsequent development of the international law of the sea. Upon gaining independence from Denmark in 1944, Iceland sought to wrest control of its surrounding waters from predatory foreign fleets that had wreaked havoc on its fisheries.[55] This initiative was a matter of supreme importance to the newly independent state, because fishing constituted the lion's share of the country's exports.[56] Iceland's aspiration to establish sovereignty over its coastal fisheries resonated with the concurrent efforts of formerly colonized peoples elsewhere in the world to achieve national self-determination, economic development, and sovereignty over their natural resources.[57] However, when Iceland

Signature concerning the Compulsory Settlement of Disputes, 450 UNTS 169, *opened for signature* 29 April 1958, entered into force on 30 September 1962.

52 Rothwell and Stephens, *The International Law of the Sea*, pp. 6–9.

53 For example, Canada signed, but did not ratify, three of the four conventions. Donald R. Rothwell, 'The Canadian-U.S. Northwest Passage Dispute: A Reassessment' (1993) 26 *Cornell Int'l L.J.* 331, 341 & n.43; see also North Sea Continental Shelf (F.R.G./Den & F.R.G./Neth.), 1969 ICJ Rep. 4, 45 (20 February) (holding that the GCLS provisions relating to continental shelf delimitation did not yet qualify as customary international law).

54 Rothwell and Stephens, *The International Law of the Sea*, pp. 9–10.

55 Burke, *New International Law of Fisheries*, p. 9.

56 Kevin Bilms, 'The Cod Wars and Lessons for Maritime Counterinsurgency' (2023) 149 *US Naval Inst. Proc.*, www.usni.org/magazines/proceedings/2023/february/cod-wars-and-lessons-maritime-counterinsurgency (observing that by the 1970s, "the fishing industry represented 80–90 percent of Iceland's export earnings").

57 See UN GA Res. 1515 (XV), 15 December 1960, para. 5 ("[T]he sovereign right of every State to dispose of its wealth and its natural resources should be respected in conformity with the rights and duties of States under international law."); UN GA Res. 1803 (XVII),

followed the lead of other established states in claiming a twelve-mile territorial sea, it encountered stiff opposition from the Federal Republic of Germany (West Germany) and the United Kingdom, which had fished in Icelandic waters for generations.[58]

In 1972, Iceland declared its intent to extend its national fishery zone out to fifty nautical miles.[59] British and German fishers initially ignored Iceland's claim and continued fishing. However, Iceland had developed a device that enabled its coast guard to sever the nets of foreign trawlers. Iceland used this invention to spectacular effect, destroying the nets of sixty-nine British and fifteen West German vessels. In response, the British Royal Navy sent frigates to protect its fishing fleet by ramming and occasionally training live fire on Icelandic coast guard vessels. The ensuing violent confrontations between Iceland and its foreign adversaries, which caused substantial property damage and injuries to sailors and fishers on both sides, came to be known as the Cod Wars.[60]

As the conflict over the Icelandic fisheries escalated, the United Kingdom and West Germany each initiated proceedings before the ICJ. Iceland refused to participate, arguing that its decision to claim exclusive fishing rights out to fifty miles was a purely domestic matter over which the ICJ lacked jurisdiction.[61] The ICJ disagreed[62] and proceeded to render judgment on the merits in July 1974.[63]

The Court opened its merits judgment by emphasizing that "[t]he delimitation of sea areas has always an international aspect; it cannot be dependent merely upon the will of the coastal State as expressed in its municipal law."[64] The Court acknowledged that the treaties that emerged from the 1958 and 1960 Conferences on the Law of the Sea left the breadth

14 December 1962, pmbl. (recognizing "the inalienable right of all States freely to dispose of their natural wealth and resources in accordance with their national interests").

58 Bilms, 'The Cod Wars'; Mark Kurlansky, *Cod: A Biography of the Fish that Changed the World* (New York: Penguin Group, 1997), pp. 148, 152–153.

59 Fisheries Jurisdiction Case (UK/Iceland), Merits, 1974 ICJ Rep. 3 (25 July), pp. 13–14, para. 27 [hereinafter Fisheries-UK].

60 Jónsson, *Friends in Conflict*, pp. 134–138; Guðmundur J. Guðmundsson, 'The Cod and the Cold War' (2006) 31 *Scand. J. Hist.* 97.

61 Fisheries-UK, p. 8, para. 14.

62 Fisheries Jurisdiction Case (UK/Iceland), Jurisdiction, 1973 ICJ Rep. 49, 66 (2 February) (finding jurisdiction over the dispute).

63 Fisheries-UK; Fisheries Jurisdiction (Fed. Rep. Germ./Iceland), Merits, 1974 ICJ Rep. 175 (25 July). As the two judgments are substantially identical, for economy's sake subsequent citations are to the UK judgment only.

64 Fisheries-UK, p. 22, para. 49 (quoting the Fisheries Case (UK/Norway), 1951 ICJ Rep. 116, 132 (18 December)).

of a coastal state's fishery jurisdiction unsettled.[65] The Court therefore rejected Iceland's position that international law recognized the right to a fifty-mile exclusive fishery zone.[66] However, the Court also concluded that a "general consensus" among states at the 1960 Conference had "crystallized as customary law" the principle that a coastal state enjoys "preferential rights of fishing in adjacent waters" whenever it has established "special dependence on its coastal fisheries."[67] Given Iceland's extraordinary economic dependence on its coastal fisheries and the evident need to limit catch levels in order to preserve the fisheries from depletion, the Court agreed that Iceland was entitled to claim such preferential fishing rights.[68]

Had the ICJ followed the classical unilateralist model of state sovereignty, its characterization of Iceland's fishing rights as "preferential" might have been fatal to the competing claims of the United Kingdom and West Germany. The Court could have construed Iceland's preferential rights as trumps that categorically superseded the competing claims of the United Kingdom and West Germany. Under this approach, Iceland would have been within its rights to exclude British and German fishers from its adjacent waters.

The ICJ, however, adopted a radically different approach. It rejected Iceland's assertion that the priority accorded to its fishing rights under customary international law meant that it was "free, unilaterally, and according to its own uncontrolled discretion, to determine the extent of [its] rights" vis-à-vis other states.[69] Preferential rights did not operate as trumps, the Court explained: characterizing a "coastal State's rights as preferential implies a certain priority, but cannot imply the extinction of the concurrent rights of other States."[70] Instead, "in order to reach an equitable solution of the present dispute it is necessary that the preferential fishing rights of Iceland, as a State specially dependent on coastal fisheries, be reconciled with the traditional fishing rights of the Applicant[s]."[71]

How, then, should these conflicting rights be reconciled? The ICJ explained that Iceland must "take into account and pay regard to the

65 Ibid. pp. 22–23, paras. 51–52.

66 Ibid. p. 29, para. 68 (holding that "Iceland's extension of its exclusive fishery jurisdiction beyond 12 miles is not opposable to the United Kingdom").

67 Ibid. p. 23, para. 52.

68 Ibid. p. 27, para. 60. The United Kingdom conceded this point. Ibid. p. 24, para. 54.

69 Ibid. p. 27, para. 62.

70 Ibid. pp. 27–28, para. 62.

71 Ibid. p. 30, para. 69; see also ibid. p. 30, para. 70 (explaining that the negotiation should seek to reconcile the states' rights "in as equitable a manner as possible").

position of [the United Kingdom and West Germany]," in recognition of their "economic dependence on the same fishing grounds."[72] Iceland should then seek to "bring[] about an equitable apportionment of the available fishing stocks based on the facts of the particular situation," according special weight to its own preferential rights, but also taking into account the need for conservation and "the interests of other States which have established fishing rights in the area."[73]

Far from leaving fishery management to Iceland's absolute discretion, the Court emphasized that the states concerned must cooperate with one another to determine how Iceland's preferential rights can be best reconciled with other states' historically established rights. In particular, the parties must "keep under review the fishery resources in the disputed waters" and "examine together, in the light of scientific and other available information, the measures required for the conservation and development, and equitable exploitation, of those resources."[74] Following this consultation and exchange of information, Iceland's preferential rights "are to be implemented by agreement between the States concerned, either bilateral or multilateral, and, in case of disagreement, through the means for the peaceful settlement of disputes provided for in Article 33 of the Charter of the United Nations."[75] In other words, Iceland and its rivals must pursue "negotiation, enquiry, mediation, conciliation, arbitration, judicial settlement, resort to regional agencies or arrangements, or other peaceful means of their own choice."[76] The Court explained that this obligation "flows from the very nature of the respective rights of the Parties" – their concurrent rights to a common resource.[77] The Court therefore directed the parties to enter negotiations for the purpose of determining an equitable apportionment of the available fishing stocks.[78]

Significantly, the ICJ was quick to acknowledge that its approach to the Icelandic fisheries dispute represented a major departure from the classical model of sovereign unilateralism, as reflected in cases like *North Pacific Fur Seals*. The Court defended its equitable approach, however, as a modernizing improvement to the law of the sea that was worth

[72] Ibid.
[73] Ibid. p. 33, para. 78.
[74] Ibid. p. 31, para. 72.
[75] Ibid. p. 27, para. 57.
[76] UN Charter art. 33.
[77] Fisheries-UK, p. 32, para. 75.
[78] Ibid. ("[T]o direct them to negotiate is . . . a proper exercise of the judicial function in this case."); see also ibid. p. 32, para. 74 ("It is implicit in the concept of preferential rights that negotiations are required in order to define or delimit the extent of those rights.").

celebrating: "It is one of the advances in maritime international law ... that the former laissez-faire treatment of the living resources of the sea in the high seas has been replaced by a recognition of a duty to have due regard to the rights of other States and the needs of conservation for the benefit of all."[79]

According to the Court, the law of the sea had entered a new era in which mandatory cooperation based on equitable principles had replaced state unilateralism as the governing legal framework for reconciling states' rights to oceanic resources.

Delimiting Maritime Boundaries

The Cod Wars were not the only international dispute during this period that gave the ICJ an opportunity to affirm mandatory cooperation in the law of the sea. Several years before the *Fisheries Cases*, a controversy between Denmark, the Netherlands, and West Germany led the Court to affirm that mandatory cooperation also applied to maritime boundary delimitation.[80]

At stake in the case were national claims to resources in the seabed and continental shelf beneath the North Sea.[81] During the first Conference on the Law of the Sea, the international community had endeavored to clarify the legal standards that governed such claims. The 1958 Convention on the Law of the Continental Shelf, part of the original GLCS, permitted coastal states to claim exclusive sovereign rights over their adjacent continental shelf.[82] States with opposite or adjacent coastlines were to determine the boundaries between their continental shelf claims by agreement.[83] Barring "special circumstances," boundaries between states' territorial jurisdiction were to be determined by the principle of equidistance.[84] For states with coastlines on opposite sides of a continental shelf, boundaries should ordinarily track "the median line, every point of which is equidistant from the nearest points of the baselines from which the breadth of the territorial sea of each State is measured."[85] States with adjacent coastlines should determine equidistance by reference to "the nearest points of

79 Ibid. p. 31, para. 72.
80 North Sea Continental Shelf Case (FRG/Den., FRG/Neth.), 1969 ICJ Rep. 3 (20 February).
81 Wolfgang Friedmann, 'The North Sea Continental Shelf Cases: A Critique' (1970) 64 AJIL 229, 229.
82 Convention on the Continental Shelf art. 2.
83 Ibid. art. 6(1)–(2).
84 Ibid.
85 Ibid. art. 6(1).

the baselines from which the breadth of the territorial sea of each State is measured."[86]

Had Denmark, the Netherlands, and West Germany all been parties to the Convention on the Law of the Continental Shelf, the ICJ's task in the *North Sea Continental Shelf Case* would have been a relatively straightforward exercise in maritime cartography. What made the case more challenging from a legal perspective was that West Germany had not joined the Convention and disputed the equidistance principle's applicability to nonparties.[87] The Court agreed with West Germany's assessment that the Convention's equidistance principle was "a purely conventional rule,"[88] which "did not embody or crystallize any pre-existing or emergent rule of customary law."[89] Accordingly, the Court had to determine what customary norms, if any, operated in the Convention's shadows as default rules for maritime boundary delimitation.

Falling back on "basic legal notions which . . . have from the beginning reflected the opinio juris in the matter of delimitation," the Court concluded that customary international law required the parties to resolve their dispute through "agreement ... in accordance with equitable principles."[90] The Court took pains to emphasize that equitable principles did not invite recourse to principles of "abstract justice,"[91] nor did it require that coastal states receive an equal or "just and equitable share" of the resources within a continental shelf.[92] For example, countries with a short coastline would not necessarily be entitled to claim the same share of a continental shelf as states with much longer coastlines.[93] Instead, references to "equitable principles" in this context should be understood as

> a rule of law which itself requires the application of equitable principles in accordance with the ideas which have always underlain the development of the legal régime of the continental shelf in this field, namely:

[86] Ibid. art. 6(2).

[87] North Sea Continental Shelf Case, p. 20, para. 15.

[88] Ibid. p. 45, para. 81.

[89] Ibid. p. 41, para. 69.

[90] Ibid. p. 46, para. 85; see also North Sea Continental Shelf Cases, 1969 ICJ Rep. at 139–140, para. 38 (Ammoun, J., dissenting) (observing that equity is a general principle of law common to all of "the great legal systems of the modern world"). The Court concluded that equitable principles also apply to unsettled land borders. Case Concerning the Frontier Dispute (Burk. Faso/Mali), 1986 ICJ Rep. 554, 633 paras. 149–150 (December 22) (citing North Sea Continental Shelf).

[91] North Sea Continental Shelf Case, p. 46, para. 85.

[92] Ibid. p. 22, para. 19.

[93] Ibid. pp. 49–50, para. 91.

(a) the parties are under an obligation to enter into negotiations with a view to arriving at an agreement, and not merely to go through a formal process of negotiation as a sort of prior condition for the automatic application of a certain method of delimitation in the absence of agreement; they are under an obligation so to conduct themselves that the negotiations are meaningful, which will not be the case when either of them insists upon its own position without contemplating any modification of it; [and]

(b) the parties are under an obligation to act in such a way that, in the particular case, and taking all the circumstances into account, equitable principles are applied, – for this purpose the equidistance method can be used, but other methods exist and may be employed, alone or in combination, according to the areas involved.[94]

The ICJ characterized these requirements of mandatory cooperation as "merely a special application of a principle which underlies all international relations" – namely, the general obligation to resolve international disputes peacefully in a spirit of mutual respect and accommodation, rather than through unilateral fiat and coercion.[95] The Court therefore directed the parties to resume negotiations for the purpose of determining to what extent equitable principles would support departing from the equidistance principle to account for West Germany's exceptionally concave coastline relative to its neighbors, Denmark and the Netherlands.[96]

In sum, the *North Sea Continental Shelf Case* and the *Fisheries Jurisdiction Cases* affirm that the international law of the sea requires states to cooperate with one another to resolve disputes over maritime resources in accordance with equitable principles. In *North Sea Continental Shelf*, the Court held that the states must cooperate to resolve an unsettled question regarding the apportionment of national jurisdiction. Should any of the parties impose their preferred solution to the boundary dispute unilaterally, such action would violate the principle of sovereign equality.[97] Mandatory cooperation also applied in the *Fisheries Jurisdiction Cases* because Iceland and the United Kingdom held

[94] Ibid. p. 47, para. 85.
[95] Ibid. p. 47, para. 86.
[96] Ibid. p. 50, para. 91; p. 53, para. 101.
[97] For the same reason, international tribunals have recognized that a state may not decide a dispute over an unsettled land border unilaterally. *See* Arbitration Between the Republic of Croatia and the Republic of Slovenia, PCA Case No. 2012-04, Final Award, p. 108, para. 334 (29 June 2017) (describing mutual state consent as "the fundamental principle applicable to the establishment of land boundaries between sovereign States").

concurrent rights to the same resources. In each of these settings, the Court recognized that the only way to harmonize the respective rights of the litigants, while respecting their authority and formal equality as sovereign states, was to direct them to resolve their disputes through negotiation based on equitable principles. With the principle of sovereign equality on the line, directing the parties to negotiate was "a proper exercise of the judicial function," the Court concluded.[98]

Codifying Mandatory Cooperation

Although mandatory cooperation makes brief appearances in the GLCS,[99] it achieves its fullest expression in UNCLOS. With well over 300 articles and nine annexes, this sprawling codex addresses almost every topic imaginable on the law of the sea. Some have characterized UNCLOS as a "synthesis" of Grotius's *mare liberum* and Selden's *mare clausum*[100] because it guarantees universal freedoms on the high seas while also expanding national jurisdiction by, among other things, extending the territorial sea to twelve miles and expanding national jurisdiction over fisheries via a 200-nautical-mile exclusive economic zone.[101] At a more fundamental level, however, UNCLOS breaks sharply with the classical model of state sovereignty exemplified in the writings of both Grotius and Selden by imposing obligations of mandatory cooperation within every maritime zone beyond the territorial sea.

Requirements to cooperate under UNCLOS can be grouped into three general categories.[102] First, whenever states hold concurrent rights or powers over maritime resources, UNCLOS requires them to cooperate in the management of those resources. For example, mandatory cooperation applies when fishing stocks straddle national jurisdictions or migrate from

[98] Fisheries-UK, p. 32, para. 75. The ICJ has also held that international cooperation is mandatory when a coastal state sets the outer boundaries of its maritime jurisdiction relative to the high seas and deep-sea floor. Fisheries Case (U.K./Nor.), Judgment, 1951 ICJ Rep. 116 (December 18).

[99] E.g., CHS, art. 3 (requiring mandatory cooperation between coastal states and land-locked states for access to the sea), art. 14 (mandatory cooperation to suppress piracy), art. 25 (requiring cooperation to prevent and suppress pollution).

[100] Helen Thornton, 'John Selden's Response to Hugo Grotius: The Argument for the Closed Seas' (2006) 18 *Int'l J. Mar. Hist.* 105, 127.

[101] UNCLOS art. 3 (territorial sea), art. 57 (exclusive economic zone).

[102] Many other provisions of the Convention reflect equitable compromises between coastal and transit states, such as the provisions governing "innocent passage" through territorial seas and archipelagic sea lanes (arts. 17–26, 52–54) and "transit passage" through international straits (arts. 37–44).

one jurisdiction to another: the states concerned must work together to establish measures necessary to conserve and develop these stocks in order to promote sustainability and optimal utilization.[103] UNCLOS entitles land-locked and geographically disadvantaged states to fish in coastal states' otherwise exclusive economic zones, but the "terms and modalities" for these activities are to be established through negotiated agreement with coastal states on an equitable basis.[104] States that border an enclosed or semi-enclosed sea are required to coordinate their management, conservation, exploration, and exploitation of the sea's living resources; coordinate protection and preservation of the marine environment; and establish joint research programs for these purposes.[105] Likewise, states that use straits and those that border straits must cooperate with one another to maintain navigational and safety aids and prevent and control pollution.[106] These measures are designed to ensure that states exercise their sovereign rights and powers under the law of the sea in a manner that reflects due regard for other states' rights and powers.

Most remarkably, mandatory cooperation applies to states even on the high seas. According to the equitable model enshrined in UNCLOS, a state's right to navigate and fish on the high seas must be exercised always "with due regard to the interests of other States in the exercise of the freedom of the high seas."[107] Far from enjoying an absolute right that may be exercised unilaterally, as was the case under Grotius's free sea, UNCLOS requires states to cooperate with one another to establish and implement regulatory measures necessary for the conservation and management of living resources in the high seas.[108] This broad obligation to cooperate entails specific requirements to exchange relevant scientific information and data on fish stocks, consult and negotiate with one another, and, "as

[103] Ibid. arts. 63–67; see also Agreement on the Implementation of the Provisions of the United Nations Convention on the Law of the Sea of 10 December 1982 Relating to the Conservation and Management of Straddling Fish Stocks and Highly Migratory Fish Stocks art. 8, 2167 UNTS 3 (1995) (reaffirming states' obligations cooperate in relation to straddling fish stocks and highly migratory fish stocks).

[104] UNCLOS arts. 69–70. But see James L. Kateka, 'Landlocked and Geographically Disadvantaged States', in David Joseph Attard et al. (eds.) (2014) 1 *IMLI Manual Int'l Mar. L.* 431, 441 ("The right to share in the living resources of the [exclusive economic zone] is indeterminate. It is subject once again to the whims of the coastal State concerned. For most [landlocked states] the rights in the [exclusive economic zone] and the freedom of the high seas remain unreal and impractical.").

[105] UNCLOS art. 123.

[106] Ibid. art. 43.

[107] Ibid. art. 87.

[108] Ibid. arts. 117–118.

appropriate, cooperate to establish subregional or regional fisheries organizations" for the purpose of promoting prudent conservation and management of living resources in the high seas.[109] In each of these respects, UNCLOS demands that states exercise their rights on the high seas in an equitable manner that reflects due regard for the equal rights of other sovereign states.

Second, UNCLOS reinforces the ICJ's judgment in the *North Continental Shelf Case* by confirming that mandatory cooperation governs maritime boundary delimitation. States with opposite or adjacent coasts must set jurisdictional boundaries for the continental shelf and their respective exclusive economic zones "by agreement on the basis of international law . . . in order to achieve an equitable solution."[110] If states struggle to reach agreement on maritime boundaries through bilateral consultation and negotiation, they must seek third-party dispute resolution.[111] Pending a final resolution, states-parties are obligated to proceed "in a spirit of understanding and cooperation," making "every effort to enter into provisional agreements of a practical nature," while taking care to avoid actions that would "jeopardize or hamper the reaching of the final agreement."[112] UNCLOS thus prohibits states from violating the principle of sovereign equality by dictating the scope of their maritime jurisdiction vis-à-vis other states unilaterally.[113]

Third, UNCLOS mandates cooperation in settings where oceanic resources are committed to the collective stewardship of the international community as a whole. This category is exemplified most clearly in the convention's articles governing the use and exploitation of resources from the seabed and ocean floor beneath the high seas.[114] To underscore the contribution that these articles make to the law of the sea, some additional historical context might be helpful.

Over a decade before UNCLOS arrived on the scene, Maltese Ambassador Arvid Pardo brought a novel proposal to the UN General Assembly: he urged the international community to reserve the seabed and ocean floor beneath the high seas with their valuable deposits of

[109] Ibid. arts. 118–119.
[110] Ibid. arts. 74(1), 83(1).
[111] Ibid. arts. 74(2), 83(2).
[112] Ibid. arts. 74(3), 83(3).
[113] Maritime Delimitation in the Indian Ocean (Somalia v. Kenya), Judgment, 2021 ICJ Rep. 206, 227 para. 49 (12 October) ("Maritime delimitation cannot be effected unilaterally by either of the States concerned.").
[114] Ibid. arts. 133–191.

cobalt, copper, lithium manganese, and zinc[115] as a "common heritage of mankind" outside national jurisdiction.[116] This common heritage concept bore a superficial resemblance to Grotius's *res communis*, but Pardo actually had in mind something fundamentally different. Rather than expose the resources of the deep seabed and ocean floor to unilateral exploitation by individual states, Pardo argued that these resources should be exempted from national appropriation. He proposed that the international community establish an international agency to assume exclusive jurisdiction over deep sea resources "as a trustee for all countries," using profits generated from the area "primarily to promote the development of poor countries."[117] Pardo's ambitious vision, in other words, called for using the resources of the deep sea to level the economic playing field between developed and less-developed states, thus mitigating persistent global inequities that can be traced, at least in part, to international law's colonialist legacy.

The General Assembly endorsed Pardo's proposal unanimously in 1970, designating the seabed and ocean floor beyond the limits of national jurisdiction as a "common heritage of mankind" to be "exploited for the benefits of mankind as a whole, and taking into particular consideration the interests and needs of the developing countries."[118] Through UNCLOS, the international community further codified this principle and established an institutional framework to operationalize Pardo's vision.[119] UNCLOS proclaims

[115] IUCN, 'Issues in Brief: Deep-Sea Mining', https://iucn.org/resources/issues-brief/deep-sea-mining.

[116] Note Verbale Dated 17 August 1967 from the Permanent Mission of Malta to the United Nations Addressed to the Secretary General, A/6695, 18 August 1967, para. 3, https://documents-dds-ny.un.org/doc/UNDOC/GEN/N67/192/09/PDF/N6719209.pdf?OpenElement [hereinafter Pardo Proposal]; see generally Arvid Pardo, 'Before and After' (1983) 46 *L. & Contemp. Probs.* 95. For excellent introductions to the concept of common heritage resources, see Jutta Brunnée, 'Common Areas, Common Heritage, and Common Concern', in Daniel Bodansky, Jutta Brunnée, and Ellen Hey (eds.), *The Oxford Handbook of International Environmental Law* (Oxford: Oxford University Press, 2007), p. 550; and Dinah Shelton, 'Common Concern of Humanity' (2009) 32 *Envt'l Pol'y & L.* 83.

[117] Pardo Proposal, paras. 3–4.

[118] UN GA Res. 2749 (XXV); *see also* UN GA Res. 2574 D (XXIV) (declaring a moratorium on exploitation of the seabed pending the establishment of "an international regime including appropriate international machinery").

[119] Pardo was deeply disappointed, however, that UNCLOS's extensions of the continental shelf and exclusive economic zone significantly reduced the resources reserved as the common heritage of mankind. Jean Buttigieg, 'Arvid Pardo-A Diplomat with a Mission' (2016) 12 *Symposia Melitensia* 13, 27 (noting Pardo's complaint that under UNCLOS "the common heritage of mankind had been whittled to 'a few fish and a little seaweed'");

the deep seabed and ocean floor and their associated resources "the common heritage of mankind" and affirms that they are "vested in mankind as a whole," rather than states individually.[120] It then establishes an international organization – the International Seabed Authority – to regulate and manage the resources as a steward or fiduciary of humanity.[121] The convention directs the Authority to "provide for the equitable sharing of financial and other economic benefit derived from activities in the Area," while "taking into particular consideration the interests and needs of developing States and of peoples who have not attained full independence or other self-governing status."[122] In carrying out these responsibilities, the Authority bears obligations to cooperate with interested states by collecting and carrying out relevant scientific research; to consult, negotiate with, and give due regard to the rights and interests of states that might be effected by its activities; to adopt regulations for protection of human life and the marine environment; and to promote international cooperation for economic development and trade, with special attention to the needs of developing states.[123]

The Authority thus facilitates international cooperation for collective management of the common heritage resources of the deep seabed and ocean floor. When a state harvests resources from the deep sea floor, other members of the international community are entitled under UNCLOS to an equitable share of the proceeds as administered by the Authority.[124] The United States and a handful of other developed states have resisted these features of the Convention, expressing reluctance to relinquish their freedom to act unilaterally.[125] However, with the deep seabed and ocean floor having already been unanimously recognized by the UN General Assembly as a common heritage of humanity, it seems clear that under customary

Pardo, *Before and After*, p. 104 (observing that "despite its many merits, [UNCLOS] is fundamentally flawed: inequality between states is increased . . . and the concept of common heritage of mankind is ineffectively implemented").

120 UNCLOS arts. 136, 137(2).

121 Ibid. arts. 140(1), 156.

122 Ibid. art. 140.

123 Ibid. arts. 142, 143, 145–146, 150; *see also* Agreement Relating to the Implementation of Part XI of the UN Convention on the Law of the Sea of 10 December 1982, UN GAOR, 48th Sess., Agenda Item 36, UN Doc. A/RES/48/263 (1994), reprinted in 33 ILM 1309 (1994) (outlining procedures for implementation of the Authority's activities).

124 See UNCLOS art. 140 (providing that such "[a]ctivities in the [seabed and ocean floor below the high seas] shall . . . be carried out for the benefit of mankind as a whole" and distributed according to the principles of "equitable sharing" and non-discrimination).

125 See Brunnée, *Common Areas, Common Heritage, and Common Concern*, p. 563 (noting that "the very countries most likely to" exploit the deep seabed "have consistently resisted the application of the concept").

international law, states – including those, like the United States, that have yet to join UNCLOS – are no longer entitled to use or exploit the resources of the deep seabed and ocean floor unilaterally. Mandatory cooperation has become the universally binding legal norm.

The New Law of the Sea

Perhaps more than any other field, the law of the sea exemplifies international law's transition from the unilateral model to the equitable model of state sovereignty. Consistent with the equitable model, UNCLOS reflects a thorough-going commitment to mandatory cooperation as a strategy for reconciling concurrent state rights, addressing unsettled boundary disputes, and managing common resources for the benefit of humanity as a whole. These features of the new law of the sea have only become further cemented through subsequent developments in international legal practice.

Recognizing mandatory cooperation's importance to the success of the new law of the sea, in 1995 states concluded an additional agreement that further clarified how requirements to cooperate applied to the conservation and sustainable exploitation of jurisdiction-straddling and highly migratory fish stocks.[126] Among other things, states-parties to the 1995 agreement committed to collect data necessary to facilitate effective fishery management,[127] consult with one another "in good faith and without delay,"[128] and "make every effort to agree on compatible conservation and management measures within a reasonable period of time."[129] Should agreement on conservation and management measures prove elusive, states-parties agreed that any one of them could take the resulting dispute to mandatory dispute resolution.[130] States-parties also pledged to cooperate with one another "to enhance the ability of developing States, in particular the least-developed among them and small island developing States, to conserve and manage straddling fish stocks and highly migratory fish stocks" and "to participate in high seas fisheries for such stocks."[131]

126 Agreement for the Implementation of the Provisions of the United Nations Convention on the Law of the Sea of 10 December 1982 Relating to the Conservation and Management of Straddling and Highly Migratory Fish Stocks, A/Conf.164/37, 8 September 1995.

127 Ibid. art. 14.

128 Ibid. art. 8(2).

129 Ibid. art. 7(3).

130 Ibid. arts. 7(4), 27.

131 Ibid. art. 25.

Since the *North Sea Continental Shelf Case* and the *Fisheries Jurisdiction Cases*, the ICJ has continued to affirm that mandatory cooperation applies to the law of the sea.[132] Indeed, the Court has characterized mandatory cooperation as the "fundamental norm" of international maritime delimitation.[133]

International arbitral tribunals have also made important contributions to clarifying the requirements associated with mandatory cooperation in the law of the sea.[134] A prominent example is the *Chagos Marine Protected Area Arbitration (Mauritius v. United Kingdom).*[135] At issue in the arbitration was Mauritius's objection to the United Kingdom unilateral declaration of a marine protected area (MPA) around the Chagos Archipelago. Mauritius argued that the proposed MPA did not reflect due regard for its legal rights as a coastal state, as required under the customary international law of the sea.[136] The arbitral panel agreed. It explained that the United Kingdom's obligation to give due regard to Mauritius' rights "does not impose a uniform obligation to avoid impairment of Mauritius' rights, nor does it uniformly permit the United Kingdom to proceed as it wishes, merely noting such rights."[137] Neither of those approaches was compatible with the principle of sovereign equality because each would uphold one state's rights while effectively extinguishing the other's rights. Respect for the equal sovereignty of both states required a more equitable, collaborative approach. The tribunal explained that the parties must take into consideration the equities involved for both sides, including the "importance [of Mauritius's rights], the extent of the anticipated impairment, the nature and importance of the activities contemplated by the United Kingdom, and the availability of alternative approaches."[138] With these considerations in mind, the two states must endeavor to reconcile their respective rights through

132 E.g., Maritime Delimitation in the Area Between Greenland and Jan Mayen Case (Den. v. Nor.), 1993 ICJ Rep. 59, para. 48 (June 14); Case Concerning Delimitation of the Maritime Boundary in the Gulf of Maine Area (Can./US), Judgment, 1984 ICJ Rep. 246, 299, para. 112 (12 October) [hereinafter Gulf of Maine]; Continental Shelf (Tunis./Libya), 1982 ICJ Rep. 18, 59, para. 70 (24 February).

133 Gulf of Maine, pp. 299–300, paras. 111–113.

134 See, e.g., South China Sea Arbitration, PCA Case No. 2013-19, Award, paras. 741–742 (12 July 2016); Request for an Advisory Opinion Submitted by the Sub-Regional Fisheries Commission (SRFC), Advisory Opinion of 2 April 2015, ITLOS Rep. 2015, para. 219; Arctic Sunrise Arbitration, Case No. 2014-02, paras. 228, 230 (Perm. Ct. Arb. 2015).

135 Chagos Marine Protected Area Arbitration (Mauritius/U.K.), Case No. 2011-03, Award, para. 534 (Perm. Ct. Arb. 2015).

136 Ibid. paras. 7–8.

137 Ibid. para. 519.

138 Ibid.

negotiation in a spirit of mutual accommodation. The United Kingdom's failure to pursue such cooperation with Mauritius in good faith before imposing the MPA violated this customary requirement of the law of the sea.[139] By proceeding unilaterally over Mauritius's objections, the United Kingdom continued to treat Mauritius, its former colony, as a political subordinate rather than as an equal sovereign.

Challenges and Opportunities

As of the date of this writing, over one hundred states have signed the new High Seas Treaty,[140] reaffirming their commitment to mandatory cooperation[141] and offering a ray of hope for marine biodiversity at a moment of great peril.[142] Yet, for every positive development like the High Seas Treaty, skeptics can point to other areas where mandatory cooperation has disappointed. For example, Arctic states have yet to resolve longstanding disputes over the Arctic Sea and the abundant resources within its continental shelf.[143] Demanding special treatment based on historical practice, China has declined to cooperate with other states to establish by agreement maritime boundaries for the South China Sea based on equitable principles,[144] and it has refused to recognize a related arbitral award from the International Tribunal for the Law of the Sea.[145] States with large fishing industries often oppose reasonable

[139] Ibid. paras. 520–536; see also Julia Gaunce, 'On the Interpretation of the General Duty of "Due Regard"' (2018) 32 *Ocean Y.B.* 27 (explaining that the due regard requirement under the law of the sea obligates states to pursue "an objectively positive interaction with another [state]'s interests and with those of the international community").

[140] Agreement Under the United Nations Convention on the Law of the Sea on the Conservation and Sustainable Use of Marine Biological Diversity of Areas Beyond National Jurisdiction, UN Treaty Collection, https://treaties.un.org/Pages/ViewDetails.aspx?src=TREATY&mtdsg_no=XXI-10&chapter=21&clang=_en#EndDec (listing 107 states-parties).

[141] High Seas Treaty arts. 7–8.

[142] Ibid. arts. 17–26.

[143] Tania Röttger and Theocharis N. Grigoriadis, 'Arctic Conflicts & Russian Foreign Policy' (2021) 50 *Ga. J. Int'l & Compar. L.* 1.

[144] Evan J. Criddle and Evan Fox-Decent, 'Mandatory Multilateralism' (2019) 113 AJIL 272, 314–317.

[145] See South China Sea (Phil. v. China), PCA Case No. 2013-19, Award, paras. 471–477 (12 July 2016) (concluding that various maritime features claimed by China were insufficient to support rights to maritime zones under international law); Ministry of Foreign Affairs, Statement of the Ministry of Foreign Affairs of the People's Republic of China on the Award of 12 July 2016 of the Arbitral Tribunal in the South China Sea Arbitration Established at the Request of the Republic of the Philippines, 12 July 2016,

limits on commercial fishing, favoring their immediate economic interests over the claims of environmental conservation and international and intergenerational equity.[146] Some critics lament, therefore, that mandatory cooperation naively "assumes a degree of good will and a spirit of accommodation that is not always available among highly competitive entities."[147]

However, even when states shirk their obligations of mandatory cooperation, they cannot fully escape them. For all its diplomatic and military bluster, China has not succeeded in convincing most other states, much less international courts and tribunals, to accept the legality of its unilateral claims to sovereignty over nearly all of the South China Sea.[148] Arctic states recognize that their contested jurisdictional claims will not achieve general international recognition until they resolve their remaining disputes through agreement or third-party dispute resolution.[149] Meanwhile, scientific cooperation has persuaded many states of the need to take aggressive collective action to prevent a massive decline in overexploited fish stocks. States that might have resisted scaling back their fishing industries a generation ago now recognize that international regulatory cooperation offers the only realistic path to restore declining fisheries for the benefit of present and future generations. While much work must still be done, the good news is that many fish stocks that were approaching depletion only a few decades ago are starting to bounce back through concerted international cooperation.[150] Whether this progress can be sustained in an era of accelerating climate change and explosive population growth is an open question. If there is hope for the oceans and the human communities that depend upon them, it lies in national authorities embracing the spirit of mandatory cooperation.

www.fmprc.gov.cn/eng/wjdt_665385/2649_665393/201607/t20160712_679470.html (declaring the arbitral award "null and void" with "no binding force").

146 E.g., Antoaneta Roussi and Louise Guillot, 'Fishy Business: EU Flashes Green Money to Support Indian Ocean Tuna Grab', Politico, 8 May 2023.

147 Vicuña, *The Changing International Law of High Seas Fisheries*, p. 45.

148 South China Sea Arbitration, PCA Case No. 2013-19, Award, paras. 771–777 (12 July 2016).

149 Röttger and Grigoriadis, 'Arctic Conflicts & Russian Foreign Policy', pp. 30–39 (discussing options for peaceful dispute resolution).

150 Hannah Ritchie and Max Roser, 'Fish and Overfishing', Our World in Data, October 2021, https://ourworldindata.org/fish-and-overfishing.

4

Landlocked States

An Unfinished Battle

In March 1879, Bolivian engineer Eduardo Abaroa Hidalgo found himself wounded and surrounded by the lifeless bodies of his compatriots as hundreds of hostile Chilean troops advanced toward his position. Weeks earlier, Chile invaded the Litoral, Bolivia's arid coastal region, occupying the port city of Antofagasta and seizing control of the Atacama Desert with its lucrative nitrate deposits. Abaroa abandoned his job at a silver mine to lead the civilian resistance. As the Chilean army progressed inland, Abaroa's men joined forces with the scanty Bolivian military presence in the region in an attempt to prevent the invaders from reaching the oasis town of Calama. After destroying two bridges across the Topáter River, Abaroa and his compatriots dug in to face the advancing army. Badly outnumbered and facing a superior force that included cavalry and heavy artillery, Abaroa's side was quickly overwhelmed. The Bolivian military withdrew, leaving Abaroa's volunteers to continue the fight alone until none but Abaroa remained standing. According to Bolivian lore, when the Chilean army demanded Abaroa's surrender, his cheeky reply sealed his fate: "Me, surrender? Let your grandmother surrender, bastards!"[1]

Over a century later, Bolivia continues to commemorate the Battle of Topáter on March 23 as "The Day of the Sea" (*El Día del Mar*). On this national holiday, Bolivians gather to celebrate Abaroa's heroism while also collectively mourning the loss of the Litoral and affirming their determination to regain this corridor to the Pacific. In La Paz, a casket bearing Abaroa's remains proceeds in full ceremony of state from the Basilica of San Francisco to the Plaza Abaroa, where a monumental bronze statue

[1] Chantelle Bacigalupo, 'Every Year on "Dia Del Mar," Bolivia Celebrates the Coastline They Lost', The World, 22 March 2019; 'Day of the Sea', Bolivia Bella, www.boliviabella.com/day-of-the-sea.html [hereinafter Bolivia Bella].

honors the hero. Marching bands with majorettes, civic groups with banners, and marines clad in snow-white uniforms with polished sabers parade past the casket as the country's president and other dignitaries look on from an elevated grandstand. Representatives of the Bolivian navy also join in the procession, proudly reaffirming their official motto: "The sea is ours by right; to take it back is our duty."[2] Meanwhile, school children throughout the country unite their voices in an anthem that every Bolivian knows by heart – the "Hymn to the Litoral" (*Hymno al Litoral*):

> *We sing the song of the sea, the sea, the sea, that will soon be ours again.*
> *Let us raise our voice in happiness for the Litoral that Bolivia will soon have again, again, again.*
> *Antofagasta, beautiful lands of Tocopilla and Mejillones next to the sea, with Cobija and Calama return to Bolivia again.*[3]

For Bolivians, reclaiming the lost Litoral is not only a matter of national pride, but also of overriding national interest. As a result of Chile's annexation of the Litoral, Bolivia has the dubious distinction of being one of two landlocked countries in South America and one of forty-four landlocked countries worldwide.[4] Many of these countries became landlocked through colonial-era borders imposed by foreign powers. Unlike the developed landlocked states of Europe, the vast majority of landlocked states – including those in Africa, Central Asia, and South America – do not have navigable rivers, advanced transportation infrastructure, or a high degree of regional economic integration. As a result, they tend to experience lower economic growth than their coastal neighbors, and many rank among the most impoverished and least developed of developing countries. Bolivia, one of the poorest countries in South America, knows these disadvantages of landlocked status all too well. Thus, reclaiming the lost Litoral has dominated Bolivia's national aspirations and foreign policy for over 140 years.

International law no longer permits states like Bolivia to shed their landlocked status by wresting territory from their neighbors through military conquest.[5] A landlocked state's access to the sea therefore depends

[2] Laetitia Perrier Bruslé, 'Bolivia: Its Lost Coastline and Nation-Building' (2013) 689 *Annales de Géographie* 47–72, 58.

[3] Bacigalupo, 'Every Year on "Dia Del Mar."'

[4] Ernesta Swanepoel, 'The Law of the Sea and Landlocked States', Policy Briefing, South African Institute of International Affairs (2020).

[5] UN Charter art. 2(4); Oona A. Hathaway and Scott J. Shapiro, *The Internationalists: How a Radical Plan to Outlaw War Remade the World* (New York: Simon and Schuster, 2018), p. 309.

upon neighboring states enabling them to transport people and goods through their territory. In this chapter, we show how mandatory cooperation explains and clarifies the legal position of landlocked states vis-à-vis transit states. We show that international law governing landlocked states offers a classic case of conflicting entitlements under international law. On the one hand, coastal states like Chile enjoy sovereignty over their territory, including the right to "territorial integrity and political independence."[6] On the other hand, landlocked states like Bolivia "have the right of access to and from the sea," including "freedom of transit through the territory of transit States by all means of transit."[7] Reconciling these conflicting entitlements is the work of mandatory cooperation.

By facilitating universal access to the sea, mandatory cooperation provides an equitable response to pathologies generated by the international legal order itself. A core function of international law is regulating the distribution of territorial sovereignty among states. The landlocked status of particular countries is the byproduct of an international legal order that validates borders established in the past through violent conquest and colonial subjugation. Absent mandatory cooperation, international law would consign landlocked states to a subservient position vis-à-vis transit states, who could arbitrarily prevent them from accessing the rest of the international community. Mandatory cooperation mitigates this structural injustice by requiring transit states to exercise their rights as territorial sovereigns in an equitable manner to facilitate foreign access to the sea.[8]

Territorial Sovereignty or Transit Rights?

Prior to the mid-twentieth century, international publicists offered diverging viewpoints about whether the law of nations required coastal states to permit foreigners to travel through their borders. Hugo Grotius argued that all people enjoyed a legal right of innocent passage through foreign territory.[9] This right encompassed not only passage of persons but also goods and

[6] UN Charter art. 2(4).

[7] UN Convention on the Law of the Sea art. 125(1), UN Doc. A/CONF. 62/122 (1982) [hereinafter UNCLOS].

[8] For a similar argument that international human rights law "attend[s] to pathologies" engendered by "the structure and operation of the international legal order" and "impose[s] obligations on sovereign . . . actors to exercise the authority they receive from international law in ways that respect the rights of all," see Patrick Macklem, *The Sovereignty of Human Rights* (New York: Oxford University Press, 2015), p. 1.

[9] Hugo Grotius, *The Rights of War and Peace* (Richard Tuck ed., Oxford: Oxford University Press 2005) (1625), p. 41 ("[A] free Passage ought to be granted to Persons, where just

merchandise intended for international commerce.[10] In Grotius's view, coastal states could not impose customs or taxes on people or goods transiting through their borders, except as reimbursement for costs incurred ensuring their security.[11] Grotius considered the right to travel and trade freely to be "clear and immutable" under the law of nations.[12]

Not everyone agreed with Grotius's assessment. A generation later, German jurist and political philosopher Samuel Pufendorf contested Grotius's view, arguing that under the law of nations a state was free to decide for itself how "free or cautious" it wished to be in welcoming foreigners into its territory.[13] According to Pufendorf, the principle of territorial sovereignty meant that "it is left in the power of all States, to take such Measures about the Admission of Strangers, as they think convenient," subject only to a narrow exception for those "who are driven on the Coasts by Necessity, or by any Cause that deserves Pity and Compassion."[14] Pufendorf also rejected Grotius's view that under the law of nations "every one has a Right of trading into foreign parts" and "of importing what the People there want."[15] Hence, "there lies no Restraint on a State, why . . . it should not favour its own Subjects more than Strangers . . . by demanding less Custom of the former, than of the latter."[16] Although Pufendorf characterized hospitality toward foreign travelers as a morally binding "Duty of Humanity," even this ethical obligation was subordinate to "good Reasons of State."[17] Thus, Pufendorf believed that the nationals of landlocked states could not claim a legal entitlement to travel or transport goods through coastal states except in cases of exceptional grave necessity and "ought to rest satisfied with [whatever] Station and Privileges [a transit state deigns to] assign them."[18]

This disagreement between Grotius and Pufendorf – the two leading lights of seventeenth-century international law – cast a shadow of uncertainty over the relationship between territorial sovereignty and transit rights.

occasion shall require, over any Lands and Rivers, or such parts of the Sea as shall be then in the Property and Possession of any other Nation.").

10 Grotius, 'The Rights of War and Peace', p. 45.

11 Grotius, 'The Rights of War and Peace', p. 47.

12 Grotius, *The Free Sea* (Richard Hakluyt transl., Indianapolis: Liberty Fund, 2004) (1609), p. 10.

13 Samuel Pufendorf, *The Law of Nature and Nations* (1729), p. 246.

14 Ibid. p. 245.

15 Ibid. p. 247.

16 Ibid.

17 Ibid. pp. 244–246.

18 Ibid.

Did peaceful travelers have a right to innocent passage through foreign territory? Or were coastal states free to exclude most foreign nationals?

The debate was mostly academic because coastal states in Europe tended to accept that it was in their national interest to welcome foreigners, including traders who wished to transport goods and merchandise through their borders. For example, when the Swedish empire controlled every major port on the Baltic Sea at the end of the seventeenth century, it permitted foreign merchants to travel freely and engage in commerce throughout the Baltic region, subject to modest customs duties, in order to maintain a steady flow of economic activity and tax revenue through its ports.[19] Yet Pufendorf's vision of territorial sovereignty still spelled trouble for the commercial interests of landlocked states. By insisting that the law of nations would permit a coastal state like Sweden to close its borders to foreign traders, Pufendorf's account threatened geographically disadvantaged states with the possibility that coastal states might eventually sever transit through their borders or impose crushing customs duties. Even when coastal states did not close their borders, the mere possibility that they might do so placed landlocked states in a vulnerable position and became a source of friction conductive to conflict.

Illustrative of this dynamic was the Great Northern War (1700–1721), when Russia allied with Denmark and Saxony to challenge Sweden's regional hegemony. In the years leading up to the war, Tsar Peter I had made no secret of his ambition to acquire a "window to the West" by retaking territory along the Baltic that Sweden had seized from Russia nearly a century earlier in the 1617 Peace of Stolbova.[20] This objective was strategically important because Russia's access to blue water was limited to Arkhangelsk, a remote port on the White Sea to the far north. Sweden's dominion over the Baltic coastline meant that Russia depended greatly on foreign intermediaries to deliver its commodities to foreign markets. Anxious to burnish Russia's reputation in the West, Peter followed the conventions of European monarchs by commissioning a formal legal-historical brief to justify Russia's intervention in the war.[21] Having studied keenly both Grotius's *Law of War and Peace* and Pufendorf's *Law of Nature and Nations*, Peter likely would have been

[19] David Kirby, *Northern Europe in the Early Modern Period: The Baltic World 1492–1772* (London: Routledge, 1990), p. 240; Michael Roberts, *The Swedish Imperial Experience 1560–1718* (Cambridge: Cambridge University Press, 1979), pp. 101–130.

[20] Kirby, *Northern Europe in the Early Modern Period*, p. 299.

[21] Petr P. Shafirov, *A Discourse Concerning the Just Causes of the War between Sweden and Russia: 1700–1721* (New York: Oceana Publications, 1973).

acquainted with their divergent perspectives on transit rights.[22] It is noteworthy, therefore, that Russia's published justification for the war cited intelligence from a Swedish prisoner of war suggesting that Sweden had been preparing to invade Russia and seize Arkhangelsk to eliminate Russia's access to the sea and "cut off the Russians from … Commerce with Foreigners."[23] Although this was not Russia's primary legal argument for entering the war, its inclusion in Russia's war manifesto underscores Peter's fear that Sweden might eventually invoke Pufendorf's theory of territorial sovereignty, forbid commerce between foreigners, and establish a stranglehold on Russia's foreign trade. The only sure way to avert this threat would be for Russia to pierce Sweden's territorial holdings to the north and establish its own sovereign corridor to the Baltic. This plan ultimately came to fruition when Russian forces drove the Swedes from the Gulf of Finland, followed by Peter's triumph over King Charles XII at Poltava.[24] These victories enabled Peter to fulfill his dream of establishing a cosmopolitan port on the Baltic – St. Petersburg, Russia's "Venice of the North" – which served as the opulent capital of Imperial Russia from 1703 to 1918.

For over 250 years after Poltava, the debate between Grotius and Pufendorf over transit rights continued to simmer without definitive resolution. Writing in 1904, John Westlake divided "the opinions of accredited authors" on this subject into two categories:

> (A) Those who deny the right of innocent passage, referring the matter entirely to convention, and consequently allowing the territorial state to refuse the passage or to exact a price for it; with whom must be classed those who assert a duty on the part of the territorial state to allow the passage subject to a reasonable convention, but make that state the final

22 William E. Butler, 'P.P. Shafirov and the Law of Nations', in Shafirov, *A Discourse Concerning the Just Causes of the War between Sweden and Russia*, pp. 1–6; E. V. Anisimov, *The Reforms of Peter the Great: Progress through Coercion in Russia* (John T. Alexander trans., Abingdon: Routledge, 1993), p. 25.

23 Shafirov, *A Discourse Concerning the Just Causes of the War between Sweden and Russia*, p. 348. This legal-historical brief was the first original document produced in Russia addressing the law of nations. Friedrich Christian Weber, *The Present State of Russia*, 2 vols. (London: Routledge, 1968), vol. 1, p. 28.

24 See Peter Englund, *The Battle that Shook Europe: Poltava and the Birth of the Russian Empire* (London; I.B. Tauris, 1988), p. 251 (explaining how Russia's victory over the formidable Swedes at Poltava in 1709 turned the tide of the Great Northern War, "signal[ling] the end of Swedish imperium" and "confirm[ing] the birth of a new great European power: Russia"); John LeDonne, 'Poltava and the Geopolitics of Western Eurasia' (2009–10) 31 *Harv. Ukrainian Stud.* 177, 188 (arguing that Russia's victory at Poltava "accelerated Muscovy's transformation into a great Eurasian power").

> judge of its duty; and (B) those who assert the right of innocent passage, of course normally to be regulated by convention, but so that a clearly wrongful refusal by the territorial state may be resented as an injury.[25]

In the former category, Westlake placed Johan Ludwig Klüber, Georg Friedrich von Martens, August Wilhelm Heffter, Carlos Calvo, Robert Phillimore, Travers Twiss, and William Edward Hall; in the latter category, he included Grotius (obviously), Pufendorf (dubiously), Emer de Vattel, Johann Kaspar Bluntschli, F. H. Geffken, Édouard Engelhardt, and Henry Wheaton, among others.[26] This debate persisted well into the twentieth century, with some commentators affirming a customary right of innocent passage and others denying the existence of such a right.[27]

Tensions between these competing views flared up during international negotiations in the latter half of the twentieth century, with disappointing results for landlocked states.[28] In negotiations leading to the 1965 Convention on Transit Trade of Land-locked States, delegations for landlocked states argued that international law already recognized a principle of free access to the sea. Transit states did not deny the existence of such a principle of free access, but they objected that the principle was subordinate to coastal states' territorial sovereignty.[29] Unable to move beyond this impasse, the Convention affirmed that landlocked countries "should have free access to the sea," but it did not establish a firm legal right.[30] Instead, it provided that states-parties "shall

[25] John Westlake, *International Law: Peace*, 2 vols. (Cambridge: Cambridge University Press, 1910), vol. 1, pp. 158–159.

[26] Westlake, *International Law*. Westlake fails to distinguish between Pufendorf's denial of a general legal right to innocent passage and his affirmation that states are morally obligated to permit innocent passage as a moral "Duty of Humanity."

[27] Compare, e.g., Elihu Lauterpacht, 'Freedom of Transit in International Law', in *Transactions of the Grotius Society* (London: Sweet & Maxwell, 1958), pp. 313–349 (affirming a right of innocent passage); with Georg Schwarzenberger, *International Law* (London: Stevens and Sons, 1957), vol. 1, p. 237 (denying a right of innocent passage).

[28] Earlier international agreements had relatively few members and limited scope. For example, the first international instrument on transit – the 1921 Barcelona Convention and its Statute on Freedom of Transit – established a right to freedom of transit by water and rail, but not road or air. James L. Kateka, 'Landlocked and Geographically Disadvantaged States' (2014) *IMLI Manual Int'l Mar. L.* 431, 435–436. The 1947 General Agreement on Tariffs and Trade (GATT) provided for freedom of transit for goods, but not for people. General Agreement on Tariffs and Trade (GATT), Geneva, 30 October 1947, in force 1 January 1948, art. V(2), 61 Stat. A3, TIAS No. 1700.

[29] Kishor Uprety, 'The Transit Regime for Landlocked States: International Law and Development Perspectives', World Bank (2006), p. 63.

[30] Convention on Transit Trade for Landlocked States, New York, 8 July 1965, in force 9 June 1967, art. 1, 1967 UNTS No. 8641.

by common agreement . . . accord: (a) [t]o the State having no sea-coast, on a basis of reciprocity, free transit through their territory," as well as (b) "access to seaports and the use of such ports."[31] Although superficially supportive of landlocked states' interests, without according substantive legal rights to landlocked states this mere agreement to agree (*pactum de contrahendo*) was unenforceable under international law.[32] Ultimately, therefore, the Convention essentially codified Pufendorf's approach to the transit interests of landlocked states: it proclaimed that coastal states and landlocked states *should* conclude transit agreements to facilitate oceanic access, but it did not establish a legal *right* to innocent passage.

Both Territorial Sovereignty and Transit Rights

Following the Convention on Transit Trade for Landlocked Countries, landlocked states continued to lobby for international recognition of a right to innocent passage to the sea. During the Third UN Conference on the Law of the Sea, landlocked states argued that their access to the sea should not depend on transit states' consent, which was too often used as leverage to bully them during negotiations.[33] Ultimately, transit states agreed to include a firm legal right to transit in the 1982 UN Convention on the Law of the Sea (UNCLOS).[34] Article 125 of UNCLOS provides that landlocked states are entitled to exercise "the right of access to and from the sea" – including "transit through the territory of transit States by all means of transport" – so that they can enjoy the full range of rights associated with "the freedom of the high seas and the common heritage of mankind."[35]

UNCLOS does not go so far as to embrace Grotius's view that a landlocked state's right of innocent passage trumps transit states' territorial sovereignty. Although Article 125 establishes transit as a genuine legal right, it also affirms that transit states retain "full sovereignty over their territory."[36] Transit states therefore "have the right to take all

[31] Convention on Transit Trade for Landlocked States.

[32] Uprety, 'The Transit Regime for Landlocked States', p. 66.

[33] Ibrahim J. Wani, 'An Evaluation of the Convention on the Law of the Sea from the Perspective of Landlocked States' (1982) 22 VJIL 627, 635.

[34] UNCLOS, art. 125(1).

[35] UNCLOS, art. 125(1). As discussed in chapters 3 and 8, "freedom of the high seas" and the "common heritage of mankind" are predicated on sovereign equality and joint stewardship.

[36] UNCLOS, art. 125(3).

measures necessary to ensure that the rights and facilities provided . . . for landlocked States shall in no way infringe their legitimate interests."[37]

By affirming *both* a legal right to transit *and* the prerogatives of territorial sovereignty, UNCLOS adopts an intermediate position. Territorial sovereignty is not hierarchically superior to transit rights nor is it subordinate to transit rights. Instead, Article 125 places these entitlements in direct conflict.[38] Landlocked states have a genuine legal "right" to access the sea "through the territory of transit States." But transit states have a no less significant right to exercise "full sovereignty" in order to protect their "legitimate interests." What emerges is a dialectic of dueling entitlements – a structural antinomy that can be reconciled only through the synthesizing praxis of mandatory cooperation.

How does UNCLOS reconcile transit states' territorial sovereignty with landlocked states' right to access the seas? Article 125 provides: "The terms and modalities for exercising freedom of transit shall be agreed between the land-locked States and transit States concerned through, bilateral, subregional or regional agreements."[39] Contrary to the assertion of some commentators, this requirement does not render landlocked states' transit rights dependent on a future agreement.[40] Article 125 is not a mere agreement to agree. Under UNCLOS, landlocked states are entitled to exercise transit rights to access the sea – full stop. But determining how this right may be exercised without undermining the transit state's legitimate sovereign interests (e.g., public health and safety) requires international cooperation. Thus, UNCLOS contemplates that the legal entitlements of landlocked states and transit states must be reconciled harmoniously through mandatory cooperation.[41]

37 UNCLOS, art. 125(3). Notably, UNCLOS does not define transit states' "legitimate interests."

38 UNCLOS, art. 125.

39 UNCLOS, art. 125(2).

40 Uprety, 'The Transit Regime for Landlocked States', p. 86.

41 Benvenisti suggests that rights of transit of landlocked states, including those articulated in Article 125 of UNCLOS, can be explained by a "restricted Pareto concept" according to which "one benefits and the other sustains no loss." Eyal Benvenisti, 'Sovereigns as Trustees of Humanity: On the Accountability of States to Foreign Stakeholders' (2013) 107 AJIL 295, 322. As Article 125(2) makes clear, however, for the transit rights of landlocked states to be reconciled with the sovereign rights of the transit state, the legally mandated path forward is through good faith, cooperative decision-making. In contexts where the passage is relatively lengthy and requires infrastructure such as a railway and port facilities, there will necessarily be a cost. If a transit state can rightfully refuse to negotiate access to the sea on the basis of this cost, a landlocked state's access right under Article 125 would be illusory.

Viewing transit rights through this lens of mandatory cooperation clarifies the legal obligations enshrined in Article 125. To satisfy their obligations to landlocked states, transit states must investigate and consult with landlocked states to fully understand and accommodate their legitimate interests with respect to the "terms and modalities for exercising freedom of transit." They may not arbitrarily withhold – or threaten to withhold – safe passage through their territory. In this way, mandatory cooperation provides an equitable safety valve against transit states exercising their territorial sovereignty in a manner that would effectively imprison the people of landlocked states within their own national territory. Landlocked states, in turn, must respect transit states' territorial integrity and political independence by accepting reasonable constraints on their passage through transit states. Article 125 thus places landlocked states and transit states under mutual obligations to establish cooperative frameworks for facilitating oceanic access. Failure to reach agreement about specific "terms and modalities" is not necessarily a violation of Article 125, as long as the parties remain committed to, and actively engaged in, the pursuit of an equitable solution. If negotiations reach an impasse, both sides arguably must pursue third-party dispute resolution in a good faith effort to achieve a mutually acceptable compromise that reflects due regard for their respective rights, consistent with equitable principles. Mandatory cooperation thus respects the rights of both landlocked states and transit states, while prohibiting either side from dictating unilaterally the terms of their interaction.

Bolivia v. Chile in the World Court

A recent proceeding between Bolivia and Chile in the International Court of Justice (ICJ) illustrates both the limits and promise of mandatory cooperation with regard to conflicts between landlocked and transit states. At issue in the proceeding is more than a century of diplomatic exchanges between Bolivia and Chile over the future of the disputed Litoral. For several decades after Chile's seizure of Bolivia's coastal region, the two countries normalized their relations through a series of agreements, while Bolivia continued to pursue a territorial outlet to the Pacific. In 1904, Bolivia and Chile concluded a Treaty of Peace and Friendship in which Bolivia formally recognized Chile's sovereignty over its former territory in exchange for financial compensation and other concessions, but without expressly addressing Bolivia's desire to acquire an independent corridor to the ocean.[42] Over the next century, Bolivia periodically renewed negotiations with Chile without success. During a temporary thaw in relations, the reigning dictator-generals of Bolivia and Chile, Hugo Banzer and Augusto Pinochet, met in 1975 at the disputed border town of Charaña to shake hands over a possible agreement to grant Bolivia a sovereign corridor to the sea.[43] The tentative agreement soon unraveled under objections from both sides. The ensuing disagreement led the two countries to the brink of war in 1979, prompting Chile to plant landmines along the border. In the 2010s, Bolivia's pretensions to the Litoral gained renewed salience as Bolivian President Evo Morales and Chilean President Sebastián Piñera each exploited the issue to stoke nationalist fervor for political gain.[44]

In 2013, Bolivia instituted proceedings against Chile in the ICJ, seeking to compel Chile to return to the negotiation table.[45] Bolivia asserted that at various critical junctures during their diplomatic exchanges, Chile had undertaken a legal obligation to negotiate with Bolivia for the purpose of ending once and for all Bolivia's unfortunate status as a landlocked state.[46] Chile, however, vigorously rejected the notion that it had undertaken any such legal duty to negotiate a land surrender. Although Chile acknowledged that it had entertained Bolivian invitations to negotiate on a number of occasions, it categorically denied that its conduct reflected an intention to undertake a legal *duty* to negotiate with Bolivia over the possible transfer of Chilean territory to Bolivia.[47]

To be clear, in the proceedings before the ICJ, Bolivia did *not* assert its transit right under UNCLOS. Instead, Bolivia set its sights on a more

42 Treaty of Peace and Friendship Between Chile and Bolivia, and Convention for the Construction and Convention for the Construction and operation of Railroad from Arica to La Paz, 20 October 1904, Chile No. 427.

43 Buslé, 'Bolivia'.

44 Anne-Laure Amilhat-Szary, 'Are Borders More Easily Crossed Today? The Paradox of Contemporary Trans-Border Mobility in the Andes' (2007) 12 *Geopolitics* 1–10; Buslé, 'Bolivia'.

45 Application Instituting Proceedings, Obligation To Negotiate Access to the Pacific Ocean (Bolivia v. Chile), 14 April 2013, www.icj-cij.org/files/case-related/153/17338.pdf. The ICJ exercised jurisdiction over the dispute pursuant to Article XXXI of the American Treaty on Pacific Settlement (Pact of Bogota) to which both Bolivia and Chile are members. Obligation To Negotiate Access to the Pacific Ocean (Bolivia v. Chile), Preliminary Objection, 2015 ICJ Rep. 592, 610 (24 September).

46 Bolivia Memorial, pp. 125–135, 138–151, 153–154.

47 Obligation To Negotiate Access to the Pacific (Bolivia v. Chile), Counter-Memorial of the Republic of Chile, 13 July 2016, Vol. I, pp. 6–7, www.icj-cij.org/files/case-related/153/153-20160713-WRI-01-00-EN.pdf [hereinafter Chile Counter-Memorial].

ambitious target: securing a judgment that it was legally entitled to negotiate with Chile toward the possible return of the Litoral. Because the unilateral aspiration to acquire foreign territory is not an issue that triggers mandatory cooperation, the success of Bolivia's strategy depended on the ICJ agreeing that Chile had, in fact, voluntarily undertaken an obligation to negotiate with Bolivia for these purposes. Had Chile undertaken such an obligation, then it would have borne a relatively modest duty to receive and consider proposals from Bolivia in good faith. Chile would not, however, have been required to endorse or give any special weight to Bolivia's proposals. Unlike settings where mandatory cooperation applies, triggering the more robust duty of due regard, Chile would have been free to decide for itself whether, or on what terms, it would relinquish some of its coastal territory to Bolivia. Ultimately, however, the ICJ concluded that Chile had not voluntarily undertaken any such duty to negotiate with Bolivia for the purpose of granting Bolivia "sovereign access" to the Pacific.[48] By rejecting the idea that mandatory cooperation applies to state efforts to acquire foreign territory, the ICJ's judgment underscored the limits of mandatory cooperation as a constraint on territorial sovereignty.

Chile bears more robust duties of cooperation when it comes to facilitating transit through its territory pursuant to Article 125. Because Bolivia's right to access the ocean under UNCLOS is in tension with Chile's right to territorial integrity, Article 125 requires that the two states reconcile their conflicting entitlements through cooperation. Bolivia and Chile must therefore cooperate in investigating, consulting, negotiating, and, if necessary, pursuing third-party dispute resolution to establish equitable "terms and modalities" that balance their respective interests.[49] In pursuing cooperative solutions, each state must respect the other's legitimate interests and manifest an openness to compromise. These equitable requirements are essential not only to reconcile the states' respective rights under international law (territorial sovereignty vs. oceanic access), but also to ameliorate historical injustices arising from Chile's violent conquest of the Litoral and to prevent Bolivia's landlocked status from perpetuating Chilean domination and suppressing Bolivia's economic development.

In many respects, Bolivia and Chile have successfully implemented these legal obligations. Pursuant to the 1904 Treaty of Peace and Friendship,

[48] Obligation To Negotiate Access to the Pacific Ocean (Bolivia v. Chile), Judgment, 2018 ICJ Rep. 507, 563 (1 October).

[49] UNCLOS, art. 125(2); *cf.* 'Obligation To Negotiate', p. 564 (observing that finding a solution to Bolivia's "landlocked situation" is "a matter of mutual interest" for both states).

Chile has connected Bolivia to the Pacific by constructing and maintaining a railway line and a paved highway between Bolivia's capitol, La Paz, and the Chilean port city of Arica.[50] Chilean lawmakers have worked with Bolivia to reduce regulatory red tape that would otherwise impede the free flow of people and goods across Chilean territory.[51] Bolivian cargo is exempt from Chilean taxes, and Chile allows Bolivia to exercise customs powers in the Chilean city of Arica over cargo traveling to or from Bolivia.[52] Pursuant to agreements negotiated in 1955 and 1957, a Bolivian state-owned company operates a pipeline from Sica in Bolivia to Arica in Chile, facilitating the shipment of Bolivian oil across the high seas to markets around the world.[53] To be sure, Bolivia clearly believes that further concessions by Chile are necessary – including a permanent transfer of coastal territory between the countries – to strengthen Bolivia's political independence and boost its economic development.[54] Yet, these lingering grievances should not overshadow the substantial progress that the states have made in reconciling their conflicting interests through diplomacy. For generations, Bolivia and Chile have managed to cooperate productively – investigating, consulting, and negotiating with one another on a wide variety of issues – in a good faith effort to balance equitably their respective sovereign interests. The fact that such a robust partnership has taken root and flourished – even as the two states remain bitterly divided over Bolivia's aspiration to acquire a territorial corridor to the Pacific – is a testament to the promise of mandatory cooperation.[55]

Mitigating Geographic Inequity

Bolivia is not the only landlocked state that has benefited from UNCLOS's endorsement of transit rights and mandatory cooperation.

50 'Chile Counter-Memorial', pp. 43–45, 53.
51 Ibid. pp. 52–54.
52 Ibid. p. 46.
53 Ibid. pp. 50–51.
54 Gideon Long, 'Bolivia-Chile Land Dispute Has Deep Roots', BBC News, 24 April 2013 (noting that Chile's complaint "reneged on agreements to give Bolivia access to ports further south on Chile's long Pacific coastline").
55 Uprety, 'The Transit Regime for Landlocked States', p. 113 (observing that because bilateral negotiations tend to favor transit states, the resulting agreements "often tend to appear like a generous gesture rather than a provision negotiated by equals," and arguing that this trend offends "general principles of international law" (i.e., sovereign equality) by making "the status of a country subject to, and conditional upon, the benevolence (or malevolence) of another State" (i.e., domination)).

Over the past four decades, government and scholarly resistance to the legal transit rights of landlocked states has faded as 170 states have become parties to UNCLOS.[56] Consistent with UNCLOS, transit states generally have abandoned the practice of subjecting goods in transit to customs duties and other taxes, except as remuneration for services rendered.[57] These developments have paved the way for a host of international, regional, and bilateral agreements that facilitate oceanic access for landlocked states. International instruments such as the World Trade Organization's Trade Facilitation Agreement have lowered customs barriers, facilitated cooperation among national transit authorities, and expedited the release and clearance of goods in transit across national borders to facilitate transit.[58] In Africa – home to sixteen landlocked states – regional transit-facilitating agreements include the Trans-Kalahari Corridor Agreement (Botswana, Namibia, South Africa) and the African Continental Free Trade Area Agreement (thirty-two states-parties, with many more pending). After decades of tension, Somalia agreed in the recent Ankara Declaration to facilitate Ethiopia's access to the Red Sea "within a spirit of friendship and mutual respect," while Ethiopia recognized Somalia's sovereign "independence and territorial integrity."[59] As these examples illustrate, the overall trend post-UNCLOS reflects coastal states cooperating to facilitate oceanic access for landlocked states.

International recognition of transit rights has enabled landlocked states to appeal to international organizations for assistance when disputes have arisen with their coastal neighbors. Even before UNCLOS, Lesotho successfully enlisted the assistance of the UN Security Council and UN General Assembly when Apartheid-era South Africa closed several border posts in an attempt to strong-arm its fiercely independent landlocked neighbor.[60] In 2001, the General Assembly provided sustained institutional support for

[56] UNCLOS, UNTS, https://treaties.un.org/pages/ViewDetailsIII.aspx?src=TREATY&mtdsg_no=XXI-6&chapter=21&Temp=mtdsg3&clang=_en.

[57] UNCLOS, art. 127(1); Kishor Uprety, 'From Barcelona to Montego Bay and Thereafter: A Search for Land-locked States' Rights to Trade through Access to the Sea: A Retrospective Review' (2003) 7 *Sing. J. Int'l & Compar. L.* 201, 225.

[58] Joann Peterson, 'The WTO Facilitation Agreement: Implementation Status and Next Steps' (2020) *J. Int'l Com. & Econ.* 1, 2–3, www.usitc.gov/publications/332/journals/wto_trade_facilitation_agreement.pdf.

[59] Republic of Türkiye, Ministry of Foreign Affairs, 'Ankara Declaration by the Federal Democratic Republic of Ethiopia and the Federal Republic of Somalia facilitated by the Republic of Türkiye'.

[60] Susan Marks, 'Transit Rights of Lesotho' (1990) 16 *Commonwealth L. Bull.* 329, 337–344.

landlocked states by establishing the Office of the High Representative for the Least Developed Countries, Landlocked Developing Countries and Small Island Developing States (UN-OHRLLS). The UN-OHRLLS has worked with landlocked states and their regional neighbors to stimulate cross-border trade and transport, establish transit transport corridors, promote regional integration and infrastructure development, and facilitate integration into regional and global value chains.[61] The UN-OHRLLS has championed the Vienna Programme of Action for Landlocked Developing Countries, a ten-year cooperative global initiative (2014–2024) to promote landlocked states' access to the sea, including by promoting regional integration, eliminating regulatory red tape, and developing essential transportation infrastructure.[62]

As international, regional, and bilateral cooperation has increased, landlocked states have been able to pursue economic opportunities that would have been unimaginable a half century ago. For example, in 2015 the world's largest landlocked state, Kazakhstan, announced an audacious plan to develop a blue-water shipping fleet[63] – no mean feat for a country located 3,750 kilometers from the ocean.[64] This remarkable initiative would be impossible without the cooperation of three transit states that separate Kazakhstan from the Persian Gulf: Uzbekistan, Turkmenistan, and Iran.

Even with mandatory cooperation facilitating oceanic access, the practical disadvantages of landlocked status should not be underestimated. There are good reasons why Bolivia continues to commemorate the Day of the Sea each year, anticipating a future (real or imagined) when the lost cities of "Antofagasta, beautiful lands of Tocopilla and Mejillones next to the sea, with Cobija and Calama return to Bolivia again."[65] Compared to the average developing country, landlocked states like Bolivia spend more than twice as much of their export earnings on transport and

[61] UN Office of the High Representative for the Least Developed Countries, Landlocked Developing Countries and the Small Island Developing States, 'Landlocked Developing Countries', www un.org/ohrlls/content/landlocked-developing-countries.

[62] Second UN Conference on Landlocked Developing Countries, Vienna Programme of Action for Landlocked Developing Countries for the Decade 2014–2024. at 7, Vienna, 3 November 2014, A/CONF.225/L.1 [hereinafter Vienna Programme].

[63] Paul Goble, 'Land-locked Kazakhstan Plans to Build a Blue-Water Commercial Fleet', Eurasia Daily Monitor, 28 July 2015.

[64] UN Office of the High Representative for the Least Developed Countries, Landlocked Developing Countries and Small Island Developing States, www.un.org/ohrlls/content/about-landlocked-developing-countries.

[65] Bacigalupo, 'Every Year on "Dia Del Mar."'

insurance services.[66] Many are at the mercy of transit delays produced by shoddy roads, bureaucratic red tape, and violent unrest in neighboring transit states. International law does not obligate transit states to construct new infrastructure to facilitate access to the sea for landlocked states. During times of port or rail congestion, coastal states may treat the needs of landlocked states as a lesser priority – particularly if they view landlocked states as competitors in the global marketplace.[67] Due to these and other factors, the United Nations estimates that "the level of development in landlocked developing countries is on average twenty per cent lower than what it would be were they not landlocked."[68] Where economic development is concerned, geography is destiny.

Mandatory cooperation cannot erase the structural inequities inherent in landlocked status.[69] However, experience has shown that international cooperation can at least mitigate the inequities of geography by enabling landlocked states to reach blue water – the gateway to international commerce.

[66] UN Office of the High Representative for the Least Developed Countries, Landlocked Developing Countries and Small Island Developing States, www.un.org/ohrlls/content/about-landlocked-developing-countries.

[67] Bojotlhe O. G. Butale, 'Bridging the Gap to the Sea for Landlocked States: A Case for Botswana' (2016), p. 29, www.un.org/oceancapacity/sites/www.un.org.oceancapacity/files/bj_butale_bridging_the_gap_for_landlocked_states.pdf.

[68] Vienna Programme, p. 4.

[69] Cf. North Sea Continental Shelf Cases (Fed. Rep. Germ./Den.; Fed. Rep. Germ./Neth.), Merits, 1969 ICJ Rep. 3, para. 91 (20 February) ("Equity does not necessarily imply equality. There can never be any question of completely refashioning nature.").

5

Pirates, Terrorists, and Hackers

Below the Green Waters

On June 19, 1864, an enthusiastic crowd of 15,000 spectators flocked to Cherbourg, France – some taking trains from as far away as Paris – to witness a naval duel between two celebrated adversaries from the American Civil War.[1] Anchored in the harbor for repairs was the *Alabama*, the Confederacy's most notorious and successful raider. Described by her captain, Raphael Semmes, as a model of "the most perfect symmetry" with "the lightness and grace of a swan," the *Alabama* had spent the previous two years pillaging Union shipping from the Caribbean to the Cape of Good Hope to the South China Sea and back again.[2] Awaiting the *Alabama* in the English Channel was the *Kearsarge*, a formidable Union warship under the command of Captain John A. Winslow. Long before the Civil War, Semmes and Winslow had cut their teeth in the US navy while serving as shipmates during the Mexican War. Their careers then followed similar trajectories: both swiftly climbed the officer ranks and received commendations for bravery before they eventually found themselves on opposite sides of the Civil War. When the *Kearsarge* tracked the *Alabama* to Cherbourg, Semmes challenged his former shipmate to battle.[3]

The *Alabama* did not fare well in the ensuing contest. Years later, Semmes recounted what transpired in elegiac prose:

> At the hour when the church-goers in Paris and London were sending up their orisons to the Most High, the sound of cannon was heard in the British Channel, and the *Alabama* was engaged in her death-struggle . . .

[1] Charles G. Summersell (ed.), *The Journal of George Townley Fullam: Boarding Officer of the Confederate Sea Raider Alabama* (University: University of Alabama Press, 1973), p. 193.

[2] Raphael Semmes, *Memories of Service Afloat, During the War Between the States* (Baltimore: Kelly, Piet & Co., 1869), p. 402.

[3] *The Journal of George Townley Fullam*, pp. 190–192.

> The sun rose, as before, in a cloudless sky, and the sea-breeze has come in over the dancing waters, mild and balmy . . . The *Alabama* steams out to meet the *Kearsarge* in mortal combat, and before the sun has set, she has gone down below the green waters, and lies entombed by the side of many a gallant craft that had gone down before her in that famous old British Channel.[4]

Thus ended the storied career of the *Alabama*, the toast of the Confederate navy.

Politicians and reporters in the Northern States preferred a less reverential epitaph for the *Alabama*: "British pirate."[5] Three years earlier, in April 1861, an agent for the Confederacy concluded a contract with Messrs. Laird & Co. of Birkenhead, Liverpool for the construction of "a wooden-hulled ship that could be readily refitted in any port around the world, built to the highest standard of the day."[6] When the US Minister to England, Charles Francis Adams, caught wind of the transaction, he urged the British government to seize the ship pursuant to the Foreign Enlistment Act of 1819, which prohibited constructing warships in British territory for a belligerent power.[7] To Adams's dismay, the British Customs Office initially demurred. While recognizing that the ship in question was clearly designed for combat, the Customs Office questioned whether it had authority to intervene under domestic law when the ship as yet carried no armaments and had been commissioned nominally for a private party, not the Confederacy itself.[8]

Union agents retained a private detective to confirm the ship's belligerent purpose. The detective collected affidavits attesting that the Lairds were secretly recruiting British seamen with fighting experience to join the ship's crew in support of the Confederacy.[9] Adams delivered these affidavits to the Customs Office in London, renewing the United States' plea to impound the vessel. He also made arrangements for the *USS Tuscarora*, a Union frigate anchored in Southampton, to set course northward to intercept the warship before it could escape out to sea.

4 Semmes, *Memories of Service Afloat*, pp. 410–411.
5 Thomas Willing Balch, *The Alabama Arbitration* (Philadelphia: Allen, Lane & Scott, 1900), p. 10.
6 Arthur Sinclair, *Two Years on the Alabama: A Firsthand Account of the Daring Exploits of the Infamous Confederate Raider* (Edinburg: Tantallon Press, 2004), p. xix.
7 Sinclair, *Two Years on the Alabama*, p. xvii; Balch, *The Alabama Arbitration*, pp. 5–6. The Foreign Enlistment Act also prohibited British citizens from serving in foreign militaries.
8 Sinclair, *Two Years on the Alabama*, p. xxii.
9 Ibid.; Charles Cotesworth Beaman, *The National and Private "Alabama Claims" and Their "Final and Amicable Settlement"* (Washington: W. H. Moore, 1871), p. 270.

Neither of these moves succeeded. Tipped off by friends in the British government, the Lairds accelerated their plans for the warship's departure. On July 29, 1862 – the very same day legal officers in London determined that the vessel should be detained – it slipped quietly out to sea with a skeleton crew. Two days later, customs officers in Liverpool watched passively as a tug picked up crewmembers and supplies to join the warship fifty miles away in Moelfre Bay. No effort was made to detain the ship at this rendezvous point before she pulled up anchor and departed for Terceira in the Azores, where she received her armament.[10] On August 24, 1862, Captain Semmes arrived at Terceira to assume command. Upon reading out his commission as a commander in the Confederate navy, Semmes raised the Confederate flag and christened the ship the *CSS Alabama.*[11]

Over the next two years, the *Alabama* traveled 75,000 miles, a distance roughly equivalent to circling the world three times.[12] Along the way, it captured and destroyed dozens of Union ships, causing losses in the millions of dollars, and planting fear in the hearts of merchants and seamen around the world.[13] In 1863 Adams wrote in protest to UK Foreign Secretary Earl Russell. The United States, he wrote:

> greatly regret to be compelled to admit the fact that the vessel known . . . as the Alabama, is roving over the seas capturing, burning, sinking, and destroying American vessels without lawful authority from any source recognized by international law, and in open defiance of all judicial tribunals established by the common consent of civilized nations as a restraint upon such a piratical mode of warfare.[14]

Adams stressed that the *Alabama* had been constructed on British soil by British subjects and operated by a British crew with the express purpose to make war against the United States.[15] In Adams's view, these considerations meant that the British government was "bound by treaty obligations and by the law of nations to prevent" the *Alabama* from leaving port. Having neglected that responsibility time and again, the British government was obligated under the law of nations to compensate "the

10 Beaman, *The National and Private "Alabama Claims,"* p. 89.
11 Ibid. pp. 92–97.
12 Sinclair, *Two Years on the Alabama*, p. 4.
13 Balch, *The Alabama Arbitration*, pp. 105, 127; Beaman, *The National and Private "Alabama Claims,"* p. 98.
14 Balch, *The Alabama Arbitration*, p. 17.
15 Ibid. p. 18.

peaceful lawabiding citizens of the United States" for the *Alabama*'s ruinous "depredations."[16]

The US government continued to press these claims after the war. In an 1869 speech, Senator Charles Sumner of Massachusetts castigated the United Kingdom for its ties to the *Alabama*. Particularly maddening, Sumner noted, was how the United Kingdom had welcomed the *Alabama* with open arms whenever she sailed around the world:

> Constantly the pirate ship was within reach of British cruisers, and from time to time within the shelter of British ports. For six days unmolested she enjoyed the pleasant hospitality of Kingston, in Jamaica, obtaining freely the coal and other supplies so necessary to her vocation. But no British cruiser, no British magistrate ever arrested the offending ship ... Audacity reached its height when iron-clad rams were built, and the perversity of the British Government became still more conspicuous by its long refusal to arrest these destructive engines of war, destined to be employed against the United States.[17]

Given the United Kingdom's failure to prevent the *Alabama* from preying on Union shipping, the consequences under the law of nations were clear: the British government "must respond in damages," Sumner declared, furnishing compensation "not only to the individuals who have suffered but also to the National Government, acting as *paterfamilias* for the common good of all the people."[18]

The two states eventually agreed to submit the *Alabama* controversy to arbitration.[19] In the Treaty of Washington of 1871, they stipulated to several rules that would govern the tribunal's decision. First, a neutral state, such as the United Kingdom, must "use due diligence to prevent the fitting out, arming, or equipping, within its jurisdiction, of any vessel which it has a reasonable ground to believe is intended to ... carry on a war against a Power with which it is at Peace," as well as to prevent any such vessel from escaping its jurisdiction.[20] Second, a neutral state may not allow belligerents to use its ports or waters as a safe harbor for recruiting, restocking, or launching attacks. And third, a neutral state must "exercise due diligence in its own ports and waters, and, as to all

[16] Ibid. p. 19.
[17] Ibid. pp. 100, 102–103.
[18] Ibid. p. 106.
[19] Ibid. p. 114.
[20] Treaty of Washington (Gr. Brit.-US) art. 6, 8 May 1871, 17 Stat. 863.

persons within its jurisdiction, to prevent any violation of the foregoing obligations."[21] The United Kingdom resisted characterizing these rules as customary international law, but it agreed to accept them for the *Alabama* controversy in the interest of nurturing "friendly relations between the two countries."[22]

In the proceedings that followed, the British government asserted that it had practiced due diligence by enforcing its Foreign Enlistment Act in good faith. The arbitral tribunal disagreed. On September 14, 1872, the tribunal issued a decision and award that endorsed the United States' position that due diligence required a higher level of vigilance commensurate with the serious threat the *Alabama* posed to the United States.[23] The tribunal concluded that the British government had not acted on the United States' pleas for assistance with "all possible solicitude."[24] In particular, the government failed "to take in due time any effective measures of prevention," and "those orders which it did give at last, for the detention of the vessel, were issued so late that their execution was not practicable."[25] These belated half-measures did not reflect due diligence. Accordingly, the tribunal concluded that the United Kingdom was liable to the United States for millions of dollars in commercial losses inflicted by the *Alabama*.[26]

Before long, the standards of state responsibility applied in the *Alabama* arbitration achieved wider acceptance as general international law. In 1875, the influential Institute de Droit International endorsed the rules applied in the arbitration.[27] States later accepted the rules in the Hague Convention of October 18, 1907:

> A neutral Government is bound to employ the means at its disposal to prevent the fitting out or arming of a vessel within its jurisdiction which it has reason to believe is intended to cruise, or engage in hostile operations, against a power with which that government is at peace. It is also bound to display the same vigilance to prevent the departure

[21] Ibid.

[22] Balch, *The Alabama Arbitration*, p. 120.

[23] Ibid. p. 135 (reprinting the Alabama Decision and Award).

[24] Ibid.

[25] Ibid. p. 137. The tribunal also concluded that Great Britain incurred legal responsibility by admitting the *Alabama* into its colonial ports, rather than repelling or arresting it, as required under international law. Ibid.

[26] Ibid. p. 138.

[27] Horst Blomeyer-Bartenstein, 'Due Diligence', in *Encyclopedia of Public International Law* (Heidelberg: Max Planck Institute, 1992), vol. 1, pp. 1110, 1111 (quoting and discussing the Institute's conclusions).

> from its jurisdiction of any vessel intended to cruise, or engage in hostile operations, which had been adapted entirely or partly within the said jurisdiction for use in war.[28]

As long as states remained neutral with respect to foreign wars, they were required to prevent their territory from being used as a staging ground for transboundary attacks. The *Alabama* controversy thus became a path-breaking precedent for the principle that states must exercise due diligence to prevent violent actors from using their territory to inflict significant harm abroad.

Taking the *Alabama* controversy as a point of departure, this chapter explores a variety of settings where international law obligates states to cooperate with one another to suppress harm caused by dangerous non-state actors, such as pirates, terrorists, and computer hackers. Since the *Alabama* dispute, the international community has recognized that international law requires states to exercise due diligence to prevent criminals in their territory from causing significant injuries to foreign states and foreign nationals. Only more recently, however, has the international community embraced the idea that states also bear legal obligations to cooperate with one another to suppress such transnational crimes. Nonetheless, this chapter shows that mandatory cooperation has now become firmly embedded in multilateral conventions on piracy and terrorism. Mandatory cooperation is also beginning to gain traction in international law governing cyberattacks, though the framework is embryonic.

From Due Diligence to Mandatory Cooperation

Following the *Alabama* arbitration, domestic courts and international tribunals extended the due diligence standard to a variety of other contexts where non-state actors threatened to inflict serious harm on foreign states or foreign nationals. For example, in the 1887 case *United States v. Arjona*, the US Supreme Court declared that this standard applied to currency counterfeiting:

> The law of nations requires every national government to use "due diligence" to prevent a wrong being done within its own dominion to another nation with which it is at peace, or to the people thereof; and because of this, the obligation of one nation to punish those who, within

[28] Convention Respecting the Rights and Duties of Neutral Powers in Naval War art. 8, (1908) 2 AJIL Supp. 202, 206.

its own jurisdiction, counterfeit the money of another nation has long been recognized.[29]

Quoting Vattel, the Court explained that if a state "allows and protects false coiners who [counterfeit foreign currency], she does that nation an injury."[30] Thus, the law of nations obligated the United States to exercise due diligence to prevent and criminalize counterfeiting, as well as to prosecute false coiners.[31]

International tribunals also have applied the due diligence standard to other transnational crimes. For example, following the assassination of an Italian general and other officials in Greece, a Commission of Jurists appointed by the League of Nations affirmed that a state is responsible for injuries to foreigners if it does not take "all reasonable measures for the prevention of the crime" and for bringing the perpetrators to justice.[32] By 1927, when the Permanent Court of International Justice (PCIJ) decided the landmark *Lotus Case*, Judge John Bassett Moore confidently observed that it was "well settled that a state is bound to use due diligence to prevent the commission within its dominion of criminal acts against another nation or its people."[33] The ICJ would endorse this principle later in the *Corfu Channel Case*[34] and the *Tehran Hostages Case*.[35] In sum, states are obligated under international law to exercise due diligence in preventing criminal activities within their jurisdiction from inflicting significant harm on foreign states or foreign nationals.

But what precisely does "due diligence" demand of states? Some requirements are uncontroversial. At a minimum, states where criminal activities originate must take reasonable steps to prevent and suppress transnational harm. They must investigate crimes to determine the nature and extent of the threats, and they must make a reasonable effort

[29] United States v. Arjona, 120 US 479, 484 (1887).

[30] Ibid. (quoting Vattel's *Law of Nations*).

[31] Ibid. at pp. 486–487.

[32] Quincy Wright, 'Opinion of Commission of Jurists on Janina-Corfu Affair' (1924) 18 AJIL 536, 543 (quoting the jurists); *see also* David Jayne Hill, 'The Janina-Corfu Affair', (1924) 18 AJIL 98.

[33] S.S. Lotus (France v. Turkey), 1927 PCIJ (ser. A) No. 10 (7 September), p. 88 (Moore, J., dissenting).

[34] Corfu Channel Case (U.K. v. Alb.), Judgment, 1949 ICJ Rep. 4, ¶ 22 (9 April) (affirming a state's obligation "not to allow knowingly its territory to be used for acts contrary to the rights of other States").

[35] United States Diplomatic and Consular Staff in Tehran (Tehran Hostages Case), 1980 ICJ Rep. 3 (24 May) (affirming that states "are required under international law to take appropriate acts in order to protect the interests" of other states from nonstate actors in their jurisdiction).

to disrupt criminal behavior through law enforcement and prosecution. These basic requirements stem from the general customary obligation to prevent significant transboundary harm.

In principle, due diligence should also require international cooperation, because states often cannot respond effectively to transnational crime without foreign assistance. The *Alabama* affair illustrates this dynamic. Recall that it was American agents who first tipped off the British government that the *Alabama* was destined for the Confederacy. Given the gravity of the threat, the British government should have undertaken a more diligent investigation of the warship. Once the British government confirmed the *Alabama*'s belligerent purpose, it should have exchanged information and cooperated with Union officials to ensure that the *Alabama* could not slip away to inflict harm abroad. If that failed, the British government should have detained the *Alabama* when it later sought safe harbor in colonial ports while inviting assistance from the United States to gather evidence necessary to prosecute the *Alabama*'s British crew. By withholding its cooperation at each of these stages, the British government defaulted on its legal obligation to diligently prevent and suppress transboundary attacks.

International law today supports the idea that at least some transnational crimes trigger mandatory cooperation. States from which transnational crime originates must exchange information, consult, and negotiate with states that are likely to suffer injury in order to ensure that their laws, policies, and practices are adequate to avert the anticipated harm. When disagreements arise, states must resolve their differences through negotiation or third-party dispute resolution. Without such cooperation, states that serve as hosts for transnational crime would be complicit in the wrongs inflicted on other states and foreign nationals, ultimately undermining the principle of sovereign equality. Respect for sovereign equality favors applying mandatory cooperation to all significant transnational boundary harms, including criminal activities that adversely impact foreign states and foreign nationals.

Joining Forces to Stop Piracy

International law now unequivocally requires mandatory cooperation to suppress piracy. Few international norms have a longer historical pedigree than the prohibition of piracy. For centuries, international lawyers have characterized pirates as "enemies of all mankind" (*hostis humani generis*) – outlaws whom all states are authorized to subdue for humanity's benefit.[36] Conventional wisdom suggests that all states have an interest in suppressing piracy, so states have strong incentives to cooperate for this purpose. Only relatively recently, however, has international law generated affirmative obligations for states to cooperate in combatting pirate attacks.

An important first step in this direction is the 1982 UN Convention on the Law of the Sea (UNCLOS), which endorses mandatory cooperation in significant respects by declaring that states must "cooperate to the fullest possible extent in the repression of piracy." However, UNCLOS defines "piracy" to include only acts of violence, detention, or depredation that take place "on the high seas" or "in a place outside the jurisdiction of any State."[37] Attacks that take place in port or within a state's internal waters or territorial sea might be punishable under domestic law, but they do not qualify as "piracy" under UNCLOS. Hence, mandatory cooperation extends only to acts committed outside states' exclusive territorial jurisdiction.[38] UNCLOS thus neglects the most promising opportunities for suppressing piracy – before pirates reach open sea.[39]

These geographic limits on mandatory cooperation might have become permanent had the international community not been shocked into action a few years later by a horrific incident in the Mediterranean Sea. In 1985, four members of the Palestinian Liberation Front (PLF) forcibly boarded an Italian passenger liner, the *Achille Lauro*, which had put into port in Alexandria, Egypt. The hijackers forced the captain to depart with twelve passengers held at gunpoint. Among the hostages was Leon Kinghoffer, a disabled sixty-nine-year-old. When the hijackers' demands were not met, the gunmen "pushed Klinghoffer's wheelchair

[36] See James Kraska, *Contemporary Maritime Piracy: International Law, Strategy, and Diplomacy at Sea* (Oxford: Praeger, 2011), pp. 7–8, 106 (asserting that international law does not define piracy as an international crime, but rather as a domestic crime that qualifies for universal jurisdiction).

[37] UN Convention on the Law of the Sea art. 101(a), opened for signature 10 December 1982, UN Doc. A/CONF. 62/122.

[38] See ibid. art. 100. With respect to territorial waters in international straits, UNCLOS provides only that user states and littoral states "should by agreement cooperate: (a) in the establishment and maintenance in a strait of necessary navigational and safety aids or other improvements in aid of international navigation; and (b) for the prevention, reduction and control of pollution from ships." Ibid. art. 43.

[39] As NATO Supreme Allied Commander for Europe John Craddock has cautioned, "You do not stop piracy on the seas. You stop piracy on the land." David Charter, 'Royal Navy Admiral Phillip Jones Heads EU Somali Pirate Task Force', The Times, 9 December 2008, www.timesonline co.uk/tol/news/world/europe/article5309165.ece (quoting Craddock).

to the edge of the deck, shot him in the back, and pitched his still-twitching body into the sea."[40]

Following the *Achille Lauro* incident, an overwhelming majority of states agreed to pursue more robust collaboration in the 1988 Convention for the Suppression of Unlawful Acts Against the Safety of Maritime Navigation (SUA Convention).[41] The SUA Convention requires states-parties to criminalize and punish certain acts, such as seizing a ship by force, destroying a ship, and killing or injuring people aboard a ship in the course of such activities.[42] States-parties also must "afford one another the greatest measure of assistance in connection with ... criminal proceedings," including through rendering assistance in obtaining evidence for criminal prosecution.[43] The SUA Convention also promotes international cooperation by creating an independent mechanism to facilitate extradition.[44] Most important for present purposes, states-parties agree to cooperate with one another in preventing piracy and terrorism at sea, including by employing "all practical measures to prevent preparations in their respective territories for the commission of those offenses," as well as by exchanging information and "co-ordinating administrative and other measures ... to prevent the commission of offenses."[45] The SUA Convention therefore brings mandatory cooperation home by requiring states to cooperate with one another to prevent and suppress piracy at its source – within their own national jurisdictions. And when disputes arise that cannot be resolved through negotiation, states-parties may take cooperation to another level by initiating binding arbitration or adjudication in the ICJ.[46]

40 Michael B. Oren, *Power, Faith, and Fantasy* (New York: W.W. Norton & Co., 2007), p. 556.

41 Convention for the Suppression of Unlawful Acts against the Safety of Maritime Navigation, Mar. 10, 1988, 1678 UNTS 222 [hereinafter SUA Convention]. As of 2017, the SUA Convention had 166 states-parties, constituting approximately 95.16 percent of the gross tonnage of the world's merchant fleet. *See* Status of Multilateral Conventions and Instruments in Respect of Which the International Maritime Organization or Its Secretary-General Performs Depositary or Other Functions 423, 11 July 2017, https://web.archive.org/web/20170713063200/http://www.imo.org/en/About/Conventions/StatusOfConventions/Documents/Status%20-%202017.pdf.

42 SUA Convention, arts. 3, 5, 7, 10.

43 Ibid. art. 12(1).

44 Ibid. art 11.

45 Ibid. art. 13(1).

46 Ibid. art. 16. A 2005 Protocol offers various amendments to supplement the SUA Convention, but it leaves intact the features discussed here. Whether these treaty-based obligations have become customary international law through general state practice and *opinio juris* is unclear at this stage. If obligations satisfy the requirements for customary international law, they would also qualify as obligations *erga omnes*.

Among the maritime spaces most vulnerable to pirate attacks are the Straits of Malacca and Singapore. The distinctive geographic features and human uses of these straits make them a congenial setting for piracy. Dividing Indonesia, Malaysia, and Singapore for 520 nautical miles, the Straits of Malacca and Singapore are strategically important highways for shipping to and from some of the world's busiest ports, including Hong Kong, Jakarta, Pusan, Shanghai, Singapore, and Tokyo. Narrow and crowded with small fishing craft and commercial vessels traveling at low speeds, the straits offer abundant opportunities for pirates to launch quietly from the coasts, blend into the bustling maritime traffic, strike targets quickly, and then disappear into hidden retreats along the shoreline. As a result of these factors, piracy became a serious problem in the region at the end of the 1990s and in the early 2000s. The vast majority of attacks in the straits did not technically qualify as "piracy" under the terms of UNCLOS, because they occurred within the territorial waters of Indonesia, Malaysia, or Singapore.[47] To make matters worse for user states, Indonesia, Malaysia, and Singapore resisted overtures to establish international counter-piracy patrols in the straits on the grounds that the straits were within their exclusive sovereign jurisdiction.[48]

Despite this hesitation, Indonesia, Malaysia, and Singapore have made important strides in preventing and suppressing piracy and armed robbery in the straits, and they have embraced multilateral cooperation by working with user states to strengthen their capacities to combat piracy. In July 2004, the three states began conducting joint naval patrols. Later the same year, they joined the Association of Southeast Asian Nations (ASEAN) sister-states and six other Southeast Asian states to conclude a Regional Agreement on Combatting Piracy and Armed Robbery Against Ships in Asia (ReCAAP). This agreement provides for information sharing, collaborative capacity building, and cooperative enforcement among the states parties.[49] In September 2005, the International Maritime Organization (IMO) also convened a meeting of littoral and user states in Jakarta to address piracy. The meeting produced a joint-statement that emphasized "the need to balance the interest of the littoral States and the user States while respecting the littoral States' sovereignty,

[47] Kraska, 'Contemporary Maritime Piracy: International Law', pp. 35–38, 41.

[48] Ibid. pp. 42, 43; Robert Beckman, 'Piracy and Armed Robbery Against Ships in Southeast Asia', in Douglas Guilfoyle (ed.), *Modern Piracy: Legal Challenges and Responses* (Cheltenham: Edward Elgar Publishing, 2013), p. 13, pp. 14–15.

[49] Kraska, 'Contemporary Maritime Piracy: International Law', pp. 145–146.

and to establish a mechanism to facilitate cooperation between them to discuss issues relating to the safety, security and environmental protection of the Straits of Malacca and Singapore, including exploring possible options for burden sharing."[50] Other multilateral initiatives have generated an Information Sharing Centre in Singapore and a formal Cooperative Mechanism consisting of three components: a Cooperation Forum, a Project Coordination Committee, and an Aids to Navigation Fund.[51] Working through the Cooperation Mechanism, littoral states have accepted valuable training and technology, such as surface search radars, from user states to assist them in their counter-piracy efforts. By the time Indonesia, Malaysia, and Singapore invited Thailand to join their regional counter-piracy patrols in 2008 under the renamed Malacca Straits Patrols, piracy in the straits had dropped precipitously, from 187 incidents in 2003 to 65 in 2008.[52] International lawyers and security experts have hailed cooperation in the Straits of Malacca and Singapore as "the great counter-piracy success story."[53]

Piracy off the Horn of Africa presents different challenges. Like the Straits of Malacca and Singapore, the Horn of Africa is a major crossroads for international shipping, with 33,000 ships transiting through the nearby Gulf of Aden each year.[54] However, when piracy exploded around the Horn of Africa in the early 2000s, it reflected a distinct set of social, political, and economic dynamics. Particularly salient were government fragility in Puntland, the region of Somalia where most piracy in the region originates, and the limited law enforcement capabilities of other coastal states in East Africa.[55] Whereas coastal states have been willing to take the lead in combatting pirate attacks and armed robbery around the Straits of Malacca and Singapore, Somalia has been unable to shoulder this responsibility along its lengthy 2,000-mile shoreline.

This resulting governance gap off the coast of Somalia has been ameliorated through international cooperation. In 2008, the UN Security Council determined that piracy and armed robbery off the coast of Somalia constituted a threat to international peace and security

[50] Yann-huei Song, 'Security in the Strait of Malacca and the Regional Maritime Security Initiative: Responses to the US Proposal' (2007) 83 *Int'l L. Stud.* 97, 128 (quoting identical letters from the Permanent Representatives of Indonesia, Malaysia, and Singapore).

[51] Kraska, 'Contemporary Maritime Piracy: International Law', pp. 43–44, 146.

[52] Ibid. p. 44.

[53] Douglas Guilfoyle, 'Introduction: Piracy, Law and Lawyers', in Guilfoyle (ed.), pp. 1, 2.

[54] Kraska, 'Contemporary Maritime Piracy: International Law', p. 46.

[55] See Douglas Guilfoyle, 'Piracy Off Somalia and Counter-piracy Efforts', in Guilfoyle (ed.), p. 35; Kraska, 'Contemporary Maritime Piracy: International Law', p. 45.

in the region.[56] Invoking its binding authority under Chapter VII of the UN Charter, the Security Council urged states to cooperate with one another and with relevant international organizations to share information about Somali pirate attacks and render assistance to threatened vessels. It also called upon states to assist in enhancing the capacities of Somalia and other coastal states to combat piracy. And it authorized user states to enter and perform law enforcement functions within Somali territorial waters, in cooperation with the Somali government, to suppress piracy and armed robbery.[57] Significantly, the Security Council explained that these measures should not be construed as impinging on Somalia's territorial sovereignty because Somalia's central government had consented to the measures. The Security Council also cautioned that the measures thus established were context-specific, in the sense that they "shall not be considered as establishing customary international law" authorizing international intervention to suppress piracy elsewhere.[58]

The Security Council's efforts to promote international cooperation have inspired a wide variety of counter-piracy missions, cooperative agreements, and informal networks for safeguarding shipping off the Horn of Africa. Prominent examples including the Combined Task Force 151 (CTF-151), which involved ships from twenty-five participating countries, and NATO's "Operation Ocean Shield," which provides naval escorts and general deterrence patrols in the region.[59] The African Union has incorporated regional cooperation against piracy into its 2050 Integrated Maritime Strategy[60] and the African Charter on Maritime Security and Safety and Development in Africa (Lomé Charter).[61] Thanks in part to these diverse commitments and institutional arrangements for cooperation,[62] piracy around the Horn of Africa has plummeted since its peak in the early 2000s.[63]

[56] SC Res. 1816, pmbl., S/RES/1816, 2 June 2008.

[57] Ibid. paras. 3, 5, 7.

[58] Ibid. para. 9.

[59] Guilfoyle, p. 48, in Guilfoyle (ed.); Jan Klabbers, 'Piracy in Global Law and Global Governance', in Guilfoyle (ed.), pp. 329, 339–340.

[60] African Union, 2050 Africa's Integrated Maritime Strategy (2012), pp. 24–25.

[61] African Charter on Maritime Security and Safety and Development in Africa art. 32(1) (2016) ("State Parties shall cooperate and coordinate their actions in combating transnational organized crimes of all kinds including ... acts of piracy and armed robbery against ships.").

[62] Bueger, *Responses to Contemporary Piracy*, pp. 91, 113 (observing more than fifty different organizations and arrangements dedicated to countering piracy).

[63] Christian Bueger, *Learning from Piracy: Future Challenges of Maritime Security Governance* (2015), p. 1, www.cardiff.ac.uk/__data/assets/pdf_file/0013/42412/dr-chris

In sum, the past twenty years have witnessed a remarkable turn toward multilateral cooperation for combatting piracy. The overwhelming majority of states have committed by treaty to assist one another in preventing and suppressing piracy not only outside their jurisdiction (UNCLOS) but also within their jurisdiction (SUA Convention). Coastal states must, at a minimum, consult and exchange information about piracy with other interested states. They must also work with other states to improve their capacity to prevent pirates in their waters from launching attacks on foreign vessels. When coastal states are incapable of preventing such attacks, due diligence requires that they pursue international cooperation, either by accepting training and resources from other states and international organizations to bolster their national antipiracy efforts (as in the Straits of Malacca and Singapore) or by allowing user states or international organizations to undertake law enforcement operations within their territorial waters (as in Somalia).[64] All of these requirements can be understood as corollaries of the *Alabama* doctrine that states must exercise due diligence to prevent their territories from being used as staging grounds for attacks on foreign states and foreign nationals.

Countering Terrorism

Mandatory cooperation also features centrally in the international law of counterterrorism. The UN General Assembly expressly embraced mandatory cooperation in its 1994 Declaration on Measures to Eliminate International Terrorism.[65] The Declaration affirms that states bear "obligations under the Charter of the United Nations and other provisions of international law with respect to combatting international terrorism," including the duty to "ensure that their respective territories are not used ... for the preparation or organization of terrorist acts ... against other States or their citizens."[66] More important for present purposes, the Declaration proclaims that states must "cooperate with one another in

tian-bueger.pdf ("The decade of large scale piracy off the coast of Somalia appears to be over. Since 2012 there has not been a successful hijacking attempt.").

64 Importantly, as the Security Council implied in Resolution 1816, mandatory cooperation does not give user states license to exercise law enforcement functions in coastal states' territorial waters without Security Council authorization or the coastal state's consent.

65 Declaration on Measures to Eliminate International Terrorism, GA Res. 49/60, UN GAOR, 49th Sess., UN Doc. A/RES/49/60 (1994) [hereinafter Declaration on Measures to Eliminate International Terrorism].

66 Declaration on Measures to Eliminate International Terrorism, para. 5

exchanging relevant information" and "endeavour to conclude special agreements [to prevent and suppress terrorism] on a bilateral, regional and multilateral basis."[67] The Declaration thus envisions states as bearing affirmative obligations under the Charter and customary international law to promote international peace and security through coordinated counterterrorism.

By making the case for mandatory cooperation, the General Assembly paved the way for a series of multilateral treaties that required international cooperation against terrorism. Within a few years, states concluded the International Convention for the Suppression of Terrorist Bombings[68] and the International Convention for the Suppression of the Financing of Terrorism.[69] Both agreements committed states parties to "afford one another the greatest measure of assistance in connection with criminal investigations or criminal or extradition proceedings," as well as to "cooperate in the prevention of [terrorism] . . . by exchanging accurate and verified information . . . to prevent the commission of [terrorist] offences."[70] The 2005 International Convention for the Suppression of Acts of Nuclear Terrorism (Nuclear Terrorism Convention) also requires states to cooperate by exchanging information, consulting and assisting one another in the investigation and prosecution of terrorists, and resolving disputes through negotiation or arbitration.[71] The Nuclear Terrorism Convention underscores that states must discharge these cooperative obligations "in a manner consistent with the principles of sovereign equality," "territorial integrity," and "non-intervention in the domestic affairs of other States."[72]

67 Declaration on Measures to Eliminate International Terrorism, para. 5; see also G.A. Res. 56/1, UN GAOR, 56th Sess., 1st mtg., Agenda Item 8, UN Doc. A/RES/56/1 (12 September 2001) (urgently calling "for international cooperation to prevent and eradicate acts of terrorism").

68 International Convention for the Suppression of Terrorist Bombings, 31 December 1999, 2149 UNTS 256 (1997) [hereinafter Terrorist Bombing Convention].

69 International Convention for the Suppression of the Financing of Terrorism, 2178 UNTS 197 (1999) [hereinafter Terrorist Financing Convention]; see also https://treaties.un.org/pages/ViewDetails.aspx?src=IND&mtdsg_no=XVIII-11&chapter=18&clang=_en (listing 190 states parties).

70 Terrorist Bombings Convention, arts. 10, 15; Terrorist Financing Convention, arts. 12, 18.

71 International Convention for the Suppression of Acts of Nuclear Terrorism, arts. 7, 14, 20, 23, 31 December 2006, 2445 UNTS 89 [hereinafter International Convention for the Suppression of Acts of Nuclear Terrorism].

72 International Convention for the Suppression of Acts of Nuclear Terrorism, art. 21.

The UN Security Council has also endorsed mandatory cooperation in this field. Security Council resolutions direct states to assist one another with counter-terrorism efforts by exchanging information, collaborating to apprehend and prosecute suspects, and working together to disrupt suspects' travel, communications, and financing.[73] The Security Council has also "call[ed] upon all States to become party, as a matter of urgency, to the international counter-terrorism conventions," including the Nuclear Terrorism Convention specifically.[74] Through these and other directives, the Security Council has played an important role in coordinating international efforts to prevent, suppress, and punish terrorist attacks.

International cooperation against terrorism, however, has a notorious dark side. Following the 9/11 terrorist attacks, the United States collaborated with foreign partners to bring about the enforced disappearance, prolonged arbitrary detention, torture, and cruel, inhuman, and degrading treatment of suspected terrorists.[75] The Security Council has also courted controversy by directing states to freeze the assets of terrorist suspects without affording them due process of law.[76] These striking abuses offer stark reminders that mandatory cooperation can be turned to pernicious ends and that safeguards are necessary to help ensure that cooperation is practiced consistent with states' other obligations under international law – including international human rights law.

Curiously, international lawyers generally give short shrift to mandatory cooperation as an emergent feature of international counter-terrorism law. When discussing transnational counter-terrorism, legal scholars and practitioners tend to focus on the options for unilateral state action. In particular, international lawyers have debated whether a state exposed to transboundary terrorist attacks (the target state) may use force against terrorists abroad without the consent of the state where terrorists are located (the host state). The ICJ has intervened in this

[73] See, e.g., SC Res. 1373, paras. 2–3, S/RES/1373 (28 September 2001); SC Res. 2178, para. 11, S/RES/2178 (24 September 2014); SC Res. 2322, S/RES/2322 (12 December 2016); SC Res 2462, S/RES/2462 (28 March 2019).

[74] SC Res. 1624, pmbl., S/RES/1624 (14 September 2005).

[75] Jane Mayer, 'Outsourcing Torture: The Secret History of America's 'Extraordinary Rendition' Program', New Yorker, 4 and 21 February 2005 (discussing extraordinary rendition practices in the "war on terrorism").

[76] For discussion and critique of this practice, emphasizing the Security Council's failure to afford due process to individual sanctions targets, see Michael Bothe, 'Security Council's Targeted Sanctions Against Presumed Terrorists: The Need to Comply with Human Rights Standards' (2008) 6 *J. Int'l Crim. Just.* 541.

debate by holding that the UN Charter does not allow a target state to use force in self-defense unless attacks from nonstate actors are imputable to the host state.[77] Some commentators contest the ICJ's position, arguing that international law permits states to use force abroad without a host state's consent if the host state is "unwilling or unable" to eliminate the threat.[78] What makes this debate so challenging is that the two dueling approaches share a common defect: taken at face value, they would both undermine the principle of sovereign equality. By narrowly defining the right of self-defense, the ICJ's approach would make a target state powerless to protect its people when a host state is unwilling or unable to eliminate transboundary attacks. This would exalt the host state's territorial sovereignty at the expense of the target state's right to territorial integrity. But the "unwilling or unable" theory of unilateral self-defense is no better, when considered from a sovereign equality perspective, because it would subordinate the host state's territorial sovereignty to the target state's security demands. Whichever path one chooses, the result is similar: one state is entitled to exercise sovereign rights, while the other is not. Transnational counter-terrorism becomes a zero-sum game that subverts the principle of sovereign equality.

Mandatory cooperation suggests a better way forward. As previous chapters have shown, it is possible to reconcile territorial sovereignty with territorial integrity, but only if states cooperate with each other in accordance with equitable principles. To respect the principle of sovereign equality, host states must refrain from invoking their territorial sovereignty as a basis for refusing to assist with preventing and suppressing terrorism. To shirk this obligation would constitute an abuse of right. Nor may target states invoke their "inherent right to self-defense"[79] as a justification for conducting unauthorized cross-border interventions in violation of host states' territorial sovereignty; this, too, would be an

[77] Legal Consequences of the Construction of a Wall in the Occupied Palestinian Territory, Advisory Opinion, 2004 ICJ Rep. 136, 201, ¶ 147 (9 July); Case Concerning Armed Activities on the Territory of the Congo (Congo v. Uganda), 2005 ICJ Rep. 168, 207 ¶ 139 (19 December).

[78] See, e.g., Daniel Bethlehem, 'Self-Defense Against an Imminent or Actual Armed Attack by Nonstate Actors' (2012) 106 AJIL 770, 776; Ashley Deeks, 'Unwilling or Unable: Toward a Normative Framework for Extraterritorial Self-Defense' (2012) 52 VJIL 483; Theresa Rheingold, 'State Weakness, Irregular Warfare, and the Right to Self-Defense Post 9/11' (2011) 105 AJIL 244, 285; Kimberley N. Trapp, 'Back to Basics: Necessity, Proportionality, and the Right to Self-Defense Against Non-State Actors' (2007) 56 ICLQ 141, 147.

[79] UN Charter art. 51.

abuse of right.[80] Instead, international law obligates states to cooperate in developing equitable, negotiated solutions for confronting transnational terrorism.

When a host state is unable to prevent transboundary attacks on its own, counterterrorism can take a page from the law and practice of counter-piracy. In both settings, there are at least two options for reconciling territorial sovereignty with territorial integrity. First, the host state may enlist international assistance to enhance its capacity for effective law enforcement (as in the Straits of Malacca and Singapore). Second, it may authorize other states to perform selective law enforcement functions within its territory (as at the Horn of Africa). Both options offer practical solutions for combatting terrorism without sacrificing sovereign equality. General principles of mandatory cooperation suggest that the choice between these options should be made through international consultation and negotiation between interested states or, if necessary, by an authoritative international body like the Security Council.

Obstacles to Mandatory Cooperation against Cybercrime

Although mandatory cooperation has made substantial inroads into the law of piracy and terrorism, the same cannot be said for many other transnational crimes.[81] In the digitally networked world of the twenty-first century, failures of international cooperation have become especially problematic with regard to transboundary cyberattacks, such as computer hacking, malware attacks, and distributed denial of service (DDOS) attacks.[82] Malware attacks launched from one country can easily

[80] Although not justified, asymmetric self-defense might still be excused under the international law of necessity in settings where a host state is unwilling and unable to cooperate in a timely and effective manner. In such cases, the target state would bear responsibility to compensate the host state for harm incurred as a result of a target state's counter-terrorist use of force. See Gabriella Blum and John C.P. Goldberg, 'The Unable or Unwilling Doctrine: A View from Private Law' (2022) 63 HILJ 63.

[81] An important exception is mandatory cooperation against transnational organized crime, which has a well-developed Convention to support it: Convention Against Transnational Organized Crime, 15 November 2000, 2225 UNTS 209.

[82] Computer hacking refers to "remote and unauthorized access to computer systems"; a malware attack involves "the dissemination of actual software such as Trojan horses and worms"; and a DDOS attack entails "an attempt to overwhelm the capacities of a server in which a large number of machines ... simultaneously ping the server, occupying the entire bandwidth." Troy Anderson, 'Fitting a Virtual Peg into a Round Hole: Why Existing International Law Fails to Govern Cyber Reprisals' (2017) 34 *Ariz. J. Int'l & Compar. L.* 135, 136.

reverberate around the world, wreaking havoc in many countries. Hackers have deployed transboundary cyberattacks to obtain illicit profit, advance political agendas, or simply for sport.[83] The global harm inflicted by cybercriminals has reached staggering proportions and increases every year. Experts estimate that in 2025 cybercrime cost the world approximately USD 10.5 trillion.[84] Yet, international lawyers have been slow to embrace the idea that states bear obligations under general international law to cooperate with one another for the purpose of combating cybercrime.

Cyber security vaulted to the top of the international community's agenda in April 2007, when a tsunami of debilitating cyberattacks struck Estonia. Reacting to the Estonian government's decision to relocate a controversial World War II monument, the Bronze Soldier, hackers in various countries, including Egypt, Peru, and (principally) Russia, overwhelmed Estonia's cyber-infrastructure with DDOS attacks and other mischief. These attacks paralyzed the office of the Estonian president and key government ministries, as well as banks, newspapers, television stations, and schools.[85] More than two weeks passed, with Estonia teetering on the brink of "a complete digital collapse," before the country's Cyber Emergency Response Team finally managed to turn the tide.[86]

In the years following Estonia's cyber siege, legal experts have gathered periodically in Tallinn to clarify and systematize the international law of cyberattacks. These consultations have produced an influential restatement of the law: the *Tallinn Manual on the International Law Applicable to Cyber Operations*, now in its second edition.[87] The *Tallinn Manual* affirms that "[a] State must exercise due diligence in not allowing its territory, or territory under its governmental control, to be used for cyber operations that affect the rights of, and produce serious adverse consequences for, other States."[88] The International Group of Experts (IGE), who prepared the *Tallinn Manual*, agreed unanimously that the requirement to exercise due diligence in

83 Anderson, 'Fitting a Virtual Peg into a Round Hole', p. 136.

84 Steve Morgan, 'Cybercrime to Cost the World $10.5 Trillion Annually by 2025', Cybercrime Magazine, 13 November 2020.

85 Susanna Bagdasarova, 'Brave New World: Challenges in International Cybersecurity Strategy and the Need for Centralized Governance' (2015) 119 *Penn St. L. Rev.* 1005, 1006–1007; Scott J. Shackelford, 'From Nuclear War to Net War: Analogizing Cyber Attacks in International Law' (2009) 27 BJIL 192, 203.

86 Shackelford, 'From Nuclear War to Net War', p. 203.

87 Michael Schmitt (ed.), *Tallinn Manual on the International Law Applicable to Cyber Operations 2.0* (Cambridge: Cambridge University Press, 2017).

88 Ibid. p. 30 (Rule 6).

combatting transboundary attacks "is a general principle that has been particularized in specialized regimes of international law" and "applies in the cyber context."[89] Hence, states must "take all measures that are feasible in the circumstances to put an end to cyber operations that affect a right of, and produce serious adverse consequences for, other States."[90] However, the IGE declined to follow this due diligence requirement to its logical conclusion by affirming that states must cooperate with one another to ensure that their efforts to suppress cyberattacks are effective. According to the IGE, "customary international law does not generally oblige States to cooperate with other States in domestic criminal law matters ... even if such matters have a transnational character."[91] Absent a treaty-based requirement or other specific legal obligation, "States are not obliged to cooperate in the investigation and prosecution of cyber crime."[92] Given the *Tallinn Manual*'s status as the leading reference on the international law of cyberattacks, many international lawyers would consider mandatory cooperation against cyber crime to be a welcome proposal for the law's future development (*lex ferenda*) but not an accurate description of the law as it exists today (*lex lata*).[93]

Even if customary international law has yet to incorporate mandatory cooperation against cyberattacks, cooperation has become obligatory for states that have joined the Council of Europe's Convention on Cybercrime, better known as the Budapest Convention.[94] With sixty-seven states-parties, including Australia, Israel, Japan, Nigeria, the United States, and dozens of European states, the Budapest Convention reflects a growing recognition among states "that an effective fight against cybercrime requires increased, rapid and well-functioning international co-operation

[89] Ibid. p. 31.

[90] Ibid. p. 43 (Rule 7). Significantly, the IGE stopped short of endorsing a strict duty of continuous network supervision or monitoring. See Antonio Coco & Talita de Souza Dias, '"Cyber Due Diligence": A Patchwork of Protective Operations in International Law' (2021) 32 EJIL 771, 784, 787.

[91] *Tallinn Manual*, p. 75 (Rule 75 cmt.1).

[92] Ibid. at 75 (Rule 75).

[93] See Rebecca Crootof, 'International Cybertorts: Expanding State Accountability in Cyberspace' (2018) 103 *Cornell L. Rev.* 565, 635 (observing that although the IGE's conclusions are "formally nonbinding, many of their pronouncements have been widely accepted as authoritative"). The *Tallinn Manual* recognizes that some cyberattacks, by virtue of their extensive scale and grave effects, may constitute "armed attacks" that activate the right to self-defense under the UN Charter. See *Tallinn Manual*, p. 339 ("Whether a cyber operation constitutes an armed attack depends on its scale and effects."). We discuss mandatory cooperation in response to such threats to international peace and security in Chapter 9.

[94] Convention on Cybercrime, 23 November 2001, ETS No. 185 [hereinafter Budapest Convention].

in criminal matters."[95] To this end, the Convention not only criminalizes cyberattacks and requires states parties to prevent attacks from their territories, but also obligates states parties to "cooperate with each other . . . to the widest extent possible for the purposes of investigations or proceedings concerning criminal offences related to computer systems and data, or for the collection of evidence in electronic form of a criminal offence."[96] States parties to the Budapest Convention also agree to "consult periodically" with each other with a view to facilitating "the effective use and implementation of the Convention" and "the exchange of information on significant legal, policy or technological developments pertaining to cybercrime and the collection of evidence."[97] Disputes over the interpretation or application of the Convention are to be resolved cooperatively through negotiation or third-party dispute resolution.[98]

A notable weakness of the Budapest Convention is its failure to gain the support of chronic offenders like China, North Korea, and Russia. Observers speculate that one reason why these states have not joined the Convention is that they are reluctant to cooperate with the international community in investigating malicious cyber activities conducted by their nationals and other users of their digital infrastructure.[99] Further complicating the deepening East/West cyber rivalry are philosophical differences over the possible goals of international cooperation. Within the past decade, China, Kazakhstan, Kyrgyzstan, Russia, Tajikistan, and Uzbekistan have proposed an alternative to the Budapest Convention: a draft International Code of Conduct for Information Security.[100] Western officials have criticized the Code for focusing exclusively on terrorism and other online content that "might contribute to political instability and regime change" to the exclusion of conventional cybercrimes, such as political and economic cyberespionage, malware attacks, and DDOS attacks.[101] The Code does call for mandatory cooperation, but principally in the service of suppressing domestic political

[95] Ibid. pmbl.
[96] Ibid. art. 23.
[97] Budapest Convention, art. 46(1).
[98] Ibid. art. 45(2).
[99] See Daniel Ortner, 'Cybercrime and Punishment: The Russian Mafia and Russian Responsibility to Exercise Due Diligence to Prevent Trans-Boundary Cybercrime' (2015) *BYU L. Rev.* 177, 178.
[100] Permanent Representatives of China, Kazakhstan, Kyrgyzstan, the Russian Federation, Tajikistan and Uzbekistan to the United Nations, Letter Dated 9 Jan. 2015 to the Secretary-General, UN Doc. A/69/723 [hereinafter International Code].
[101] Kristen E. Eichensehr, 'The Cyber-Law of Nations' (2015) 103 GLJ 317, 356–357 (quoting then-US Director of National Intelligence James Clapper).

dissent.[102] These features have made the proposed Code anathema to liberal democracies. In the near term, therefore, the prospects are not promising for mandatory cooperation to become customary international law for cyberattacks; as long as the world's major powers cannot agree about what kinds of online activities require prevention and suppression, mandatory cooperation will struggle to gain a firm foothold in general international law.

Mandatory Cooperation as Global Governance

A common feature of the transnational crimes discussed in this chapter – piracy, terrorism, and cyberattacks – is that they all depend on states for further specification and enforcement. Unlike international crimes, such as genocide and crimes against humanity, which are defined by treaty and fall within the jurisdiction of international criminal tribunals, states are expected to take the lead in criminalizing, investigating, and prosecuting transnational crimes. Therefore, transnational criminal law might seem to embrace decentralization as an alternative to multilateral governance.[103]

As this chapter has shown, however, the decentralized features of transnational criminal law are paired with a complementary practice: mandatory cooperation. International treaties codify obligations to cooperate in combatting transnational crimes, including by exchanging information, sharing resources and expertise, consulting on matters of common concern, and resolving disputes through negotiation or third-party dispute resolution.[104] These aspects of mandatory cooperation complement the otherwise decentralized structure of transnational criminal law, providing a framework that enables states to address transnational crime collectively while respecting sovereign equality.

[102] International Code, para. 3 (requiring states "to cooperate in combating criminal and terrorist activities which use ICTs including networks, and curbing dissemination of information which incites terrorism, secessionism, extremism or undermines other countries' political, economic and social stability, as well as their spiritual and cultural environment").

[103] This is essentially how Jan Klabbers characterizes the international law of piracy as global governance. See Klabbers, *Piracy in Global Law and Global Governance.*

[104] Other examples of treaties codifying mandatory cooperation against transnational crime include the Optional Protocol to the Convention on the Rights of the Child on the Sale of Children, Child Prostitution and Child Pornography art. 10, GA Res. 54/263, UN Doc. A/RES/54/263 (25 May 2000) (requiring states-parties to cooperate to prevent, detect, investigate, prosecute, and punish perpetrators of transnational sex crimes against children); and the United Nations Convention Against Illicit Traffic in Narcotic Drugs and Psychotropic Substances arts. 7, 9–10, 17, 19, 20 December 1988, 28 ILM 493 (entered into force 1 November 1990) (requiring states-parties to provide mutual legal assistance and provide other cooperation to combat drug trafficking).

6

Pollution

Ashes of Death

When the Japanese fishing craft *Lucky Dragon* (*Fukuryu Maru*) reached Tokyo Bay on March 14, 1954, the entire crew and 4,000 pounds of tuna onboard were dangerously radioactive. Two weeks earlier, the United States had conducted the first detonation of a hydrogen bomb at Bikini Atoll in the Marshall Islands, deep in the South Pacific.[1] The US Atomic Energy Commission (AEC) had previously announced plans to use the islands as a testing ground for nuclear weapons, and it had advised foreign governments to keep ships outside a 50,000-square-mile "danger area" for their safety. This designated danger area proved to be woefully inadequate. The magnitude of the hydrogen bomb's thermonuclear explosion more than doubled scientific projections, and due to an unforeseen shift in atmospheric conditions, the resulting radiation cloud traveled outside the official danger area to drop a "ghostly white rain, thick with ash" on the *Lucky Dragon*.[2] When the rain subsided, crew members experienced dizziness, vomiting, and fever – the first visible symptoms of severe radiation exposure. By the time the *Lucky Dragon* returned to Japan, most of the crew suffered from headaches, skin burns, bleeding gums, and other afflictions.[3] Six months later, crew member Aikitchi Kuboyama died, and twenty-two others continued to receive hospital treatment for serious injuries.[4] Reflecting on Kuboyama's

[1] At the time of the nuclear test, the Marshall Islands were a UN trusteeship under the United States' administrative authority.

[2] David Ropeik, 'How the Unlucky Lucky Dragon Birthed an Era of Nuclear Fear', Bull. of the Atomic Scientists, 28 February 2018.

[3] Ibid.

[4] Emmanuel Margolis, 'The Hydrogen Bomb Experiments and International Law' (1955) 64 YLJ 629, 637–638; Myers S. McDougal and Norbert A. Schlei, 'The Hydrogen Bomb Tests in Perspective: Lawful Measures for Security' (1955) 64 YLJ 648, 651–652. Many Americans and Marshallese on islands outside the designated danger zone also reported

untimely passing, a Japanese newspaper inquired, "Has the death of a citizen ever been watched by so many eyes? They are the eyes of a strong anger and protest against the 'ashes of death.'"[5]

The botched nuclear test at Bikini Atoll was among the first in a series of highly publicized environmental disasters that fixed the world's attention on the growing threat of transboundary pollution. In 1967, the *Torrey Canyon*, an American-owned and chartered tanker manned by an Italian crew, attracted international infamy when it ran aground on the Seven Stones reef in international waters. Approximately 80,000 tons of crude oil spilled into the Atlantic, befouling resort beaches and decimating sea bird populations along the coast of Cornwall, England.[6] A decade later, another oil spill eclipsed the *Torrey Canyon* incident when the *Amico Cadiz*, an American-owned supertanker, collided with a submerged reef and broke in half, dropping nearly all of its 230,000-ton load of crude oil to contaminate the French coastline for hundreds of miles. The year 1986 brought two environmental calamities in quick succession: the Chernobyl nuclear meltdown near Kyiv, Ukraine, which scattered its own "ashes of death" and eventually radiation throughout Europe, and the Sandoz chemical plant fire in Switzerland that sent thousands of liters of highly toxic pesticides down the Rhine to poison wildlife and drinking water in Germany, France, and the Netherlands. In each of these incidents, pollution from one state traversed international borders to inflict grave harm.

Like international disputes over the apportionment of watercourses and fisheries, transboundary pollution presents a classic clash of sovereign entitlements. On the one hand, international law gives states sovereign authority over activities within their territorial jurisdiction – including activities that produce pollution. But on the other hand, international law also entitles states to territorial integrity.[7] This means states are entitled to demand the cessation of transboundary pollution that causes significant harm within their borders.[8]

radiation-related injuries from the test. Margolis, 'The Hydrogen Bomb Experiments', p. 637.

5 Ropeik, 'How the Unlucky Lucky Dragon Birthed an Era of Nuclear Fear'.

6 Ved P. Nanda, 'The Torrey Canyon Disaster: Some Legal Aspects' (1967) 44 *Denver L. Rev.* 400, 400–401.

7 UN Charter art. 2(4).

8 Tamar Meshel, 'Swimming Against the Current: Revisiting the Principles of International Water Law in the Resolution of Fresh Water Disputes' (2020) 61 HILJ 135, 140 ("The no

The unilateralist theory of sovereignty would resolve this tension, for all intents and purposes, in favor of the state where transboundary pollution originates. Recall that under the unilateralist theory, states may decide how to exercise their sovereign powers without regard to foreign interests. Accordingly, the unilateralist theory would empower states to engage in practices, such as atmospheric nuclear testing, that generate harmful transboundary pollution. The unilateralist theory would threaten to render illusory the sovereign right to territorial integrity because the enjoyment of the right would depend on the mercy or grace of other states. The "no significant harm" principle from international environmental law would be subordinated to the originating state's discretion. In an international legal order based on unilateral sovereignty, strong states would be free to do as they please within their borders, while weak states would "suffer what they must."[9]

International environmental law rejects this vision of sovereign unilateralism, embracing an equitable approach that respects and reconciles states' sovereign interests. Although states have exclusive authority to regulate pollution within their borders, international law requires them to exercise this authority in a manner congenial to other states' territorial integrity. The primary mechanism for achieving this reconciliation is the requirement that states must exercise due diligence to prevent activities in their territory from producing significant transboundary harm.

This chapter shows how due diligence leads to mandatory cooperation. To satisfy the due diligence standard, states must take into account foreign interests when they regulate activities that may produce transboundary harm. Due diligence also imposes procedural obligations to conduct environmental impact assessments, provide notice to states that may be impacted by transboundary pollution, engage in meaningful consultation and negotiation, and resolve disputes through mediation, arbitration, adjudication, or other third-party dispute resolution. The requirements of mandatory cooperation thus apply to transboundary pollution under international law.

significant harm principle prohibits states from using their territory in such a way as to cause significant harm to another state.").

9 Thucydides, *History of the Peloponnesian War* (London, J. M. Dent; New York, E. P. Dutton, 1910) bk. 5, ch. 89 (431–404 BC) (claiming that right exists only among equals, "while the strong do what they can and the weak suffer what they must").

Good Neighbors

Less than ten miles north of the Canada-US border lies Trail, a modest mining town in British Columbia. For over a century, Trail has hosted the world's largest zinc and lead smelter, a sprawling complex adjacent to the Columbia River. Celebrated as "the jewel of the British Columbian mining industry," the Trail smelter has served as a "locus of regional growth, a pillar of provincial development, and an instrument of Canadian economic policy."[10] For environmentalists and international lawyers, Trail has also become synonymous with industrial pollution. In the late 1920s, the Trail smelter provoked international controversy when it became apparent that the sulfur dioxide fumes emitted in prodigious quantities from its 409-foot smokestack were devastating timber lots, orchards, gardens, pastures, and farmland in neighboring Washington State.[11] Aggrieved American homesteaders demanded that the smelter cut back its emissions to protect them from further harm. When private negotiations between the smelter and the homesteaders stalled, attention shifted toward international diplomacy. Canada and the United States eventually concluded a bilateral treaty, which provided for the smelter to compensate private claimants for harm incurred before 1932 while referring questions about subsequent injuries to arbitration.

The arbitral tribunal delivered its final decision in 1941. Citing national court decisions that held sovereigns responsible for private transboundary pollution, the tribunal reasoned that "under the principles of international law . . . no State has the right to use or permit the use of its territory in such a manner as to cause injury by fumes in or to the territory of another or the properties or persons therein, when the case is of serious consequence and the injury is established by clear and convincing evidence."[12] This affirmation of the prohibition against transboundary pollution has become a canonical cornerstone of international environmental law.[13]

[10] James R. Allum, '"An Outcrop of Hell": History, Environment, and the Politics of the Trail Smelter Dispute', in Rebecca M. Bratspies and Russell A. Miller (eds.), *Transboundary Harm in International Law: Lessons from the Trail Smelter Arbitration* (Cambridge: Cambridge University Press, 2006), pp. 13, 18.

[11] Trail Smelter Case (US v. Can.), 3 RIAA 1905, 1917 (Trail Smelter Arb. Trib. 1941); Allum, 'An Outcrop of Hell', pp. 14–15.

[12] Trail Smelter, p. 1965.

[13] Daniel Bodansky, Jutta Brunnée and Ellen Hey, 'International Environmental Law: Mapping the Field', in Daniel Bodansky et al. (eds.), *The Oxford Handbook of International Environmental Law* (Oxford: Oxford University Press, 2007), pp. 1, 9.

Trail Smelter envisions an international legal order in which states must interact as good neighbors, consistent with principles of equity and sovereign equality.[14] As Günther Handl has explained,

> the notion of "neighborliness" simply implies that the exercise of sovereign territorial rights, as indeed of any rights, cannot be separated from the social context in which the rights are being asserted and that it is only in the concrete circumstances of a specific situation that rights may find their exact delimitation. From this it follows logically that where, in the context of an international society based on the sovereign equality of states, the exercise of a sovereign right ... conflict[s] with similar rights of an equal rank, insistence on individual rights must be considered unreasonable and reprehensible [as an abuse of right].[15]

Being a good neighbor, in this sense, means states must live with some inconveniences that are inevitable features of communal life. It would be unreasonable, for example, to expect states to exercise such complete control over their territory as to eliminate all risk of transboundary harm. But being a good neighbor also means that states may not simply play territorial sovereignty as a trump card to avoid taking responsibility for serious transboundary harm. They must exercise due diligence, using the resources at their disposal – including legal regulation – to ensure that dangerous activities do not inflict significant injury abroad. When transboundary harm does occur, they must take steps to curtail further injury and provide compensation.[16] These obligations are necessary to respect the principle of sovereign equality under international law.

Elementary Considerations of Humanity

Canada and the United States used the *Trail Smelter* arbitration to bolster their shared commitment to good neighborly relations. However, the legal principles articulated in *Trail Smelter* would soon receive broader application when the ICJ extended these principles to a dispute between embittered geopolitical adversaries on the other side of the Atlantic.[17]

On October 22, 1946, two British destroyers struck submerged mines in the Corfu Channel off the coast of Albania. The ensuing blast caused

[14] Linda J. Pike, 'Neighbor States', in *Max Planck Encyclopedia of Public International Law vol. 10* (Amsterdam: Elsevier North Holland, 1988), pp. 311, 311–312.

[15] Günther Handl, 'Territorial Sovereignty and the Problem of Transnational Pollution' (1975) 69 AJIL 50, 56.

[16] Trail Smelter, pp. 1965–1966.

[17] Corfu Channel Case (UK v. Alb.), 1949 ICJ Rep. 4 (9 April).

major damage to the destroyers and claimed the lives of over three dozen crew members. The incident marked the culmination of a series of tense standoffs between Albania and the United Kingdom, which had squared off on opposite sides of the nascent Cold War. Earlier the same year, an Albanian battery had fired in the direction of two British cruisers passing through the channel without connecting. The British made a formal diplomatic protest and, in further defiance, sent four warships steaming through the channel. When two of these ships – the *Saumarez* and the *Volage* – struck mines, suffering casualties and major damage, the United Kingdom initiated proceedings against Albania in the ICJ.[18]

A central question in the *Corfu Channel Case* was whether Albania could be held responsible for the mine blasts. The United Kingdom did not offer any direct evidence to establish that Albania had planted the mines in the channel.[19] Nonetheless, the Court concluded that Albania must pay compensation for the United Kingdom's injuries due to a combination of factors. First, by all accounts, the minefield had been laid in Albanian territorial waters not long before the deadly explosions. Second, during the relevant period, Albania exercised exclusive jurisdiction and continuous oversight over the waters, such that the mines could not have been placed without its knowledge.[20] Third, Albania did not warn the United Kingdom about the minefield.[21] Under these circumstances, the Court concluded, Albania had a duty to warn the United Kingdom of the impending danger. Albania's duty to provide notice rested "on certain general and well-recognized principles, namely: elementary considerations of humanity, even more exacting in peace than in war; the principle of the freedom of maritime communication; and every State's obligation not to allow knowingly its territory to be used for acts contrary to the right of other States."[22] Having failed to notify the United Kingdom that its navy risked serious harm by traversing the Corfu Channel, Albania assumed legal responsibility for injuries suffered by the *Saumarez*, the *Volage*, and their crews.

By holding that Albania was obligated to provide notice of threats emanating from its territory, the ICJ took a substantial step toward mandatory cooperation. The *Corfu Channel* judgment gave states like Albania a choice: either eliminate serious dangers themselves

18 The ICJ upheld the United Kingdom's right to innocent passage. See ibid. pp. 29–32.
19 Ibid. p. 17.
20 Ibid. pp. 18–19.
21 Ibid. pp. 19–20.
22 Ibid. p. 22.

(e.g., by removing submerged mines) or cooperate with other states (e.g., by consenting to foreign minesweeping). In either scenario, states could not act without regard to foreign interests. They must take actions reasonably calculated to prevent serious harm to other states, including by affirmatively warning other states of dangers. As the ICJ recognized in *Corfu Channel*, these minimal requirements to suppress serious threats and provide notice to other states are necessary to respect "elementary considerations of humanity" and honor other states' equal rights.

Cooperating for Environmental Conservation

States cannot satisfy their due diligence obligations in many contexts without robust cooperation. Consider again the *Trail Smelter* dispute. In theory, Canada could have shut down the Trail smelter, but this would have delivered a crushing blow to the British Columbian mining industry. Economic and political considerations dictated that Canadian regulators should pursue an intermediate solution, setting emissions standards at levels that would maximize the smelter's capacity for zinc and lead production without inflicting serious harm across the border in violation of international law. But how much would the smelter have to reduce its emissions to achieve this objective? To answer this question, Canadian regulators would have to conduct a rigorous environmental impact assessment, taking into account wind patterns, terrain, flora, fauna, human settlement, and other factors on the American side of the border. Collecting this information would require the United States' cooperation. Canada could not realistically satisfy its obligation to regulate harmful transboundary pollution from the smelter without consulting and exchanging information with the United States.

Due diligence also constrained how Canada could handle US objections to its governance of the Trail smelter. As noted above, Canada accepted responsibility for the smelter's adverse environmental impacts in the 1920s and early 1930s. Nonetheless, Canada continued to resist the United States' requests to make even more aggressive cuts to the smelter's pollution. The dispute between the two states centered partly on scientific uncertainty about the smelter's environmental impact under various atmospheric conditions. However, Canada and the United States also disagreed about what level of harm would be serious enough to trigger the duty to prevent significant harm. Given the indeterminacy of "significant harm" and the triggering conditions of the duty, due diligence required Canada to strive in good faith to pursue further consultation, negotiation, or third-party dispute resolution, such as an independent fact-finding commission, mediation, arbitration, or adjudication. By cooperating with the United States to resolve their factual and legal disagreements in the Court of Arbitration, Canada satisfied the due diligence standard.

The Trail smelter controversy thus illustrates how, in practice, the duty to prevent transboundary harm may generate cooperation that satisfies the due diligence requirements of the prevailing regime of mandatory cooperation. To satisfy the due diligence standard, states must make a reasonable, good-faith effort to investigate risks of significant transboundary harm. They must notify, exchange information, and consult, negotiate, and accept third-party dispute resolution with other states. Only by taking these kinds of steps can they demonstrate due regard for other states' equal sovereignty and avoid an impermissible abuse of right.

Codifying Mandatory Cooperation

Within the past half-century, mandatory cooperation has become deeply embedded in international environmental law. In June 2022, the international community celebrated the fiftieth anniversary of the first global summit on environmental conservation: the UN Conference on the Human Environment, held in Stockholm, Sweden, June 5–16, 1972. A crowning achievement of the Stockholm Conference was its landmark declaration enshrining "common principles to inspire and guide the peoples of the world in the preservation and enhancement of the human environment."[23] The Stockholm Declaration recognizes the need for "extensive cooperation among nations and action by international organizations in the common interest."[24] Although the Stockholm Declaration does not spell out precisely which forms of international cooperation are essential, it does affirm that states have a "responsibility to ensure that activities within their jurisdiction or control do not cause damage to the environment of other States or of areas beyond the limits of national jurisdiction."[25]

After the Stockholm Conference, the international community elaborated duties of cooperation for environmental conservation in a series of treaties, declarations, and other instruments. That same year, the UN

[23] Declaration of the United Nations Conference on the Human Environment, Stockholm, 16 June 1972, 11 ILM 1416, pmbl. [hereinafter Stockholm Declaration].
[24] Ibid. pmbl. para. 7.
[25] Ibid. Principle 21.

General Assembly recognized that international cooperation for the environment, as contemplated in the Stockholm Declaration, demanded that states exchange technical data related to transboundary pollution "in the best spirit of co-operation and good-neighborliness."[26] In 1979, the UN Economic Commission for Europe's (UNECE) Long Range Transboundary Air Pollution Agreement (LRTAP) committed member-states to combat air pollution by exchanging information, consulting, and pursuing collaborative research to identify and eliminate significant threats.[27] Under LRTAP's cooperative framework, member states have subsequently established additional protocols to combat some of the most deadly atmospheric pollutants, including sulfur, nitrogen, and volatile organic compounds.[28] UNECE's 1992 Convention on Transboundary Effects of Industrial Accidents also obligates states to identify risks of transboundary harm from industrial accidents, share relevant information, and consult with one another to develop effective prevention and mitigation strategies.[29] When accidents occur, states-parties must notify other interested states, assess transboundary harm, and solicit assistance to address the harm.[30]

Mandatory cooperation also features prominently in treaties addressing oceanic pollution, including the 1982 UN Convention on the Law of the Sea (UNCLOS).[31] In addition to requiring states-parties to prohibit and penalize pollution of the marine environment, UNCLOS demands that they cooperate to prevent significant oceanic pollution and eliminate or reduce its adverse effects on the marine environment.[32] When

[26] Cooperation Between States in the Field of the Environment, 15 December 1972, UNGA Res. 2995 (XXVII), A/RES/2995, paras. 2–3.

[27] Long-Range Transboundary Air Pollution Agreement, Geneva, 13 November 1979, 18 ILM 1442, arts. 3–5, 7–9, 13 [hereinafter LRTAP]. The UNECE's membership draws from Eastern and Western Europe, Canada, and the United States.

[28] See, e.g., 1985 Helsinki Protocol on the Reduction of Sulphur Emissions or Their Transboundary Fluxes by at Least 30 Per Cent, Helsinki, 8 July 1985, 27 ILM at 698 (sulfur); 1991 Geneva Protocol concerning the Control of Emissions of Volatile Organic Compounds or their Transboundary Fluxes, Geneva, 18 November 1991, 31 ILM at 569 (VOCs).

[29] Convention on the Transboundary Effects of Industrial Accidents, Helsinki, 17 March 1992, UN/E/ECE/1268, arts. 3–4.

[30] Ibid. arts. 10–12; see also UN Environment Programme, Basel Convention the Control of Transboundary Movements of Hazardous Wastes and Their Disposal, Basel, 22 March 1989, 1673 UNTS 126, arts. 6, 10, 13 [hereinafter Basel Convention] (requiring states to provide timely notice, exchange information, and consult with other states before shipping hazardous wastes into foreign territory).

[31] UN Convention on the Law of the Sea, 10 December 1982, 1833 UNTS 3.

[32] Ibid. arts. 199, 207–211.

states-parties become aware of imminent dangers to the marine environment, they must immediately notify other states that are likely to be impacted.[33] In addition, states-parties are obligated to cooperate in "promoting studies, undertaking programmes of scientific research and encouraging the exchange of information and data acquired about pollution of the marine environment" to assess better "the nature and extent of pollution, exposure to it, and its pathways, risks and remedies."[34] They must conduct environmental impact assessments for pollution of the marine environment,[35] and they must cooperate to formulate and elaborate international rules, standards, and best practices for protecting the marine environment.[36] Similar cooperative obligations appear in other treaties that address marine pollution.[37] Based on these developments in treaty law and consistent state practice, the International Tribunal for the Law of the Sea (ITLOS) has characterized mandatory cooperation as "a fundamental principle in the prevention of pollution of the marine environment under . . . general international law."[38]

Another important codification of mandatory cooperation is the Convention on Environmental Impact Assessment in a Transboundary Context, the product of a UN-sponsored conference in Espoo, Finland (Espoo Convention).[39] The Espoo Convention requires states-parties to provide notice of activities that are likely to cause a significant adverse transboundary impact.[40] They must also conduct environmental impact assessments for such activities, consult with other interested states regarding preventing or mitigating transboundary harms, and provide mutual assistance in eliminating or reducing such harms.[41] When states-parties decide whether to proceed with an activity that may have transboundary impacts, they must take "due account" of the likely effect on

[33] Ibid. art. 198.
[34] Ibid. art. 200.
[35] Ibid. arts. 204–206.
[36] Ibid. art. 197.
[37] Convention on the Prevention of Marine Pollution by Dumping of Wastes and Other Matter, 29 December 1972, 1340 UNTS 61, art. 12 [MARPOL Convention]; Convention for the Protection of the Mediterranean Sea Against Pollution, 16 February 1976, 1102 UNTS 27, arts. 9–11.
[38] MOX Plant Case (Ireland v. UK), Provisional Measures, ITLOS Case No. 10, 3 December 2001, 41 ILM 405, 416, para. 89 (2002).
[39] Convention on Environmental Impact Assessment in a Transboundary Context, 25 February 1991, 1989 UNTS 310 (1997). As of January 2024, the Espoo Convention's membership currently included the European Union and 44 other states-parties.
[40] Ibid. art. 3.
[41] Ibid. arts. 4–5.

other states.[42] Final decisions must be communicated to other states in writing, explaining the reasons and considerations on which decisions are based.[43] If other states object, states-parties must pursue further consultations to consider alternative courses of action.[44] The Espoo Convention thus offers a detailed roadmap for international cooperation concerning transboundary pollution.[45]

In 2008, the UN International Law Commission (ILC) incorporated central features of this burgeoning treaty practice into its Draft Articles on the Prevention of Transboundary Harm from Hazardous Activities (Draft Articles).[46] Consistent with *Trail Smelter* and *Corfu Channel*, the Draft Articles provide that states must "take all appropriate measures to prevent significant transboundary harm or at any event to minimize the risk thereof," and they characterize this obligation as "one of due diligence."[47] In addition, the Draft Articles demand that states cooperate by providing notice of possible transboundary harm, transmitting relevant technical information about risks, and consulting with one another to "seek solutions based on an equitable balance of interests."[48] If consultations do not lead to an agreed solution, the state of origin may decide how to proceed, but it must account for the interests of other states.[49] As the ILC has recognized, this approach to transboundary harm draws inspiration from the *Lake Lanoux Case* discussed in Chapter 2. Like *Lake Lanoux*, the Draft Articles respect territorial jurisdiction by denying potentially affected states veto power over activities outside their territory. But the Draft Articles also guard against the abuse of territorial sovereignty by requiring states to exercise due diligence to stop activities

[42] Ibid. art. 6(1).

[43] Ibid. art. 6(2).

[44] Ibid. art. 6(3).

[45] A year after completion of the Espoo Convention, the UN Conference on Environment and Development endorsed these requirements in the 1992 Rio Declaration. Report of the United Nations Conference on Environment and Development, 12 August 1992, A/CONF.151/26/Rev.1 (vol. 1), Principles 18–19.

[46] Draft Articles on the Prevention of Transboundary Harm from Hazardous Activities, with Commentaries, Rep. of the Int'l Law Comm'n on the Work of its Fifty-Third Session, UN Doc. A/56/10, pp. 370–377 (2001).

[47] Ibid. art. 3 & cmt. 7.

[48] Ibid. arts. 4, 8–10, 12. In commentary accompanying the Articles, the ILC explains that this cooperation is necessary, in part, because states likely to be affected by transboundary harm "may know better than anybody else . . . which features of the activity may be damaging to it, or which zones of its territory close to the border may be affected by the transboundary activity, such as a specially vulnerable ecosystem." Ibid. art. 4, cmt. 1.

[49] Ibid. art. 9(3).

within their jurisdiction from generating significant transboundary harm.[50] When disputes arise concerning these requirements, the Draft Articles contemplate that states may convene an impartial fact-finding commission or they may settle their disputes through other "peaceful means . . . chosen by mutual agreement," such as negotiation, mediation, conciliation, arbitration, or adjudication.[51]

Cooperating through Courts and Tribunals

In recent years, international courts and tribunals have applied mandatory cooperation to transboundary pollution in a variety of settings. The most important and influential case is the ICJ's 2010 judgment in a dispute concerning Uruguay's construction of pulp mills on the River Uruguay.[52] Decades earlier, Argentina and Uruguay had concluded a bilateral treaty establishing detailed rules to govern the river's use and environmental conservation, and they had established the Administrative Commission of the River Uruguay (CARU) to facilitate conciliation and judicial settlement of disputes.[53] They also agreed to prepare environmental impact assessments for projects that might impact the river's water and work through CARU to notify the other party, exchange relevant information, and consult and negotiate over any unresolved concerns.[54] Uruguay took significant steps to comply with these requirements before proceeding with plans to build two pulp mills: it prepared preliminary environmental impact assessments, delivered these assessments to CARU for review, and engaged in consultations with Argentina. Uruguay began constructing the mills, however, before Argentina had a reasonable opportunity to study the possible environmental impacts and before differences between the two states had been resolved.

Fearing significant pollution to the Uruguay River, Argentina initiated proceedings in the ICJ. Argentina asked the ICJ for a judgment that Uruguay had violated the 1975 Statute by proceeding with construction of the two pulp mills without sufficient bilateral cooperation to ensure the river's environmental conservation. The Court agreed

50 Ibid. art. 9, cmt. 10.
51 Ibid. art. 19.
52 Case Concerning Pulp Mills on the River Uruguay, 2010 ICJ Rep. 14 (20 April).
53 Ibid. p. 32, paras. 26–27 (discussing art. 7 of the treaty concluded between Argentina and Uruguay, Montevideo, 7 April 1961, 635 UNTS 9074, p. 98, and the Statute of the River Uruguay, 26 February 1975, 1295 UNTS No. I-21425, p. 340).
54 Ibid. pp. 49–51, para. 80.

> that the procedural obligations of informing, notifying and negotiating constitute an appropriate means, accepted by the Parties, of [ensuring environmental conservation under the 1975 Statute]. These obligations are all the more vital when a shared resource is at issue, as in the case of the River Uruguay, which can only be protected through close and continuous co-operation between the riparian States.[55]

Citing *Corfu Channel*, the Court linked these procedural duties to "the principle of prevention," which, "as a customary rule, has its origins in the due diligence that is required of a State in its territory."[56] Uruguay's failure to provide timely notice before authorizing construction was significant, in the Court's opinion, because "the obligation to notify is intended to create the conditions for successful co-operation between the parties, enabling them to assess the plan's impact on the river on the basis of the fullest possible information and, if necessary, to negotiate the adjustments needed to avoid the potential damage that it might cause."[57] Until this consultation and negotiation had concluded, Uruguay was obligated to withhold its authorization for construction; otherwise, "the negotiations between the parties would no longer have any purpose."[58] Ultimately, however, because Argentina had not presented any conclusive evidence showing that Uruguay's pulp mills threatened substantial harm to Argentina, the Court declined Argentina's request to grant compensatory damages and order the closing of the pulp mills.[59] Instead, the Court concluded its judgment by simply affirming that Uruguay had violated its obligations of mandatory cooperation and reminding the parties of their continuing "duty to co-operate with each other" to prevent future pollution.[60] Thus, *Pulp Mills* cleared the way for Uruguay to continue constructing and operating the disputed pulp mills while encouraging continued cooperation with Argentina through CARU.[61]

[55] Ibid. p. 51, para. 81.

[56] Ibid. p. 55, para. 101; see also ibid. p. 83, para. 204 (observing that "due diligence, and the duty of vigilance and prevention which it implies, would not be considered to have been exercised, if a party planning works liable to affect the régime of the river or the quality of its waters did not undertake an environmental impact assessment on the potential effects of such works").

[57] Ibid. p. 58, para. 113.

[58] Ibid. p. 68, paras. 144–149.

[59] Ibid. pp. 102–105, paras. 267–280.

[60] Ibid. pp. 105–106, para. 281.

[61] Alan Boyle and Catherine Redgwell, *Birne, Boyle & Redgwell's International Law and the Environment*, 4th ed. (Oxford: Oxford University Press, 2021), p. 206.

Although *Pulp Mills* involved legal duties enshrined in a bilateral treaty, international courts and tribunals have recognized that the obligation to cooperate in addressing transboundary pollution applies to the entire international community as a general requirement of customary international law. For example, in the *Case Concerning Land Reclamation by Singapore in and Around the Straits of Johor* (*Land Reclamation*),[62] an ITLOS tribunal characterized the duty to cooperate in preventing transboundary environmental harm as a "fundamental principle" not only under UNCLOS but also under "general international law."[63] At issue in the case was Malaysia's challenge to Singapore's efforts to expand its territory by reclaiming land from the Straits of Johor.[64] Malaysia argued that the project would degrade the marine environment in the straits by adversely impacting the usual patterns of coastal erosion, sedimentation, and water flow through the straits. Malaysia also challenged Singapore's failure to provide notice, exchange information, and consult and negotiate with Malaysian authorities as required under UNCLOS. While the proceedings were pending, the parties managed to resolve their differences by agreeing to jointly sponsor an environmental impact assessment by an independent body.[65] Singapore also agreed to share relevant information, consult with Malaysian authorities, consider their views, and negotiate toward a mutually acceptable resolution.[66] Accordingly, by the time the tribunal was ready to rule on Malaysia's claims, the parties had already reached a mutually acceptable path forward consistent with their duties of mandatory cooperation under customary international law. All that remained was for the ITLOS tribunal to incorporate the parties' agreement into its October 2003 order granting provisional measures.[67]

In other proceedings, the ICJ has agreed that under customary international law, the requirements of mandatory cooperation apply to all

[62] Case Concerning Land Reclamation by Singapore in and Around the Straits of Johor (Malaysia v. Singapore) (Provisional Measures), 8 October 2003, ITLOS_F3-F4_6-64, p. 10, paras. 76–78, 92.

[63] Ibid. p. 25, para. 92 (quoting MOX Plant Case, para. 82).

[64] Ibid. p. 10, paras. 76–78, 92.

[65] Ibid. p. 25, para. 86.

[66] Ibid. p. 23, paras. 76–78; ibid. p. 24, para. 85. Malaysia indicated that it was prepared to accept these assurances if the tribunal incorporated them into the formal record. Ibid. p. 23, para. 79.

[67] Ibid. pp. 27–28, para. 106(1). In the meantime, the tribunal unanimously directed "Singapore not to conduct its land reclamation in ways that might cause irreparable prejudice to the rights of Malaysia or serious harm to the marine environment, taking especially into account the reports of the group of independent experts." Ibid. p. 28, para. 106(2).

states in disputes concerning significant transboundary harm. In *Certain Activities Carried Out by Nicaragua in the Border Area (San Juan River)*, Costa Rica and Nicaragua each claimed that the other had violated international law by failing to conduct an environmental impact assessment for works undertaken along the San Juan River.[68] Costa Rica faulted Nicaragua for not undertaking a sufficiently robust environmental impact assessment before commencing a dredging project in the San Juan that might cause harm to the Colorado River and vulnerable wetlands within Costa Rica's borders.[69] Nicaragua counterclaimed that Costa Rica had failed to conduct an environmental impact assessment for a road it had constructed alongside the river.[70] Quoting *Pulp Mills*, the Court agreed with the parties that the obligation to undertake an environmental impact assessment for activities that risk transboundary harm "may now be considered a requirement under general international law" that applies even without a binding treaty.[71] Nicaragua satisfied this obligation by undertaking a preliminary assessment before beginning its dredging project, the Court concluded,[72] but Costa Rica violated international law by failing to undertake an environmental impact assessment before building the road.[73]

In sum, *Pulp Mills*, *Land Reclamation*, and *San Juan River* illustrate how mandatory cooperation can facilitate peaceful dispute resolution in accordance with equitable principles. When states conduct environmental impact assessments, notify one another of ecological risks, and share other relevant information, they can better understand the harmful impacts of transboundary pollution and develop more effective prevention and mitigation strategies. Through negotiation and third-party dispute resolution, they can reach solutions that equitably accommodate their respective rights and interests.

[68] Certain Activities Carried Out by Nicaragua in the Border Area (Costa Rica v. Nicaragua), 2015 ICJ Rep. 665, 705, 719, paras. 101–102 (16 December).

[69] Ibid. p. 705, para. 102.

[70] Ibid. p. 719, para. 146.

[71] Ibid. p. 706, para. 104 (quoting Judgment, ICJ Rep. 2010 (I), p. 83, para. 204).

[72] Ibid. p. 707, para. 105.

[73] Ibid. p. 721, para. 156; p. 723, para. 162. The Court concluded that because no environmental impact assessment had been undertaken, it was not necessary to address whether Costa Rica had also violated general international law by failing to notify or consult with Nicaragua about the road project. Ibid. p. 724, para. 168.

Catalyzing Environmental Cooperation

At the opening session of the 1972 Stockholm Conference, Secretary-General Maurice Strong declared that the Conference's aim was "to reconcile man's legitimate, immediate ambitions with the rights of others, with respect for all life supporting systems, and with the rights of generations yet unborn."[74] Strong explained that the Stockholm Declaration "holds that all nations must accept responsibility for the consequences of their own actions on environments outside their borders," and he asserted that "it is essential that this fundamental principle be accepted here if we are to establish a minimum basis for effective international cooperation following this conference."[75] As Strong correctly perceived, and as this chapter has shown, there is a vital link between state responsibility to prevent transboundary pollution, on the one hand, and international cooperation for environmental protection, on the other. States cannot satisfy their due diligence obligations with respect to transboundary pollution unless they also embrace international cooperation. Put another way, cooperation is necessary for international law to govern transboundary pollution. Once states recognized in Stockholm that they must prevent transboundary pollution, it followed that they would also have to share information, consult, negotiate, and accept third-party dispute resolution to ensure their efforts were effective. Cooperation thus became mandatory under international environmental law.[76]

These developments have transformed global governance. As this chapter has shown, states have enshrined the requirements of mandatory cooperation in international environmental treaties; the ILC has endorsed mandatory cooperation in its *Draft Articles on Transboundary Harm*; and international courts and tribunals have applied the requirements of mandatory cooperation as customary international law. There is no longer any serious doubt that international law obligates states to cooperate with one another to ensure that activities within their jurisdiction do not introduce

[74] Maurice F. Strong, 'Opening Statement, Stockholm Conference on the Human Environment 1972', in Alon Tal (ed.), *Speaking of Earth: Environmental Speeches that Moved the World* (New Brunswick: Rutgers University Press, 2006), p. 48.

[75] Ibid. p. 50.

[76] See Günther Handl, 'Transboundary Impacts', in Daniel Bodansky et al. (eds.), *The Oxford Handbook of International Environmental Law* (Oxford: Oxford University Press, 2007), pp. 531, 542 ("[I]t would seem undeniable that all three transboundary impact-related procedural obligations of assessment, notification, and consultation are part of present-day customary international law.").

harmful pollution abroad. But the ramifications of mandatory cooperation for environmental protection run deeper still. Mandatory cooperation has accelerated the progressive development of international environmental law by pressing states to share information, consult, and negotiate with one another. Since Stockholm, states have concluded a host of agreements to combat transboundary pollution, including air pollution,[77] water pollution,[78] hazardous wastes,[79] and nuclear safety.[80] The rapid proliferation of environmental treaties and institutions following the Stockholm Conference reflects the new reality that states are expected to work together as committed partners to address transboundary pollution. Mandatory cooperation has become both a cornerstone of international environmental law and a powerful catalyst for the law's progressive development.

Much of the development of international environmental law consists of "soft law" instruments rather than legally binding treaties.[81] Nonbinding declarations, such as the Stockholm Declaration, the 1992 Rio Declaration on Environment and Development,[82] and the 2002 Johannesburg Declaration on Sustainable Development,[83] articulate broad principles and suggest best practices for responsible environmental stewardship. Critics sometimes dismiss such nonbinding declarations as phantom laws that compromise international law's integrity as a normative system.[84] However, reliance on soft commitments need not be viewed as a "pathological phenomenon" that enfeebles international legal order.[85] In the environmental arena, soft law instruments usually reflect serious efforts to bolster states' political commitments and practical capacities to prevent transboundary environmental harm. When these efforts are successful, they can reduce the need for binding treaties.

77 E.g., Canada–US: Agreement on Air Quality, 13 March 1991, 30 ILM 676; ASEAN Agreement on Transboundary Haze Pollution, 10 June 2002; LRTAP.

78 E.g., Agreement on Great Lakes Water Quality, 22 November 1978, 30 UST 1383, TIAS No. 9257; Convention on the Law of the Non-navigational Uses of International Watercourses, New York, 21 May 1997, UN Doc. A/RES/51/229, arts. 2(a), 21–23.

79 E.g., Basel Convention.

80 E.g., Convention on Nuclear Safety, 17 June 1994, 1963 UNTS 293, art. 7.

81 See, e.g., International Law Association, Report of the Fifty-Second Conference, Helsinki, 14–20 August 1966, p. 477; International Law Association, Report of the Sixtieth Conference, Montreal, 1982, p. 1.

82 Report of the UN Conference on Environment and Development, above note 45, Annex I.

83 World Summit on Sustainable Development, Johannesburg Declaration on Sustainable Development, 4 September 2002, UN Doc. A/CONF.199/20.

84 E.g., Prosper Weil, 'Towards Relative Normativity in International Law?' (1983) 77 AJIL 413, 414–423.

85 Ibid. p. 416.

To the extent states relate to each other as neighbors, they may find ways to resolve their differences through friendly cooperation based on informal norms and practices rather than resort to legal obligations and enforcement.[86] Even if treaties might be preferable in a perfect world, soft law commitments are sometimes the most robust form of normative consensus that states can achieve through diligent cooperation. Mandatory cooperation thus helps to explain and contextualize soft law's prevalence in international environmental governance, showing why it may be worth celebrating, or at least having, even as the international community continues to pursue more intensive commitments to prevent or minimize transboundary pollution.

Yet despite evident progress, the dangers of transboundary pollution have never been greater. In the next chapter, we consider how mandatory cooperation applies to the supreme existential danger of our time: atmospheric pollution and its devastating contribution to global warming. As we will see, in principle, states must exercise due diligence to prevent carbon emissions from exacerbating global warming. This obligation flows, in part, from the general duty to prevent transboundary harm. Additionally, states now accept that climate change and its adverse effects qualify as a common concern of humanity that is entrusted to the joint stewardship of the international community as a whole. Accordingly, joining the fight against climate change is no longer an option states can take up or refuse; it is mandatory under international law.

[86] Cf. Robert C. Ellickson, *Order Without Law: How Neighbors Settle Disputes* (Cambridge: Harvard University Press, 1994), p. 4 ("Neighbors in fact are strongly inclined to cooperate, but they achieve cooperative outcomes … by developing and enforcing adaptive norms of neighborliness that trump formal legal entitlements.").

PART II

Collective Stewardship

7

Climate Change

Paradise Lost

Consisting of thirty-two atolls and one raised coral island dispersed over an area of the central Pacific larger than India, Kiribati (pronounced *KIRR-ih-bass*) is a breathtaking tropical paradise.[1] Straddling the equator, its atolls are surrounded and laced through with shimmering turquoise waters. Towering coconut palm trees and stilt houses line its beaches. Marine life is abundant; fishers in sarongs gather shellfish at low tide. But for Kiribati's roughly 119,000 permanent residents, the beauty and wonder of their ancestral homeland is overshadowed by impending cataclysm: the devastating impacts of global climate change.

Historically, Kiribati has not suffered from cyclones and similar severe weather, since those rarely occur near the equator.[2] However, climate scientists have long warned of changing weather patterns in the Pacific, predicting that global warming would cause island nations to experience severe weather events with greater frequency.[3] In 2015, heavy seas and winds from Tropical Cyclone Pam struck Kiribati, flooding and destroying homes and buildings, contaminating freshwater wells, and destroying sea walls.[4] Already reliant on significant development assistance, with the lowest gross domestic product of any sovereign state in Oceania, Kiribati lacks the resources needed to recover from a natural disaster of this magnitude.[5]

[1] *See* 'Kiribati', Wikipedia, https://en.wikipedia.org/wiki/Kiribati. The Kiribati archipelago covers 3,441,810 square kilometers. Ibid.

[2] Karen Allen, 'We need to talk about cyclones', ReliefWeb, 12 March 2016.

[3] See, e.g., Wenju Cai et al., 'Anthropogenic Impacts on Twentieth-Century ENSO Variability Changes' (2023) 4 *Nat. Rev. Earth & Env't* 407.

[4] Ron K. Hoeke et al., 'Severe Flooding in the Atoll Nations of Tuvalu and Kiribati Triggered by a Distant Tropical Cyclone Pam' (2020) *Front. Mar. Sci.*, 22 January 2021.

[5] Ibid.

More terrifying yet for Kiribati is the rising sea. Kiribati is a low-lying nation, with most land less than two meters above sea level.[6] According to the Intergovernmental Panel on Climate Change (IPCC), between 1901 and 1971 the average rate of sea level rise was 1.3mm per year, increasing to 1.9mm per year between 1971 and 2006, and further accelerating to 3.7mm per year between 2006 and 2018.[7] By 2100, the sea level around Kiribati is estimated to rise between 520 mm (20.5 inches) and 910 mm (36 inches), and possibly much more.[8] In 1999, two of Kiribati's islands, Abanuea and Tebua Tarawa, flooded and disappeared underwater entirely.[9] As these trends continue, much more of Kiribati's landmass will be lost to the rising sea.[10] Nonetheless, the most probable and imminent existential crisis Kiribati faces is the threat of higher seas and more frequent extreme weather combining to render its islands uninhabitable long before they are buried by the sea.[11]

The principal cause of rising sea levels is global warming.[12] The IPCC reports global surface temperature reaching 1.1°C above 1850–1900 levels in 2011–2020.[13] Rising global temperature is melting glaciers and ice sheets at an unprecedented pace, all the while expanding the volume of the ocean as sea water warms. The IPCC's leading headline in its 2023 Synthesis Report is that "[h]uman activities, principally through emissions of greenhouse gases, have unequivocally caused global warming."[14] Greenhouse gases (GHGs) – carbon dioxide, methane, nitrous oxide, and fluorinated gases – trap heat energy from the sun within the earth's

[6] Rodney Dekker, 'Island neighbours at the mercy of rising tides', Austrl. Broadcasting Corp., 9 December 2011.

[7] Intergovernmental Panel on Climate Change, 'Climate Change 2023 Synthesis Report' (2023), p. 46.

[8] 'IPCC 6th Assessment Report Sea Level Projections: Median projections of global and regional sea level rise, relative to 1995–2014 baseline', NASA, https://sealevel.nasa.gov/ipcc-ar6-sea-level-projection-tool.

[9] 'Tarawa, Kiribati', European Space Agency, 25 September 2020, www.esa.int/ESA_Multimedia/Images/2020/09/Tarawa_Kiribati.

[10] Mark Nevitt, 'Key Takeaways from the Glasgow Climate Pact', Lawfare, 17 November 2021 [hereinafter Key Takeaways] (reporting the finding that 20 percent of some Pacific Island nations' landmass is likely to disappear underwater by 2040).

[11] Jane McAdam, *Climate Change, Forced Migration, and International Law* (Oxford: Oxford University Press, 2012), p. 119.

[12] Rebecca Lindsey, 'Climate Change: Global Sea Level', National Oceanic and Atmospheric Administration, 19 April 2022, www.climate.gov/news-features/understanding-climate/climate-change-global-sea-level.

[13] Intergovernmental Panel on Climate Change, 'Climate Change 2023 Synthesis Report: Summary for Policymaker', IPCC (2023), p. 4 [hereinafter IPCC, SPM].

[14] Ibid.

atmosphere, raising global surface temperatures.[15] GHGs are created by a host of industrial, agricultural, and consumer practices, including the harvesting, transporting, and burning of coal, oil, natural gas, solid waste, and trees. Past and present GHG emissions have already locked in considerable environmental damage. The IPCC concludes that "[s]ea level rise is unavoidable for centuries to millennia due to continuing deep ocean warming and ice sheet melt, and sea levels will remain elevated for thousands of years."[16] However, the IPCC also affirms that "deep, rapid, and sustained GHG emissions reductions would limit further sea level rise acceleration and projected long-term sea level rise commitment."[17]

Put concretely, whether Kiribati faces half a meter, a full meter, or more than a meter of sea level rise by 2100 depends on the extent to which the international community is prepared to mitigate global warming by making "deep, rapid, and sustained" reductions to global GHG emissions. Even under optimistic forecasts, however, Kiribati will need robust sea walls and elevated dwellings to remain habitable. If Kiribati's citizens are to remain on their islands, the international community must assist Kiribati in implementing adaptation measures to cope with higher sea levels. Mitigation and adaptation are essentially the two policy choices available to address climate change constructively.

Kiribati is sometimes referred to as the "canary in the coal mine" of climate change, since it was among the first countries to suffer devastating harm from global warming, serving as a warning to others.[18] Many other countries are now experiencing similar effects, however, and there is mounting evidence that global warming is accelerating faster than expected just a few years ago. Three years after authoring a widely publicized "warning of a climate emergency" that attracted 15,000 expert signatories,[19] seasoned climate scientists William Ripple and Christopher Wolf offered this alarming assessment:

> In 2023, we witnessed an extraordinary series of climate-related records being broken around the world . . . This year, exceptional heat waves have

[15] Katharine Hayhoe, *Saving Us: A Climate Scientist's Case for Hope and Healing in a Divided World* (New York: Simon and Schuster, 2021), p. 49.

[16] IPCC, SPM, p. 18

[17] Ibid.

[18] Danny Rose, 'Pacific Nations Like "Canary in Coal Mine"', News.com.au, 19 November 2015.

[19] William J. Ripple et al., 'World Scientists Warning of a Climate Emergency' (2020) 70 *Bioscience* 8–12.

> swept across the world, leading to record high temperatures. The oceans have been historically warm, with global and North Atlantic sea surface temperatures both breaking records and unprecedented low levels of sea ice surrounding Antarctica ... In addition, June through August of this year was the warmest period ever recorded, and in early July, we witnessed Earth's highest global daily average surface temperature ever measured, possibly the warmest temperature on Earth over the past 100,000 years ...
>
> We are venturing into uncharted climate territory. Global daily mean temperatures never exceeded 1.5-degree Celsius (°C) above pre-industrial levels prior to 2000 and have only occasionally exceeded that number since then. However, 2023 has already seen 38 days with global average temperatures above 1.5 °C by 12 September – more than any other year – and the total may continue to rise ... Similarly, on 7 July 2023, Antarctic sea ice reached its lowest daily relative extent since the advent of satellite data ... Other variables far outside their historical ranges include the area burned by wildfires in Canada, which may indicate a tipping point into a new fire regime.[20]

These accelerating changes to the global environment pose grave dangers not only for low-lying island nations, such as Kiribati, but also for countries elsewhere, whether they be in the Global North or the Global South. Climate change knows no borders, and its adverse effects threaten to leave no people or territory unharmed.

This chapter examines the international community's efforts to address climate change. As we shall see, the overarching method is international cooperation within an institutional framework supplied by international law. States and international organizations have established a supranational framework – the UN Framework Convention on Climate Change (UNFCCC) and related instruments – to articulate and implement mitigation and adaptation policies. We argue that this framework reflects the norms of mandatory cooperation, and it holds cautious promise for equitably allocating the costs of mitigation and adaptation in developing countries hard hit by climate change, such as Kiribati.

Governing the Climate Commons

When the UNFCCC entered into force in 1994, the international community formally recognized that "change in the Earth's climate and its adverse effects are a common concern of humankind" and that this

[20] William J. Ripple et al., 'The 2023 State of the Climate Report: Entering Uncharted Territory' (2023) *Bioscience* 1–10 (references omitted) [hereinafter Uncharted Territory].

common concern requires "the widest possible cooperation by all countries and their participation in an effective and appropriate international response."[21] Similarly, the Convention on Biodiversity identifies the "conservation of biological diversity" (not animal life per se) as "a common concern of humankind."[22] By explicitly specifying in treaties that these issues constitute common concerns of humanity, the international community has signaled that states' sovereign rights to exploit resources within their domestic jurisdiction are coupled with a concomitant obligation to cooperate with other states in advancing sustainable development and preventing catastrophic environmental harm.

In 2015, representatives from 196 states met near Paris to negotiate and draft an agreement that would address climate change at the global level. These talks ultimately produced the Paris Agreement.[23] Its principal aim is to promote the adoption of policies that will reduce GHG emissions, thereby "[h]olding the increase in the global average temperature to well below 2°C above pre-industrial levels and pursuing efforts to limit the temperature increase to 1.5°C above pre-industrial levels."[24] The scientific consensus is that warming above 2°C will result in "irreversible, catastrophic harm."[25]

A further objective of the Paris Agreement is "[i]ncreasing the ability to adapt to the adverse impacts of climate change and foster climate resilience and low greenhouse gas emissions development."[26] The Global Commission on Adaptation points to several serious harms likely to occur if the international community does not provide adequate resources for adaptation:

- Without adaptation, climate change may depress growth in global agriculture yields up to 30 percent by 2050. The 500 million small farms around the world will be most affected.

[21] UN Framework Convention on Climate Change, New York, 9 May 1992, 1771 UNTS 107, pmbl. [hereinafter UNFCCC].

[22] UN Conference on Environment and Development: Convention on Biodiversity, 6 June 1992, 31 ILM 822, pmbl.

[23] Adoption of the Paris Agreement, Paris, 12 December 2015, FCCC/CP/2015/L.9/Rev.1, Annex.

[24] Paris Agreement to the United Nations Framework Convention on Climate Change, 13 December 2015, art. 2(a), *in* Rep. of the Conference of the Parties on the Twenty-First Session, Paris, 29 January 2016, UN Doc. FCCC/CP/2015/10/Add.1, Annex [hereinafter Paris Agreement].

[25] Key Takeaways.

[26] Paris Agreement, art. 2(b).

- The number of people who lack sufficient water at least one month per year will soar from 3.6 billion today to more than 5 billion by 2050.
- Rising seas and greater storm surges could force hundreds of millions of people in coastal cities from their homes, with a total cost to coastal urban areas of more than USD 1 trillion each year by 2050.
- Climate change could push more than 100 million people in developing countries below the poverty line by 2030.[27]

As the chief means of attaining mitigation and adaptation goals, the Paris Agreement envisions all countries developing and periodically ratcheting up "nationally determined contributions" (NDCs) to address climate change.[28] NDCs are to be submitted to the United Nations every five years and then used to assess states-parties' compliance with their ongoing commitments, as we explain in this section.[29] Sensitive to the concerns of developing countries, the preamble affirms "the principle of equity and common but differentiated responsibilities and respective capabilities."[30] More concretely, the Paris Agreement provides a framework for preexisting commitments of USD 100 billion a year in climate finance for developing countries by 2020, and for further financial assistance subsequently.[31] Although the plan's success depends on the willingness of countries to follow through on these commitments and develop and adhere to meaningful NDCs, we have suggested in previous writing that the obligation of states to do so is explained by the idea that states, severally and jointly, are fiduciaries of humanity.[32]

Implementation of the Paris Agreement is followed and pursued by the institutional framework inaugurated by the UNFCCC. The centerpiece of this framework is the annual Conference of the Parties to the UNFCCC (COP). The COP is the supreme decision-making body of the UNFCCC. Running concurrently is the Conference of the Parties, serving as the Meeting of the Parties of the Paris Agreement (the CMA series), and the Conference of the Parties to the Kyoto Protocol (the CMP series). So, for example, in Glasgow in 2021 there were concurrent meetings of the 26th

[27] 'Adapt Now: A Global Call for Leadership on Climate Resilience', Report, Global Commission on Adaptation (September 2023), p. 3.

[28] Paris Agreement, arts. 3, 4.

[29] Ibid. art. 4(9).

[30] Ibid. pmbl.

[31] Joe Thwaites et al., 'What Does the Paris Agreement Do for Finance?', World Resource Inst., 18 December 2015.

[32] Evan J. Criddle and Evan Fox-Decent, *Fiduciaries of Humanity: How International Law Constitutes Authority* (Oxford: Oxford University Press, 2016), pp. 348–349.

session of the Conference of the Parties to the UNFCCC (COP26), the 16th session of the Conference of the Parties serving as the Meeting of the Parties to the Kyoto Protocol (CMP16), and the 3rd session of the Conference of the Parties serving as the Meeting of the Parties to the Paris Agreement (CMA3). The main result of COP26/CMA3 was the Glasgow Climate Pact, an agreement of the 197 Parties in attendance that built on various commitments found in the Paris Agreement.[33] Before turning to some of the specific measures in the Glasgow Pact, however, we set out now the numerous ways the legal regime established by the Paris Agreement reflects the norms of mandatory cooperation.

Like the UNFCCC, the Paris Agreement acknowledges that mitigating climate change and its adverse effects is "a common concern of humankind."[34] Although the Paris Agreement is careful to protect developing countries with the principle of "common but differentiated responsibilities," all states parties are expected to participate in the Agreement's regime of international cooperation. Nonetheless, while the Kyoto Protocol establishes legally binding GHG emission-reduction targets for developed countries,[35] the Paris Agreement does not. The Kyoto Protocol adopts a "top-down" approach that imposes emission-reduction targets on wealthier nations. The Paris Agreement, by contrast, relies on a "bottom-up" method that requires all states to develop NDCs, either by themselves or jointly with others, including through the use of "internationally transferred mitigation outcomes" (typically, a developed country would finance realization of a developing country's NDC).[36] The Agreement calls for each party's successive NDC to ratchet up or "represent a progression beyond" the prior NDC.[37] States parties are likewise legally required to submit their NDCs to the United Nations and a public registry, report on progress every two years, and have their progress reports reviewed by technical experts and peers.[38] In fact, each state's NDCs and progress toward them are transparently displayed and

[33] Glasgow Climate Pact, 13 Nov. 2021, in Report of the Conference of the Parties serving as the meeting of the Parties to the Paris Agreement on its third session, Glasgow, 13 November 2021, UN Doc. FCCC/PA/CMA/2021/10/Add.1 [hereinafter Glasgow Pact].

[34] Paris Agreement, pmbl.

[35] Kyoto Protocol to the United Nations Framework Convention on Climate Change, Kyoto, 10 December 1997, UN Doc FCCC/CP/1997/7/Add.1, 37 ILM 22, art. 3.

[36] Paris Agreement, art. 6.

[37] Ibid. art. 4(4).

[38] Ibid. art. 13.

assessed on a publicly available website.[39] The Agreement further envisions a "global stocktake" every five years to assess collective progress toward its objectives.[40]

The Paris Agreement seeks to strike a balance that takes into account state autonomy and self-determination, on the one hand, and the urgent need for a global response to climate change, on the other. State autonomy is respected through the use of NDCs that states are legally entitled to design and implement as they wish. The demands of climate change are reflected in the legal requirement to establish, implement, and report periodically on progress toward NDCs. This activity is wedded to the annual COP meetings under the UNFCCC framework, as described above. In this context, states retain an overarching obligation from the UNFCCC to "protect the climate system for the benefit of present and future generations of humankind,"[41] and to do so cooperatively, such as through the negotiated use of "internationally transferred mitigation outcomes."[42] Thus, explicitly and implicitly, the UNFCCC and the Paris Agreement require states to negotiate with one another in good faith, and on an ongoing basis, for the purpose of developing and implementing NDCs capable of achieving collectively the goals of the Paris Agreement. In the event of a dispute concerning the interpretation or application of the UNFCCC or the Paris Agreement, the controversy is remitted to the International Court of Justice (ICJ), arbitration, or conciliation.[43] The Paris Agreement thus embraces a form of mandatory cooperation akin to the form established under the UN Convention on the Law of the Sea,[44] where contending parties are obligated to negotiate in good faith, resorting to third-party dispute resolution only if necessary.

The principle of sovereign equality is respected under the Paris Agreement because no state is entitled to dictate terms to another, and every state is ultimately responsible for the content of its NDC. The principle of joint stewardship is put into action by the Paris Agreement's delegation to states of the responsibility to craft meaningful

39 See 'Climate Action Tracker', https://climateactiontracker.org/about/ ("The Climate Action Tracker is an independent scientific project that tracks government climate action and measures it against the globally agreed Paris Agreement aim of 'holding warming well below 2°C, and pursuing efforts to limit warming to 1.5°C.'").

40 Paris Agreement, art. 14.

41 UNFCCC, art. 3(1).

42 Paris Agreement, art. 6.

43 Ibid. art. 24 (referring to UNFCCC, art. 16).

44 UN Convention on the Law of the Sea, 10 December 1982, 1833 UNTS 3.

NDCs to reduce GHG emissions and address the adverse effects of climate change. Joint stewardship assumes an institutional and democratic form through the Paris Agreement's annual COP and CMA conference series. Every party has one vote, allowing the COP/CMA conferences to speak collectively on behalf of all.[45]

The Glasgow Climate Pact

Six years after the signing of the Paris Agreement, COP26 in Glasgow gave the international community an opportunity to assess progress, grapple with challenges, and strengthen NDCs. Held during the COVID-19 pandemic, COP26 demonstrated states' willingness to take new decisions and strengthen commitments. Over fifty formal decisions were adopted.[46] In addition, COP26 secured near-global net zero NDCs from 153 countries, such that over 90 percent of world gross domestic product and around 90 percent of global emissions are now covered by net zero commitments.[47] Significantly, the Glasgow Pact cemented 1.5°C as the primary global temperature ceiling, with the more severe impacts of 2°C warming emphasized.[48] The Pact also emphasized near-term

[45] Paris Agreement, art. 25. Of course, mandatory emission standards established under Kyoto could also be said to reflect sovereign equality (the equality of sovereigns to negotiate and enter treaties) and could be subject to joint stewardship via the UNFCCC Conference of Parties. Organizing principles can explain and justify any number of reasonable policies that fall within their ambit. Our thesis here is that NDCs operate within a multilateral framework that has significant mandatory components, notwithstanding the discretion left to states to craft their own NDCs. NDCs can be fairly characterized, therefore, as operating within a regime of mandatory cooperation that is helpfully explained by sovereign equality and joint stewardship.

[46] See 'Outcome of the Glasgow Climate Change Conference—Advance Unedited Versions (AUVs) and list of submissions from the sessions in Glasgow', United Nations Climate Change, https://unfccc.int/process-and-meetings/conferences/glasgow-climate-change-conference-october-november-2021/outcomes-of-the-glasgow-climate-change-conference.

[47] UN Climate Change Conference UK 2021, 'COP26: The Glasgow Climate Pact', pp. 5–7, https://webarchive.nationalarchives.gov.uk/ukgwa/20230311050139mp_/https://ukcop26.org/wp-content/uploads/2021/11/COP26-Presidency-Outcomes-The-Climate-Pact.pdf [hereinafter Glasgow Pact explainer]. The term "net zero" refers to GHG emissions being reduced or removed from the air through various means – e.g., improved energy efficiency, use of renewables, electrification – with the result that the GHG emissions produced by humans are balanced to zero (or close to it) by GHG emissions removed from the air. See UN Climate Action, 'For a livable climate: Net-zero commitments must be backed by credible action', www.un.org/en/climatechange/net-zero-coalition.

[48] Glasgow Pact, paras. 20–22.

action aimed at 2030, such as "reducing global carbon dioxide emissions by 45 per cent by 2030 relative to the 2010 level and to net zero around mid-century as well as deep reductions in other greenhouse gases."[49] The Paris Agreement, by contrast, only refers to achieving net-zero "in the second half of this century."[50] The Glasgow Pact also invited the Parties to "consider further actions to reduce by 2030" methane and other non-carbon dioxide GHGs, whereas the Paris Agreement is silent on methane and other non-carbon dioxide GHGs.[51] Possibly the most significant novelty in the Pact, however, is its call on the Parties to accelerate "efforts towards the phasedown of unabated coal power and phase-out of inefficient fossil fuel subsidies."[52] This is the first time an international instrument has expressly called for a reduction in the use of coal, which alone is responsible for roughly 40 percent of all current carbon dioxide emissions.[53]

The many joint commitments in the Glasgow Pact are the product of negotiation and cooperation that aims for consensus within the COP/CMA framework. Crucially, these multilateral decisions and commitments include major GHG producers, such as China, India, Russia, and the United States. In the case of the provision on coal, China and India resisted the original language that called for a phasing out of coal power but did agree to a progressive "phasedown."[54] This is consistent with mandatory cooperation's norm calling on states to negotiate matters of common concern in good faith without prescribing predetermined outcomes.

Mandatory cooperation in this context assumes that states wear two hats. One is the hat of their people's representative, a role that requires them to bargain zealously for their people's welfare. The other hat is worn as a joint steward of humanity, where they are called on, with other states, to safeguard the earth's environment. As their people's representative, they are entitled to seek reasonable accommodations consistent with "the principle of equity and common but differentiated responsibilities."[55] As

[49] Ibid. para. 22.
[50] Paris Agreement, art. 4(1).
[51] Glasgow Pact, para. 37.
[52] Ibid. para. 36.
[53] Ripple et al., 'Uncharted Territory', p. 8.
[54] Joanna Depledge et al., 'Glass Half Full or Glass Half Empty? The 2021 Glasgow Climate Conference' (2022) 22 *Climate Pol'y* 147. A positive bilateral surprise was an agreement between the United States and China to take steps on a series of issues including methane emissions, transition to clean energy, and decarbonization. See Key Takeaways.
[55] Paris Agreement, pmbl.

a steward of humanity, they are tasked with ensuring that equity and reasonableness frame the claims made by individual states, including their own. Plausibly, China and India's insistence on "phasedown" rather than "phase out" falls within the margin of maneuver they enjoy as both their people's representatives and good stewards of humanity.

Some might be surprised that China and India compromised at all. Why did they not just walk away and refuse to set up any standard for measuring the reduction of coal power? Let us assume that China and India believed that it was in their interest to compromise, either for the sake of reputational gain or because they themselves were being affected by climate change or were otherwise concerned about its possible effects on them. Whatever their actual motivation, the presence of a self-interested reason for compromising does not imply that they did not have an obligation to negotiate in good faith. By agreeing to take part in the COP/CMA process, they agreed to negotiate and participate in good faith, and thereby incurred an obligation to do so. Moreover, they would likely present themselves and their interlocutors as having an obligation to negotiate in good faith, since good faith is the least that can be reasonably expected of contending parties who must negotiate a collective approach to a common concern. Accordingly, for Parties within the COP/CMA framework, good faith and mandatory cooperation are the overarching practices to which they are committed.

It is equally clear from the record of proceedings and negotiations that the Parties view the provisions of the Glasgow Pact as binding and authoritative. The Parties' self-understanding of the Pact is noteworthy because, unlike the Paris Agreement, which is formally a treaty within the UN system, the Glasgow Pact is not a treaty but rather a "soft law" instrument of international law. As a decision of COP26/CMA3 (Decision 1/CMA.3), it resembles in form a resolution of the UN General Assembly. Now, many of the Pact's provisions recall and seek urgent implementation of articles from the Paris Agreement. For example, paragraph 26 "[e]mphasizes the urgent need for Parties to increase their efforts to collectively reduce emissions through accelerated action and implementation of domestic mitigation measures in accordance with . . . the Paris Agreement."[56] In these cases, the Pact can piggyback on the Agreement by serving as an authoritative interpretation of the relevant articles of the Agreement, which unquestionably are legally binding under international law.

[56] Glasgow Pact, para. 26 (emphasis omitted).

The open-textured nature of many of the Agreement's provisions means that even the novel and specific commitments from the Pact, such as the coal phasedown, may be read as giving content to those provisions. For example, the coal phasedown may be understood as part of the commitment from Article 4(1) of the Agreement to "reach global peaking of greenhouse gas emissions as soon as possible."[57] Moreover, even where the Glasgow Pact enshrines commitments that cannot be brought into the four corners of the Paris Agreement, Joanna Depledge, Miguel Saldivia, and Cristine Peñasco rightly observe that "COP decisions still shape the obligations and expectations of parties and stakeholders, and have the advantage of immediate and global applicability, since they do not require domestic ratification to take effect."[58]

Regrettably, not everything on which states agreed prior to Glasgow has come to pass, exposing the relative frailty of UNFCCC framework. The Glasgow Pact notes "with deep regret" the failure of developed countries to meet the goal previously set of mobilizing jointly USD 100 billion per year by 2020 to support mitigation in developing countries, while welcoming increased transparency and pledges that surpass this goal.[59] The Pact also calls on developed countries "to at least double their collective provision of climate finance for adaptation of developing parties from 2019 levels by 2025."[60] It is far from clear that even this apparently ambitious goal is adequate. The International Energy Agency estimates that "[b]y the end of the 2020s, annual capital spending on clean energy in [developing] economies needs to expand by more than seven times, to above USD 1 trillion, in order to put the world on track to reach net-zero emissions by 2050."[61] While price-tags such as this are eye-watering, the Global Commission on Adaptation has calculated that investing USD 1.8 trillion globally in five adaptation areas – early warning systems, infrastructure resiliency, dryland crop production, protecting mangroves, and water resource management resiliency – would

57 Paris Agreement, art. 4(1).

58 Depledge et al., 'Glass Half Full or Glass Half Empty?', p. 151.

59 Glasgow Pact, paras. 43–48. The OECD confirmed that climate finance in 2019 totaled USD 79.6 billion. See OECD 'Climate finance provided and mobilised by developed countries: Aggregate trends updated with 2019 data', Report (2021) *Climate Finance and the USD 100 Billion Goal.*

60 Glasgow Pact, para. 18.

61 International Energy Agency, 'Financing Clean Energy Transitions in Emerging and Developing Economies' (2021), p. 14.

produce total net benefits of USD 7.1 trillion.[62] The challenge for policymakers will be harnessing the ambition underlying the Glasgow Pact to convince developed countries to invest jointly in mitigation and adaptation measures that are in their long-term economic as well as climate interest.

COP28 and the First Global Stocktake

Held in Dubai in December 2023, COP28 brought together more than 150 heads of state and government and some 85,000 participants, including representatives of national delegations, civil society organizations, business, indigenous peoples, and international organizations. The major outcome from the conference was the first global stocktake on climate matters prescribed by the Paris Agreement.[63] In what the United Nations hailed as "a demonstration of global solidarity," nearly two hundred parties reached consensus on the stocktake, which provides assessments of mitigation and adaptation efforts to date, the state of the climate, and prescriptions on what needs to done.[64] The headline-grabbing novelty was the stocktake's call for "[p]hasing out inefficient fossil fuel subsidies" and "[t]ransitioning away from fossil fuels."[65] Expressing "serious concern that 2023 is set to be the warmest year on record," the agreement calls on parties to implement "deep, rapid and sustained reductions in global greenhouse gas emissions of 43 per cent by 2030 and 60 per cent by 2035" so as to limit warming to 1.5°C with limited overshoot.[66] Reaffirming "equity and the principle of common but differentiated responsibilities," the stocktake recognizes that time frames for peaking temperatures in different countries "may be shaped by sustainable development, poverty eradication needs and equity and be in line with different national circumstances."[67] Mitigation prescriptions include "[t]ripling renewable energy capacity globally and doubling the global

[62] Global Commission on Adaptation, pp. 3–4.

[63] First global stocktake, 13 December 2023, in Conference of the Parties serving as the meeting of the Parties to the Paris Agreement on its fifth session, United Arab Emirates, 12 December 2023, UN Doc. FCCC/PA/CMA/2023/L.17 [hereinafter Stocktake].

[64] UN Climate Change Press Release, 13 December 2023, 'COP28 Agreement Signals "Beginning of the End" of the Fossil Fuel Era', UN Climate Change, 13 December 2023 [hereinafter Beginning of the End].

[65] Stocktake, para. 28.

[66] Ibid. paras. 5, 28.

[67] Ibid. para. 26.

average annual rate of energy efficiency improvements by 2030."[68] The stocktake likewise affirms ambitious adaptation measures to contend with the effects of climate change, especially on the most vulnerable states, such as Kiribati. For example, the Parties acknowledge "that climate change impacts are often transboundary in nature and may involve complex, cascading risks that require knowledge-sharing and international cooperation for addressing them."[69] In fact, the agreement devotes an entire section to "International Cooperation," recognizing "the importance of international cooperation, including transboundary cooperation, for contributing to progress towards the goals of the Paris Agreement."[70]

At COP29 in 2024, states established a new climate finance goal to increase the scale of international assistance to developing countries from the previous goal of USD 100 billion annually to 300 billion annually by 2035.[71] At COP30, in 2025, governments have committed to present new NDCs that are "economy-wide, cover all greenhouse gases and are fully aligned with the 1.5°C temperature limit."[72] On our view, states bear a legal obligation to both their people and humanity to advance these goals through good faith cooperation. We consider now the argument in favor of viewing their cooperation as mandatory.

Recalcitrant States

Arguably, the international community has elected to place climate change policy under joint stewardship precisely because a healthy global environment is a non-excludable public good, and so the reduction of GHG pollution and adaptation poses a serious collective action problem. Self-interested states would prefer to free ride, letting others bear the cost of mitigation measures, while they themselves avoid those costs while benefitting from a relatively healthy environment. The logic of the prisoner's dilemma encourages states to pursue their narrow self-interest, since whether or not other states shoulder the burden of climate mitigation, a state will typically do better economically by avoiding the burden. But, of course, if a plurality of heavily polluting states adopted

[68] Ibid. para. 28(a).
[69] Ibid. para. 52.
[70] Ibid. para. 156.
[71] 'COP29 UN Climate Change Conference Agrees to Triple Finance to Developing Countries, Protecting Lives and Livelihoods', UN Climate Change, 24 November 2024.
[72] Ibid.

this policy, climate mitigation would be severely threatened if not doomed. The mandatory cooperation of the Paris Agreement and Glasgow Pact addresses this collective action problem by providing a framework for joint stewardship that makes the development and implementation of NDCs transparent, with the hope that national policymakers may be held accountable. Of course, this approach depends on policymakers caring about climate change and the Agreement's multilateral process, or at least caring about the consequences of refusing to participate in good faith. The quality of states-parties' participation in the COP/CMA framework, their ability to reach consensus on deeply contentious and high budget matters, and their public commitment to the goals of mitigation and adaptation suggest that, in general, most states at most times care a lot about climate change and want to be known as good global climate actors. But, regrettably, not all states at all times.

Pursuant to his "America First" policy, US President Donald Trump indicated early in his first term that the United States would withdraw from the Paris Agreement.[73] Article 28 of the Agreement provides that a party may give notice of withdrawal "any time after three years from the date on which the Agreement has entered into force" for that party, but the withdrawal takes effect only one year after notification.[74] The United States submitted its withdrawal notification on November 4, 2019, and formally withdrew from the Paris Agreement on November 4, 2020, one day after the presidential elections in which Joseph Biden prevailed. Withdrawal made the United States a free rider on the mitigation efforts of others, and was a brazen assertion of unilateralism in breach of the United States' joint stewardship obligations. The assertion was especially brazen because, as noted, the Paris Agreement does not subject states-parties to emission-reduction quotas or targets. States must merely develop some climate change mitigation policy in nonbinding (but good faith) negotiations with others and subject the policy's implementation to public review. Withdrawal from the Paris Agreement was therefore an outright rejection by the United States of international legal norms requiring mandatory cooperation in the field of climate change. This jeopardized collective action on the environment, in part because the United States is one of the world's largest carbon emitters,

[73] Jonathan Easley, 'Trump cements "America First" doctrine with Paris withdrawal', The Hill, 2 June 2017.

[74] Paris Agreement, art. 28(1)–(2). The United States formally stated its intention to withdraw in an official note to the United Nations delivered on August 4, 2017. See UN Depositary Notification, 4 August 2017, C.N.464.2017.TREATIES-XXVII.7.d.

and in part because defections from collective action regimes and open free riding breed resentment and may prompt further defections.

The United States' withdrawal did not have grave practical implications in the short term because the Biden administration signaled during and immediately after the 2020 election that it would rejoin the Paris Agreement.[75] Nonetheless, upon his return to the White House in January 2025, President Trump initiated a second US withdraw from the Paris Agreement,[76] potentially prompting other states to follow.[77] It is worth reflecting, therefore, on whether a recalcitrant state is entitled to go it alone and do as it pleases with respect to climate policy.

We suggest that the substantive and procedural norms of mandatory cooperation are binding independent of their codification in the Paris Agreement or the Glasgow Pact. The rationale for the theory proceeds from the premise that states' GHG emissions spill over into the global atmosphere possessed in common by all. As discussed in Chapter 6, transboundary environmental harm triggers duties of mandatory cooperation, such as duties to share information, negotiate in good faith, demonstrate due regard for other states and their nationals, and reduce harm where practicable.[78] In the climate change context, where transboundary pollution harms all states, the duties of mandatory cooperation become omnilateral. A practical way to specify and satisfy these duties within a regime that respects sovereign equality and avoids unilateralism is to authorize states to serve as coequal joint stewards of the atmosphere within an institutional framework such as the UNFCCC. For this charge to be legally meaningful, states must have some obligation to take it seriously.

The legal obligation to cooperate with other states in addressing the harmful effects of climate change derives in part from the issue's longstanding status under the UNFCCC, the Convention on Biodiversity, the

[75] President Biden signed an executive order to this effect on January 20, 2021, his first day in office. See Joseph R. Biden, Jr., 'Acceptance on Behalf of the United States', The White House, 20 January 2021, www.whitehouse.gov/briefing-room/statements-releases/2021/01/20/paris-climate-agreement/#:~:text=Biden%20Jr.%2C%20President%20of%20the,20th%20day%20of%20January%2C%202021.

[76] Max Bearak, 'Trump Orders a U.S. Exit From the World's Main Climate Pact', NY Times, 20 January 2025. At the time of writing the United States remains a party to the UNFCCC. Ibid.

[77] See Daniel Politi and Ana Ionova, 'Argentina Mulls Exiting Paris Climate Deal', NY Times, 15 November 2024.

[78] See, e.g., Convention on Environmental Impact Assessment in a Transboundary Context, Espoo, 25 February 1991, 1989 UNTS 310 (1997).

Paris Agreement, and the Glasgow Pact as a "common concern of humankind." This status is evidence of a customary rule that states have an obligation to work together in good faith to mitigate climate change because the environment is an important and nonexcludable public good on which humanity depends. Further evidence of such a customary rule is discernible from the relationship between a state and its people, on the one hand, and the state and humanity, on the other. As fiduciaries of their people and joint stewards of humanity, states owe both their people and humanity an obligation to do what is reasonably necessary to safeguard the environment. Because climate change is quintessentially a collective action problem, addressing it effectively necessarily requires states to negotiate mitigation and adaptation measures together in good faith.

Mandatory cooperation in a context in which the United States has withdrawn from the Paris Agreement would require the United States to take good faith steps to mitigate climate change and provide for adaptation. The United States would enjoy wide discretion to design and implement mitigation measures, much as states-parties to the Paris Agreement enjoy broad authority over the development and implementation of NDCs. The United States would also, however, be under an obligation to exercise that discretion in a way that did not subvert the collective mitigation efforts of other states, and in a manner that demonstrated due regard for other states touched by its GHGs. In addition, mandatory cooperation would entail procedural obligations of investigation, consultation, negotiation, and possibly third-party dispute resolution. Thus, even if the United States were to again withdraw from the Paris Agreement, and for a lengthier duration, it may still be bound by substantive and procedural customary norms of mandatory cooperation that call on the United States to have due regard for the environmental interests of other states, including Kiribati and others suffering climate harms now.

This again raises the question of compliance. What if the United States withdraws and explicitly refuses to recognize the validity or applicability of any international legal obligations in this sphere? Such a move could have far-reaching, and potentially disastrous consequences for global efforts to combat climate change. Purely as a conceptual matter, however, the compliance problem does not appear any more or less pressing here than in other areas of international law. Moreover, issues of compliance go to states' motivations for complying with international norms and the likelihood of their compliance with them, whereas our project has been to theorize norms that are already part of international legal practice. While practical concerns counsel publicists to take compliance seriously, elaborating the nature and implications of legal principles, as we have tried to do, is a separate inquiry.

A further issue raised by the prospect of customary norms of mandatory cooperation concerns whether the persistent objector doctrine would apply, such that unwilling states can legally opt out of multilateral regimes. In our view, these states would be in the same legal position as states that attempt to negotiate a settlement of a dispute in good faith but simply cannot reach amenable terms with the counterparty. Like these states, persistent objectors would remain subject to norms that prohibit them from adopting measures or positions that undermine the efforts of other states to develop an equitable multilateral framework. They would also remain subject to the obligation to continue to pursue good faith efforts to reach a mutually acceptable outcome. We recognize that, as a general matter, holding states to a customary obligation to seek third-party dispute resolution over climate change mitigation measures might appear, at this point in the evolution of international law, more prescription than description. However, it is a prescription wholly consonant with the principles of sovereign equality and joint stewardship that underlie mandatory cooperation's other norms. And, as we explain now, it is also a prescription that international courts and tribunals appear ready to endorse, just as they have affirmed duties of mandatory cooperation for other matters of international concern, such as maritime delimitation and transboundary pollution.

Adjudicating Climate Change Mitigation

Within the past several years, international courts and tribunals have received several requests for advisory opinions on states' international obligations concerning climate change mitigation. In December 2022, the Commission of Small Island States on Climate Change and International Law (COSIS), an organization that represents climate-vulnerable states like Kiribati, requested an advisory opinion from the International Tribunal for the Law of the Sea (ITLOS).[79] COSIS asked the tribunal to specify states' obligations to preserve and protect the marine

[79] Request for an Advisory Opinion Submitted by the Commission of Small Island States on Climate Change and International Law, Advisory Opinion, 21 May 2024, ITLOS [hereinafter ITLOS Advisory Opinion].

environment under the UN Convention on the Law of the Sea (UNCLOS) in light of the deleterious impact of GHGs on the global climate.[80] A month later, Chile and Colombia requested that the Inter-American Court of Human Rights (IACtHR) prepare an advisory opinion concerning states' climate-related obligations under the American Convention on Human Rights.[81] The request for an advisory opinion specifically invited the Court to clarify, inter alia, states' "cooperative obligations" for mitigating climate change.[82] On March 29, 2023, the UN General Assembly adopted resolution 77/276 with the support of 150 states, requesting an advisory opinion from the ICJ on "the obligations of States under international law to ensure the protection of the climate system and other parts of the environment from anthropogenic emissions of greenhouse gases for States and for present and future generations."[83] Within just four months, these requests for advisory opinions vaulted states' obligations with respect to climate change to the center stage of international adjudication.

The ITLOS tribunal, the IACtHR, and the ICJ have now delivered landmark advisory opinions concerning climate change. The ITLOS tribunal unanimously affirmed that states-parties to UNCLOS bear duties to "prevent, reduce, and control" the emissions that contribute to oceanic warming and acidification.[84] States' duties to curb GHGs are not limited to their voluntarily determined contributions under the Paris Agreement; to satisfy UNCLOS, states must "take *all necessary measures* to prevent, reduce and control marine pollution from anthropogenic GHG emissions, including measures to reduce such emissions."[85] The measures states take to prevent, reduce, and control GHG emissions must be reasonably calculated to protect the marine environment,

[80] Ibid.

[81] Request for an Advisory Opinion on Climate Emergency and Human Rights to the Inter-American Court of Human Rights from the Republic of Columbia and the Republic of Chile (9 January 2023), Advisory Opinion, 29 May 2025, IACtHR [hereinafter IACtHR Advisory Opinion].

[82] Ibid.

[83] UN Gen. Assembly, Request for an Advisory Opinion of the International Court of Justice on the Obligations of States in Respect of Climate Change, UN Doc. A/77/L.58 (1 March 2023); see also Maria A. Tigre, 'It Is (Finally) Time for an Advisory Opinion on Climate Change: Challenges and Opportunities on a Trio of Initiatives' (2024) 17 *Charleston L. Rev.* 623 (offering background on the three requests for advisory opinions).

[84] ITLOS Advisory Opinion, para. 197.

[85] Ibid. para. 223 (citing UNCLOS article 194, para. 1) (emphasis added).

consistent with the requirement of due diligence under customary international law.[86]

Significantly, the ITLOS tribunal also offered a resounding endorsement of mandatory cooperation for climate change mitigation. The tribunal emphasized that "the duty to cooperate is a fundamental principle in the prevention of pollution of the marine environment under [both UNCLOS] and general international law."[87] The "core" of this obligation, the tribunal explained, is states' duty to cooperate in "developing a common regulatory framework 'for the protection and preservation of the marine environment.'"[88] Under UNCLOS, states must "endeavour to harmonize" their regulatory responses to climate change, exercising "stringent" due diligence to adopt common rules, standards, and recommended practices and procedures to protect and preserve the marine environment from the adverse impacts of GHGs.[89] Due diligence requires states to expend substantial effort, consult with one another in good faith,[90] and cooperate in undertaking and promoting scientific research and exchanging information and data about oceanic pollution.[91] Perhaps most striking, the tribunal declared that these obligations of mandatory cooperation are not fully exhausted by the UNFCCC and the Paris Agreement:

> The adoption of a particular treaty, such as the UNFCCC or the Paris Agreement, does not discharge a State from its obligation to cooperate, as the obligation requires an ongoing effort on the part of States in the development of new or revised regulatory instruments, in particular in light of the evolution of scientific knowledge.[92]

Thus, mandatory cooperation may require the international community to take more aggressive measures now and in the future to prevent, reduce, and control the escalating impacts of GHGs on the global environment.

86 Ibid. paras. 206, 258.

87 Ibid. para. 296 (citing MOX Plant (Ireland v. United Kingdom), Provisional Measures, Order of 3 December 2001, ITLOS Rep. 2001, p. 95, at p. 110, para. 82).

88 Ibid. paras. 300–01 (quoting UNCLOS article 197); see also paras. 302, 305 (concluding that the resulting rules, standards, and procedures may be binding or nonbinding, and involve both global and regional frameworks).

89 Ibid. paras. 230 (citing UNCLOS art. 194, para. 1), 241, 243, 256–258, 307, 309.

90 Ibid. para. 308 (citing Request for Advisory Opinion Submitted by the Sub-Regional Fisheries Commission, Advisory Opinion of 2 April 2015, ITLOS Reports 2015, p. 4, at pp. 59–60, para. 210).

91 Ibid. paras. 313–321 (discussing the application of UNCLOS arts. 200–201).

92 Ibid. para. 311.

The advisory opinions of the IACtHR and the ICJ were released as this book went to press and go further still. Linking state obligations to address climate change to human rights enshrined in the American Convention of Human Rights, the IACtHR frames its analysis as responding to "the climate emergency" of "climate change, pollution, and biodiversity loss."[93] Breaking new ground, the IACtHR finds that states are subject to a peremptory or *jus cogens* norm of international law to safeguard humanity against "anthropogenic conducts with irreversible impacts on the vital equilibrium of the planetary ecosystem," since these conducts "undermine the conditions required *sine qua non* for the enforceability of fundamental human rights that are already protected under international law by peremptory provisions."[94] Further, the IACtHR dedicates a lengthy section to "The Obligation of Cooperation," finding that "[t]he obligation of States to cooperate in good faith forms part of customary international law" and that "cooperation is a cardinal principle established in the OAS Charter."[95] The Court observes that, as a general matter, "the obligation of cooperation has special relevance in all contexts in which the international community pursues common objectives or faces problems that require collective solutions," and that this is "precisely the case in relation to addressing the causes and impacts of climate change."[96]

The ICJ's Advisory Opinion is likewise unequivocal in its prescription of mandatory cooperation to address climate change.[97] The Court observes at the outset that states-parties to the UNFCCC, the Kyoto Protocol, the Paris Agreement, UNCLOS and other environmental treaties have interlocking treaty-based obligations of mitigation and adaption to address climate change.[98] The ICJ also finds that states have a duty under customary international law "to prevent significant harm to the environment" that applies "to global environmental concerns."[99] And, just as significantly, the Curts affirms "that the duty of States to co-operate for the protection of the environment is a rule whose customary character has been established."[100] Emphasizing the customary status of

93 IACtHR Advisory Opinion, para. 42.

94 Ibid. para 290.

95 Ibid. paras. 247, 248.

96 Ibid. para. 253.

97 Obligations of States in Respect of Climate Change, Advisory Opinion, 2025 ICJ Rep. (23 July) [hereinafter ICJ Advisory Opinion].

98 ICJ Advisory Opinion, paras. 116–270.

99 ICJ Advisory Opinion (Summary), p. 6.

100 ICJ Advisory Opinion, para. 140.

the duty to co-operate, the Court notes that the "duty to co-operate is intrinsically linked to the duty to prevent significant harm to the environment, because unco-ordinated individual efforts by States may not lead to a meaningful result."[101] The customary duty to cooperate "is applicable to all States," the Court says, although its demands are sensitive to "the common but differentiated responsibilities and respective capabilities principle."[102] The customary duty applies "regardless of whether a State is a party to the climate change treaties."[103] The ICJ concludes that "[c]o-operation is not a matter of choice for States but a pressing need and a legal obligation."[104]

Conclusion

It is far beyond the remit of this chapter to offer a forecast of our climate future. However, let us return for a moment to Kiribati, the "canary in the coal mine."[105] Should the worst or even the fairly bad come to pass in the near future, the world will have to choose between very costly adaptation measures or providing space and status elsewhere for a people who will have become climate refugees.[106] For now, the President of Kiribati, Taneti Maamau, seeks funding from developed countries "in the billions" to physically raise some portion of Kiribati's land mass to escape the encroaching sea.[107] "The wealthy countries are after all responsible for what we are facing," President Maamau says.[108] Whether developed countries step up may depend, in part, on whether they recognize and embrace their obligation to cooperate on fair terms as joint stewards of the environment.

101 Ibid. para 141.
102 Ibid. para 305.
103 Ibid. para. 315.
104 Ibid. para 308.
105 Danny Rose, 'Pacific Nations Like "Canary in Coal Mine"'.
106 We address some of the options on forced migration in Chapter 11.
107 Oliver Milman, '"No Safe Place": Kiribati Seeks Donors to Raise Islands from Encroaching Seas', The Guardian, 18 November 2022.
108 Ibid.

8

Common and Disputed Territories

At the Brink of Doomsday

In April 2018, an extraordinary initiative was launched in western Antarctica: the International Thwaites Glacier Collaboration (ITGC). The Thwaites Glacier is 3,900 feet thick, has a surface area equivalent to Great Britain, and is teetering on the brink of collapse due to global warming. Since the turn of the century, the glacier has lost over a billion tons of ice to the adjacent Amundsen Sea. With warming waters undermining the glacier's outer tongue from below and cracks expanding across its surface, scientists anticipate that the glacier could shatter like a broken windshield within the next five years. When this happens, it is expected to release thousands of towering icebergs into the Southern Ocean, causing global sea levels to rise by as much as twenty-six inches. If the glacier's collapse destabilizes neighboring glaciers, it could trigger a chain reaction of accelerated ice flow that would elevate sea levels by up to ten feet by the end of the century, with catastrophic consequences for coastal communities around the world. Seeking to better understand these potential dangers, the ITGC has assembled over a hundred scientists from seven countries to study the glacier using overflight imaging, seismometers, radar, ocean gliders, drill-implanted sensors, and submersible semi-autonomous probes. Researchers anticipate that technologies developed for the ITGC might eventually be used by national space agencies in the search for extraterrestrial life on Europa, Jupiter's ice-encrusted, oceanic moon. For now, however, the international community has more pressing concerns: determining how much time remains before this aptly nicknamed "Doomsday Glacier" inflicts a global sea level crisis.[1]

[1] See Ben Hurwitz, 'About the International Thwaites Glacier Collaboration', 16 November 2017, https://schmidt.eas.gatech.edu/about/about-the-international-thwaites-glacier-collab

Located in a remote sector of western Antarctica that has yet to be claimed by any country, the Thwaites Glacier is effectively the last unclaimed land on earth. The legal status of the rest of Antarctica is hotly contested. Over the past two centuries, dozens of states have sent expeditions to Antarctica, often with the purpose of establishing or fortifying claims to territorial sovereignty. Some national claims to Antarctic territory overlap with other states' claims. To complicate matters further, two powerful states with permanent research stations in Antarctica – Russia and the United States – have refrained from asserting territorial claims but have reserved the right to do so in the future. Meanwhile, other states universally reject the territorial partition of Antarctica, insisting that the international community should instead work together through international institutions to preserve the continent's fragile natural environment.

This unresolved controversy has been placed on hold for the time being by the Antarctica Treaty of 1959 and associated instruments – known collectively as the "Antarctic Treaty System" (ATS).[2] The ATS safeguards Antarctica as a demilitarized and environmentally protected preserve for scientific study through at least 2048.[3] Legal scholars and political scientists tend to characterize the ATS as a pragmatic *modus vivendi* that appeals to states-parties' rational self-interest – that is, their shared concern for avoiding armed conflict and facilitating scientific cooperation.[4] As this chapter will show, however, the ATS also reflects legal requirements enshrined in the UN Charter obligating states to respect sovereign equality and resolve territorial disputes through peaceful cooperation rather than the use of force. In Antarctica, states cooperated to freeze the status quo and promote scientific expeditions pending development of a permanent and comprehensive legal framework to resolve the continent's disputed status. The ATS thus offers an important

oration/; Sarah Kaplan, 'Crucial Antarctic Ice Shelf Could Fail Within Five Years, Scientists Say', Washington Post, 13 December 2021.

2 Antarctic Treaty, Washington, 1 December 1959, 402 UNTS 71, art. IV [hereinafter Antarctic Treaty]; Convention for the Conservation of Antarctic Seals, London, 1 June 1972, 29 UST 441 [hereinafter Seals Convention]; Convention for the Conservation of Antarctic Marine Living Resources, Canberra, 20 May 1980, 1329 UNTS 47 [hereinafter CCAMLR]; Protocol on Environmental Protection to the Antarctic Treaty, Madrid, 4 October 1991, 30 ILM 1455 [hereinafter Madrid Protocol].

3 Antarctic Treaty, arts. II–III; Madrid Protocol, art. 25.

4 Christopher C. Joyner and Ethel R. Theis, *Eagle Over the Ice: the U.S. in the Antarctic* (Hanover: University Press of New England, 1997), p. 31; David J. Bederman, 'Antarctica in International Law and Relations' (1999) 39 VJIL 467, 501.

case study, illustrating how mandatory cooperation applies to territorial disputes even in the absence of a foreseeable permanent resolution.

This chapter also surveys other settings in which states are legally obligated to cooperate with one another to administer territory in accordance with equitable principles. Some territorial disputes do not implicate duties of mandatory cooperation because international law supplies a dispositive rule of decision or assigns decision-making authority exclusively to one party. For example, *Bolivia v. Chile* (discussed in Chapter 4) affirms that states are free to rebuff foreign offers to annex their territory.[5] When multiple states plausibly claim sovereignty over the same territory, however, international law does not authorize any single state to impose its will unilaterally; instead, states must consult with one another, share information relevant to their legal claims, and pursue a peaceful negotiated settlement or submit their dispute to arbitration or adjudication.[6] Mandatory cooperation also applies when territories are entrusted to the joint-stewardship of multiple states. In these contexts, pursuing cooperation in accordance with equitable principles is necessary to make sovereign equality meaningful under international law.

Res Communis

Long before the Antarctic Treaty, the international community addressed a similar territorial dispute at the opposite end of the world. Halfway between continental Norway and the North Pole in the extreme north of the Arctic Ocean lies an archipelago of rugged islands known today as Svalbard – "cold coast" in Old Norse.[7] Lacking pre-European indigenous people, Svalbard remained largely uninhabited until the seventeenth

[5] *See* Chapter 4 (discussing Obligation To Negotiate Access to the Pacific Ocean (Bolivia v. Chile), Judgment, 2018 ICJ Rep. 507, 563 (1 October); UN Charter art. 2(4) ("All Members shall refrain in their international relations from the threat or use of force against the territorial integrity or political independence of any state.").

[6] Arbitration Between the Republic of Croatia and the Republic of Slovenia, PCA Case No. 2012-04, Final Award, p. 108, para. 334 (29 June 2017) (describing mutual state consent as "the fundamental principle applicable to the establishment of land boundaries between sovereign States"); Steven R. Ratner, 'Land Feuds and Their Solutions: Finding International Law Beyond the Trial Chamber' (2006) 100 AJIL 808, 811 ("[T]he belief by one state that it has legal title to the territory of another does not legitimate the unilateral use of force.").

[7] Christopher R. Rossi, '"A Unique International Problem": The Svalbard Treaty, Equal Enjoyment, and Terra Nullius: Lessons of Territorial Temptation from History' (2015) 15 *Wash. U. Glob. Stud. L. Rev.* 93, 113.

century when European whalers began hunting its surrounding waters for walruses and Bowhead whales.[8] As the populations of walruses and whales dwindled, so too did European interest in Svalbard. Norwegians and Russians continued to visit Svalbard in small numbers during the eighteenth and nineteenth centuries, but under international law the islands remained *terra nullius*, which is to say, outside the jurisdiction of any particular state.

In 1871, the Swedish-Norwegian government directed diplomatic notes to several European powers, expressing interest in acquiring Svalbard. Russia pushed back, demanding that the islands be preserved as "*un domaine indécis*."[9] Through additional diplomatic exchanges, the two countries eventually agreed to preserve the status quo.[10] An 1872 treaty established Svalbard as an international commons or *res communis* open for exploitation but exempt from territorial acquisition. Adventurers and profit seekers of all nationalities were free to build settlements, perform scientific research, and conduct commerce.[11] They could hunt seals, set fur traps, and put down mine shafts in Svalbard. The one thing they could not do under the 1872 treaty was lay claim to Svalbard on behalf of their respective sovereigns.

The *res communis* approach began to show its flaws at the turn of the twentieth century when coal and other valuable mineral deposits were discovered on Spitsbergen, the largest island in the Svalbard archipelago. As commercial enterprises from Europe and the United States arrived to exploit the islands' resources, controversies over conflicting private claims to land and resources multiplied. Without any legal or institutional mechanisms for establishing or adjudicating title to property, companies and individuals were often at a loss to protect their interests from foreign encroachment. Making Svalbard an international commons turned out to be a recipe for incessant conflict, as well as enabling domination and exploitation by the most powerful commercial actors.[12] No public or private interests in Svalbard could be fully

[8] Ibid. pp. 113–115.

[9] Elen C. Singh, *The Spitsbergen (Svalbard) Question: United States Foreign Policy, 1907–1935* (Oslo: Universitetsforlaget, 1980), p. 24.

[10] A.N. Vylegzhanin and V.K. Zilanov, *Spitzbergen: Legal Regime of Adjacent Marine Areas* (W. E. Butler, transl., Utrecht: Eleven International Publishing, 2007), p. 7.

[11] Ibid. p. 9 (quoting R. V. Dekanozov, *Mezhdunanordnoe Pravovoe polozhenie Shpitsbergena morskoi mezhdunarodno-pravnoi spravochnik* (Sverdlovsk, 1956), pp. 199–201).

[12] Rossi, 'A Unique International Problem', pp. 118–119.

secure while the territory lacked shared legal norms and institutions to ensure fair and equitable treatment.

Seeking to correct these deficiencies, Norway convened a series of diplomatic gatherings in Oslo between 1910 and 1914.[13] Norway's representatives initially proposed to place Svalbard under an international administrative regime that would facilitate unlimited access to the islands for all states on the basis of sovereign equality.[14] When other states gave the proposal a cool reception, however, efforts to break the resulting impasse faded with the onset of World War I.

Only toward the end of the war did the Svalbard question resurface as a subject of serious international discussion. Enjoying the good will of the victorious Allies and exploiting the Bolsheviks' eagerness to secure recognition for their new government, Norway succeeded in securing international support for its bid to annex Svalbard.[15] However, this historic achievement was subject to a major caveat: in exchange for international recognition, Norway agreed to guarantee full access to the islands for nationals of foreign treaty-parties, enabling them to hunt, fish, conduct scientific research, and exploit the islands' natural resources on an equal playing field with Norwegians.[16] Norway also agreed to establish mining regulations and to endorse the property claims of foreign nationals who had established proprietary interests in land by virtue of their past activities.[17] In the treaty's preamble, the states-parties expressed their hope that this framework would establish an "equitable regime" to facilitate the islands' cooperative "development and peaceful utilisation."[18]

In sum, Svalbard's human history reflects the territory's transition from a *res communis* to an equitable regime administered under Norwegian sovereignty. States ultimately opted for a cooperative legal order that would respect equitable principles, securing their practical

13 Thor B. Arlov, *A Short History of Svalbard* (Oslo: Norsk Polarinstitutt, 1989), pp. 63–64; Robert Lansing, 'A Unique International Problem' (1917) 11 AJIL 763, 763.

14 Méir Ydit, *Internationalised Territories: From the "Free City of Cracow" to the "Free City of Berlin"* (Leyden: A W. Sythoff, 1961), p. 35.

15 Rossi, 'A Unique International Problem', pp. 131–132.

16 Treaty Concerning the Archipelago of Spitsbergen, Paris, 9 February 1920, 2 LNTS 7 [hereinafter Spitsbergen Treaty]; Geir Ulfstein, *The Svalbard Treaty: From Terra Nullius to Norwegian Sovereignty* (Oslo: Scandinavian University Press, 1995), p. 49.

17 Spitsbergen Treaty arts. 6–7.

18 Ibid., pmbl.

interests against foreign domination. For over a century, these features of the Spitsbergen Treaty have facilitated peaceful international cooperation in Svalbard.[19]

Who Rules Antarctica?

Concerns for international equity and multilateral cooperation have also shaped the legal regime for Antarctica. Like Svalbard, Antarctica has transitioned from an essentially unregulated *res communis* to a multilateral treaty-based regime that better guarantees respect for sovereign equality. In the case of Antarctica, however, this result has been achieved not by vesting sovereign jurisdiction in a particular state or group of states, but instead by providing a framework for international cooperation and environmental stewardship without resolving the underlying territorial disputes.

The story of humanity's engagement with Antarctica begins just two centuries ago. On January 28, 1820, one day after leading just the second maritime expedition across the Antarctic Circle, Russian naval commander Fabian Gottlieb von Bellingshausen sighted a "solid stretch of ice running from east through south to west."[20] Stretched out before his view was a vast continent roughly the size of Mexico and the United States combined.[21] Nearly all of Antarctica is concealed beneath an ancient ice dome that averages 6,600 feet in thickness and contains 90 percent of the world's freshwater reserves.[22] This icy mantle gives Antarctica the highest average elevation of any continent in the world – nearly twice the median height of Asia, the world's next highest continent. Blasted by ferocious winds, subfreezing temperatures, and total darkness during its long winter months, Antarctica ranks among the least hospitable environments for human habitation in the world.[23] After sighting this bleak polar desert, Bellingshausen and his crew reversed course without making landfall.

19 Donald Rothwell, *The Polar Regions and the Development of International Law* (Cambridge: Cambridge University Press, 1996), p. 170. Some states have questioned, however, whether the Spitsbergen treaty empowers Norway to claim sovereign rights to the continental shelf and an exclusive economic zone around Svalbard.

20 David Day, *Antarctica: A Biography* (Oxford: Oxford University Press, 2013), p. 22.

21 Christopher C. Joyner, *Governing the Frozen Commons: The Antarctic Regime and Environmental Protection* (Columbia: University of South Carolina Press, 1998), p. 1; Joyner and Theis, *Eagle Over the Ice*, p. 11.

22 Joyner and Theis, *Eagle Over the Ice*, p. 11.

23 Joyner, *Governing the Frozen Commons*, pp. 3–4.

Despite these extreme conditions, explorers, scientists, and sealers from around the world soon flocked to Antarctica in pursuit of adventure, profit, and glory. Some of these expeditions laid the groundwork for sponsoring states to stake claims to territorial sovereignty. Seven states would eventually lay claim to pie-slice sectors of Antarctica, beginning with the United Kingdom in 1908, followed by France, Norway, Chile, Argentina, Australia, and New Zealand.

Throughout the period of Antarctica's early exploration, international law permitted states to claim sovereignty over *terra nullius* unilaterally. This rule was designed by and for European nations to enable colonialism and mediate claims between colonial powers, with little or no regard for prior indigenous occupation.[24] To establish and maintain sovereignty, however, states were required to "effectively occupy" territory.[25] This meant taking actual possession and making a "continuous and peaceful display of sovereignty" by establishing a permanent administration *in situ* to govern the territory in the name of the claimant state.[26] Given the daunting challenges presented by Antarctica's inhospitable natural environment, none of the seven claimant states attempted to establish continuous sovereign governance in Antarctica prior to asserting territorial claims.[27] Instead, they argued that this was impractical and legally unnecessary to establish territorial sovereignty in the Antarctic context.[28] In support of this view, claimant states would later cite Max Huber's observation in the *Island of Palmas Case* (1928) that "[m]anifestations of territorial sovereignty" may vary depending

[24] See Antony Anghie, *Imperialism, Sovereignty and the Making of International Law* (Cambridge: Cambridge University Press, 2004), p. 103 (explaining how the doctrine of *terra nullius* was designed "to erase the non-European world from any subjectivity or personality").

[25] See Thomas Willing Balch, 'The Arctic and Antarctic Regions and the Law of Nations' (1910) 4 AJIL 265, 266 ("[D]iscovery alone is not sufficient to give a good title to a new, unoccupied land. The custom among nations for centuries, that gradually crystallized into a part of the Law of Nations, is that in order to perfect the right given by discovery, it must be followed by occupation.").

[26] The Arbitral Award Rendered in Conformity with the Special Agreement Concluded on January 23, 1925 Between the United States of America and the Netherlands Relating to the Arbitration of Differences Respecting Sovereignty over the Island of Palmas (or Miangas), 2 RIAA 829 (Perm. Ct. Arb. 1928), reprinted in (1928) 22 AJIL [hereinafter Island of Palmas Case].

[27] Balch, 'The Arctic and Antarctic Regions', pp. 267–268 (observing that "none of the nations who can bring forward the claim of discovery to various parts of that continent, have as yet perfected, or even attempted seriously, owing to the immense impeding power of nature, to perfect their respective titles of discovery by effective occupation").

[28] Note, 'Thaw in International Law? Rights in Antarctica Under the Law of Common Spaces' (1978) 87 YLJ 804, 819–822.

on "conditions of time and place."[29] In view of Antarctica's extreme climate, claimant states asserted that what constituted effective occupation could be relaxed in this context. Some measures that would not suffice to create or maintain sovereign title elsewhere – including discovery, exploration, proximity to sovereign territory, scientific study, the erection of physical markers, or the construction of a permanent research station – might suffice to confer sovereign rights over the continent's expansive and largely unexplored hinterlands.[30]

By the mid-twentieth century, claimant states encountered three formidable obstacles to their efforts to carve up Antarctica. First, claimant states could not agree among themselves about how a flexible approach to effective occupation would apply to their Antarctic claims. For example, Argentina and Chile failed to persuade other states that large sections of Antarctica fell under their sovereignty because those sections were natural extensions of their sovereign territories in South America.[31] European claimants based their claims on their asserted first discovery of the sectors of the continent.[32] The United Kingdom, in particular, resisted the Argentine-Chilean claims, arguing that it had already established sovereignty over much of the same territory based on its first discovery.[33] These divergent positions proved to be irreconcilable.

Further complicating the state of play was the possibility that other states might assert competing claims to Antarctica in the future. By the 1950s, both the Soviet Union and the United States had engaged in significant expeditions in Antarctica. Although the Soviet Union and the United States refrained from formally asserting territorial claims in Antarctica, both asserted the right to do so in the future, and their political influence posed a major deterrent against claimant states advancing their claims with greater force.

29 Island of Palmas Case, p. 877.

30 Charles Cheney Hyde, 'Acquisition of Sovereignty over Polar Areas' (1933) 19 *Iowa L. Rev.* 286; Peter Kikkert, '*Grasping for the Ends of the Earth: Framing and Contesting Polar Sovereignty, 1900-1955*' (unpublished PhD dissertation, University of Western Ontario, 2016), pp. 468–469.

31 See Joyner, *Governing the Frozen Commons*, p. 17 (explaining that Chile advanced a claim to part of Antarctica in 1940); Robert D. Hayton, 'The Antarctic Settlement of 1959' (1960) 54 AJIL 349, 350 ("The Chileans first put an expedition into the area in 1947."). At the time Chile gave notice of its claim, none of its nationals had ever set foot on the continent. Steve Heavens, 'Brian Roberts and the Origins of the 1959 Antarctic Treaty' (2016) 52 *Polar Record* 717, 718.

32 Note, 'A Thaw in International Law?', pp. 816–817.

33 Joyner, *Governing the Frozen Commons*, p. 14.

The third challenge confronting claimant states was the absence of international political or diplomatic recognition for their claims. Non-claimant states uniformly rejected Antarctic territorial claims. Legal commentators agreed that claimant states had not established the kind of effective occupation necessary to establish territorial jurisdiction.[34] By the 1920s, the US government threw its weight behind the view that Antarctic claims must be accompanied by actual settlement to be effective under international law.[35] Other non-claimant states argued that none of the claimants had established the kind of functioning government in Antarctica that could ground a plausible claim to effective occupation.

As long as the legal rules governing Antarctica remained unsettled, no state claim could be secure from foreign interference. This was not merely a hypothetical concern. In 1952, Argentineans at Hope Bay fired warning shots over the heads of a British group that was attempting to establish a research station in the disputed area. The following year, an Argentinean expedition erected a hut on Deception Island a short distance away from a new British base. The British Colonial Office characterized this move as an act of "aggression" against its territorial sovereignty that justified the responsive use of force in self-defense.[36] The United Kingdom dispatched Falkland Islands Governor Colin Campbell aboard the H.M.S. Snipe, accompanied by fifteen marines and two police officers, to dismantle Argentina's hut and arrest its two occupants. When news of this action reached Argentina, protests erupted in the streets of Buenos Aires.[37]

Skirmishes like these raised fears that Antarctica might become a flashpoint for international conflict during the second half of the twentieth century. That these fears were not realized is a testament to the power of international cooperation. During the 1950s, an era otherwise defined by bitter Cold War rivalries, Antarctic states succeeded in establishing the ATS – a multilateral regime that has facilitated peaceful scientific cooperation ever since.

[34] E.g., Balch, 'The Arctic and Antarctic Regions', p. 266 (explaining that "discovery alone is not sufficient to give a good title to a new, unoccupied land").

[35] Day, *Antarctica: A Biography*, p. 144.

[36] Kikkert, *Grasping for the Ends of the Earth*, p. 457.

[37] Ibid.

The Miracle on Ice

This happy result was hardly inevitable. During the first half of the twentieth century, many proposals to resolve the Antarctica question were promoted and debated, but none was deemed acceptable to all interested states. Some advocated internationalizing Antarctica under the administration of the League of Nations or the United Nations, perhaps as a trusteeship under the UN Trusteeship Council.[38] Another proposal would have placed the whole continent under a joint condominium for the collective benefit of the claimant states.[39] However, some of the claimant states adamantly opposed any measures that would extinguish or dilute their asserted entitlements to territorial sovereignty.[40]

Stymied on the negotiation front, the United Kingdom on several occasions attempted to take its disputes with Argentina and Chile to the International Court of Justice (ICJ), but the South Americans repeatedly refused to cooperate in submitting a joint-application to the ICJ.[41] The United Kingdom eventually gave up and submitted a unilateral application to the Court in May 1955,[42] but Argentina and Chile successfully contested the ICJ's jurisdiction, prompting the Court to remove the case from its list.[43] This result reverberated beyond the instant dispute. Had the Court addressed the case on the merits, it might have clarified how the international law of territorial acquisition applied to Antarctica. Once it became clear that an authoritative statement from the Court would not be forthcoming, and with no realistic prospect that Argentina and Chile would submit to adjudication or arbitration elsewhere, the international community confronted the unsettling possibility that the international law governing Antarctica would remain unsettled indefinitely. This state of affairs cast a shadow over all claims to Antarctic territory.

At this moment of uncertainty, an ambitious scientific initiative laid the groundwork for the international community to establish a new legal

38 Joyner and Theis, *Eagle Over the Ice*, p. 30.

39 Kikkert, *Grasping for the Ends of the Earth*, p. 447.

40 Ibid.; Heavens, 'Brian Roberts and the Origins', p. 726.

41 Kikkert, *Grasping for the Ends of the Earth*, pp. 449–463.

42 Antarctica Case (UK v. Chile), 1956 ICJ Rep. 15, 15–16 (16 March); Kikkert, *Grasping for the Ends of the Earth*, pp. 458–62. At the time, Argentina and Chile expressed concern that the ICJ showed "no guarantees at all to small powers." Kikkert, *Grasping for the Ends of the Earth*, p. 449.

43 Antarctica Case, 1956 ICJ Rep. at 17.

regime for Antarctica. Beginning in 1950, scientists championed a plan to designate 1957–1958 as an "International Geophysical Year" (IGY) to study holistically how the earth operates as a system. With phenomena like geomagnetism, meteorology, and polar auroras featuring prominently in the IGY's research agenda, it was evident from the start that Antarctic research would be critical to the initiative's success. International negotiations led eventually to a simple solution: for the duration of the IGY, states would suspend their territorial disputes so that scientists from all over the world could engage in Antarctic research. Activities conducted during the IGY, including the construction of scientific research stations, would not have any bearing on preexisting territorial claims.[44]

In preparation for the IGY, the United States and the Soviet Union both established permanent bases in Antarctica. The United States placed one of these research bases – the Amundsen-Scott South Pole Station – at the South Pole itself, the strategic intersection point for all seven preexisting territorial claims. The Soviet Union established a base at the "pole of inaccessibility," the central point of the continent where temperatures fall as low as −70 degrees Celsius.[45] By the end of the IGY, over fifty research stations had been established in Antarctica by twelve different states.[46]

As the IGY came to a close, US President Dwight D. Eisenhower gathered representatives of the twelve IGY states in Washington, DC, to discuss building on the initiative's success by continuing to cooperate for the peaceful, nonpolitical study of Antarctica.[47] The discussions that followed produced the Antarctic Treaty of 1959, which entered force two years later when the final three signatories – Argentina, Australia, and Chile – deposited their instruments of ratification.[48] Fifty-eight states have now become parties to the treaty.[49]

[44] Sir Arthur Watts *International Law and the Antarctic Treaty System* (Cambridge: Grotius Publications, 1992), p. 4.

[45] Charlotte Connelly, 'How Antarctica Became Home to a New Kind of Scientific Diplomacy', The Guardian, 1 July 2017.

[46] Kikkert, *Grasping for the Ends of the Earth*, p. 464.

[47] Robert D. Hayton, 'Polar Problems and International Law' (1958) 53 AJIL 746, 756 (discussing 38 Dep't of State Bulletin 910–911 (1958) (White House Press Release, 3 May 1958)).

[48] Joyner and Theis, *Eagle Over the Ice*, p. 33.

[49] 'The Antarctic Treaty', Secretariat of the Antarctic Treaty, www.ats.aq/devAS/Parties?lang=e.

For an agreement that governs an entire continent, the Antarctic Treaty is remarkably short, with only fourteen brief articles. The preamble affirms that "international cooperation in scientific investigation in Antarctica" has benefited humankind, and it asserts that "it is in the interest of all mankind that Antarctica shall continue for ever to be used exclusively for peaceful purposes and shall not become the scene or object of international discord."[50] The centerpiece of the treaty is Article IV, which freezes Antarctic territorial claims by declaring that "[n]o acts or activities taking place while the present Treaty is in force shall constitute a basis for asserting, supporting or denying a claim to territorial sovereignty in Antarctica or create any rights of sovereignty in Antarctica."[51] Article IV does not require claimant states to renounce their sovereignty claims, but it does not validate those claims either; it simply sets aside for the time being whether any of the claims or potential claims are effective under international law. In the meantime, the treaty opens the continent to continued scientific investigation (Article II), requires states to cooperate and share the fruit of their scientific activities (Article III), and prohibits states-parties from militarizing and nuclearizing the continent (Articles I and V). The treaty thus allows international scientific cooperation to continue apace without resolving the sovereignty controversy. In short, the Antarctic Treaty establishes Antarctica as a *res communis*, but rather than deploying this legal form for the sake of resource exploitation, as occurred in pre-1917 Svalbard, the Antarctic Treaty sets up a joint-stewardship regime to facilitate scientific cooperation.

Over the years, states-parties have supplemented the Antarctic Treaty with a variety of other agreements, including a convention to conserve Antarctic seals and marine living resources[52] and a comprehensive environmental protocol, known as the Madrid Protocol.[53] Antarctic states have committed to guarantee "the comprehensive protection of the Antarctic environment and dependent and associated ecosystems," thereby preserving "Antarctica as a natural reserve, devoted to peace and science."[54] To this end, the Madrid Protocol bans mining and drilling activities except for scientific purposes.[55] States-parties must "cooperate in the planning and conduct of activities in the Antarctic Treaty

[50] See Antarctic Treaty, pmbl.
[51] Ibid. art. IV(2).
[52] See generally Seals Convention; CCAMLR.
[53] See generally Madrid Protocol.
[54] Protocol on Environmental Protection, art. 2.
[55] Ibid. art. 7.

area," conduct environmental impact assessments for their activities, and "share information that may be helpful to other Parties in planning and conducting their activities in the Antarctic Treaty area, with a view to the protection of the Antarctic environment and dependent and associated ecosystems."[56] When disputes arise concerning the Protocol's "interpretation or application," states-parties must "consult among themselves as soon as possible with a view to having the dispute resolved by negotiation, inquiry, mediation, conciliation, arbitration, judicial settlement, or other peaceful means to which the parties to the dispute agree."[57] These requirements are to remain in place until at least 2048.[58]

Some scholars have characterized Antarctic cooperation as "the closest thing to a 'world order miracle' that the world has known."[59] In truth, however, under international law states had no lawful alternative other than to pursue a peaceful solution to the Antarctic sovereignty question through negotiation or third-party dispute resolution.[60] Concerns of national self-interest also supported this result. It was not apparent at the time that claimant states stood to gain much from attempting to enforce their territorial claims unilaterally. Antarctica's natural resources were largely unknown, concealed beneath two kilometers of ice. Moreover, pressing Antarctic territorial claims would mean risking confrontation with the two global superpowers, the Soviet Union and the United States, which threatened to assert their own claims. Thus, at the time states concluded the Antarctic Treaty, both international law and concerns for national self-interest supported moving territorial claims to the back burner so that scientists could conduct research on the continent.

The Antarctic "miracle" of peaceful cooperation has been replicated in some other contexts, from the Beaufort Sea controversy between Canada and the United States[61] to the pending case in the ICJ between Gabon and

[56] Ibid. arts. 6, 8.

[57] Ibid. art. 18.

[58] Ibid. art. 25(5).

[59] Rothwell, *The Polar Regions*, p. 457 (quoting with approval Richard Falk, 'The Antarctic Treaty System: Are There Viable Alternatives?', in Arnfinn Jorgensen-Dahl and Willy Østreng (eds.), *The Antarctic Treaty System in World Politics* (New York: Palgrave Macmillan, 1991), p. 399).

[60] UN Charter art. 2(3) (declaring that states must "settle" their disputes "by peaceful means").

[61] Betsy Baker, 'Filling an Arctic Gap: Legal and Regulatory Possibilities for Canadian-US Cooperation in the Beaufort Sea' (2009) 34 *Vt. L. Rev.* 57.

Equatorial Guinea over islands in the Gulf of Guinea.[62] Even some bitter enemies have managed to handle territorial disputes through cooperation. For example, India and Pakistan have committed to manage their acrimonious contest over Kashmir in accordance with the UN Charter "through bilateral negotiations or by any other peaceful means mutually agreed upon between them," respecting "each other's national unity, territorial integrity, political independence and sovereign equality."[63] Under the 1972 Simla Agreement, India and Pakistan have agreed that, "[p]ending the final settlement of any of the problems between the two countries, neither side shall unilaterally alter the situation and both shall prevent the organization, assistance or encouragement of any acts detrimental to the maintenance of peaceful and harmonious relations."[64] Although these commitments have been sorely tested by a limited war in 1999, sporadic violence along the border that continues into the present, and political maneuvering on both sides, thus far the legal framework of mandatory cooperation has prevented hostilities between India and Pakistan from spiraling out of control. Ultimately, international law and national self-interest have combined in these settings to promote international peace and security.

Granted, it is not realistic to expect that states will always respect their legal obligations to manage territorial disputes peacefully through negotiation or third-party dispute resolution. Too often, states assert the prerogative to determine their own borders unilaterally. Beyond Russia's controversial annexation of Crimea in 2014 (discussed in Chapter 1), prominent examples of unilateral territorial settlement include Azerbaijan's occupation of the Nagorno-Karabakh region, Israel's expanding settlements in the West Bank, and Morocco's long-standing presence in Western Sahara. Territorial settlements like these reproduce the wrongs of colonialism: states claim territorial sovereignty unilaterally without regard to the rights and legitimate interests of indigenous political communities. Unilateral territorial settlement essentially treats disputed territories as *res nullius*, ignoring the principle of sovereign equality and the right to self-determination under contemporary international law. Mandatory cooperation outlaws this form of neocolonialism. Whenever states delimit their shared borders on land or at sea,

62 See 'Land and Maritime Delimitation and Sovereignty Over Islands (Gabon/Equatorial Guinea)', International Court of Justice, www.icj-cij.org/en/case/179.

63 Agreement on the Bilateral Relations between the Government of India and the Government of Pakistan (Simla Agreement), Simla, 2 July 1972, 858 UNTS 71, art. 1.

64 Ibid. para. 1(ii).

they must resolve disputes through negotiation or third-party dispute resolution in accordance with equitable principles.[65] Although embittered rivals cannot always be convinced to meet at the negotiating table or submit their disputes to arbitration or adjudication, international law nudges them in that direction by denying legal validity and legitimacy to territorial settlements achieved through unilateral action such as aggression and occupation.

Internationalization

Mandatory cooperation also applies when states internationalize territory. A territory is considered to have been "internationalized" when it is removed from national jurisdiction, in whole or in part, in favor of international administration.[66] During the twentieth century, states experimented with internationalization in a variety of settings, with mixed success. For example, at the conclusion of World War I, the Allied Powers designated the port city of Danzig (currently Gdańsk) as an independent "Free City."[67] From its establishment in 1920 until the Nazi annexation of 1939, Danzig enjoyed local democratic government subject to the League of Nations' authority to supervise the city's administration and guarantee compliance with its Constitution.[68] In virtue of Danzig's internationalized status, members of the League of Nations were legally obligated to cooperate with efforts to guarantee the city's autonomous legal status and government.

Unlike the internationalization of Danzig, most exercises in international territorial administration have been designed as temporary solutions to aid conflict resolution, protect human rights, and pave the way for national self-determination. For instance, the Mandate System of the League of Nations authorized selected states to serve as "Mandatories

[65] See North Sea Continental Shelf Cases (Fed. Rep. Germ./Den; Fed. Rep. Germ./Neth.), Merits, 1969 ICJ Rep. 3 (20 February) (maritime boundaries); Case Concerning the Frontier Dispute (Burk. Faso/Mali), 1986 ICJ Rep. 554, 633, paras. 149–150 (22 December) (land borders).

[66] For similar definitions of "internationalized territory," see Carsten Stahn, *The Law and Practice of International Territorial Administration: Versailles to Iraq and Beyond* (Cambridge: Cambridge University Press, 2010), pp. 538–539; Ydit, *Internationalised Territories*, p. 21.

[67] Treaty of Peace with Germany (Treaty of Versailles), Versailles, 28 June 1919, 1919 UST 7, art. 100.

[68] Stahn, *The Law and Practice of International Territorial Administration*, p. 7; Ydit, *Internationalised Territories*, pp. 50–51.

of the League" in administering territories that had been wrested from Germany and the Ottoman Empire during World War I.[69] The UN Charter later replaced the Mandate System with a Trusteeship System that commissioned some states to administer former mandates and colonial holdings of the defeated Axis Powers.[70] Subsequently, the Security Council has authorized the Secretariat to conduct territorial administration on an ad hoc basis in countries such as Cambodia (1992–1993), Somalia (1993–1995), Eastern Slavonia (1996–1998), East Timor (1999–2002), and Kosovo (1999–present).[71] Across these and other contexts, international law requires states to cooperate with one another and with international organizations to ensure the success of international territorial administration.[72]

Between the Moon and the Deep Blue Sea

Within the past half century, technological advances have opened new frontiers for human exploration and exploitation. From the deep ocean floor to the surface of the moon, it is now possible to imagine humanity exploiting natural resources in environments that were previously inaccessible. These developments raise important legal questions. Are such spaces *terra nullius* subject to national acquisition? Should they be understood as an international commons or *res communis* similar to the high seas or Svalbard at the turn of the twentieth century – that is, subject to exploitation but not state sovereignty? Should the international

[69] League of Nations Covenant, 28 April 1919, art. 22; Aaron M. Margalith, *The International Mandates* (Baltimore: Johns Hopkins Press, 1930), p. 31.

[70] UN Charter art. 76. Many have argued that the Mandate and Trusteeship Systems merely perpetuated colonial domination. Antony Anghie, *Imperialism, Sovereignty, the Making of International Law* (Cambridge: Cambridge University Press, 2012), ch. 3. The last UN trusteeship – the Trust Territory of the Pacific Islands (Palau) – was dismantled in 1994. The United Nations and Decolonization: International Trusteeship System, www.un.org/dppa/decolonization/en/history/international-trusteeship-system-and-trust-territories.

[71] UNMIK Fact Sheet: 'United Nations Interim Mission in Kosovo', https://peacekeeping.un.org/en/mission/unmik#:~:text=Originally%2C%20the%20Security%20Council%2C%20by,under%20which%20the%20people%20of; Ralph Wilde, *International Territorial Administration: How Trusteeship and the Civilizing Mission Never Went Away* (Oxford: Oxford University Press, 2008), p. 155.

[72] The ICJ affirmed this responsibility for mandatory/trustee powers, in particular, in the South-West Africa Cases. See, e.g., Namibia, 1971 ICJ Rep. 16 (21 June); South West Africa Cases (Ethiopia v. South Africa, Liberia v. South Africa), Second Phase (SWA Second Phase), 1966 ICJ Rep. 6 (July 18).

community entrust these spaces to international institutions? Or would a different legal regime be preferable?

In 1963, the UN General Assembly addressed some of these issues in a *Declaration of Legal Principles Concerning the Activities of States in the Exploration and Use of Outer Space.*[73] "Desiring to contribute to broad international cooperation in the scientific as well as in the legal aspects of exploration and use of outer space for peaceful purposes," the General Assembly "[s]olemnly declare[d] that in the exploration and use of outer space States should be guided by the following principles":

1. The exploration and use of outer space shall be carried on for the benefit and in the interests of all mankind.
2. Outer space and celestial bodies are free for exploration and use by all States on a basis of equality and in accordance with international law.
3. Outer space and celestial bodies are not subject to national appropriation by claim of sovereignty, by means of use or occupation, or by any other means.
4. The activities of States in the exploration and use of outer space shall be carried on in accordance with international law, including the Charter of the United Nations, in the interest of maintaining international peace and security and promoting international cooperation and understanding.[74]

Through these principles, the General Assembly envisioned a new legal paradigm for outer space territory and resources. Like Svalbard in the late-nineteenth and early-twentieth centuries, resources in outer space would be "free for exploration and use" by all states without being subject to national appropriation. Unlike Svalbard, however, states would not be permitted to exploit resources in outer space exclusively for their own national gain. Any activities conducted in outer space would have to "be carried out for the benefit and in the interests of all mankind."[75]

A few years later, these principles were incorporated into the "Magna Carta of space law"[76] – the Outer Space Treaty of 1967.[77] The Outer Space

[73] Declaration of Legal Principles Concerning the Activities of States in the Exploration and Use of Outer Space, 13 Dec. 1963, UNGA Res 1962 (XVIII), A/RES/18/1962.
[74] Ibid. (one principle omitted).
[75] Ibid.
[76] Tanja Masson-Zwaan and Mahulena Hofmann, *Introduction to Space Law*, 4th ed. (Alphen aan den Rijn: Wolters Kluwer, 2019), p. 3.
[77] Treaty on Principles Governing the Activities of States in the Exploration and the Use of Outer Space, Including the Moon and Other Celestial Bodies, 27 January 1967, 610 UNTS 205 [hereinafter Outer Space Treaty].

Treaty declares "outer space, including the Moon and other celestial bodies," to be "the province of all mankind."[78] It affirms that outer space resources are "not subject to national appropriation by claim of sovereignty, by means of use or occupation, or by any other means."[79] Like the General Assembly principles, it also authorizes states to engage in "free ... exploration and use" of outer space resources on the basis of equality, while emphasizing that that these activities "shall be carried out for the benefit and in the interests of all countries, irrespective of their degree of economic or scientific development."[80] As of January 2025, the Outer Space Treaty has 116 states parties.[81]

International lawyers have debated what it means for states to explore and use the moon and other celestial bodies "for the benefit and in the interests of all countries," as required under the Outer Space Treaty. Some argue that resources harvested from outer space are the "common heritage of mankind" and therefore must be shared equitably with the rest of the international community.[82] The 1979 Moon Agreement endorses this position, declaring that resources from the moon are subject to "equitable sharing by all States Parties," including developing countries.[83] The Moon Agreement's legal authority is limited, however, by the fact that only seventeen states have ratified it and few states have accepted its contents as expressive of customary international law.[84] Some other international lawyers contend that the Outer Space Treaty declares space resources to be "the province of mankind" only with respect to "exploration and use," not exploitation. On this interpretation, outer space is a *res communis* comparable to the high seas, where states are free to take resources without sharing the benefits with other states as long as they respect other states' freedom to do likewise.[85] An

[78] Ibid. art. I.

[79] Ibid. art. II.

[80] Ibid. art. I.

[81] 'Status of International Agreements Relating to Activities in Outer Space', United Nations Office for Outer Space Affairs, www.unoosa.org/oosa/en/ourwork/spacelaw/treaties/status/index.html.

[82] Stephan Hobe and Kuan-Wei Chen, 'Legal Status of Outer Space and Celestial Bodies', in Ram S. Jakhu and Paul Stephen Dempsey (eds.), *Routledge Handbook of Space Law* (London: Routledge, 2017), pp. 25, 30 (asserting that customary international law "prohibits claims to ownership in outer space, unless an international regime for exploitation of the resources of the Moon and other celestial bodies is established").

[83] Agreement Governing the Activities of States on the Moon and Other Celestial Bodies, 5 December 1979, 1363 UNTS 3, art. 11(1), 11(7).

[84] Status of International Agreements; Joyner and Theis, *Eagle Over the Ice*, p. 164.

[85] Masson-Zwaan and Hofmann, *Introduction to Space Law*, pp. 35–36, 99. Under President Donald J. Trump, the United States rejected the common heritage position and essentially

intermediate view is that states are obligated to share benefits derived from their activities in outer space but it is up to them, and them alone, to determine how to do so in accordance with equitable principles.[86]

Regardless of how the international community defines the "common province of mankind," it is clear that the concept activates legal duties of international cooperation. States with active space programs cannot respect sovereign equality without recognizing the equal right of other states to explore, use, and benefit from outer space. At a minimum, this means that states may not interfere arbitrarily with other states' peaceful space programs. But the requirements of mandatory cooperation do not end there: states must also notify and consult with one another about their space activities, share information, render assistance, and seek to resolve disputes through peaceful cooperation. In this spirit, the Outer Space Treaty requires states-parties to practice "cooperation and mutual assistance" and "conduct all their activities . . . with due regard to the corresponding interests of all other States Parties."[87]

The "common heritage of humanity" concept has achieved broader acceptance in another area: the deep seabed. In 1966, US President Lyndon Johnson gave a speech in which he argued that "the prospects of rich harvest and mineral wealth" from the deep seafloor should not be allowed "to create a new form of colonial competition among maritime nations . . . We must ensure that the deep seas and ocean bottom are, and remain, the legacy of all human beings."[88] A year later, Maltese Ambassador Arvid Pardo echoed these sentiments in a celebrated address to the General Assembly, proposing that resources in the deep seabed be

endorsed the *res communis*/high seas position. Donald J. Trump, 'Executive Order on Encouraging International Support for the Recovery and Use of Space Resources', White House Press Release, 6 April 2020 (rejecting the Moon Agreement and declaring that "it shall be the policy of the United States to encourage international support for the public and private recovery and use of resources in outer space, consistent with applicable law").

86 Jennifer Frakes, 'The Common Heritage of Mankind Principle and the Deep Seabed, Outer Space and Antarctica: Will Developed and Developing Nations Reach a Compromise?' (2003) 21 *Wisc. J. Int'l L.* 409, 412.

87 Outer Space Treaty, art. IX. The General Assembly has reaffirmed these principles repeatedly, placing particular emphasis on the need for "exploration and use of outer space" to proceed "on an equitable and mutually acceptable basis," affording due regard to the interests of other states, including developing nations. Declaration on International Cooperation in the Exploration and Use of Outer Space for the Benefit and in the Interest of All States, Taking into Particular Account the Needs of Developing Countries, 4 February 1997, UNGA Res. 51/122, A/RES/51/122, para. 1.

88 Joyner and Theis, *Eagle Over the Ice*, p. 163.

recognized as the common heritage of humanity.[89] The General Assembly unanimously endorsed this proposal in 1970, declaring the deep seabed the common heritage of humanity and therefore not subject to national appropriation. To facilitate the seabed's exploitation, the General Assembly called for an international regime that would "ensure equitable sharing by States in the benefits derived therefrom."[90] All of these elements of Part XI of the General Assembly's proposal would later be incorporated into the 1982 UN Convention on the Law of the Sea (UNCLOS).[91] Once the international community designated the deep seabed as the common heritage of humanity – a resource vested in humanity "as a whole" and exempt from national appropriation – the necessary consequence was that states were obligated to cooperate with one another to achieve mutually acceptable solutions in accordance with equitable principles.

One final example of common heritage resources deserves special mention: cultural heritage sites. Under contemporary international law, significant cultural sites and natural wonders, such as India's Taj Mahal, the Great Wall of China, and Victoria Falls in Zambia/Zimbabwe, are governed by a series of international agreements that include UNCLOS[92] and various treaties adopted under the auspices of the UN Educational, Scientific, and Cultural Organization (UNESCO).[93] These conventions require states not only to protect cultural heritage sites, but also to cooperate with one another for this purpose, suggesting that the preservation of cultural heritage is a joint-stewardship responsibility of the entire international community.[94] Duties to cooperate in preserving cultural heritage do not deprive states of their sovereign authority over sites within their territory. Instead, they constrain how national authorities may exercise their sovereign rights over cultural heritage sites to

89 Ibid.

90 Declaration of Principles Governing the Sea-Bed and the Ocean Floor, and the Subsoil Thereof, Beyond the Limits of National Jurisdiction, 17 December 1970, UNGA Res. 2749 (XXV).

91 United Nations Convention on the Law of the Sea, Montego Bay, 10 December 1982, 1833 UNTS 397, part. XI [hereinafter UNCLOS].

92 Ibid. arts. 149, 303.

93 Convention for the Protection of Cultural Property in the Event of Armed Conflicts, 14 May 1954, 249 UNTS 240; Convention Concerning the Protection of the World Cultural and Natural Heritage, 16 November 1972, 27 UST 37, pmbl. [World Heritage Convention]; UNESCO Convention on the Protection of the Underwater Cultural Heritage, 2 November 2001, 41 ILM 40 [hereinafter Underwater Cultural Heritage Convention].

94 UNCLOS art. 303(1); Underwater Cultural Heritage Convention, art. 19(1); World Heritage Convention, art. 6.

ensure that they fulfill their joint-stewardship responsibilities and respect the interests of humanity as a whole. In this sense, states' duties to cooperate for the preservation of cultural heritage sites are similar to the equitable obligations that govern international rivers (see Chapter 2) and landlocked states (see Chapter 4).

Looking to the Future

Each of the case studies discussed in this chapter reflect a transition from legal frameworks involving unilateral state action (e.g., *terra nullius*, unregulated *res communis*) to legal frameworks that require multilateral cooperation (e.g., agreements guaranteeing equitable use and apportionment of resources). In Antarctica, states embraced multilateralism, in part, because international law did not permit them to resolve disputed claims or potential future claims unilaterally. Given the serious uncertainty over what constitutes effective occupation for Antarctica, no state could establish its territorial sovereignty unilaterally without violating the principle of sovereign equality. A lawful and legitimate solution to the Antarctica controversy therefore required cooperation. Similarly, once the international community designated the moon and other celestial bodies, the deep seabed, and cultural heritage sites as common concerns of humanity, it followed that states were required to cooperate with one another to regulate these spaces in accordance with equitable principles.

Time will tell whether this shift in international law is durable. A common characteristic of Antarctica, the deep seabed, and the moon is that they are all extreme environments where the commercial exploitation of natural resources is not yet financially viable on a large scale. As technology advances, humanity may well face conditions that invite a new colonial era of unilateralism at the South Pole, on the ocean floor, or in outer space. With the ATS's expiration date on the horizon and global warming exposing more of the continent and its surrounding waters to drilling and mining, the future of Antarctica hangs in the balance. If states simply allow the ATS to lapse without replacing it with a new legal framework, this could spark a race to establish territorial control through unilateral displays of force and occupation, undermining international peace and security. Alternatively, the international community could pursue other options that would better respect sovereign equality under international law. For example, claimant states could cooperate with non-claimant states to recognize Antarctica as the common heritage of humanity, designating it as a "world park" under the administration of an international organization. This is the preferred outcome of the Organization of African Unity and G-77 developing states.[95] Whatever the future holds, the key point for present purposes is that international law obligates states to resolve the Antarctic sovereignty question through peaceful cooperation in accordance with equitable principles.

[95] See Moritaka Hayashi, 'The Antarctica Question in the United Nations' (1986) 19 *Cornell Int'l L.J.* 275 (discussing the OAU's 1985 declaration proclaiming Antarctica a "common heritage of mankind"); Michael T. Kyriak, 'The Future of the Antarctic Treaty System: An Examination and Evaluation of the "Common Heritage" and "World Park" Proposals for an Alternate Antarctic Regime' (1992) 7 *Auckland U. L. Rev.* 105 (discussing the G-77 proposal to designate Antarctica as a "World Park").

9

Peace, Security, and Human Rights

The Federation of the World

On June 25, 1945, a hulking C-54 military transport plane descended through foggy skies to touch down at Hamilton Airforce Base north of San Francisco. Waiting on the tarmac were US Secretary of State Edward Stettinius, California Governor Earl Warren, and the heads of forty-nine foreign delegations from around the world.[1] As a military guard saluted and a brass band played, US President Harry Truman emerged from the plane wearing a grey double-breasted suit, a blue bowtie, and an exultant smile. Although war with Japan raged on in the Pacific, Truman's spirits were high, and for good reason. He had come to witness the birth of a new world order – one intended to end war for generations to come.

Nine weeks earlier, diplomats and heads of state had gathered in San Francisco at the invitation of Truman's predecessor, Franklin Roosevelt, with an ambitious goal: to lay the foundation for a peaceful postwar order.[2] Almost overnight, the City by the Bay cast aside years of wartime austerity, exchanging food rationing and blackouts for decadent parties awash with light and music, where foreign diplomats rubbed shoulders with Hollywood stars. Reporters from around the world descended in record numbers, including the young Navy hero and future US president, John Kennedy. While the press flocked to the conference's plenary sessions at the stately San Francisco Opera House, the most consequential proceedings took place across town in Secretary Stettinius's penthouse

[1] Stephen C. Schlesinger, *Act of Creation: The Founding of the United Nations* (Boulder: Westview Press, 2003), p. 252.

[2] Roosevelt envisioned the birth of this new international organization as the crowning achievement of his presidency. Just thirteen days before the San Francisco Conference was to begin, however, Roosevelt suddenly collapsed and died while working on his speech for the Conference. David L. Bosco, *Five to Rule Them All: The UN Security Council and the Making of the Modern World* (Oxford: Oxford University Press, 2009), p. 32.

suite at the Fairmont Hotel on Nob Hill.[3] Representatives of the "Big Five" – China, France, the Soviet Union, the United Kingdom, and the United States – met daily to hammer out the final details of a plan, announced two years earlier in Moscow, for "a general international organization, based on the principle of sovereign equality of all peace-loving states, and open to membership by all such states, large and small, for the maintenance of international peace and security."[4]

Truman championed the conference's agenda. From his youth, Truman had carried in his wallet a folded copy of several stanzas from a favorite poem by Lord Tennyson that envisioned international cooperation fostering a more peaceful world:

For I dipt into the future, far as human eye could see,
Saw the Vision of the world, and all the wonder that would be;

Saw the heavens fill with commerce, argosies of magic sails,
Pilots of the purple twilight dropping down with costly bales;

Heard the heavens fill with shouting, and there rain'd a ghastly dew
From the nations' airy navies grappling in the central blue;

Far along the world-wide whisper of the south-wind rushing warm,
With the standards of the peoples plunging thro' the thunder-storm;

Till the war-drum throbb'd no longer, and the battle-flags were furl'd
In the Parliament of man, the Federation of the world.

There the common sense of most shall hold a fretful realm in awe,
And the kindly earth shall slumber, lapt in universal law.[5]

In the months preceding the San Francisco Conference, Truman had urged his compatriots to embrace this vision of a "Federation of the world" as the formula for enduring peace and security.[6] "The policy we hope and believe will emerge from the San Francisco Conference and others to follow will embody cooperation among nations to keep down aggressors," he explained to an audience in his home state of Missouri.

3 Edward Epstein, 'When Nations United: The Historic Gathering of Delegates from 50 Countries to Sign the U.N. Charter Half a Century Ago Was One of San Francisco's Finest Hours', San Francisco Gate, 23 April 2019.

4 Joint Four-Nation Declaration Moscow Conference, US-UK-USSR-China, 30 October 1943, para. 4.

5 Schlesinger, 'Act of Creation', pp. 7, 9 (quoting Alfred, Lloyd Tennyson, *Lockesley Hall* (1842)).

6 Tennyson, of course, channeled Immanuel Kant's proposal for a federation of states in *Perpetual Peace: A Philosophical Essay* (1795).

"The only rational alternative to existing anarchy lies in some reasonable form of international organization among so-called sovereign states."[7]

Thus, it was with great excitement that Truman arrived in San Francisco to join the final sessions of the conference. After greeting the assembled dignitaries, Truman led a motorcade of nearly a hundred limousines flanked by motorcycle police across the Golden Gate Bridge, where 500,000 residents – the largest crowd in the city's history – gathered to cheer on the procession.[8] Later that evening, thousands packed into the Opera House to see the fifty national delegations rise from their seats to adopt the Charter of the United Nations unanimously.[9]

The following day, as delegates reassembled for the Charter's signing ceremony, the conference's secretary-general, Alger Hiss, praised the participants for changing the course of history. He reminded them that the Charter affirms the proposition that "we all have to recognize – no matter how great our strength – that we must deny ourselves the license to do always as we please . . . This is the price which each nation will have to pay for world peace."[10] Truman then rose to underscore the importance of international cooperation to ensure the venture's ultimate success. He declared: "We have tested the principle of cooperation in this war, and we have found it works."[11]

Eighty years later, the Charter's ambitious framework for international cooperation remains formally intact, but its promise only partly fulfilled.[12]

[7] Schlesinger, *Act of Creation*, p. 7.

[8] Ibid. p. 253.

[9] Ibid. p. 254.

[10] Ibid. p. 256 (citing *New York Times*, 27 June 1945).

[11] Ibid.

[12] Although this chapter for brevity's sake focuses on the UN Charter and other international agreements with universal or near-universal membership, we recognize that mandatory cooperation also features prominently in and arguably operates more effectively through regional regimes. See, e.g., Organization of American States' American Treaty on Pacific Settlement, 30 April 1948, OAS Treaty Series No. 17 & 61 (establishing mandatory procedures for pacific dispute settlement); Inter-American Treaty of Reciprocal Assistance arts. 2 & 3(1), TIAS No. 1838, 21 UNTS 77 (committing states-parties "to submit every controversy which may arise between them to methods of peaceful settlement," as well as to "assist in meeting [an] attack [against another member state] in the exercise of . . . collective self defense"); Revised Treaty of the Economic Community of West African States (ECOWAS) art. 4, 24 July 1993, 2373 UNTS 233 (affirming the principles of "inter-State co-operation," "promotion and strengthening of good neighborliness," and "peaceful settlement of disputes"); ibid. arts. 56, 58 (requiring international cooperation for regional security). A more comprehensive survey of mandatory cooperation for collective security and human rights would require further attention to regional international law.

Mandatory cooperation under the Charter entails essentially the same legal requirements as in other domains where it arises: states must consult, evaluate risks, share relevant information, and pursue peaceful dispute resolution with one another. When threats to peace and security emerge, states must cooperate through the United Nations to keep "a fretful realm in awe." In addition, states must work together to address the root causes of human immiseration which undermine international peace and security, including atrocity crimes and global poverty. If the United Nations has struggled to deliver international peace and security and universal respect for human rights, the fault lies in large measure with states that have defaulted on their obligations of mandatory cooperation.

Uniting for International Peace and Security

Just as international cooperation at the San Francisco Conference gave birth to the United Nations, the Charter relies on international cooperation "to save succeeding generations from the scourge of war" and to "reaffirm faith in fundamental human rights, in the dignity and worth of the human person," and "in the equal rights of men and women and of nations large and small."[13] In the Charter's preamble, UN member states express their determination "to practice tolerance and to live together in peace with one another as good neighbours."[14] Article 2(4) obligates them to "refrain in their international relations from the threat or use of force against the territorial integrity or political independence of any state, or in any other manner inconsistent with the Purposes of the United Nations."[15] When international disputes arise, states must strive "in good faith" to resolve their differences "by peaceful means in such a manner that international peace and security, and justice, are not endangered."[16] These requirements of mandatory cooperation safeguard the sovereign equality of individual UN member states[17] while also

[13] UN Charter, 24 October 1945, 1 UNTS XVI, pmbl.

[14] Ibid.

[15] Ibid. art. 2(4). This article reaffirmed states' earlier pledge in the Kellogg-Briand Pact to "condemn recourse to war for the solution of international controversies, and renounce it, as an instrument of national policy in their relations with one another." General Treaty for Renunciation of War as an Instrument of National Policy, 27 August 1928, 46 Stat. 2343, art. 1.

[16] UN Charter, art. 2(2)–(3).

[17] See Leland M. Goodrich and Edvard Hambro, *Charter of the United Nations: Commentary and Documents* (Boston: World Peace Foundation, 1946), p. 48 (explaining

attending to the international community's collective interest in preserving a peaceful world order.[18]

Recognizing that states might be tempted to violate these obligations, the Charter establishes the United Nations as a secondary guarantor of international peace and security. The preamble conveys the international community's aspiration "to unite our strength" to preserve the peace, thereby ensuring "that armed force shall not be used, save in the common interest."[19] To this end, Article 1 specifies four general purposes of the United Nations:

1. To maintain international peace and security, and to that end: to take effective collective measures for the prevention and removal of threats to the peace, and for the suppression of acts of aggression or other breaches of the peace, and to bring about by peaceful means, and in conformity with the principles of justice and international law, adjustment or settlement of international disputes or situations which might lead to a breach of the peace;
2. To develop friendly relations among nations based on respect for the principle of equal rights and self-determination of peoples, and to take other appropriate measures to strengthen universal peace;
3. To achieve international co-operation in solving international problems of an economic, social, cultural, or humanitarian character, and in promoting and encouraging respect for human rights and for fundamental freedoms for all without distinction as to race, sex, language, or religion; and
4. To be a centre for harmonizing the actions of nations in the attainment of these common ends.[20]

The Charter tasks the Security Council with coordinating the United Nations' efforts to preserve international peace and security.[21] Some of

that the Charter is "an instrument of cooperation between the Members of the United Nations Organization who, according to the first principle of Article 2, retain their 'sovereign equality'").

[18] See Heike Krieger, 'Rights and Obligations of Third Parties in Armed Conflicts', in Eyal Benvenisti and Georg Nolte (eds.), *Community Interests Across International Law* (Oxford: Oxford University Press, 2018), pp. 448, 452 (observing that "the protection of states and their sovereignty from military attacks is seen as part of the community interest to protect international peace and security, the realization of which is entrusted to the Security Council").

[19] Ibid. pmbl.

[20] UN Charter, art. 1.

[21] Ibid. art. 24. A familiar critique of the Charter is that it violates the principle of sovereign equality by conferring veto power on the Security Council's five permanent members (P5) – China, France, Russia, the United Kingdom, and the United States. We discuss in Chapter 12 the P5's veto and its challenge to the legitimacy of international legal order.

the Security Council's powers relate to encouraging states to settle their disputes through peaceful cooperation. For example, the Security Council may call upon states to embrace negotiation, mediation, conciliation, arbitration, adjudication, or other peaceful means of dispute resolution.[22] If these efforts fail, states must refer their disputes to the Security Council so that it can "recommend such terms of settlement as it considers appropriate."[23] The Security Council may also take action on its own initiative to investigate "any situation which might lead to international friction or give rise to a dispute, in order to determine whether the continuance of the dispute or situation is likely to endanger the maintenance of international peace and security."[24]

Chapter VII of the Charter empowers the Security Council to compel recalcitrant states to take whatever steps it deems necessary to maintain international peace and security. When the Security Council identifies a threat to the peace, a breach of the peace, or an act of aggression, it may not only "make recommendations" to states but also "decide what measures shall be taken ... to maintain or restore international peace and security."[25] This may include provisional measures "to prevent an aggravation of the situation" or coercive "measures not involving the use of force" (e.g., economic sanctions, travel bans).[26] The Security Council may even authorize using military force to preserve or restore international peace and security (e.g., naval blockades, air strikes, peacekeeping, and peacebuilding missions).[27]

Significantly, the Charter obligates *all* states to cooperate with the Security Council's efforts to prevent and suppress threats to international peace and security – not just those directly responsible for the threats. Under Article 25, "Members of the United Nations agree to accept and carry out the decisions of the Security Council."[28] States also pledge in Article 2(5) "to give the United Nations every assistance in any action it takes" to maintain international peace and security, as well as to "refrain from giving assistance to any state against which the United Nations is taking preventive or enforcement action."[29] States that violate these

22 UN Charter, art. 33(2).
23 Ibid. art. 37.
24 Ibid. art. 34.
25 Ibid. art. 39.
26 Ibid. arts. 40–41.
27 Ibid. art. 42.
28 Ibid. art. 25.
29 Ibid. art. 2(5); see also ibid. art. 43 ("All Members of the United Nations ... undertake to make available to the Security Council, on its call and in accordance with special

obligations expose themselves to international censure, as well as sanctions and other coercive measures, as directed by the Security Council.[30] Thus, when the Security Council finds a threat to the peace or a breach of the peace, all states are obligated under the Charter to follow its lead.[31]

In its landmark 1970 Declaration on Principles of International Law Concerning Friendly Relations and Co-operation Among States in Accordance with the Charter of the United Nations (Friendly Relations Declaration), the UN General Assembly affirmed that states bear due diligence obligations to promote the Charter's general purposes. In particular, the Friendly Relations Declaration states that "[a]ll states shall comply in good faith with their obligations under the generally recognized principles and rules of international law with respect to the maintenance of international peace and security, and shall endeavor to make the United Nations security system based on the Charter more effective."[32] Hence, states must settle their disputes peacefully "on the basis of the sovereign equality of States and in accordance with the principle of free choice of means" and cooperate with other states and the United Nations to maintain international peace and security.[33]

Some international lawyers might object that the Charter's cooperative framework for collective security is undermined by Article 51, which permits states to defend themselves from attack without awaiting

agreement or agreements, armed forces, assistance, facilities, including rights of passage, necessary for the purpose of maintaining international peace and security."); art. 49 (requiring states to "join in affording mutual assistance in carrying out the measures decided upon by the Security Council").

30 Ibid. arts. 39–42.

31 The UN General Assembly has also declared that if, due to "lack of unanimity of the permanent members," the Security Council "fails to exercise its primary responsibility for the maintenance of international peace and security . . . the General Assembly shall consider the matter immediately with a view to making appropriate recommendations to Members for collective measures, including in the case of a breach of the peace or act of aggression the use of armed force when necessary, to maintain or restore international peace and security." Uniting for Peace, 3 Nov. 1950, GA Res. 377A(V); see also Michael P. Scharf, 'Power Shift: The Return of the Uniting for Peace Resolution' (2023) 55 *Case W. J. Int'l L.* 1, 7–10 (observing that the General Assembly has used the Uniting for Peace mechanism about a dozen times between 1951 and 2022). Unlike Security Council resolutions, General Assembly declarations under the Uniting for Peace framework are not formally binding on member states.

32 Declaration on Principles of International Law Concerning Friendly Relations and Co-operation among States in Accordance with the Charter of the United Nations, 24 October 1970, GA Res. 2625(XXV) [hereinafter Friendly Relations Declaration].

33 Ibid.

Security Council authorization.[34] In principle, however, a state's "inherent right" of self-defense under Article 51 is compatible with the Charter's commitment to mandatory cooperation through the United Nations.[35] Article 51 authorizes self-defense only when an actual or imminent attack has already ruptured international peace and security and only until the Security Council intercedes.[36] The Charter stipulates that an act of "self-defense shall be immediately reported to the Security Council and shall not in any way affect the authority and responsibility of the Security Council" to prescribe a multilateral response.[37] Self-defense under Article 51 is also subject to customary requirements of necessity and proportionality, which require states to consider the impact of their defensive measures on foreign interests.[38] Therefore, even when states act in self-defense, international law channels their response through multilateral norms and processes to prevent states from using force "save in the common interest" to liberate humanity "from the scourge of war."[39]

An Early Victory

Less than two months after the San Francisco Conference, the United Nations received an early stress test in Indonesia. On the morning of August 7, 1945 – two days after the surrender of Japan's occupying forces – Indonesian nationalist republicans assembled at the home of their leader, Sukarno, in Djakarta. Sukarno read from a slip of paper: "We the Indonesian people proclaim the independence of Indonesia." He then stood at attention while a simple red-and-white flag rose into the sky, asserting the birth of a new state – one that demanded independence not only from Japan but also from its British "liberators" and the Dutch

[34] See ibid. art. 51 ("Nothing in the present Charter shall impair the inherent right of individual or collective self-defence if an armed attack occurs against a Member of the United Nations, until the Security Council has taken measures necessary to maintain international peace and security.").

[35] Ibid.

[36] Ibid. Although the Charter does not expressly address imminent attacks, conventional wisdom holds that Article 51 permits self-defense in response to imminent attacks. See, e.g., Christine Gray, *International Law and the Use of Force*, 3rd ed. (Oxford: Oxford University Press, 2008), p. 161; Yoram Dinstein, *War, Aggression and Self-Defence*, 3rd ed. (Cambridge: Cambridge University Press, 2001), p. 168.

[37] UN Charter, art. 51.

[38] See William C. Banks and Evan J. Criddle, 'Customary Constraints on the Use of Force: Article 51 with an American Accent' (2016) 29 LJIL 67, 74–76.

[39] UN Charter, pmbl.

colonialists who had governed before the war.[40] Before long, hostilities broke out between Indonesia's independence movement and British occupying forces. Meanwhile, the Netherlands readied plans for its own military action to retake the Indonesian archipelago.[41]

Such were the circumstances in Indonesia in January 1946, when the Security Council gathered for its first session at Church House, its temporary London headquarters near Westminster Abbey. On the agenda were several pressing topics, including a proposal from Ukraine to address the escalating violence in Indonesia. Ukraine accused Japan and the United Kingdom of threatening international peace and security by occupying Indonesia illegally and conducting military operations against Indonesian civilians. The British vigorously disputed these charges, insisting that they had no intention of remaining in Indonesia and were simply trying to restore order and protect their troops from attack pending an orderly withdrawal.[42] Although the United Kingdom formally recognized Dutch sovereignty over Indonesia, British leaders attempted to prevent the Dutch from landing in Java and Sumatra and sought to broker a peaceful settlement between the Netherlands and Indonesian republicans.[43]

Ukraine's proposal for Security Council action on Indonesia came up short of the necessary votes. However, when negotiations between the Netherlands and the Indonesian independence movement collapsed, prompting the Dutch to attempt to reestablish colonial rule by force, the Security Council revisited the matter at the request of Australia and India.[44] The Netherlands, which then occupied a non-permanent seat on the Security Council, argued that the United Nations lacked jurisdiction to intercede because Indonesia fell within the Netherlands' sovereign jurisdiction, making the issue a matter of exclusively domestic concern.[45] No other Security Council member accepted this argument. Instead, on August 1, 1947, the Security Council, for the first time in its history, adopted a resolution demanding a ceasefire and calling on the

40 Evan Luard, *A History of the United Nations Volume 1: The Years of Western Domination, 1945-1955* (Oxford: Oxford University Press, 1982), pp. 132–133; Alistair M. Taylor, *Indonesian Independence and the United Nations* (Westport: Greenwood Press, 1960), pp. 3, 8–9.

41 Taylor, 'Indonesian Independence and the United Nations', pp. 8–12.

42 The Indonesian Question, UN Security Council, 7 February 1946, S/PV.12, pp. 174–182.

43 Luard, 'A History of the United Nations', pp. 132–133.

44 Ibid. p. 135; Taylor, 'Indonesian Independence and the United Nations', pp. 47–49.

45 See Luard, 'A History of the United Nations', p. 136.

parties to settle their dispute by arbitration or other peaceful means.[46] Within days, both sides complied with the Security Council's directive.[47] The *New York Times* reported "that the United Nations had probably won its first major victory and through this victory had given the new international organization a sorely needed boost in prestige."[48]

The next several years in Indonesia witnessed recurring cycles of negotiation, violent clashes, and UN-brokered ceasefires. The Security Council demanded that the Netherlands and Indonesian republicans cooperate with an international mission established to investigate and mediate their dispute.[49] After the Security Council set a timetable for Indonesian independence, the Netherlands eventually agreed to withdraw its military and formally transferred sovereignty to the Indonesian state on December 27, 1949.[50] International cooperation through the Security Council thus ended violent conflict and Dutch colonial rule, paving the way for international recognition of the sovereign Republic of Indonesia. On September 28, 1950, Indonesia became the sixtieth member of the United Nations.[51]

Collective Enforcement in Fits and Starts

The Security Council's engagement with Indonesia offered proof of concept that mandatory cooperation through the United Nations could perform a constructive role in maintaining international peace and security. The Security Council used various tools to achieve a peaceful settlement in Indonesia, including consultation, investigation, mediation, and legally binding resolutions. Encouraged by the preliminary results, the Security Council over the next several years applied these and other tools (albeit with mixed results) in various conflict zones, including the Balkans, Greece, Kashmir, and Palestine.[52] Among the Security Council's early efforts at crisis management, however, it was the

[46] UN Security Council Resolution 27 (The Indonesian Question), 1 August 1947, S/RES/27; Luard, 'A History of the United Nations', p. 136.

[47] Taylor, 'Indonesian Independence and the United Nations', p. 51.

[48] Ibid. (quoting George Barrett, 'U.N. Circles Happy over Java Action,' NY Times, 4 August 1947).

[49] Luard, 'A History of the United Nations', pp. 139, 142–145.

[50] Taylor, 'Indonesian Independence and the United Nations', p. 264.

[51] Ibid. p. 265.

[52] Luard, 'A History of the United Nations', pp. 121–123; Ramesh Thakur, *The United Nations, Peace and Security* (Cambridge: Cambridge University Press, 2006), p. 35.

Korean War that most seriously tested the Charter's framework for mandatory cooperation.

When North Korea invaded South Korea on June 25, 1950, it committed the kind of unprovoked aggression that the Charter's drafters had in mind when they outlawed the "use of force against the territorial integrity or political independence of any state."[53] The United States requested a meeting of the Security Council and circulated a draft resolution condemning the North Korean attack. The draft demanded North Korea's immediate and total withdrawal and called upon "all Member States to render every assistance to the United Nations in the execution of this resolution and refrain from giving assistance to the North Korean authorities."[54] With the People's Republic of China not represented at the Security Council (the seat designated for China was occupied by Taipei rather than Beijing) and the Soviet Union boycotting the United Nations, the United States' draft sailed through the Security Council to become Resolution 82.[55] Two days later, the Security Council recommended that UN member states "furnish such assistance to the Republic of Korea as may be necessary to repel the armed attack and to restore international peace and security in the area."[56] For the first time in its history, the Security Council had invited states to defend a state under attack.[57] By mid-September 1950, fourteen states had contributed ground forces to South Korea's defense, and dozens of others had furnished material assistance.[58]

Whatever hopes the United States and its allies may have placed in the Security Council to rally international cooperation against North Korean aggression, the limits of this strategy soon became apparent. In Resolution 82 and subsequent resolutions, the Security Council stopped short of mandating bystander state cooperation under Articles 40–42 of the Charter. Once the Soviet Union resumed participating in Security Council meetings, its veto power prevented the Security Council from further addressing the Korean War. As a result, the Security Council lost

53 UN Charter, art. 2(4).

54 UN Security Council Resolution 82 [Complaint of Aggression upon the Republic of Korea], 25 June 1950, S/RES/82; Luard, 'A History of the United Nations', p. 240.

55 Wilson Centre, 'The Lost Battle: The Soviet Union and the United Nations under Stalin, 1945–1953', Wilson Center, 13 March 2006; Bosco, *Five to Rule them All*, p. 55.

56 UN Security Council Resolution 83 (Complaint of Aggression upon the Republic of Korea), 27 June 1950, S/RES/83.

57 Ibid. p. 241.

58 Luard, 'A History of the United Nations', pp. 241–243.

meaningful supervisory control over South Korea's collective defense.[59] Just five years removed from the halcyon days of the San Francisco Conference, several of the "Big Five" states that had brought the UN Charter into the world already found themselves on opposite sides of a bloody conflict.

The incipient Cold War tensions that fueled the Korean War significantly impacted the Security Council as an institution. For the next four decades, the Security Council rarely mustered the votes necessary to respond to threats to international peace and security. However, the Security Council often invited states to cooperate in peaceful dispute resolution, and it occasionally deployed peacekeeping missions to conflict zones.[60] For example, in the United Nations' first formal peacekeeping mission (UNEF I), international peacekeepers helped to defuse the 1956 Suez Crisis by supervising the orderly withdrawal of British, French, and Israeli armed forces from Egypt.[61] A decade later, the Security Council, for the first time, imposed mandatory economic sanctions against Southern Rhodesia (present-day Zimbabwe) to compel its white-dominated apartheid government to relinquish power.[62] These measures demonstrated the United Nations' potential to galvanize international cooperation for international peace and security. More often than not, however, hardened rivalries among the Security Council's P5 hamstrung the Security Council's ability to prevent and suppress violent conflicts worldwide. Perhaps the Security Council's primary contribution during this era, therefore, was simply to foster dialogue, reducing the risks of misunderstanding and direct military confrontation among the world's great powers.[63]

[59] Bosco, *Five to Rule Them All*, pp. 60–63.

[60] The United Nations conducted fourteen peacekeeping missions between 1945 and 1987. Alex J. Bellamy, Paul Williams and Stuart Griffin, *Understanding Peacekeeping* (Cambridge: Polity Press, 2004), p. 72.

[61] 'Middle East–UNEF I', United Nations, https://peacekeeping.un.org/en/mission/past/unef1mandate.html. This first peacekeeping mission was deployed by the Secretary-General at the invitation of the UN General Assembly pursuant to "Uniting for Peace" procedures, not by the Security Council. UN GA Res.–First Emergency Special Session, 7 November 1956, A/RES/1001(ES-1).

[62] UN Security Council Resolution 232 (Southern Rhodesia), 16 December 1966, S/RES/232.

[63] Ibid. p. 74 (discussing insights from Adam Roberts and Benedict Kingsbury, 'Introduction: The UN's Roles in International Society', in Adam Roberts and Benedict Kingsbury (eds.), *United Nations, Divided World*, 2nd ed. (Oxford: Oxford University Press, 2000), pp. 1, 41).

As relations among the P5 began to thaw in the late 1980s, the Security Council became more assertive in countering threats to international peace and security. When Iraq invaded Kuwait in August 1990, the Security Council held an emergency meeting and quickly passed a resolution ordering Iraq to withdraw "immediately and unconditionally."[64] Hard on the heels of this resolution came additional directives, urged by the United States and the United Kingdom but supported by most other states, declaring the annexation of Kuwait null and void, imposing a comprehensive sanctions regime on Iraq, and establishing a special committee to monitor compliance.[65] By the end of November, the Security Council invoked its authority under Chapter VII of the Charter and gave Iraq until January 15, 1991, to withdraw from Kuwait. The Security Council authorized other states to use "all necessary means" – including military action – to expel Iraq once the deadline for voluntary withdrawal passed.[66] Backed by the Security Council, a coalition of thirty-six nations proceeded to drive the Iraqi army from Kuwait through several weeks of aerial bombardment and an intense but brief 100-hour ground campaign.[67]

In 2003, the United States led a second military campaign against Iraq with significantly less international support. In the lead up to the war, the United States sent Secretary of State Colin Powell to the United Nations to make the case for military action to topple the regime of Saddam Hussein. Powell testified based on faulty evidence that "the facts and Iraq's behavior show that Saddam Hussein and his regime are concealing their efforts to produce more weapons of mass destruction."[68] With a majority of the Security Council including Russia and France opposed to military action in Iraq, the United States, United Kingdom, and Spain abandoned last-ditch efforts to win UN backing, with British

[64] UN Security Council Resolution 660 (Iraq-Kuwait), 2 August 1990, S/RES/660.

[65] UN Security Council Resolution 662 (Iraq-Kuwait), 9 August 1990, S/RES/662; UN Security Council Resolution 661 (Iraq-Kuwait), 6 August 1991, S/RES/661.

[66] UN Security Council Resolution 678, 29 November 1990, S/RES/678 (adopted by a vote of 12–2, with China abstaining).

[67] Roger Normand and Chris de Jochnick, 'The Legitimation of Violence: A Critical Appraisal of the Gulf War' (1994) 35 HILJ 387, 389–390.

[68] Colin L. Powell, 'Remarks to the United Nations Security Council', US Dep't of State Archive, 5 February 2003. In the months following the invasion, no stockpiles of weapons of mass destruction were found, and the evidence on which Powell's testimony relied was revealed to be "seriously flawed." Parliament, House of Commons, 'Review of Intelligence on Weapons of Mass Destruction' (London: The Stationary Office, 2004), p. 101, para. 409.

Ambassador Jeremy Greenstock advising that the trio "reserve their right to take their own steps to secure the disarmament of Iraq."[69] While the Security Council did not authorize military action against Iraq in 2003, it also proved incapable of thwarting two Great Powers from using military force to impose regime change and a lengthy occupation on Iraq. The Iraq War is a potent reminder that the effectiveness of the UN system depends on the willingness of its more powerful members to abide by its Charter and international law generally.

Cooperating to Respect, Protect, and Fulfill Human Rights

Since the 1990s, the Security Council has devoted increasing attention to preventing and suppressing human rights crises around the world. The groundwork for this effort was laid during the San Francisco Conference. Recall that a core purpose of the United Nations, as set forth in Article 1 of the Charter, is to "achieve international co-operation in solving international problems of an economic, social, cultural, or humanitarian character, and in promoting and encouraging respect for human rights and for fundamental freedoms for all without distinction as to race, sex, language, or religion."[70] The drafters of the Charter believed that these "conditions of stability and well-being" within states were an essential prerequisite for "peaceful and friendly relations among nations based on the principle of equal rights and self-determination of peoples."[71] States are primarily responsible under the Charter for ensuring that their people enjoy the full protection of international human rights within their respective jurisdictions. Under Articles 55 and 56, however, they also "pledge themselves to take joint ... action in co-operation with the [United Nations]"[72] to guarantee "universal respect for, and observance of, human rights and fundamental freedoms for all."[73] Thus, just as states must cooperate with the Security Council's efforts to maintain international peace and security, the Charter also requires states to cooperate

69 'US, Britain and Spain Abandon Resolution', Associated Press, 17 March 2003.
70 UN Charter, art. 1(3).
71 Goodrich and Hambro, 'Charter of the United Nations', p. 39; see also Schlesinger, 'Act of Creation', p. 48 (observing that ECOSOC was designed to address "the causes of war, such as poverty and famine").
72 UN Charter, art. 56.
73 Ibid. art. 55; see also Friendly Relations Declaration ("Every state has a duty to promote through joint and separate action universal respect for and observance of human rights and fundamental freedoms in accordance with the Charter.").

with one another and the United Nations to protect and fulfill human rights worldwide.

Early in the United Nations' history, states worked through the General Assembly and the UN Economic and Social Council (ECOSOC) to specify international human rights norms in landmark agreements, such as the Universal Declaration of Human Rights,[74] the International Covenant on Civil and Political Rights,[75] and the International Covenant on Economic, Social and Cultural Rights (ICESCR).[76] Over the past several decades, however, the United Nations' focus generally has shifted from norm-specification and legal codification to securing compliance with established human rights obligations. Protecting human rights has become a core purpose of UN peacekeeping.[77] The Security Council has exercised its Chapter VII authority with increasing regularity to mandate collective enforcement measures (e.g., economic sanctions, travel restrictions, military action) and to prevent and suppress serious breaches of international human rights norms (e.g., crimes against humanity and war crimes).[78] Along the way, the international community has accepted that all states must cooperate when the Security Council decides that international cooperation is necessary to advance universal respect for international human rights.[79]

[74] Universal Declaration of Human Rights, 10 December 1948, UN GA Res. 217 A (III), UN Doc. A/810.

[75] International Covenant on Civil and Political Rights, 16 December 1966, 999 UNTS 171.

[76] International Covenant on Economic, Social and Cultural Rights, 16 December 1966, 993 UNTS 3 [hereinafter ICESCR]; see also ibid. art. 60 (assigning responsibility to the General Assembly and ECOSOC to discharge this norm-specification function).

[77] See, e.g., Gérard Prunier, *The Rwanda Crisis: History of a Genocide* (New York: Columbia University Press, 1995), p. 234 (explaining how UN peacekeepers failed to prevent the Rwandan genocide that claimed a million lives).

[78] See, e.g., UN Security Council Resolution 2085, 20 December 2012, S/RES/2085, para. 9 (authorizing "the deployment of an African-led International Support Mission in Mali" to support local authorities' efforts to protect civilians); UN Security Council Resolution 1970, 26 February 2011, S/RES/1970 (imposing sanctions in response to crimes against humanity in Libya).

[79] See, e.g., 2005 UN Secretary-General, Implementing the Responsibility to Protect, 12 January 2009, UN Doc. A/63/677, para. 10 (embracing this principle); 2005 World Summit Outcome, 24 Oct. 2005, A/RES/60/1, para. 139 ("The international community, through the United Nations," bears "responsibility . . . to help to protect populations from genocide, war crimes, ethnic cleansing and crimes against humanity."). With respect to the right to self-determination, the international community has declared that "[e]very State has the duty . . . to render assistance to the United Nations in carrying out the responsibilities entrusted to it by the Charter regarding the implementation of the principle." Friendly Relations Declaration; see also Legal Consequences Arising from

One of the ways states have pledged to promote respect for international human rights is by cooperating with one another and with international tribunals to facilitate the prosecution of those who commit international crimes. During the 1990s, the UN Security Council established ad hoc criminal tribunals to investigate and prosecute mass atrocities in Rwanda and the former Yugoslavia.[80] In both settings, the Security Council issued binding regulations requiring states to cooperate with the tribunals, including by complying with requests for assistance with pretrial investigation and prosecution.[81] States later incorporated duties of cooperation into the Rome Statute of the International Criminal Court (ICC).[82] The Rome Statute requires states-parties to "cooperate fully with the Court in its investigation and prosecution of crimes within the jurisdiction of the Court,"[83] including by gathering evidence, securing witnesses for trial, and arresting and surrendering suspects upon the Court's request.[84] Mandatory cooperation also features prominently in the Convention Against Torture and Other Cruel, Inhuman, or Degrading Treatment or Punishment.[85] States-parties must not only prevent, criminalize, and prosecute domestic acts of torture[86] but also grant reasonable extradition requests and "afford one another the greatest measure of assistance in connection with criminal proceedings brought" to enforce the Convention, including by providing "all evidence at their disposal necessary for the proceedings."[87] Similar duties of international cooperation appear in the International Convention for

the Policies and Practices of Israel in the Occupied Palestinian Territory, Including East Jerusalem, 2024 ICJ (19 July), para. 275 (explaining that "while it is for the General Assembly and the Security Council to pronounce on the modalities required to ensure . . . the full realization of the right . . . to self-determination, all States must co-operate with the United Nations to put those modalities into effect").

80 UN Security Council Resolution 827, 25 May 1993, S/RES/827, para. 2 (establishing the International Criminal Tribunal for the Former Yugoslavia); UN Security Council Resolution 955, 8 November 1994, S/RES/955, para. 1 (establishing the International Criminal Tribunal for Rwanda).

81 UN Security Council Resolution 827, 25 May 1993, S/RES/827, para. 4; UN Security Council 955, 8 November 1994, S/RES/955, para. 2.

82 Rome Statute of the International Criminal Court, 17 July 1998, 2187 UNTS 90, arts. 86, 89, 93 [hereinafter Rome Statute].

83 Ibid. art. 86.

84 Ibid. arts. 89, 93.

85 Convention Against Torture and Other Cruel, Inhuman or Degrading Treatment or Punishment, 10 December 1984, S. Treaty Doc. No. 100-20 (1988), 1465 UNTS 85.

86 Ibid. arts. 2, 4, 7.

87 Ibid. arts. 8, 9(1); see also art. 20 (outlining procedures for state cooperation with fact-finding investigations of the Committee Against Torture).

the Protection of All Persons from Enforced Disappearance[88] and the Convention on the Prevention and Punishment of the Crime of Genocide (Genocide Convention).[89]

The Bosnian Genocide Case

On July 11, 1995, at the height of the violence unleashed by Yugoslavia's dissolution, Bosnian Serbs under the command of General Radko Mladić captured the weakly fortified town of Srebrenica on the eastern fringe of present-day Bosnia and Herzegovina. Stationed at Srebrenica was a small contingent of Dutch peacekeepers operating under UN mandate but without authorization to use force for the town's defense. Two years earlier, the Security Council had adopted a resolution designating "Srebrenica and its surroundings as a safe area which should be free from any armed attack or any other hostile act."[90] As Mladić entered town, however, he looked directly into a journalist's video camera and declared, "We give this town to the Serb nation as a gift. The time has come to take revenge on the Muslims."[91] Over the next five days, Mladić's troops systematically rounded up and executed over 7,000 unarmed Muslim men of all ages.[92]

Even before the massacre at Srebrenica, Bosnia and Herzegovina had instituted proceedings in the ICJ, claiming that Serbia was legally responsible for atrocities committed on Bosnian soil by Bosnian Serb separatists.[93] These proceedings gained even greater urgency after the much-publicized Srebrenica massacre. Bosnia and Herzegovina argued that Serbia violated the Genocide Convention by failing to prevent acts of genocide by Bosnian Serbs and declining to arrest and surrender General Mladić for prosecution in the International Criminal Tribunal for the

88 UN General Assembly, International Convention for the Protection of All Persons from Enforced Disappearance, 20 December 2006, GA Res. 61/177, Annex, UN Doc. A/RES/61/177, arts. 11, 13–15.

89 Convention on the Prevention and Punishment of the Crime of Genocide, 9 December 1948, in force 12 January 1951, 78 UNTS 277, arts. 1, VI–VII [hereinafter Genocide Convention].

90 UN Security Council Resolution 819, 16 April 1993, S/RES/819, para. 1.

91 'Ratko Mladic trial told of Srebrenica chaos', BBC, 17 May 2012.

92 Prosecutor v. Kristić, IT-98-33-T, Judgment, para. 12, August 2001.

93 Application of the Convention on the Prevention and Punishment of the Crime of Genocide (Bosn. & Herz. v. Serbia & Montenegro), 2007 ICJ Rep. 43, 49, para. 1 (26 February) [hereinafter Bosnian Genocide Case]. When Bosnia and Herzegovina first instituted the proceedings, Serbia was part of the Federal Republic of Yugoslavia. Ibid.

Former Yugoslavia (ICTY).[94] These legal claims raised important questions about the scope of mandatory cooperation as applied to mass atrocities. Did Serbia indeed have an affirmative obligation to prevent the Srebrenica genocide and punish those responsible? Should it make a difference that the genocidal acts were committed by foreign nationals (Bosnian Serbs) outside Serbian territory?

In its landmark judgment of February 26, 2007, the ICJ agreed that Serbia violated the Genocide Convention by failing to cooperate fully with international efforts to prevent the massacre at Srebrenica and punish Mladić.[95] Although the Court found insufficient evidence to attribute the Srebrenica genocide to Serbia,[96] it underscored Serbia's affirmative obligation to prevent and punish genocide:

> [T]he obligation of States parties is . . . to employ all means reasonably available to them, so as to prevent genocide so far as possible. A State does not incur responsibility simply because the desired result is not achieved; responsibility is however incurred if the State manifestly failed to take all measures to prevent genocide which were within its power, and which might have contributed to preventing the genocide. In this area the notion of "due diligence," which calls for an assessment *in concreto*, is of critical importance.[97]

The ICJ acknowledged that a state's legal responsibility to prevent others from committing genocide varies depending upon its "capacity to influence effectively the action of persons likely to commit or already committing, genocide," as well as "its particular legal position vis-à-vis the situations and persons facing the danger, or the reality, of genocide." However, the fact that a state might not be able to prevent genocide through its efforts alone would not suffice to excuse a failure to act. Instead, the proper inquiry was whether "the combined efforts of several States, each complying with its obligation to prevent, might have achieved the result – averting the commission of genocide – which the efforts of only one State were insufficient to produce."[98] Put simply, when a state cannot prevent genocide unilaterally, it must pursue international cooperation.[99] In the case of Srebrenica, the ICJ concluded that Serbia

[94] Ibid. p. 65, para. 65.
[95] Ibid. p. 228, para. 449.
[96] Ibid. pp. 214–215, paras. 413–415.
[97] Ibid. p. 221, para. 430.
[98] Ibid. p. 221, paras. 413–415, 219, 424.
[99] The Court concluded that the Genocide Convention's requirements to prevent and punish genocide are not territorially constrained, but instead "apply to a State wherever

violated its obligations under the Genocide Convention by failing to devote "the best efforts within [its] power to try and prevent the tragic events then taking shape."[100]

This was not Serbia's only violation of international law. The ICJ also concluded that Serbia "failed in its duty to co-operate with the ICTY."[101] According to the Court, states-parties to the Genocide Convention must "arrest persons accused of genocide who are in their territory – even if the crime of which they are accused was committed outside it – and, failing prosecution of them in the parties' own courts," they must "hand them over for trial by the competent international tribunal."[102] The Court found "plentiful, and mutually corroborative, information suggesting that General Mladić, indicted by the ICTY for genocide," had been living freely in Serbian territory with the knowledge of Serbia's intelligence service but without Serbia taking reasonable steps to make an arrest.[103] This failure to cooperate fully with the ICTY violated Serbia's duties "as a member of the United Nations" and "under Article VI of the Genocide Convention."[104]

Cooperating to Prevent and Punish Other Atrocity Crimes

The *Bosnian Genocide Case* confirms that states bear due diligence obligations to prevent and suppress genocide and that they must cooperate with one another and with international organizations to make those efforts effective. The judgment does not directly address whether states must unite to prevent and suppress other international crimes. Still, there are strong signals elsewhere in the ICJ's jurisprudence that all such

it may be acting or may be able to act in ways appropriate to meeting the obligations in question." Bosnian Genocide Case, p. 120, para. 183; see also Application of the Convention on the Prevention and Punishment of the Crime of Genocide (Bosn. & Herz. v. Yugoslavia), Preliminary Objections, Judgment, 1996 ICJ Rep. 595, 616, para. 31 (11 July) [hereinafter Bosnian Genocide Preliminary Objections]. Thus, unlike most due diligence obligations under international law, such as the requirements to prevent transboundary pollution and attacks by non-state actors (see Chapters 6 and 7), the obligation to prevent genocide is not limited to threats arising within a state's own territory. See Marko Milanovic, 'State Responsibility for Genocide: A Follow-Up' (2007) 18 EJIL 669, 685 (emphasizing the exceptional nature of this extraterritorial obligation to prevent genocide).

100 Bosnian Genocide Case, pp. 225–226, paras. 438–439.

101 Ibid. p. 229, para. 449.

102 Ibid. p. 227, para. 443.

103 Ibid. p. 229, para. 448.

104 Ibid. p. 229, para. 449.

crimes trigger mandatory cooperation. For example, in the *Reservations to the Genocide Convention Case* (*Reservations Case*), the Court explained that mandatory cooperation is a "consequence" of the Genocide Convention's "conception" of genocide as an international crime which "shocks the conscience of mankind and results in great losses to humanity, and which is contrary to moral law and to the spirit and aims of the United Nations."[105] Based on this logic, it would seem to follow that states must cooperate to prevent, suppress, and punish other mass atrocities, as well. Genocide is not the only universally recognized international crime that shocks the conscience, generates great losses to humanity, and violates the spirit and aims of the United Nations; the crime of aggression, crimes against humanity, and at least some war crimes clearly satisfy these criteria.[106] The ICJ's reasoning in the *Reservations Case* suggests, therefore, that those other international crimes also trigger an obligation to cooperate in good faith "to liberate mankind from such an odious scourge."[107]

Consistent with the *Reservations Case*, customary international law may be in the process of establishing positive duties of cooperation for grave breaches of international human rights and international criminal law. In its influential 2001 Articles on State Responsibility for Internationally Wrongful Acts (the Articles), the UN International Law Commission (ILC) concluded that under international law, states must "cooperate to bring to an end through lawful means any serious breach" "of an obligation arising under a peremptory norm of general international law."[108] The ILC's commentary accompanying the Articles acknowledges that reasonable minds might question whether

[105] Reservations to the Genocide Convention, 1951 ICJ Rep. 15, 23 (28 May) [hereinafter Reservations Case]. Another "consequence" of this conception, the Court suggested, is that the prohibition against aggression is a peremptory norm "recognized by civilized nations" that binds states "even without any conventional obligation." Ibid.; see also Case Concerning Armed Activities on the Territory of the Congo (DRC v. Rwanda), 2006 ICJ Rep. 6, 31, para. 64 (3 February) (reaffirming these principles from the Reservations Case); Bosnian Genocide Preliminary Objections, p. 616, para. 31 (same).

[106] Rome Statute, arts. 5–8 (codifying these international crimes).

[107] Reservations Case, p. 23 (quoting UN Charter pmbl.).

[108] International Law Commission, 'Articles on Responsibility of States for Internationally Wrongful Acts', in *Report of the International Law Commission on the Work of Its Fifty-Third Session*, UNGAOR, 56th Sess., Supp. No. 10, UN Doc. A/56/10, p. 113, arts. 40–41 (2001); see also ibid. art. 41, cmt. 2 ("Cooperation could be organized in the framework of a competent international organization, in particular the United Nations. However, paragraph 1 also envisages the possibility of non-institutionalized cooperation.").

"[customary] international law at present prescribes a positive duty of cooperation," and it concedes that the Articles' articulation of this duty "may reflect the progressive development of international law."[109] Nonetheless, the ILC's commentary observes that "in fact such cooperation, especially in the framework of international organizations, is carried out already in response to the gravest breaches of international law."[110]

Since the ILC finalized the Articles, the idea that states must cooperate to prevent mass atrocities has received some additional support from the UN General Assembly. In the 2005 World Summit Outcome, 191 states unanimously endorsed the "Responsibility to Protect" (R2P) doctrine, affirming that states are responsible for protecting their people from genocide, war crimes, ethnic cleansing, and crimes against humanity, and that "[t]he international community, through the United Nations, also has the responsibility to use appropriate ... means" – including "collective action ... through the Security Council" – to protect vulnerable populations from these threats.[111] A year after the 2005 World Summit Outcome, the General Assembly clarified further that "[i]n cases of gross violations of international human rights law and serious violations of international humanitarian law constituting crimes under international law, ... States should, in accordance with international law, cooperate with one another and assist international judicial organs competent in the investigation and prosecution of these violations."[112] At a minimum, these General Assembly resolutions express a shared political commitment to cooperate to prevent and punish international crimes.

Whether states accept the idea that they have a legal obligation to cooperate to prevent and suppress atrocity crimes is less clear. In practice, bystander states rarely treat international cooperation as a legal requirement absent a binding Security Council resolution. The international community's flagrant failures to prevent genocide and crimes against humanity in Cambodia, Rwanda, Bosnia, Darfur, Syria, Myanmar, and

109 Ibid. art. 41, cmt. 3.

110 Ibid.

111 2005 World Summit Outcome, 24 October 2005, A/RES/60/1, paras. 138–139.

112 UN General Assembly, Basic Principles and Guidelines on the Right to a Remedy and Reparation for Victims of Gross Violations of International Human Rights Law and Serious Violations of International Humanitarian Law, 21 March 2006, A/RES/60/147, p. 5, para. 4.

elsewhere are well documented.[113] As these crises have unfolded, many states have turned a blind eye to imminent catastrophe. Security Council members have opposed or slow-rolled proposals to protect vulnerable populations. Reflecting on these tragedies in a 2016 Report titled *Mobilizing Collective Action: The Next Decade of the Responsibility to Protect*, UN Secretary-General Ban Ki-Moon lamented that "although Member States have repeatedly emphasized their support for the prevention of atrocity crimes, this has not been sufficiently translated into concrete support for preventive strategies – even when there have been credible assessments of imminent threats to populations."[114] Experience thus reveals a wide gap between international institutions' strong affirmations of mandatory cooperation to prevent and punish atrocity crimes, on the one hand, and tepid state practice, on the other hand.

The genocide in Sudan's Darfur region (2003–2005) illustrates this challenge. In October 2003 – at least three months before international news media began reporting ethnic cleansing by Janjaweed militia in Darfur, and a full eleven months before Western governments officially labeled the attacks "genocide" – the US State Department was aware that escalating ethnic violence in the region could soon cause death rates to spike into the hundreds of thousands. The European Commission also tracked developments in Darfur closely and anticipated imminent calamity. Nonetheless, early warnings about the approaching genocide were "swept under the carpet" based on "a conscious decision to address Darfur silently using quiet diplomacy and not bring it to the UN Security Council."[115] Had the European Commission and the United States recognized that the looming crisis triggered mandatory cooperation – including a firm due diligence obligation to notify the entire international community of the approaching calamity and seek timely action from the Security Council – this might have helped to avert or contain the atrocities that followed. Attending to the requirements of mandatory cooperation might have helped to persuade Security Council

[113] See, e.g., Samantha Power, *A Problem from Hell: America and the Age of Genocide* (New York: Basic Books, 2002); David Lanz, *The Responsibility to Protect in Darfur: From Forgotten Conflict to Global Cause and Back* (London: Routledge, 2020); UN Human Rights Committee, Report of the Independent International Fact-finding Mission on Myanmar, 12 September 2018, A/HCR/39/64.

[114] Report of the Secretary General, Mobilizing Collective Action: The Next Decade of the Responsibility to Protect, 22 July 2016, A/70/999–S/2016/620, p. 8, para. 28.

[115] Fred Grünfeld and Wessel N. Vermeulen, *Failure to Prevent Gross Human Rights Violations in Darfur: Warnings to and Responses by International Decision Makers (2003-2005)* (Brill, 2014), pp. 70–75, 78, 82, 150.

members, as "trustees of the international community," to act more decisively to condemn, prevent, and suppress mass murder in Darfur.[116]

Or perhaps not. Even when requirements of mandatory cooperation are well recognized and uncontroversial, states are not always eager to comply with their obligations. For example, in March 2009, the ICC issued a warrant for the arrest of Sudanese President Omar al-Bashir for his role in the Darfur genocide.[117] Under the Rome Statute and the Genocide Convention, all states-parties are obligated to cooperate in bringing al-Bashir to justice. Nonetheless, in the years that followed, over twenty countries welcomed visits from al-Bashir without executing his arrest, including China, Egypt, Ethiopia, Indonesia, Iran, Kenya, Russia, Saudi Arabia, the United Arab Emirates, and South Africa.[118] Although Sudan has pledged to deliver al-Bashir to the ICC for trial,[119] thus far it has not followed through on this commitment. The ICC has referred instances of state noncooperation to the Security Council, but its requests have been brushed aside. These failures of cooperation suggest that some states lack the political will to prioritize punishing atrocity crimes.

Cooperating for Economic, Social, and Cultural Rights

Economic, social, and cultural rights also trigger mandatory cooperation under international human rights law. The ICESCR enshrines a wide variety of rights, such as the right to work and the right to "an adequate standard of living . . . , including adequate food, clothing and housing, and to the continuous improvement of living conditions."[120] Article 2(1)

116 Anne Peters, 'The Security Council's Responsibility to Protect' (2011) 8 *Int'l Org. L. Rev.* 15, 25; see also Evan J. Criddle and Evan Fox-Decent, *Fiduciaries of Humanity: How International Constitutes Authority* (New York: Oxford University Press, 2018), pp. 283–352 (explaining how international organizations like the Security Council serve as fiduciaries of humanity); Jennifer Trahan, *Existing Legal Limits of the Security Veto Power in the Face of Mass Atrocities* (Cambridge: Cambridge University Press, 2020) (arguing that the P5 lack authority to use their veto power to prevent collective action against atrocity crimes).

117 Prosecutor v. Omar Hassan Ahmad Al Bashir, Warrant of Arrest for Omar Hassan Ahmad Al Bashir, ICC-02/05-01/09-1, 4 March 2009.

118 See The Office of the Prosecutor, 'Twenty-First Report of the Prosecutor of the International Criminal Court to the UN Security Council Pursuant to UNSCR 1593 (2005)', International Criminal Court, 29 June 2015; '75 Trips to 22 Countries in 7 Years: An Indicted War Criminal's Travels', NUBA Reports, 7 March 2016.

119 'Omar al-Bashir: Sudan Agrees Ex-President Must Face ICC', BBC, 11 February 2020.

120 ICESCR, arts. 6(1), 11(1).

declares that these rights are subject to mandatory cooperation: "Each State Party to the present Covenant undertakes to take steps, individually *and through international assistance and co-operation*, especially economic and technical, to the maximum of its available resources, with a view to achieving progressively the full realization of the rights recognized in the present Covenant by all appropriate means, including particularly the adoption of legislative measures."[121] In addressing the right to an adequate standard of living, the Convention provides that international assistance and cooperation could improve methods of food production, conservation, and dissemination; disseminate agricultural techniques and best practices; and "ensure an equitable distribution of world supplies in relation to need."[122] States-parties "agree that international action for the achievement of the rights recognized in the ... Covenant includes such methods as the conclusion of conventions, the adoption of recommendations, the furnishing of technical assistance and the holding of regional meetings and technical meetings for the purpose of consultation and study organized in conjunction with the Governments concerned."[123]

Some states have characterized these features of the ICESCR as mere political commitments, not legal obligations.[124] However, the Committee on Economic, Social and Cultural Rights has affirmed that the Covenant's requirements for international cooperation are legally binding. In its *General Comment No. 3*, the Committee has stated

> that in accordance with Articles 55 and 56 of the Charter of the United Nations, with well-established principles of international law, and with the provisions of the Covenant itself, international cooperation for development and thus for the realization of economic, social and cultural rights is an obligation of all States. It is particularly incumbent upon those States which are in a position to assist others in this regard.[125]

[121] Ibid. art. 2(1) (emphasis added); see also ibid. art. 11(1) (obligating states-parties to "take appropriate steps to ensure the realization of th[e] right [to an adequate standard of living], recognizing to this effect the essential importance of international co-operation based on free consent").

[122] Ibid. art. 11(2).

[123] Ibid. art. 23.

[124] See, e.g., Report of the Open-ended Working Group to consider options regarding the elaboration of an optional protocol to the International Covenant on Economic, Social and Cultural Rights on its third session, 14 March 2006, UN Doc. E/CN.4/2006/47, para. 82 (memorializing Canada's position "that international cooperation and assistance was a moral obligation, not a legal one").

[125] General Comment No. 3: The nature of States parties' obligations, 14 December 1990, UN Doc. E/1991/23, para. 14.

This is so, the Committee observes, because "in the absence of an active programme of international assistance and cooperation on the part of all those States that are in a position to undertake one, the full realization of economic, social and cultural rights will remain an unfulfilled aspiration in many countries."[126] In other words, mandatory cooperation is essential to achieve the ICESCR's object and purpose.

The Committee on the Rights of the Child has reached the same conclusion for economic, social, and cultural rights enshrined in the UN Convention on the Rights of the Child (UNCRC).[127] Article 4 of the UNCRC requires states-parties to "undertake all appropriate legislative, administrative, and other measures for the implementation of the rights recognized in the present Convention. With regard to economic, social and cultural rights, States Parties shall undertake such measures to the maximum extent of their available resources and, where needed, within the framework of international co-operation."[128] "When States ratify the Convention," the Committee explains, "they take upon themselves obligations not only to implement it within their jurisdiction but also to contribute, through international cooperation, to global implementation."[129]

In 2011, a group of forty eminent international law experts from around the world gathered in the Netherlands to "clarify [the] extraterritorial obligations of States on the basis of standing international law."[130] The resulting Maastricht Principles on the Extraterritorial Obligations of States in the Area of Economic, Social and Cultural Rights (Maastricht Principles) confirms that states must cooperate in good faith to protect and fulfill economic, social, and cultural rights for those both inside and outside their territories.[131] Consistent with general principles of mandatory cooperation, the Maastricht Principles indicate that states' cooperative obligations

[126] Ibid.

[127] Convention on the Rights of the Child, 20 November 1989, in force 2 September 1990, 1577 UNTS 3.

[128] Ibid. art. 4.

[129] General Comment No. 5: General Measures of Implementation of the Convention on the Rights of the Child, 27 November 2003, UN Doc. CRC/GC/2003/5, p. 3, para. 7; see also ibid. p. 14, para. 60 (explaining that "implementation of the Convention is a cooperative exercise for the States of the world" consistent with states' obligations under arts. 55 and 56 of the UN Charter).

[130] Maastricht Principles on the Extraterritorial Obligations of States in the Area of Economic, Social and Cultural Rights, 28 September 2011, p. 3, www.fidh.org/IMG/pdf/maastricht-eto-principles-uk_web.pdf.

[131] Ibid. arts. 23, 27–28, 30, 33, 35.

must be ascertained based on equitable principles, accounting for factors such as states' respective "economic, technical and technological capacities, available resources, and influence in international decision-making processes."[132] Mandatory cooperation thus gives states common but differentiated responsibilities to protect and fulfill economic, social, and cultural rights.

Mandatory Cooperation in the Real World

In the closing days of the San Francisco Conference, when negotiations over the draft Charter teetered on the brink of collapse, Truman dispatched an envoy to Moscow with instructions to "make it clear to Uncle Joe Stalin that I knew what I wanted – and that I intended to get [from the United Nations] – peace for the world for at least 90 years."[133]

If perpetual peace is the standard by which the United Nations must be judged, then surely it will be found wanting. Mandatory cooperation has not saved succeeding generations from the scourge of war. Less than two months after the San Francisco Conference, Truman shocked the world by authorizing the use of nuclear weapons against Hiroshima and Nagasaki. Since World War II and the Korean War, the world has endured hundreds of devastating conflicts, including the Algerian War, the Vietnam War, the Iran-Iraq War, the Bosnian War, the Iraq War, recurring armed struggles in Afghanistan and Congo, and civil wars in Burundi, El Salvador, Guatemala, Libya, Nigeria, Sri Lanka, Somalia, Sudan, Syria, and Yemen, to name just a few. Nor has international cooperation solved the puzzle of mass atrocities. As this volume goes to print, diplomats continue to wring their hands in futility as North Korea systematically murders, rapes, and tortures detainees in prison camps;[134] Israel continues to restrict the delivery of humanitarian aid to starving Palestinians in defiance of provisional measures indicated by the ICJ;[135] and Russia refuses to comply with an ICC warrant to arrest

[132] Ibid. art. 31.

[133] Schlesinger, 'Act of Creation', p. 252.

[134] Ewelina U. Ochab, 'Crimes Against Humanity Continue Unabated in North Korea: Will Kim Jong-Un Face Justice?', Forbes, 16 July 2022.

[135] See Application of the Convention on the Prevention and Punishment of the Crime of Genocide in the Gaza Strip (South Africa v. Israel), Provisional Measures, 2024 ICJ Rep. 3, 29, 31, paras. 80, 86 (26 January) (directing Israel to "take immediate and effective measures to enable the provision of urgently needed basic services and humanitarian assistance to address the adverse conditions of life faced by Palestinians in the Gaza Strip"); Integrated

Putin for war crimes.[136] Sadly, states sometimes conspire with one another to defeat international efforts to suppress aggression and human rights abuse – including through their abuse of the P5 veto power.[137] As long as states decline to condemn wars of territorial conquest, such as Russia's invasion of Ukraine,[138] it is plain that we are nowhere near the future Tennyson foresaw in which "the war-drum throbb'd no longer" and "the kindly earth shall slumber, lapt in universal law."[139]

Still, as hard as it may be to achieve, cooperation is necessary if the international community hopes to secure sovereign equality, maintain international peace and security, and safeguard humanity from oppression. This is why the Charter enshrines mandatory cooperation as a cornerstone principle – arguably *the* cornerstone principle – of our international legal order.

And there is some basis for cautious (if limited) optimism. For all their shortcomings, UN peacekeeping missions have made valuable contributions to curtailing armed conflicts, reducing civilian casualties, and strengthening peace agreements, thereby saving countless lives.[140] Dozens of the worst human rights abusers have been prosecuted successfully for atrocity crimes, including Mladić, who, with Serbia's assistance, was finally tried and sentenced to life in prison for genocide by the ICTY in 2017.[141] Mandatory cooperation has also advanced economic, social, and cultural rights worldwide. Since 1990, international cooperation of the kind envisioned in the ICESCR has lifted more than 1.1 billion people

Food Security Phase Classification Famine Review Committee: Gaza Strip, August 2025: Conclusions and Recommendations (22 August 2025), www.ipcinfo.org/fileadmin/user_upload/ipcinfo/docs/IPC_Famine_Review_Committee_Report_Gaza_Aug2025.pdf (finding famine conditions in Gaza due, in part, to "severe restrictions" imposed by Israel on humanitarian access).

136 Francesca Ebel, Robyn Dixon, and Lauren Tierney, 'Putin, Charged with War Crimes, Must Limit Travel to Avoid Arrest', Washington Post, 24 March 2023.

137 E.g., 'UN: Russia and China's Abusive Use of Veto "Shameful"', Amnesty Int'l, 28 February 2017 (discussing collaboration between China and Russia to suppress Security Council action to address atrocities in Syria).

138 See above Chapter 1.

139 Alfred, Lloyd Tennyson, *Lockesley Hall* (1842).

140 'Does UN Peacekeeping Work? Here's What the Data Says', UN News, 10 December 2022.

141 See Griff Witte, 'Ratko Mladic, the "Butcher of Bosnia", Guilty of Genocide in Last Balkan War Crimes Trial', NY Times, 22 November 2017; Colum Lynch, 'Serbia Arrests Ratko Mladic on War Crimes Charges', Washington Post, 26 May 2011.

out of extreme poverty.[142] Over fifty million lives have been saved through international cooperation to combat HIV, tuberculosis, and malaria in low- and middle-income countries.[143] If there is a path toward a more decent and peaceful world, it runs through mandatory cooperation.

[142] See UN General Assembly, Implementation of the Third United Nations Decade for the Eradication of Poverty (2018–2027), 18 October 2018, A/C.2/73/L.9. para. 7.

[143] See 'Results Report 2022', The Global Fund, September 2022.

PART III

Future Directions

10

Refugees

A Massacre of Unspeakable Brutality

With Bangladesh and India to the west, and China, Laos, and Thailand to the east, Myanmar (formerly Burma) is the largest country in mainland Southeast Asia.[1] Myanmar's history since independence in 1948 has been dominated by military dictatorship, ethnic strife, and civil war.[2] During this time, Myanmar's military – known as the Tatmadaw – has steadily resisted democratic reform while supporting and participating in extreme sectarian violence against minority ethnic groups. The Tatmadaw's decades-long targeting of the predominately Muslim Rohingya people has been especially unyielding, amounting to what has been characterized by a UN fact-finding mission as "severe, systemic and institutionalized oppression from birth to death."[3] The Rohingya are barred from obtaining Myanmar citizenship, rendering them stateless.[4] Their travel within and outside Rakhine state, where most Rohingya live, is subject to strict and discriminatory limitation, as is their right to public assembly.[5] In June and October 2012, two waves of pogrom-like violence against the Rohingya erupted with the encouragement of a government-supported campaign of "hate and dehumanization," resulting in the internal displacement of more than 140,000 and further severe violations of the Rohingya's human rights.[6]

[1] See 'Myanmar', Wikipedia. Myanmar has a total area of 678,500 square kilometers, making it roughly the size of Afghanistan or Texas. Ibid.

[2] Yun Sun, 'The Civil War in Myanmar: No End in Sight', Brookings Institution, 13 February 2023, www.brookings.edu/articles/the-civil-war-in-myanmar-no-end-in-sight/ [hereinafter No End in Sight].

[3] UN Human Rights Council, 'Report of the independent international fact-finding mission on Myanmar', 12 September 2018, A/HRC/39/64, para. 20 [hereinafter UN 2018 Fact-finding Report].

[4] Ibid. para. 21.

[5] Ibid. para. 23.

[6] Ibid. paras. 24–30.

On August 25, 2017, Rohingya militants attacked a number of security force outposts across northern Rakhine State, killing twelve security personnel. Within hours, Myanmar's military launched a response the UN described as "immediate, brutal and grossly disproportionate."[7] The Tatmadaw began what it called "clearance operations," resulting in 392 Rohingya villages – 40 percent of all settlements in northern Rakhine – being partially or totally burned to the ground.[8] Mass killings were common, while "[l]arge-scale gang-rape was perpetrated by Tatmadaw soldiers in at least ten village tracts of northern Rakhine State."[9] One of the sites of this terror was the village of Tula Toli.

On August 30, 2017, Myanmar military forces and local villagers armed with machetes descended on Tula Toli.[10] Advancing soldiers trapped several hundred unarmed Rohingya villagers on the sandy bank of a turbulent river that surrounds the village on three sides. What unfolded over the next several hours, Human Rights Watch lamented, was "a massacre of unspeakable brutality."[11] Hassina Begum, a twenty-year-old Rohingya woman, was one of few survivors. She and other survivors described how soldiers separated women and children from men, and then systematically murdered the men over several hours, dumping their bodies into pits and setting them on fire. Soldiers then took the women and children away in small groups, killing some children on the beach, and tossing others into the rushing river to drown.[12]

Human Rights Watch summarized the horror inflicted on Ms. Begum and her family:

> Hassina tried hiding her 1-year-old daughter Sohaifa under her shawl. A soldier noticed and tore the infant from her, throwing the girl alive on a fire. Five soldiers took Hassina, her mother-in-law, Fatima, 35, and her sister-in-law, Asma, 18, together with Fatima's three young sons, ages 7, 10, and 14, from the water to a nearby bamboo house in the village. Hassina says that on arrival a group of ethnic Rakhine men at the house beat the three boys to death. The soldiers proceeded to sexually assault Hassina and the women inside the house. When Fatima resisted, the

7 Ibid. para. 32.
8 Ibid. para. 42.
9 Ibid. para. 38.
10 'Massacre by the River: Burmese Army Crimes against Humanity in Tula Toli', Human Rights Watch, December 2017, www.hrw.org/sites/default/files/report_pdf/burma1217_web.pdf.
11 Ibid. p. 1.
12 Ibid.

> soldiers stabbed her to death before beating the others unconscious, and knifing Hassina.
>
> As they left, the soldiers locked the unconscious and dead women inside the house and set it on fire. Hassina and Asma regained consciousness when their clothes caught on fire, and fought their way out through the burning bamboo walls. They were the sole survivors from that house. When interviewed by Human Rights Watch, the two women showed their wounds, which included burns and machete cuts.
>
> What happened to Hassina and her relatives that day was repeated many times in Tula Toli.[13]

The UN mission later confirmed that Tula Toli was not an isolated case, but one of many villages razed to the ground amidst organized mass killing and "large-scale gang rape."[14] The UN considered the estimate of 10,000 deaths by *Médecins Sans Frontières* to be "conservative," and characterized the government's "clearance operations" as "a human rights catastrophe."[15] Ultimately, the mission concluded that there was ample evidence of genocidal actions and intent to warrant investigation and prosecution of senior Tatmadaw officials for genocide.[16]

More than 742,000 Rohingya – half of them children – fled the terror to neighboring Bangladesh.[17] Many had fled violence years before, and today almost a million Rohingya (of a total estimated population of 1.4 million) live in crowded refugee camps in Bangladesh.[18] At the time of this writing, liberal reformers and various ethnic groups were locked in civil war against the Tatmadaw, with "no end in sight."[19] There is no reasonable prospect of the Rohingya returning *en masse* to Myanmar soon, if ever. Many will need to find a permanent home elsewhere.

This chapter considers how the burden of taking in and caring for almost a million Rohingya refugees is to be distributed and shared across the international community. More specifically, we consider the manner and extent to which norms of mandatory cooperation establish a framework for "burden-sharing" – by distributing the

13 Ibid. pp. 1–2.
14 UN 2018 Fact-finding Report, paras. 36–38.
15 Ibid. para. 36.
16 Ibid. paras. 84–87
17 'Rohingya Refugee Crisis Explained', UNHCR, 23 August 2023, www.unrefugees.org/news/rohingya-refugee-crisis-explained/#Rohingya.
18 '2023 Joint Response Plan Rohingya Humanitarian Crisis January—December 2023', Inter Sector Coordination Group, p. 14 (noting that as of September 30, 2022, approximately 945,953 Rohingya refugees/forcibly displaced Myanmar nationals were registered as residing in one of thirty-three "extremely congested camps").
19 No End in Sight, *above* note 2.

burden of taking in the Rohingya and others who are forced to flee their country of origin. We first set out briefly the core features of the legal regime created by the UN Convention Relating to the Status of Refugees (Refugee Convention)[20] and the subsequent UN Protocol Relating to the Status of Refugees (Protocol).[21] We argue that ensuring protection for refugees is a "common concern of humanity" under the international community's collective stewardship, not merely a burden that falls on states of first refuge, such as Bangladesh for Rohingya refugees.

In a nutshell, we suggest that international refugee law carves out an exception to state authority to exclude outsiders, and that this exception is an especially poignant example of equitable norms proscribing the abuse of sovereign rights (in this case, the right to exclude). Consistent with equitable principles, states may exercise their sovereign right to exclude only in a manner that reflects due regard for the interests of other states and foreign nationals. We argue that this equitable framework not only grounds the international prohibition against returning refugees to territories where they would face persecution[22] but also supports a requirement of equitable burden-sharing. According due regard to the equitable interests of other states and foreign nationals means, in part, that states must do their fair share to make good on international refugee law's promise, which is that people fleeing persecution will have access to a decent safe harbor. Thus, refugee burden-sharing is a strong candidate for mandatory cooperation under international law.

The argument for recognizing a legal obligation for states to participate in refugee burden-sharing is largely aspirational, but enjoys some support in state practice. We argue that the 2016 New York Declaration for Refugees and Migrants (New York Declaration),[23] the 2018 Global Compact for Safe, Orderly and Regular Migration (Global Compact for

[20] UN Convention Relating to the Status of Refugees, 189 UNTS 150, 19 UST 6259 (28 July 1951).

[21] UN Protocol Relating to the Status of Refugees, 31 January 1967, 19 UST 6223, TIAS No. 6577 (1968). The Refugee Convention and Protocol enjoy widespread acceptance, with 149 states having signed one or both of these agreements. UN High Commissioner for Refugees, 'The 1951 Refugee Convention and Key International Conventions', UN High Commissioner for Refugees, 25 November 2023, www.unhcr.org/il/en/1951-refugee-convention-and-international-conventions.

[22] Refugee Convention, art. 33(1).

[23] New York Declaration for Refugees and Migrants, New York, 13 September 2016, A/RES/71/L/1.

Migration),[24] and the 2018 Global Compact on Refugees[25] represent substantial efforts to bring a measure of mandatory cooperation to burden-sharing. Indeed, by establishing burden-sharing frameworks based on nationally defined contributions, these instruments arguably reflect states' recognition that they bear joint stewardship obligations to ensure that all refugees have access to a decent safe harbor. In the final part, we assess some of the ways this approach to burden-sharing in the case of the Rohingya satisfies the demands of mandatory cooperation.

International Refugee Law

The cornerstone of international refugee law is the Refugee Convention's duty of *non-refoulement*, which obligates states-parties to refrain from returning refugees to places where their life or freedom would be threatened.[26] This duty is widely recognized as a customary norm because states generally do not forcibly repatriate refugees, and they do not do so, in part, because they believe themselves under a legal obligation not to do so.[27] There is also a growing consensus that the duty has a peremptory or *jus cogens* character, as affirmed in various Conclusions of the Executive Committee of the UNHCR,[28] the Cartagena Declaration,[29] and scholarship.[30] It follows from the duty's customary

[24] Global Compact on Safe, Orderly, and Regular Migration (GCM), New York, 19 December 2018, A/RES/73/195.

[25] Global Compact on Refugees, New York, 2 August 2018, A/73/12 (Part II).

[26] Refugee Convention, art. 33(1).

[27] See Jean Allain, 'The Jus Cogens Nature of Non-refoulement' (2001) 13 *Int'l J. Refugee L.* 533, 538, citing Guy S. Goodwin-Gil, *The Refugee in International Law*, 2nd ed. (Oxford: Oxford University Press, 1996), pp. 166–167; Elihu Lauterpacht and Daniel Bethlehem, 'The Scope and Content of the Principle of Non-Refoulement: Opinion', in Erika Feller et al. (eds.), *Refugee Protection in International Law: UNHCR Global Consultations on International Protection* (Cambridge: Cambridge University Press, 2009), pp. 87, 158.

[28] See, e.g., Executive Committee on the High Commissioner's Programme, 'General Conclusion on International Protection No. 79 (XLVII)', 11 October 1996, www.refworld.org/docid/3ae68c430.html ("[T]he principle of *non-refoulement* is not subject to derogation.").

[29] See Cartagena Declaration on Refugees, 22 November 1984, para. 5, Annual Report of the Inter-American Commission on Human Rights, OAS Doc. OEA/Ser.L/V/II.66/doc.10, rev. 1, pp. 190–193 (1984–1985) ("This principle [of non-*refoulement*] ... should be acknowledged and observed as a rule of jus cogens.").

[30] See, e.g., Arthur Helton and Eliana Jacobs, 'What Is Forced Migration' (1999) 13 *Geo. Immigr. L.J.* 526; Alice Farmer, 'Non-refoulement and Jus Cogens: Limiting Anti-Terror Measures that Threaten Refugee Protection' (2008) 32 *Geo. Immigr. L.J.* 1; Evan J. Criddle and Evan Fox-Decent, *Fiduciaries of Humanity: How International Law Constitutes*

status that it binds states that have not ratified the Refugee Convention and Protocol, as well as those that have done so. Moreover, if the duty is peremptory, then it applies to all states without the possibility of limitation or derogation. Reflecting the nascent rise of international human rights law at the time of its drafting, the Refugee Convention enshrines principles of nondiscrimination and nonpenalization. Under Article 3, states must apply the Convention "without discrimination as to race, religion, or country of origin."[31] And Article 31 bars states from penalizing asylum-seekers who have entered the state without authorization, so long as those persons "present themselves without delay to the authorities and show good cause for their illegal entry or presence."[32]

Importantly, however, the Refugee Convention's protection is limited in a variety of other ways. It does not expressly provide a permanent or even temporary right of asylum, nor rights to permanent resident status or citizenship.[33] Moreover, the weaker duty of *non-refoulement* provided under Article 33(1) does not apply to every person threatened with serious harm abroad. An individual counts as a "refugee" protected under the Refugee Convention only if they are outside their country of nationality or habitual residence and "owing to a well-founded fear of being persecuted for reasons of race, religion, nationality, membership of a particular social group or political opinion . . . [are] unable or unwilling to avail [themselves] of the protection of that country."[34] Thus, people who face risks arising from climate change or natural disasters are excluded. Other historically marginalized persons, such as women and sexual minorities, have to show that their persecution stems from their "membership of a particular social group."[35] Furthermore, the prohibition of *refoulement* does not apply to any person of "whom there are reasonable grounds for regarding as a danger to the security of the country in which he is, or who, having been convicted by a final judgment of a particularly serious crime, constitutes a danger to the community of that country."[36] Other possible claimants to refugee status are barred by

Authority (New York: Oxford University Press, 2016), pp. 269–271 [hereinafter *Fiduciaries of Humanity*].

31 Refugee Convention, art. 3.

32 Ibid. art. 31.

33 Guy S. Goodwin-Gill and Jane McAdam, *The Refugee in International Law*, 3rd ed. (Oxford: Oxford University Press, 2007), p. 370 (affirming that a general and universal right to asylum was too controversial for states to reach agreement on it).

34 Refugee Convention, art. 1(A)(2).

35 Ibid.

36 Ibid. art. 32(2).

the Refugee Convention's Article 1(F) "exclusion clauses," which exclude persons from claiming refugee status if they have engaged in crimes against peace, war crimes, crimes against humanity, serious nonpolitical crimes, or acts "contrary to the purposes and principles of the United Nations."[37]

Wider protection is available under the Convention Against Torture and Other Cruel, Inhuman, or Degrading Treatment or Punishment (CAT)[38] in cases where "there are substantial grounds for believing that [the individual would be in danger of being subjected to torture."[39] The inquiry mandated by the CAT does not concern itself with the grounds of persecution; the test is simply whether there are "substantial grounds for believing" that an individual may be tortured if deported.[40] For cases falling outside the CAT, however, the restrictive definition from the Refugee Convention is the default standard of international refugee law.

Significantly for present purposes, there is no bar in the Refugee Convention on a receiving state closing its borders to claimants arriving from a safe third country. Nor does the Refugee Convention expressly prohibit states from interdicting possible claimants on the high seas or in foreign jurisdictions so as to prevent them from reaching the host state, or from using carrier sanctions and visa requirements for the same purpose.[41] The lack of an express right to asylum in the receiving country, the absence of a bar on returning a claimant to a safe third country, and the positive law's silence regarding non-entrée policies combine to supply the receiving state with a strong textual argument in favor of its alleged entitlement to determine whether an asylum-seeker is eligible to make an asylum claim in the receiving state or must instead make the claim somewhere else. In other words, the Refugee Convention does not expressly grant asylum-seekers the right to choose where they will seek asylum, resulting in some policymakers

37 Ibid. art. 1(F).

38 Convention Against Torture and Other Cruel, Inhuman or Degrading Treatment or Punishment, 10 December 1984, 1465 UNTS 85.

39 Ibid. art. 3(1).

40 Ibid.

41 But see Hirsi Jamaa v. Italy, 55 Eur. Ct. Hum. Rts. 627 (2012) (concluding that returning refugees interdicted on the high seas may violate the European Convention on Human Rights); Center for Human Rights v. United States, Inter-Am. Comm'n H.R., Report No. 51/96, OEA/Ser.L/VII.95, doc. 7, rev. p. 550 (1997) (same); 'UNHCR Note on the Principle of Non-Refoulement', UN High Commission for Refugees, November 1997, www.refworld.org/docid/438c6d972.html (concluding that interdiction on the high seas may constitute *refoulement* under the Refugee Convention).

filling the void with absolutist state authority to create burden-sharing arrangements that determine the country in which refugees can seek asylum.[42] Proponents of maritime interdiction and non-entrée policies argue, therefore, that burden-sharing lies within the state's prerogative, so long as the state does not violate the duty of *non-refoulement*.[43]

Cooperation for Burden-Sharing

Burden-sharing is sometimes considered problematic because its enforcement may involve states forcibly deporting refugees to countries where they lack meaningful ties and face "warehousing" in primitive camps that resemble prisons.[44] Cooperation agreements billed as "burden-sharing" may erect roadblocks that prevent asylum-seekers from accessing refuge from persecution. States have conspired with one another to disrupt global migration routes, preventing asylum-seekers from reaching countries in the Global North where they could access asylum and establish a minimally decent life.[45] Cooperation in this context reveals its potential to erode refugee

[42] E.g., Agreement Between the Government of the United Kingdom of Great Britain and Northern Ireland and the Government of the Republic of Rwanda for the Provision of an Asylum Partnership to Strengthen Shared International Commitments on the Protection of Refugees and Migrants art. 2(3)(a), https://assets.publishing.service.gov.uk/media/656f51d30f12ef07a53e0295/UK-Rwanda_MEDP_-_English_-_Formatted__5_Dec_23__-_UK_VERSION.pdf ("creating a mechanism for the relocation to Rwanda of asylum seekers whose claims are not being considered by the United Kingdom, and by providing a mechanism for an asylum seeker's claim for protection to be determined in Rwanda").

[43] See, e.g., James C. Hathaway and R. Alexander Neve, 'Making IRL Relevant Again: A Proposal for Collectivized and Solution-Oriented Protection' (1997) 10 *Harv. Hum. Rts. J.* 115, 117; Peter H. Shuck, 'Refugee Burden-Sharing: A Modest Proposal' (1997) 22 YJIL 243. For an opposing view defending a defeasible right to remain in the receiving state, a right based on the moral cost of forcible deportation, as well as the ordinary Northern practice of permanent settlement, see our *Fiduciaries of Humanity*, *above*, pp. 263–264.

[44] See, e.g., Gregor Noll, 'Why Refugees Still Matter: A Response to James Hathaway' (2007) 8 *Melb. J. Int'l L.* 536, 538.

[45] See Maggy Lee, 'The Externalization of Border Control in the Global South: The Cases of Malaysia and Indonesia' (2022) 26 *Theoretical Criminology* 537; Monique Failla, 'Outsourcing Obligations to Developing Nations: Australia's Refugee Resettlement Agreement with Cambodia' (2016) 42 *Monash U. L. Rev.* 638; Jason Zubata, 'Is There a Safe Haven for Asylees Elsewhere? Assessing the International Legal Implications of Trump-Era Removal Practices' (2022) 25 *Harv. Latin Am. L. Rev.* 81; Margherita Matera et al., 'Is Australia a Model for the UK? A Critical Assessment of Parallels of Cruelty in Refugee Externalization Policies' (2022) 36 *J. Refugee Stud.* 271.

protection in violation of international human rights law and international refugee law.[46]

In principle, however, international cooperation need not render refugees less safe or less free. Burden-sharing can take a variety of forms. It includes measures that promote refugee welfare, such as direct humanitarian assistance to refugee populations, indirect assistance through international organizations like the Office of the UN High Commissioner for Refugees (UNHCR), and resettlement programs that allow refugees to voluntarily relocate to safe third-countries. Burden-sharing also includes states establishing legal pathways whereby refugees at their borders may obtain asylum and a path to citizenship. Such measures honor the spirit of the Refugee Convention and Protocol by ensuring that refugees have access to a decent safe harbor.

Conventional wisdom suggests that states have broad discretion to choose whether or to what extent they will embrace these mechanisms for refugee burden-sharing. International lawyers tend to assume that states are free to decide for themselves whether they will provide humanitarian assistance to distant refugees, give asylum to refugees at their borders, and offer resettlement to refugees interned abroad. Aside from the peremptory duty to refrain from *refoulement*, states are not thought to bear legal obligations to cooperate in refugee burden-sharing.

However, there are good reasons to question this conventional wisdom. To the extent that forced migration jeopardizes refugees' human rights, international cooperation is often necessary to fulfill states' joint stewardship obligation under the UN Charter and international human rights treaties to ensure "universal respect for, and observance of, human rights and fundamental freedoms for all."[47] At a minimum, states must "take steps, individually and through international assistance and cooperation," to ensure that vulnerable refugees have access to adequate food, clothing, housing, primary and secondary education, and medical care.[48] States that refuse to contribute resources to assist needy refugees, such as the Rohingya in Bangladesh, violate this requirement under international human rights law. Likewise, to the extent that refugee warehousing, maritime interdiction, and non-entrée policies threaten

46 David Cantor et al., 'Externalisation, Access to Territorial Asylum, and International Law' (2022) 34 *Int'l J. Refugee L.* 120.

47 UN Charter arts. 55–56. For more on the joint stewardship obligation to respect, protect, and fulfill human rights, see Chapter 9.

48 International Covenant on Economic, Social and Cultural Rights arts. 2(1), 11–13, 16 December 1966, 993 UNTS 3.

refugees' human rights, mandatory cooperation arguably requires states to cooperate in other ways, including by admitting and offering asylum to vulnerable refugees. In this sense, international human rights law both constrains how states may conduct burden-sharing and imposes affirmative requirements to cooperate in protecting and fulfilling refugees' human rights.

In the next section, we sketch a joint stewardship theory of international refugee law that lends further support for mandatory cooperation.[49] We argue that this joint stewardship theory and norms of mandatory cooperation mutually support one another, providing a framework for limited and principled burden-sharing. Roughly, joint stewardship provides the legal basis and structure for burden-sharing, while mandatory cooperation supplies the means and methods. Both are premised on an equitable and constitutional conception of sovereign equality, and both conceptualize international law as tracing its ultimate justification back to the individuals it serves.

Refugee Protection as a Joint Stewardship

Our theory of international refugee law is premised on the state's occupation of dual but complementary stewardship (or fiduciary) positions.[50] One is local, the other global. The local position is the state's role as a public steward entrusted and authorized by international law with sovereignty over a given territory and the people amenable to its jurisdiction, including foreign nationals who arrive at the state's border. The second position occupied by the receiving state – the global position – is that of joint stewardship of the earth's surface held with all other states on behalf of humanity.[51] Eyal Benvenisti calls the state in this position "a trustee of humanity"[52] and concludes that the state is under an "obligation not to deny entry to migrants and refugees without taking

[49] We develop this joint stewardship theory in greater detail in *Fiduciaries of Humanity*, pp. 265–281; and Evan J. Criddle and Evan Fox-Decent, 'The Authority of International Refugee Law' (2021) 62 *Wm. & Mary L. Rev.* 1067.

[50] *Fiduciaries of Humanity*, pp. 265–281.

[51] See Evan Fox-Decent, 'From Fiduciary States to Joint Trusteeship of the Atmosphere: The Right to a Healthy Environment Through a Fiduciary Prism', in Ken Coghill, Charles Sampford, and Tim Smith (eds.), *Fiduciary Duty and the Atmospheric Trust* (London: Routledge Press, 2012), p. 253 (arguing that states are joint trustees of the atmosphere on behalf of humanity).

[52] Eyal Benvenisti, 'Sovereigns as Trustees of Humanity: On the Accountability of States to Foreign Stakeholders' (2013) 107 AJIL 295.

into account the asylum seekers' individual concerns and at least providing justification for their exclusion."[53]

The argument for joint stewardship proceeds from the normative consequences of a particular kind of spillover effect produced by state possession of sovereign power. In our view, states are not entitled to set policies unilaterally that have spillover effects prejudicial to the rights or justice claims of foreign nationals. Policies related to greenhouse gas emissions are a prominent example of measures that have these kinds of spillover effects, as discussed in Chapter 7.[54]

This spillover principle applies to borders and a state's sovereign right to exclude. Mattias Kumm observes that borders present a "structural" justice-sensitive externality, one that arises as a consequence of international law's organization of the world into multiple territorially sovereign states.[55] The global territorial regime under which every state has the right to exclude outsiders raises the specter of a refugee with no place to exist lawfully. At the limit, if the refugee were forcibly driven from her home state and denied a right of asylum by all others, the territorial jurisdiction exercised over the earth's surface by sovereign states would convert her very physical existence into an illegality. Her body occupies space and must exist somewhere, but she herself (on the present assumption) has no right to be anywhere. And so her mere and unavoidable presence somewhere would constitute a permanent trespass.[56] She would do wrong by merely existing.

The possibility of doing wrong by merely existing is a structural spillover effect arising from international law's distribution of territorial sovereignty to states. Under the joint stewardship model, that distribution can be legitimate only if it can be understood to be made on behalf of every person subject to it, which is to say, on behalf of humanity. For this to be possible, international law must guarantee that every individual has a reasonable opportunity to pursue a decent life *somewhere*. Ordinarily, this opportunity is provided in the first instance through an individual's

[53] Ibid. p. 311.

[54] See Matthias Kumm, 'Constitutionalism and the Cosmopolitan State', NYU Public Law Research Paper, 10 October 2013, p. 18 [hereinafter Kumm, Constitutionalism]; Matthias Kumm, 'The Cosmopolitan Turn in Constitutionalism: An Integrated Conception of Public Law' (2013) 20 *Ind. J. Glob. Legal Stud.* 605.

[55] Kumm, Constitutionalism, pp. 15–17.

[56] See Arthur Ripstein, *Force and Freedom: Kant's Legal and Political Philosophy* (Cambridge, MA: Harvard University Press, 2009), pp. 279–280 (arguing that if all land were privately held and the landless were denied permission to be anywhere, "they would do wrong simply by being wherever they happened to be").

home state. But if a person is forced to flee or is stripped of citizenship, international law must step in to provide the refugee somewhere safe to live. Without the availability of surrogate protection, international law would not guarantee to every individual a reasonable opportunity to live a life of dignity somewhere. International law would lose its claim to universal legitimacy because it could not be said to authorize territorial sovereignty on behalf of every person subject to it; refugees and the stateless would be excluded.

A plausible way to avoid this result is to conceive of states, at the global level, as joint stewards of the earth's surface on behalf of humanity. Under this conception, international law grants states a general right to exclude as part of their territorial sovereignty, but requires as a condition of the grant that states participate in a collective regime of surrogate protection in the service of exiled outsiders. International refugee law supplies the legal framework for a regime of surrogate protection by carving out an exception to exclusive territorial sovereignty in favor of refugees. While states retain a *general* claim to exclusive territorial jurisdiction, the claim is not *absolute*. States are barred by equitable principles from exercising their right to territorial sovereignty in a way that would refuse entry to refugees. Any such use of state power would amount to an abuse of right, and, from the perspective of mandatory cooperation, would infringe the duty of all states to have due regard for the interests of vulnerable foreign nationals. The joint stewardship model explains the refugee's standing to make a claim on international refugee law's equitable limitation on states' exercise of territorial sovereignty by positing states as joint stewards of the earth's surface on behalf of humanity, and in particular on behalf of asylum-seekers entitled to resort to surrogate protection. Properly understood, the stewardship theory does not place limits on otherwise unbridled sovereign power, since under this approach there is no de jure sovereign power to exclude asylum-seekers unilaterally. Rather, the stewardship model reconceives territorial sovereignty in a manner that makes it consistent with equitable principles that affirm the universal entitlement of every member of humanity to have their bare physical existence never treated as a wrong.

The New York Declaration and the Global Compacts

Within the past several years, states have affirmed their joint stewardship responsibility for refugees, endorsing the principle that they should share the burdens of refugee protection equitably. In response to the mass movement of asylum-seekers and the high loss of life in the Mediterranean Sea in 2015, the United Nations convened a Global Summit on Refugees and Migrants in September 2016. The Summit resulted in the unanimous adoption by all 193 UN member states of the New York Declaration for Refugees and Migrants, a statement of principle committing the international community to address jointly global migration issues.[57] The parties to the New York Declaration recognized "a shared responsibility to manage large movement of refugees and migrants in a humane, sensitive, compassionate and people-centred manner."[58] The parties likewise underlined "the centrality of international cooperation to the refugee protection regime."[59] They pledged to work together to "ensure … protection for all who need it,"[60] including asylum-seekers still in transit.[61] They noted the disproportionate burden of refugee hosting undertaken by developing countries, and committed to "a more equitable sharing of the burden and responsibility for hosting and supporting the world's refugees."[62] Committing to "actively promote durable solutions" compatible with equitable burden-sharing, the parties declared their intent "to expand the number and range of legal pathways available for refugees to be admitted to or resettled in third countries," with the goal to "provide resettlement places and other legal pathways for admission on a scale that would enable the annual resettlement needs identified by [UNHCR] to be met."[63]

Two years after the summit in New York, states adopted two global compacts: the Global Compact for Migration, and the Global Compact on Refugees.[64] Like the New York Declaration, the global compacts are non-binding political agreements that seek to "foster[] international cooperation among all the relevant actors on migration, acknowledging

57 New York Declaration for Refugees and Migrants, New York, 13 September 2016, A/RES/71/L/1.

58 Ibid. para. 11.

59 Ibid. para. 68.

60 Ibid. para. 66.

61 Ibid. para. 28 (committing to "intensifying international cooperation on the strengthening of search and rescue mechanisms" for asylum seekers at sea); ibid. para. 29 (agreeing to "take steps to address the particular vulnerabilities of women and children" in transit, such as "their potential exposure to discrimination and exploitation, as well as to sexual, physical and psychological abuse, violence, human trafficking and contemporary forms of slavery").

62 Ibid.

63 Ibid. paras. 77–78.

64 Ibid. Appendix I, para. 19 (Global Compact on Refugees); Appendix II (Global Compact for Migration).

that no State can address migration alone."[65] The global compacts also track the New York Declaration in expressing states' collective commitment and shared responsibility for safeguarding refugees' human rights and fundamental freedoms.[66]

The Global Compact for Migration lays out twenty-three multilateral policy objectives aimed at promoting safe, orderly, and regular migration. The objectives include commitments to "[e]nhance availability and flexibility of pathways for regular migration," "[a]ddress and reduce vulnerabilities in migration," and, most generally, "[s]trengthen international cooperation and global partnerships for safe, orderly and regular migration."[67] A further objective, significant for our purposes, requires states to "[m]inimize the adverse drivers and structural factors that compel people to leave their country of origin."[68]

The parties' commitments to achieve this last objective include investing in programs geared toward "climate change mitigation and adaptation."[69] States undertake to "[s]trengthen joint analysis and sharing of information to better map, understand, predict and address migration movements, such as those that may result from sudden-onset and slow-onset natural disasters, the adverse effects of climate change [and] environmental degradation."[70] With an explicit nod toward low-lying countries and other regions on the frontlines of climate change, the parties commit to "[d]evelop adaptation and resilience strategies to sudden-onset and slow-onset natural disasters, the adverse effects of climate change, and environmental degradation, such as desertification, land degradation, drought and sea level rise."[71] These provisions are significant because people forced to migrate as a result of climate change do not ordinarily qualify for protection under the Refugee Convention and the Global Compact on Refugees. Implementation of these provisions is overseen by the International Migration Review Forum, an international conference convened by the United Nations every four years.[72]

65 Global Compact for Migration, para. 7.
66 Ibid. paras. 8, 11–12.
67 Ibid. para. 16.
68 Ibid.
69 Ibid. para. 18(b).
70 Ibid. para. 18(h).
71 Ibid. para. 18(i).
72 Format and Organizational Aspects of the International Migration Review Forums, 19 July 2019, A/RES/73/326.

Thus far, the Global Compact on Migration's cooperative framework for addressing climate change-related migration has yielded disappointing results. The most significant international cooperation in this domain has arisen from the UN Framework Convention on Climate Change (UNFCCC), and more specifically from the Paris Agreement and the annual Conference of Parties meetings (COPs). As discussed in Chapter 7, the UNFCCC seeks to prevent global warming by encouraging states to set targets so as to reduce global carbon emissions overall. The international community has made less progress in addressing the effects of global warming on forced migration. Regrettably, the Forum concluded at its first meeting in 2022 that "efforts to mitigate and adapt to the adverse effects of climate change have been insufficient, including in climate finance."[73] Perhaps the most that can be reasonably expected from the Global Compact on Migration in this domain is that its Forum might offer periodic assessments of mitigation and adaptation efforts that relate to climate-induced migration.

The Global Compact on Refugees begins by announcing that "[t]he predicament of refugees is a common concern of humankind."[74] The central policy challenge facing the international community is the development and implementation of a framework to facilitate "more equitable sharing of the burden and responsibility for hosting and supporting the world's refugees, while taking account of existing contributions and the differing capacities and resources among States."[75] The overarching methodology proposed for the development of this policy is international cooperation, which is characterized as "a core purpose of the United Nations, as set out in its Charter, and is in line with the principle of sovereign equality of States."[76] However, the mission of the Global Compact on Refugees extends far beyond states, identifying a wide range of "relevant stakeholders" envisioned to play a role in equitable burden-sharing, including "international organizations within and outside the United Nations system . . . ; other humanitarian and development actors; international and regional financial institutions; regional organizations; local authorities; civil society, including faith-based organizations; academics and other experts; the private sector; media;

[73] Progress Declaration of the International Migration Review Forum, 7 June 2022. A/RES/76/266, para. 27.

[74] Global Compact on Refugees, para. 1.

[75] Ibid.

[76] Ibid. para. 2.

host community members and refugees themselves."[77] This multisectoral strategy is sometimes referred to as a "whole-of-society approach," since it enlists civil society actors and organizations to contribute to the stewardship of migration, along with member states and the UN Migration Network.[78]

Like the Global Compact for Migration, the Global Compact on Refugees is "soft law," in that it is not legally binding. Instead, the Global Compact on Refugees purports to represent "the political will and ambition of the international community as a whole for strengthened cooperation and solidarity with refugees and affected host countries."[79] The "interlinked and interdependent" objectives of the Global Compact on Refugees are to "(i) ease pressures on host countries; (ii) enhance refugee self-reliance; (iii) expand access to third-country solutions; and (iv) support conditions in countries of origin for return in safety and dignity."[80] To achieve these objectives, this Global Compact adopts a *modus operandi* similar to the Paris Agreement. Whereas under the Paris Agreement states are called on to specify and realize "nationally determined contributions (NDCs)," under the Global Compact on Refugees, states and relevant stakeholders are asked to make voluntary contributions or pledges that they themselves determine, "taking into account their national realities, capacities and levels of development, and respecting national policies and priorities."[81]

Much like the way NDCs are monitored at the yearly COP under the UNFCCC framework, voluntary pledges are monitored at the Global Refugee Forum that convenes every four years to oversee implementation of the Global Compact on Refugees.[82] The first Global Refugee Forum met in 2019. The second met in December 2023. More than 4,200 participants from 168 countries attended the 2023 Refugee Forum.[83] Over 1,600 pledges were undertaken to support refugees and host countries, including 43 multi-partner commitments led by governments. An estimated USD 2.2 billion in new financial commitments were

[77] Ibid. para. 3.
[78] J. Kevin Appleby, 'Implementation of the Global Compact on Safe, Orderly, and Regular Migration: A Whole-of-Society Approach' (2020) 8 *J. Migration & Hum. Sec.* 214 (discussing the Global Compact on Migration with emphasis on irregular migration).
[79] Ibid. para. 4.
[80] Ibid. para. 7.
[81] Ibid. para. 4.
[82] Ibid. para. 17.
[83] 'About the Global Refugee Forum', UNHCR, www.unhcr.org/global-refugee-forum-2023.

made by states and other stakeholders, including some 250 million pledged by the private sector.[84]

In his closing remarks at the December 2023 Refugee Forum, UN High Commissioner for Refugees Filippo Grandi lamented that since October 2023 alone, 700,000 people had been displaced by conflict in Myanmar, bringing the total of internally displaced persons within Myanmar to more than 2.5 million.[85] At the same time, he applauded the "multistakeholder whole-of-society pledging approach" taken by stakeholders.[86] The case of the nearly one million Rohingya exiled in camps in Bangladesh is instructive.

Under the Global Compact on Refugees framework, forty-nine states and civil society organizations have pledged to support the Rohingya and Bangladesh, including thirty-five new pledges in 2023.[87] The pledges address a wide range of socioeconomic needs arising from protracted confinement in refugee camps. They support diverse programs in the camps that aim to provide or improve the delivery of crucial public goods, including elementary education and literacy, occupational and agricultural skills training, healthcare, mental health and psychosocial support, hygiene, nutritional and food-security services, assistance for survivors of gender-based violence, child welfare and safety initiatives, climate adaptation agricultural and economic programs, disaster-response services, community strengthening and resilience measures (e.g., enhancing digital communication capacity), and disability support programs.[88] Some of the pledges address resettlement, such as the pledge from Amnesty International Australia "to mobilize our movement to advocate to the Australian government to increase Australia's annual humanitarian program to 40,000."[89]

Within Bangladesh, the UN Strategic Executive Group (SEG) provides overall guidance to the international community's Rohingya response. Consisting of UNHCR, the International Organization for Migration (IOM), and the UN Resident Coordinator, the SEG in 2023 pledged "to continue bolstering and mobilizing solidarity with the

84 Ibid.

85 UNHCR, 'Global Refugee Forum 2023 Closing Statement by UN High Commissioner for Refugees Filippo Grandi', UNHCR, 15 December 2023, www.unhcr.org/news/speeches-and-statements/global-refugee-forum-2023-closing-statement-un-high-commissioner.

86 Ibid.

87 'Pledges & Contributions', UNHCR, https://globalcompactrefugees.org/pledges-contributions (Search pledges: "Rohingya").

88 Ibid.

89 Ibid.

Government of Bangladesh – as the largest host of Rohingya refugees globally – to sustain support to the Rohingya humanitarian response."[90] The SEG also pledged concrete assistance to refugee resilience and empowerment programs, but plainly understands its mission to include international advocacy to support Bangladesh as host. In other words, the SEG understands its mandate to include attracting economic and political support for equitable burden-sharing, whether that happens through resettlement in other host countries, support for camps in Bangladesh, or eventual return to Myanmar. This multisectoral, whole-of-society effort is grounded within the overarching institutional structure created by the Global Compact on Refugees and its periodic Refugee Forum.

From Soft Law to Mandatory Cooperation

The Global Compact on Refugees, like the New York Declaration that generated it, is an expressly nonbinding agreement. In the lexicon of international lawyers, it is "soft law" inasmuch as it is not a formally binding treaty. Pledges made within its framework are often characterized as humanitarian in nature, which can convey the idea that they are praiseworthy but not obligatory. Nonetheless, there are good reasons to think that the Global Compact on Refugees is legally significant from the standpoint of mandatory cooperation. As with various international declarations addressing transboundary pollution,[91] the Global Compact on Refugees evinces a serious effort on the part of the international community to coordinate publicly joint action around urgent matters, and these efforts can bolster sometimes-flagging political will. State commitments to the Global Compact on Refugees are normatively significant under international law – even if in practice they are nonjusticiable or otherwise unenforceable – insofar as they reflect a good faith effort by the participating states to satisfy their obligations to cooperate for the benefit of refugees and other forced migrants.

When the Global Compact on Refugees was presented for the approval of the UN General Assembly, it was approved overwhelmingly by a vote of 181 in favor to 2 against (United States and Hungary), with three

[90] Ibid.

[91] We explain why soft law declarations are legally relevant to mandatory cooperation at the end of Chapter 6.

abstentions (Eritrea, Liberia, Libya).[92] However, even states that opposed the Global Compact on Refugees arguably have an obligation to support its successful implementation based on their role as joint stewards of the earth's territory. Recall that under the joint stewardship theory of international refugee law, states' duty of *non-refoulement* is justified as an equitable implication of states' exclusive jurisdiction over the earth's habitable territories: persons to whom all states closed their doors would trespass and do wrong just by existing, because their presence anywhere would be illegal. For the international legal order to be legitimate, we claimed, asylum-seekers must be able to find decent safe harbor somewhere. Decent safe harbor, however, is not costless. It is an international public good. For the cost of that good to be distributed in a manner that is more equitable than letting first receiving states such as Bangladesh shoulder the burden alone, an international institution is required in which states-parties can hold each other to account publicly as they negotiate fair contributions. For now, that institution is the regime of pledging and monitoring created by the Global Compact on Refugees. Becoming a member in good standing within that institution is an obligation that falls on every state because every state claims exclusive territorial jurisdiction, and therefore every state is subject to the equitable restriction on exclusive territorial jurisdiction that asylum-seekers can rightfully claim. It follows that every state has an obligation to participate in good faith as an equal in an international policy-setting institution that aims to distribute equitably the cost of providing decent safe harbor to refugees. A recalcitrant state that refuses to cooperate with others on equal terms subverts its claim to exclusive jurisdiction over its territory, since the claim to exclusive jurisdiction relies on making good on the promise of an equitable limit on territorial sovereignty in favor of asylum-seekers.

This theory is supported by states' broad participation in the Global Refugee Forum's framework of national pledges and contributions.[93]

92 Nayla Rush, 'Global Compact for Refugees Adopted Today: Even Without U.S. Assent, It Will Likely Shape Global Regulation', Ctr. Immigr. Studs., 17 December 2018.

93 Global Refugee Forum 2023, UNHCR, www.unhcr.org/events/global-refugee-forum-2023 (observing that 168 countries participated in the latest forum meeting). For example, after initially opposing the Global Compact on Refugees, the United States subsequently has participated in the Global Refugee Forum, making pledges that include robust commitments to increase Rohingya resettlement to the United States and to encourage Rohingya resettlement in third countries. United States Announces New Pledges at 2023 Global Refugee Forum, US Dep't of State, 15 December 2023. The United States will likely suspend its participation, however, for the duration of the Trump administration.

A possible explanation for this emerging practice is that states recognize a general obligation to burden-share, but, as was the case with the Paris Agreement and NDCs, they wish to retain ultimate legislative control over the specific content of that obligation through a system of pledges. The fact that neither the general obligation to burden-share nor specific pledges under the Global Compact on Refugees are presently enforceable as a matter of international law does not necessarily mean they lack legal significance. For example, should states-parties generally continue to pledge and deliver on their pledges in a manner akin to the way they perform NDC-type treaty obligations under the Paris Agreement, a future court could find that pledges on which other stakeholders or refugees detrimentally rely are in some cases enforceable as a matter of customary law, or possibly under a doctrine of promissory estoppel.[94] Over time, soft law can harden, which itself suggests that soft law is an inchoate or embryonic form of law.

Some might reject the analysis above on realist grounds, suggesting perhaps that cooperation under the Global Compact on Refugees is driven by states' self-interested motive to advance their reputations rather than any sense of legal obligation or constraint. The frequent characterization of pledges as humanitarian supports this understanding, since humanitarianism responds to an imperfect duty of beneficence or charity under which the humanitarian agent does good whether they give a little or a lot. However, the mere existence of the Global Compact on Refugees can be read to suggest that states acknowledge a collective obligation to provide decent safe harbor for refugees. The difficulty arises at the moment of interpreting and applying the general injunction to provide decent safe harbor to the specific circumstances of each state. And since each state can determine its own pledges, this too seems to reinforce a realist reading under which states make humanitarian gestures to improve their reputations. A legalist account of burden-sharing is nonetheless available.

The key to understanding the legal quality of good faith deliberations and negotiation over burden-sharing is appreciating the distinction between legislation and interpretation. By coming together to establish the Global Compact on Refugees, the injunction to provide decent safe harbor to which states have jointly subscribed is legislative in nature: it directs states, collectively, to provide decent safe harbor. The all-purpose means for them to do so is international cooperation, but the specific

[94] Nuclear Tests, Austr. v. Fr., 1974 ICJ Rep. 253 (20 December).

contributions of each state are subject to each state's interpretation of its own fair share, taking into account the burden-sharing capacity and willingness of other states. At the stage of interpretation and application of the general injunction to provide decent safe harbor, every state in effect adopts the judicial role of interpreter.

Using the analogy of children arguing over the interpretation of a rule in a winner-take-all game that is played without a referee, David Dyzenhaus claims that states in international law, even without the benefit of separate dispute-resolution institutions, will sometimes occupy a judicial interpretive role with respect to the rules of international law.[95] The judicial role brings with it a variety of implicit commitments, such that children and states alike who adopt that role necessarily undertake to abide by the following principles: "to offer reasonable interpretations of what a rule requires . . . ; to take into account for the sake of fairness the way in which the rule has been previously interpreted in analogous situations; to treat each participant as an equal when it comes to interpretation."[96] States and game-playing children alike who occupy the judicial role have "accepted the onus of showing precisely why the different interpretations were not reducible to a player's [or state's] interests."[97] They occupy this role jointly with other states, and on equal terms, such that none is entitled to dictate unilaterally the interpretation of a rule that will bind the group. In short, the various norms internal to and constitutive of the joint judicial role show why interpretations offered by good faith states (or game-playing children) cannot be reduced to their interests, and count as legal interpretations, properly so-called.

This is so whether the ultimate legislative genesis of such interpretations is a formal treaty, such as the Paris Agreement, or a nonbinding agreement, such as the Global Compact on Refugees. The substantively legal quality of good faith deliberations is similar in both cases because the basic norms governing the judicial role of states and legal interpretation are similar in both. This too helps explain how the soft law from the Global Compact on Refugees could harden over time as customary law. States operating in good faith within the regime set by the Global Compact on Refugees will understand and abide by the norms governing their judicial role when they interpret the burden-sharing rule and apply

[95] See David Dyzenhaus, 'Hobbes and the International Rule of Law' (2014) 23 *Ethics & Int'l Affs.* 53–64.

[96] Ibid. p. 60.

[97] Ibid.

it to themselves in accordance with equitable principles. Because the reasons for their interpretation of the rule commanding decent safe harbor are conditioned by legality and therefore distinct from whatever interest they have in defending a favored interpretation, that interpretation cannot be reduced to their self-interest. A state's reasonable, good faith interpretation of its burden-sharing contribution is most easily explicable by attributing to the state a commitment to the form of legality intrinsic to the judicial role. And this conclusion paves the way for the eventual recognition of the norms of cooperation under the Global Compact on Refugees – norms governing multilateral pledging and the performance of pledges – as binding international customary law. Although duties of mandatory cooperation have yet to fully crystallize at this stage of international refugee law's development, the Rohingya people and Bangladesh may one day be able to demand that the international community contribute its fair share to the Rohingya refugee crisis as a matter of right.

Conclusion

The plight of the Rohingya people is terrible and ongoing. In the Global Compact on Refugees the international community acknowledges that the "predicament of refugees" like the Rohingya "is a common concern of humankind."[98] Through its multisectoral whole-of-society approach, the Global Compact on Refugees supplies a framework through which a significant number of states-parties, international organizations, and civil society organizations have joined forces to support the nearly one million Rohingya exiled in Bangladesh. While Bangladesh is still shouldering a massively disproportionate amount of the burden of hosting and caring for the Rohingya, there is at least now an international regime in place to facilitate burden-sharing through consultation, negotiation, and collective implementation. Formally, this regime is nonbinding soft law. Nonetheless, we have suggested that it has a legal character that may in time give rise to obligations under customary international law.

In the last section of this chapter, we discussed briefly the possible implications of states adopting a judicial role as joint interpreters of the rules of international law. Of course, international law now has arbitral and judicial institutions of its own. In Chapter 12 we suggest

[98] Global Compact on Refugees, para. 1.

that, contrary to conventional wisdom, states have an obligation to resort to such institutions if a dispute turns intractable. Before taking up that argument, however, in the next chapter we explain how mandatory cooperation applies to settings where multiple states have regulatory jurisdiction over the same people, property, or activities, posing a risk of international regulatory conflicts.

11

Extraterritorial Lawmaking

Dorm Rooms, Boardrooms, and Back Room Deals

In 1996, Stanford graduate students Sergey Brin and Larry Page developed an innovative search engine for navigating the Internet. Two years later, they dropped out of school, filed articles of incorporation, and moved their fledgling business from their dorm rooms to a friend's garage in Menlo Park, California. Public demand for their search engine soon exploded. By 2022, it received 8.5 billion search requests daily, accounting for nearly 90 percent of all searches in the United States and 70 percent worldwide. So great was its global popularity that the company's name – Google – became synonymous with searching the Internet.

Google leveraged its success as a search platform to become an advertising powerhouse. As the Internet drew consumers away from print media and television, global online advertising surged from approximately USD 6 billion in 2000 to USD 360 billion in 2020.[1] Much of this revenue went to Google, which enjoyed significant advantages over its competitors due to its dominant position in the search market and its ability to leverage user data for targeted advertising. But Google was not content to rest on these competitive advantages alone. It worked to cement its market dominance by buying up would-be competitors and expanding into adjacent markets, such as operating systems, mobile phone apps, and hardware for phones and tablet computers. These moves grew the Google family of companies – now consolidated under the holding company Alphabet – into a trillion-dollar corporate behemoth.[2]

[1] William L. Hosch, 'Google', Brittanica, www.britannica.com/topic/Google-Inc.

[2] Nick Statt, 'The Rise, Disappearance, and Retirement of Google Co-Founders Larry Page and Sergei Brin', The Verge, 4 December 2019.

As Google's empire expanded, its activities attracted regulatory scrutiny. The US Department of Justice (DOJ) filed multiple lawsuits against Google, arguing that the company has engaged in anticompetitive behaviors that violate American antitrust law. Antitrust law is concerned with prescribing terms of fair competition to protect consumers from exploitation by dominant firms. The law seeks to achieve this goal by prohibiting mergers and acquisitions that lead to monopolies, prohibiting anticompetitive tactics to achieve or sustain monopolization (e.g., abuse of a dominant position), and banning collusion between competitors to restrain trade (e.g., price-fixing). Because the international community has not developed binding general rules for antitrust, the regulations that national authorities apply arise from domestic or regional sources, not international law.

In the case of Google, the DOJ alleges that the firm has contracted with mobile device manufacturers, wireless carriers, and browser developers to become the default search engine for their smartphones and other devices.[3] Combined with Google's Android mobile platform and Chrome browser, these agreements have made Google the default search engine for over 80 percent of all devices in the United States, further entrenching its dominant market position.[4] US regulators also accuse Google of other anticompetitive practices, such as blocking or downranking search results from competitors and driving up advertising prices by representing both buyers and sellers for its advertising services. If these allegations were not troubling enough, regulators claim that Google has conspired with Meta, the parent company of Facebook, to give the latter preferential treatment in its advertising auctions in exchange for Meta's agreement not to compete with Google's advertising business. Collectively, these accusations paint an unsettling picture of the global tech titan exploiting its dominant position as the "gatekeeper of the internet" to deliberately stifle competition, suppress innovation, and inflate the prices it charges for its services.[5] Based on these concerns,

[3] Gilad Edelman, 'Google's Antitrust Cases: A Guide for the Perplexed', Wired, 10 December 2020; 'The Google Antitrust Lawsuit: Initial Observations', Cong. Res. Serv., 23 October 2020.

[4] Mark Sullivan, 'How Google Will Fight Off the DOJ's Claims of Monopoly in Search', Fast Company, 21 October 2020.

[5] Brian Fung, 'The Antitrust Lawsuits Against Google Just Keep Coming', CNN, 17 December 2020. (quoting New York State Attorney General Leticia James). Whether US regulators will succeed in these lawsuits is by no means clear. See Sullivan, 'How Google Will Fight' (reviewing the case against Google's antitrust liability).

a federal district court held in August 2024 that Google's anticompetitive practices violated American antitrust law.[6]

Google's controversial tactics have also drawn fire from European regulators. In June 2017, the European Commission fined Google €2.4 billion under EU competition law for using its search algorithm to funnel users toward its comparison shopping service, "Google Shopping," to the detriment of competitor sites.[7] The following year, Google incurred an additional €4.3 billion fine for illegally requiring Android manufacturers and network operators to preinstall its search app on mobile devices.[8] In March 2022, authorities in the European Union and the United Kingdom launched parallel investigations into the alleged conspiracy between Google and Meta to carve up the online advertising market.[9] Thus, European authorities have not shied away from enforcing their competition laws against Google, a corporation headquartered across the Atlantic.

This chapter uses antitrust law as a case study to explain why and how mandatory cooperation should apply to settings where states have concurrent regulatory jurisdiction under international law. Within the past century, the United States and the European Union have extended their domestic antitrust laws to foreign actors operating abroad.[10] Rising powers, such as Brazil, China, and India, have also asserted jurisdiction to regulate the anticompetitive behavior of foreign firms.[11] Supporters of these

[6] United States v. Google L.L.C., Memorandum Opinion, Case No. 20-cv-3010, at 276 (D.C.D.C. Aug. 5, 2024).

[7] European Commission, 'Antitrust: Commission Fines Google €2.42 Billion for Abusing Dominance as Search Engine by Giving Illegal Advantage to Own Comparison Shopping Service', European Commission, 27 June 2017; see also Jack Denton, 'Google Just Lost a Major EU Antitrust Appeal. It's Bigger Than the $2.8 Billion Fine in a Major Win for Regulators', Barron's, 10 November 2021.

[8] European Commission, 'Antitrust: Commission fines Google €4.34 Billion for Illegal Practices Regarding Android Mobile Devices to Strengthen Dominance of Google's Search Engine', European Commission, 18 July 2018.

[9] Pietro Lombardi, 'EU, UK Open Antitrust Probes Into Google, Meta Ad-Services Agreement', Politico, 11 March 2022.

[10] See United States v. Aluminum Company of America (Alcoa), 148 F 2d 416 (2d Cir. 1945); Joanne Scott, 'Extraterritoriality and Territorial Extension in E.U. Law' (2014) 62 *Am. J. Compar. L.* 87, 88.

[11] See Austen Parrish and Cedrick Ryngaert (eds.), *Research Handbook on Extraterritoriality in International Law* (Cheltenham: Edward Elgar Publishing, 2023), chs. 9–12 (discussing extraterritoriality in Africa, Asia, Australia, Latin America, New Zealand, and the United Kingdom); Angela Huyue Zhang, *Chinese Antitrust Exceptionalism: How the Rise of China Challenges Global Regulation* (Oxford: Oxford University Press, 2021), pp. 34–35, 217–221 (noting the rise of Chinese extraterritorial antitrust regulation).

practices argue that extraterritorial regulation is necessary to enable states to protect their people from foreign-sourced harm and generate public goods that benefit the entire international community.[12] Left unchecked, however, extraterritorial lawmaking can also undermine sovereign equality by subjecting a state to unilateral foreign governance.[13] Both extraterritorial regulation and its absence can enable neo-imperialism: the former by subjecting people to foreign rule and the latter by removing legal obstacles to exploitation by multinational corporations.[14] In this chapter, we argue that the equitable model of sovereignty requires a different approach: states must resolve disputes over their concurrent regulatory jurisdiction through mandatory cooperation.

Does Equal Sovereignty Require Exclusive Jurisdiction?

Prior to the twentieth century, the principle of sovereign equality was generally understood to impose limits on a state's prescriptive jurisdiction.[15] As early as the fourteenth century, Bartolus declared that "it is not for one city to make the law upon another, for an equal has no power over an equal."[16] In 1825, the US Supreme Court reiterated this view in *The Antelope*: "No principle of general law is more universally acknowledged, than the perfect equality of nations . . . It

[12] See, e.g., Cedric Ryngaert, *Selfless Intervention: The Exercise of Jurisdiction in the Common Interest* (Oxford: Oxford University Press 2020), pp. 7–8 (arguing that extraterritorial prescriptive jurisdiction can be deployed to promote cosmopolitan norms); Roger O'Keefe, 'Cooperative National Regulation to Secure Transnational Public Goods: A Reply to Nico Krisch' (2002) 33 EJIL 515, 524 (arguing that extraterritoriality advances states' "respective and collective regulatory interests in the effective securing of public goods, including transnational ones").

[13] One of us has argued that extraterritorial lawmaking in some settings also violates a people's international right to self-determination. See Evan J. Criddle, 'Extraterritoriality's Empire: How Self-Determination Limits Extraterritorial Lawmaking' (2024) 118 AJIL 607. In this chapter, we table that objection to focus on sovereign equality and the associated requirements of mandatory cooperation.

[14] See Jenny S. Martinez, 'The New Territorialism and Old Territorialism' (2014) 99 *Cornell L. Rev.* 1387, 1400 (observing that "anti-imperialist rhetoric in [US] courts" and the absence of extraterritorial US regulation "helped create the so-called 'banana republics' in Latin America").

[15] International lawyers use the term "prescriptive jurisdiction" to describe a state's legal competence to legislate and apply its law to particular people, property, and conduct. Prescriptive jurisdiction is distinguished from a state's authority to adjudicate disputes ("adjudicatory jurisdiction") or enforce legal norms ("enforcement jurisdiction").

[16] James Crawford, *Brownlie's Principles of Public International Law*, 9th ed. (Oxford: Oxford University Press, 2019), p. 433 (translating Bartolus).

results from this equality, that no one can rightfully impose a rule on another."[17] Justice Joseph Story derived two general maxims of prescriptive jurisdiction from sovereign equality: first, "that every nation possesses an exclusive sovereignty and jurisdiction within its own territory," and second, "that no state or nation can, by its laws, directly affect, or bind property out of its own territory, or bind persons not resident therein" except perhaps its own subjects.[18] Giving municipal laws extraterritorial effect would be unthinkable, Story asserted, because it "would at once annihilate the sovereignty and equality of every nation, which should be called upon to recognize and enforce them."[19] Max Huber endorsed this assessment in the *Island of Palmas* arbitration: "Sovereignty in the relations between States signifies independence. Independence in regard to a portion of the globe is the right to exercise therein, to the exclusion of any other State, the functions of a State."[20] Thus, for centuries, international lawyers tended to accept that the concept of sovereignty and the principle of sovereign equality required that states must be free to govern their respective territories without interference from foreign law.[21]

The Permanent Court of International Justice (PCIJ) dealt a significant blow to this idea in *The Lotus* when it concluded by the narrowest of margins that international law did not forbid Turkey from applying its criminal law to foreign nationals aboard a vessel flying the French flag (and therefore under French sovereignty). The Court recognized that "the first and foremost restriction imposed by international law upon a State is that – failing the existence of a permissive rule to the contrary – it may not exercise its power in any form in the territory of another State."[22] However, the Court rejected the idea that states exercise "power"

17 The Antelope, 23 US (10 Wheat) 66, 122 (1825).

18 Joseph Story, *Commentary on the Conflict of Laws* (Boston: Hilliard, Gray & Co., 1834), §§ 18, 20–21.

19 Ibid. § 32; see also The Schooner Exchange v. McFaddon, 11 US 116, 136 (1812) ("The jurisdiction of the nation within its own territory is necessarily exclusive and absolute.").

20 Island of Palmas Case (Neth./US), 2 RIAA 829, 838 (4 April 1928); see also Joseph H. Beale, 'The Jurisdiction of a Sovereign State' (1923) 36 HLR 241, 241 (reasoning that a state's prescriptive jurisdiction is limited to the extent that it "infringes the rights of other sovereigns").

21 The principle was subject to some notable exceptions, including for pirates and slave traders, who were considered "enemies of all mankind" (*hostis humani generis*). John H. Knox, 'A Presumption Against Extrajurisdictionality' (2010) 104 AJIL 351, 367 (discussing traditional exceptions to the strict territoriality rule).

22 The Case of the S.S. Lotus (Fr./Turk.), 1927 PCIJ (ser. A) No. 10 (7 September), p. 18, para. 45.

if they merely "extend the application of their laws and the jurisdiction of their courts to persons, property and acts outside their territory" without enforcing those laws extraterritorially.[23] By distinguishing lawmaking from enforcement in this manner, the Court suggested that states were free under international law to exercise unlimited prescriptive jurisdiction. *The Lotus* thus gave states *carte blanche* to use their national laws to regulate the rest of the world.

The Lotus arrived at the apex of the colonial era, a moment in history when there were relatively few recognized states and the voluntarist model of sovereign equality was ascendant. As discussed in Chapter 1, legal scholars often cite the "Lotus principle" that "whatever is not explicitly prohibited by international law is permitted"[24] as the high-water mark for voluntarist approaches to international law.[25] In contrast, international lawyers today generally take the PCIJ's sweeping pronouncements on extraterritorial prescriptive jurisdiction with a grain of salt. Most legal scholars prefer to read *The Lotus* as standing for the narrower proposition that states may exercise prescriptive jurisdiction over conduct that causes substantial harm within their borders. This narrower reading accords with subsequent developments at the national level, where legislation authorizing effects-based jurisdiction has become increasingly common.

The 1945 *Alcoa* judgment of the US Court of Appeals for the Second Circuit marked a turning point in the rise of effects-based jurisdiction.[26] At issue in the case was an international price-fixing conspiracy between Alcoa, an American company, its Canadian sister company, and several foreign aluminum producers.[27] The central legal question before the court was whether American antitrust law applied to the extraterritorial conduct of foreign corporations.[28] The court concluded, as a matter of

[23] Ibid. p. 19, para. 46.

[24] Prosper Weil, '"The Court Cannot Conclude Definitively" . . . Non Liquet Revisited' (1998) 36 CJTL 109, 112.

[25] See, e.g., Arrest Warrant of 11 April 2000, 2002 ICJ Rep. 63, p. 78 para. 51 (14 Feb.) (joint separate opinion of Higgins, Kooijmans & Buergenthal, JJ.) (suggesting that the Lotus "dictum represents the high water mark of laissez-faire in international relations, and an era that has been significantly overtaken by other tendencies"); Mehrdad Payandeh, 'The Concept of Law in the Jurisprudence of H.L.A. Hart' (2010) 21 EJIL 967, 971 (observing that the "voluntarist approach to international law found its expression in the famous *Lotus* decision").

[26] United States v. Aluminum Co. of America (Alcoa), 148 F 2d 416 (2d Cir. 1945).

[27] Ibid. pp. 421–422.

[28] Ibid. p. 443.

statutory interpretation, that foreign corporations were subject to antitrust liability under the Sherman Act if their actions "were intended to affect imports [into the United States] and did affect them."[29] *Alcoa* thus established the precedent that transboundary harm could support extraterritorial prescriptive jurisdiction under American antitrust law.

European regulators eventually embraced a similar effects-based approach to prescriptive jurisdiction. In 1964, the European Commission held that European Economic Community (EEC) rules apply to "all agreements which are apt to affect commerce between Member States and which have as their object or result to prevent, restrict or distort competition within the Common Market."[30] Two decades later, the European Court of Justice (ECJ) adopted a modified effects-based approach to prescriptive jurisdiction in *Wood Pulp.*[31] The ECJ concluded that although the defendants – numerous wood pulp producers and two associations of producers – were headquartered outside the EEC, their price-fixing agreement was subject to EEC competition law to the extent that the parties implemented the agreement through prices charged to EEC customers.[32] The ECJ thus accepted that at least two states could exercise prescriptive jurisdiction over a price-fixing conspiracy: the state where the parties organized their conspiracy and the state where the parties implemented their agreement.

By the end of the twentieth century, conventional wisdom held that international law permitted a state to exercise extraterritorial prescriptive jurisdiction in various contexts where "there is a genuine connection between the subject of the regulation and the state seeking to regulate."[33] Not only could a state regulate the activities of its nationals wherever they might be located (*nationality jurisdiction*),[34] but, more controversially, a state could also extend its law extraterritorially to protect its expatriate

29 Ibid. p. 444.

30 European Economic Community: Commission Decision in Grosfillex Case (Cartels and Dominant Positions; First Decision Under Regulation No. 17), 3 ILM (1964), 418, 419–420 (translating Grosfillex-Fillistorf, 1964 J.O. (58) 915, 3 CMLR 237, 238–339 (1964)).

31 Åhlström v. Commission (Wood Pulp), 1985 O.J. (L 85) 1, 14–15, 54 CMLR 474, 499–500 (1985), aff'd in part, void in part 1988 ECR 5193.

32 Wood Pulp, p. 5243.

33 *Restatement (Fourth) of the Foreign Relations Law of the United States* (2018) § 402(1) n. 2 [hereinafter *Fourth Restatement*]; see also James Crawford, *Brownlie's Principles of Public International Law*, 9th ed. (Oxford: Oxford University Press, 2019), p. 441 ("If there is a cardinal principle emerging, it is that of genuine connection between the subject matter of jurisdiction and the territorial base or reasonable interests of the state in question.").

34 *Fourth Restatement*, § 410; Alex Mills, 'Rethinking Jurisdiction in International Law' (2014) 84 BYBIL 187, 196.

nationals from harm (*passive personality jurisdiction*), safeguard essential sovereign interests from foreign-sourced threats (*protective principle jurisdiction*), and enforce peremptory norms of general international law (*universal jurisdiction*).[35] This expansion of states' prescriptive jurisdiction has divided international lawyers. Critics argue that extraterritorial prescriptive jurisdiction undermines national sovereignty and self-determination by subjecting states to foreign imperialism.[36] Supporters counter that a strict territorial approach would also have sovereignty costs because it would make states dependent on foreign powers to suppress extraterritorial activities that inflict transboundary harm.[37]

What makes this debate so intractable is that there is merit on both sides. Alone, neither strict territoriality (the classical approach) nor concurrent regulatory jurisdiction (the modern approach) can explain and honor sovereign equality as the organizing idea of international law that impedes powerful states and their firms from dictating terms to others. Strict territoriality prevents states from regulating foreign-sourced harm, placing them at the mercy of states where the harm originates. However, concurrent regulatory jurisdiction also fails to curb domination: allowing a state to regulate people and conduct outside its borders, at its sole discretion, would subject other states and their people to alien control. Both the classical and modern approaches to extraterritorial jurisdiction, without more, invite unilateralism and subvert a constitutional understanding of sovereign equality that takes seriously the "equal rights and self-determination of peoples."[38] Extraterritorial regulation therefore raises concerns like those that arise in other settings, such as transboundary rivers and border-straddling fisheries, where states' overlapping rights or powers trigger mandatory cooperation.[39]

35 *Fourth Restatement*, §§ 411–413.

36 See, e.g., Alejandro Chehtman, *The Philosophical Foundations of Extraterritorial Punishment* (Oxford: Oxford University Press, 2010), pp. 20, 28 (arguing that sovereignty entails a claim to juridical independence and that states therefore "hold a prima facie immunity against extraterritorial authorities dictating criminal legal rules which are binding on their territory"); Criddle, 'Extraterritoriality's Empire', pp. 633–634, 636–648 (arguing that some bases for extraterritorial prescriptive jurisdiction violate the right to self-determination).

37 Roger P. Alford, 'The Extraterritorial Application of Antitrust Laws: The United States and European Community Approaches' (1992) 33 VJIL 1, 1–2, 10–11 (discussing the positions).

38 UN Charter, art. 1(2).

39 See Chapters 2–3.

The difficulty in this context parallels the controversy discussed in Chapter 5 with respect to the authority of target states to use force against hostile groups from another state (the "host state") whose actions cannot be imputed to that state. The ICJ avers that the UN Charter does not authorize target states to use force against nonstate hostiles within the territory of the host state without the host state's consent, while some commentators claim that international law permits target states to use force without the host state's consent if the host state is unwilling or unable to address the threat. The ICJ treats the host state's territorial sovereignty as an absolute at the expense of the target state's territorial integrity, while the "unwilling or unable" approach would subject the host state's territorial sovereignty to the target state's unilateral view of its security needs. Both approaches undermine sovereign equality because both subject one state to the discretion of the other. The way forward, we argued, is to take seriously international law's demand that target states and host states cooperate to negotiate equitable solutions that forgo treating territorial sovereignty and territorial integrity as legal absolutes.

The classical and modern approaches to prescriptive jurisdiction also treat as absolutes strict territoriality, on the one hand, and an entitlement to extraterritorial prescriptive jurisdiction, on the other (whether delimited by an effects-based criterion or not). Here too, the way forward is good faith cooperation between the state asserting extraterritorial regulation and the host state from which transboundary harm originates. Generally, the territorial claim of the host state must yield to equitable interests of the state that suffers transboundary harm. The state that seeks to exercise prescriptive jurisdiction must also demonstrate due regard for the host state's sovereignty and its people's right to self-determination. Under the now-familiar norms of mandatory cooperation, the process called for is one of good faith information sharing, consultation, negotiation, mediation, conciliation, and if necessary third-party arbitration or adjudication. With equitable principles supervening on sovereign rights and with a process that treats the parties as legal equals throughout, mandatory cooperation coordinates the parties' contending sovereignties so they may fit together commodiously as part of a unified legal order, rather than subjugate one sovereignty to the other. Mandatory cooperation thereby offers the promise of interstate relations that live up to the demands of sovereign equality understood as a constitutional ideal that privileges the "equal rights and self-determination of peoples."

The remainder of this chapter discloses that international legal practice only partially subscribes to the framework of mandatory cooperation, and that global competition law as such is largely soft law and so, strictly speaking, not binding and mandatory. Nonetheless, to the extent that international law is committed to a constitutional understanding of sovereign equality, mandatory cooperation offers a laudable institutional framework through which sovereign equality can unfold into constitutional form in the context of extraterritorial regulation.

Tempering Extraterritoriality Through Adjudication

Recognizing the tensions between extraterritorial regulation and sovereign equality, American courts have used canons of statutory construction to rein in the geographic reach of domestic laws. The US Supreme Court has established a strong presumption that federal legislation does not apply to people and activities outside the United States.[40] Even when statutes reach outside the United States, courts have resisted applying them when the resulting imposition on another state's territorial sovereignty would be "unreasonable."[41] Lower courts have assessed whether extraterritoriality is unreasonable based on various considerations, including the links between the regulated activity and the regulating state, the character of the activity to be regulated, the importance of the regulation to the regulating state, and the likelihood of conflict with foreign law.[42] In the landmark 2004 decision, *F. Hoffman-La Roche Ltd. v. Empagran*, the Supreme Court held that extraterritorial regulation is unreasonable if foreign conduct lacks a genuine connection to the United States.[43]

Empagran is especially notable because the Supreme Court linked its interpretive canons to international law. The Court asserted that the presumption against extraterritoriality and the canon against unreasonable extraterritoriality are both based on "prescriptive comity" – that is, states' responsibility to "take account of the legitimate interests of other

[40] See Morrison v. Nat'l Australia Bank Ltd., 561 US 247, 255–261 (2010); Kiobel v. Royal Dutch Petroleum Co., 569 US 108, 115–117 (2013); Nestlé USA, Inc v. Doe, 141 S Ct. 1931, 1936 (2021).

[41] F. Hoffman-La Roche Ltd. v. Empagran, 542 US 155, 164 (2004) (citing *Restatement (Third) of Foreign Relations Law of the United States* §§ 403(1), 403(2) (1986) [hereinafter *Third Restatement*]).

[42] Timberlane Lumber Co. v. Bank of America, 549 F 2d 597, 614–15 (9th Cir. 1976); Mannington Mills, Inc. v. Congoleum Corp., 595 F 2d 1287, 1297–98 (3d Cir. 1979); *Third Restatement*, § 403(2).

[43] 542 US 155, 164–165 (2004).

nations when they write [domestic] laws."[44] The canon against unreasonable extraterritoriality, in particular, "reflects customary international law – law that (we must assume) Congress ordinarily seeks to follow."[45] Narrowing the extraterritorial scope of domestic legislation in deference to foreign interests "helps the potentially conflicting laws of different nations work together in harmony – a harmony particularly needed in today's highly interdependent commercial world."[46]

Some legal scholars have challenged the Supreme Court's view that prescriptive comity reflects customary international law.[47] For example, Bill Dodge argues that *Empagran* erroneously conflates international comity and international law.[48] Whereas international law establishes binding obligations, international comity is "a matter for each nation's discretion" and "does *not* bind the United States on the international plane or give rise to international responsibility."[49] According to Dodge, the presumption against extraterritoriality and the presumption against unreasonable extraterritoriality are comity-based canons rather than reflecting international legal obligations.[50] The influential *Restatement of the Law (Fourth)—Foreign Relations of the United States* (*Restatement*) concurs that the presumption against extraterritoriality is not designed "to avoid violations of international law" but instead to prevent "unintended clashes between our laws and those of other nations which could result in international discord."[51] The *Restatement* acknowledges that "prescriptive comity . . . accounts for the legitimate sovereign interests of other nations and helps the potentially conflicting laws of different nations work in harmony," but it stops short of characterizing

[44] Ibid. p. 164.

[45] Ibid. (citing, *inter alia*, *Third Restatement*, §§ 403(1)–(2)); see also Hartford Fire Ins. Co. v. California, 509 US 764, 800, 815 (1993) (Scalia, J., dissenting) (arguing that prescriptive comity rests on principles of "customary international law" that impose "limitations on a nation's exercise of its jurisdiction to prescribe").

[46] Ibid. pp. 164–165.

[47] See, e.g., William S. Dodge, 'Extraterritoriality and Conflict-of-Laws Theory: An Argument for Judicial Unilateralism' (1998) 39 HILJ 101, 137 n. 224 (arguing that the rule-of-reason "balancing approach is not required by international law"); Michael D. Ramsey, 'Escaping "International Comity"' (1998) 83 *Iowa L. Rev.* 893, 925 ("[D]escribing the inquiry as one of 'comity' disconnects it from international law.").

[48] William S. Dodge, 'International Comity in American Law' (2015) 115 *Colum. L. Rev.* 2071, 2120.

[49] Ibid. p. 2121 (emphasis in original).

[50] Ibid. pp. 2122, 2128.

[51] *Fourth Restatement*, § 404, rptr. n. 2 (quoting E.E.O.C. v. Arabian American Oil Co., 499 US 244, 248 (1991)). The *Restatement* also suggests that the presumption "reflects the assumption that Congress is primarily concerned with domestic conditions." Ibid.

prescriptive comity as reflecting international law.[52] This approach accords with the jurisprudence of most European courts, which do not recognize reasonableness as limiting a state's prescriptive jurisdiction.[53] Thus, international lawyers tend to agree that international law does not require states to consider foreign interests when determining the extraterritorial reach of their domestic law.

The conventional wisdom that international law does not require states to exercise prescriptive comity makes sense only if we accept the waning voluntarist view of sovereign equality. Under the voluntarist view, a state may exercise prescriptive jurisdiction however it pleases as long as it does not violate a prohibitive rule of international law.[54] In contrast, the ascending constitutional view of sovereign equality requires a state to pay due regard to foreign rights and interests whenever it holds prescriptive jurisdiction concurrently with another state. This equitable obligation is a legal requirement emanating from the principle of sovereign equality; it is not committed to a state's unilateral discretion.

The constitutional view of sovereign equality explains the Supreme Court's oft-cited dictum that prescriptive comity is "neither a matter of absolute obligation, on the one hand, nor of mere courtesy and good will, upon the other."[55] States are not absolutely obligated to abstain from applying their domestic law extraterritorially, but that does not mean they may disregard foreign interests entirely. To respect the principle of sovereign equality, each state must find a way to reconcile its rights and powers with other states' rights and powers in accordance with equitable principles. Insofar as the presumption against extraterritoriality and the canon against unreasonable extraterritoriality respond to these concerns, they answer to the demands of the constitutional view of sovereign equality expressed through customary international law. In this sense, the Supreme Court was correct to reason that "principles of international law" impose binding "limitations on a nation's exercise of its [prescriptive] jurisdiction."[56]

52 Ibid. § 204, cmt. A.

53 Cedric Ryngaert, *Jurisdiction in International Law*, 2nd ed. (Oxford: Oxford University Press, 2015), pp. 171–180 (summarizing the practice of European courts).

54 See Chapter 1 (discussing the "Lotus principle").

55 Hilton v. Guyot, 159 US 113, 163–164 (1895).

56 Hartford Fire Ins. Co. v. California, 509 US 764, 800, 815 (1993) (Scalia, J., dissenting).

Where Adjudication Falls Short

Nonetheless, judicial canons of statutory interpretation are poor vehicles for resolving international regulatory conflicts. Mandatory cooperation's substantive and procedural requirements are addressed primarily to diplomats and regulators, not judges. To satisfy international law, national authorities must consult with one another, share information about their national interests and policy preferences, pay due regard to foreign interests and preferences, and pursue an equitable solution that manifests due regard for their respective national interests. Courts are ill-equipped to perform these sensitive political functions.[57] The most national courts can do, consistent with their institutional role, is nudge lawmakers toward international cooperation. Courts can give lawmakers the benefit of the doubt by presuming that they would not have extended domestic law unilaterally to settings where international law requires international cooperation. When domestic law does extend extraterritorially, courts can apply the "rule of reason" canon to curb manifestly inequitable interference with another state's territorial sovereignty.[58] Yet, these judicial stopgaps, however beneficial, are no substitute for international regulatory cooperation.

The problem with relying on domestic courts to reconcile extraterritorial regulation with sovereign equality is that evaluating whether extraterritorial regulation is reasonable is, to some extent, in the eye of the beholder, and domestic judges struggle to conduct this inquiry impartially. In antitrust cases, for example, American judges rarely decide that applying domestic antitrust law to extraterritorial activities would be unreasonable. Plaintiffs therefore enjoy a clear home-field advantage when they ask US courts to enforce the Sherman Act against foreign defendants based on extraterritorial activities that cause domestic injury.

A notable illustration of this problem is the *Uranium Antitrust Litigation*.[59] In 1976, confidential documents leaked from an Australian uranium company found their way to the California Energy Commission,

[57] Brainerd Currie, 'Notes on Methods and Objectives in the Conflict of Laws' (1959) 2 *Duke L.J.* 171, 176 (arguing that "assessment of the respective values of the competing legitimate interests of two sovereign states is a political function of the highest order" outside the competence of courts).

[58] See *Fourth Restatement*, § 405, cmt. a (observing that the rule of reason canon "accounts for the legitimate sovereign interests of other nations and helps the potentially conflicting laws of different nations work in harmony").

[59] In re Uranium Antitrust Litigation, 617 F 2d 1248, 1253–1256 (7th Cir. 1980); In re Uranium Antitrust Litigation, 473 F Supp. 382 (N.D. Ill. 1979).

which shared them with the world. The documents confirmed the existence of an international cartel composed of uranium producers from Australia, Canada, France, South Africa, and the United Kingdom.[60] When an American firm filed an antitrust lawsuit against cartel members, the international reaction was heated. Foreign governments complained that American regulators had been suppressing the price of uranium for years by prohibiting nuclear power reactors in the United States from using foreign uranium. Without international cooperation to maintain uranium prices at levels comparable to those in the United States, the uranium industry outside the United States would "bleed to death for sure."[61] Critics of the United States also noted that the companies' home governments firmly supported the uranium cartel. Enforcing the Sherman Act thus imperiled the uranium industry outside the United States and manifested flagrant disregard for the considered policy judgments of foreign governments. Despite these concerns, the trial court entered a default judgment against the cartel members,[62] and the Court of Appeals affirmed, concluding, over the objections of foreign governments, that applying the Sherman Act to the international uranium cartel was not an abuse of discretion under a "jurisdictional rule of reason" analysis.[63]

In fairness to the judges who presided over the *Uranium Antitrust Litigation*, they were saddled with an impossible task. There was no way they could craft a judgment that would reconcile the contending states' exercise of their equal sovereign powers when the national interests and regulatory policies of the United States and other uranium-producing countries were diametrically opposed.[64] The judges could not simply rewrite the Sherman Act to fashion a compromise between the states' conflicting policies. The limited tools of statutory construction at their disposal – the presumption against extraterritoriality and the canon against unreasonable extraterritoriality – offered only two options: (1) apply domestic law or (2) don't apply domestic law. The first option would subordinate foreign regulators' policy judgments to the demands

[60] Earle Gray, *The Great Uranium Cartel* (Toronto: McClelland & Stewart, 1982), pp. 95, 105–106.

[61] Ibid. pp. 103–104.

[62] In re Uranium Antitrust Litigation, 473 F Supp. at 392.

[63] In re Uranium Antitrust Litigation, 617 F 2d at 1253–1256.

[64] In parallel uranium cartel litigation before the UK House of Lords, Lord Wilberforce observed that "[i]t is axiomatic that in anti-trust matters the policy of one state may be to defend what is the policy of another state to attack." In re Westinghouse Elec. Corp. Uranium Contract Litig. [1978] AC 547, 617 (H.L.).

of US antitrust law, while the second would put domestic uranium markets at the mercy of a foreign cartel. Neither option would reconcile the competing interests of the states concerned in a manner congenial to sovereign equality.

The Promise of Regulatory Cooperation

A better pathway for reconciling antitrust regulation with sovereign equality runs through international cooperation. When states cooperate to resolve antitrust disputes based on equitable principles, they can develop solutions responsive to their national interests without subordinating other states to their unilateral will.

After the *Uranium Antitrust Litigation*, the United States worked to patch things up by establishing bilateral cooperation agreements with Australia and Canada.[65] The Australia-US agreement acknowledged the parties' past conflicts over antitrust policy and affirmed "the need for such conflicts to be resolved with mutual respect for each other's sovereignty and with due regard for considerations of comity."[66] Australia agreed to notify and consult with the United States when it adopted a policy that "may have antitrust implications for the United States," and the United States committed to provide notice and consult with Australia when it undertook antitrust investigations impacting Australian interests.[67] Both sides resolved to "seek earnestly to avoid a possible conflict between their respective laws, policies and national interests and for that purpose to give due regard to each other's sovereignty and to considerations of comity."[68] Two years later, Canada and the United States concluded a memorandum of understanding with similar provisions, emphasizing the need for notice, consultation, good faith consideration of the other party's interests, and the cooperative pursuit of conflict avoidance, accommodation, and compromise.[69] Today, the

[65] See Agreement Relating to Cooperation on Antitrust Matters (US-Austl.), 29 June 1982, 34 UST 388 [hereinafter US-Austl. Agreement]; Canada-United States: Memorandum of Understanding as to Notification, Consultation and Cooperation with Respect to the Application of National Antitrust Laws, 9 March 1984, 23 ILM 275 (1984) [hereinafter Can.-US Agreement).

[66] US-Austl. Agreement, pmbl.

[67] Ibid. paras. 1–4.

[68] Ibid. para. 5.

[69] Can.-US Agreement, paras. 2–7. The 1984 memorandum of understanding between Canada and the United States has since been replaced by the more detailed and legally

United States has cooperation agreements with dozens of other states.[70]

The most important international competition agreement to date is the bilateral 1991 Competition Laws Cooperation Agreement between the European Communities and the United States (EC-US Agreement).[71] The EC-US Agreement outlines requirements of notification, consultation, exchange of information, and cooperation and coordination in enforcement activities.[72] It also requires each party to consider the other's interests when deciding whether to enforce its laws extraterritorially. Factors relevant to this inquiry include whether parties engaged in anticompetitive activities are intended "to affect consumers, suppliers, or competitors within the enforcing Party's territory" and "the relative significance of the effects of the anticompetitive activities on the enforcing Party's interests as compared to the effects on the other Party's interests."[73] The agreement also adopts a procedure now known as "positive comity": "If a Party believes that anticompetitive activities carried out on the territory of the other Party are adversely affecting its important interests, [it] may notify the other Party and may request that the other Party's competition authorities initiate appropriate enforcement activities [at the other Party's discretion]."[74] By encouraging intergovernmental cooperation in this manner, the EC-US Agreement reduces the parties' reliance on extraterritorial antitrust regulation.

Efforts to establish global standards for competition law have yet to bear fruit. Beginning in the mid-1990s, the World Trade Organization (WTO) hosted negotiations to develop treaty-based rules against cartels, the abuse of market dominance, and other anticompetitive activities impacting international trade. This initiative encountered a tepid reception outside Europe. Developing states feared global competition rules would impose onerous regulatory burdens while entrenching global inequality. The United States worried that a multilateral convention would water down antitrust enforcement by ensconcing suboptimal

binding Agreement Regarding the Application of Their Competition and Deceptive Marketing Practices Laws (US-Can.), 3 August 1995.

70 Maher M. Dabbah, *International and Comparative Competition Law* (Cambridge: Cambridge University Press, 2010), pp. 494–509.

71 Agreement Between the Government of the United States of America and the Commission of the European Communities Regarding the Application of their Competition Laws 23 September 1991, *reprinted in* 30 ILM 1487 (1991).

72 Ibid. arts. II–IV.

73 Ibid. art. VII.

74 Ibid. art. V(2), (4); see also US-European Commission Enhanced Positive Comity Agreement, 4 June 1998 (fleshing out the requirements of positive comity).

competition norms and institutions. As a result, the WTO abandoned the effort in 2003.[75]

With hopes fading for a global competition treaty, the international community has attempted to fill the gap with nonbinding "soft law" standards. For example, the Organisation for Economic Co-operation and Development (OECD) has recommended measures to suppress hard-core cartels and strengthen international cooperation for corporate merger reviews.[76] It has also collaborated with the International Competition Network, an association of public and private competition experts, to study state practices, identify opportunities for enhancing cooperation, and promote regulatory harmonization.[77] These initiatives have reduced the urgency for concluding a multilateral competition treaty. Still, more robust international cooperation will be needed in the years to come to reduce powerful states' reliance on extraterritoriality and protect weaker states from foreign domination.[78]

Thus far, the international community has yet to recognize international cooperation as a mandatory feature of global competition law. When states weigh options for international regulatory cooperation in this domain, they assume they are free to opt out and proceed unilaterally, if they choose. Yet, without international cooperation, competition laws imposed unilaterally by a state or regional organization (or the absence of national regulation) would subject other states to domination. To respect sovereign equality in accordance with equitable principles, states must accord due regard for other states' rights and powers when establishing competition rules. Accordingly, states must consult with one another, share relevant information, and negotiate mutually acceptable regulatory standards that are responsive to their respective interests.

If these requirements have been slow to take root in global competition law, as compared to other fields like the international law of the sea, this

[75] Anu Bradford, 'International Antitrust Negotiations and the False Hope of the WTO' (2007) 48 HILJ 383, 406–408; Eleanor M. Fox, 'Antitrust Without Borders: From Codes to Networks', in Andrew T. Guzman (ed.), *Cooperation, Comity, and Competition Policy* (Oxford: Oxford University Press, 2011), pp. 265, 272.

[76] 'Recommendation of the Council Concerning Effective Action Against Hard Core Cartels', OECD, 1 July 2019; 'Recommendation of the Council on Merger Review', OECD, 22 March 2005.

[77] See, e.g., OECD and International Competition Network, 'OECD/ICN Report on International Co-operation in Competition Enforcement', Report (2021).

[78] See Anu Bradford, *Digital Empires: The Global Battle to Regulate Technology* (Oxford: Oxford University Press, 2023) (explaining how China, the EU, and the United States are vying for regulatory control over the digital economy).

may be attributable, in part, to the fact that international courts and tribunals lack jurisdiction over disputes involving national competition rules. Until international courts and tribunals assume jurisdiction to resolve these disputes, there will be no landmark cases comparable to the *Fisheries Jurisdiction Cases* or the *North Sea Continental Shelf Case* to affirm that states must cooperate to establish shared regulatory frameworks for global economic competition. Meanwhile, without judicial guidance, the pathways for mandatory cooperation to become entrenched in global competition law are limited. States could conclude a multilateral treaty codifying obligations to cooperate in managing regulatory conflicts, as they have done in many other fields of international law. Alternatively, mandatory cooperation could become a generally accepted feature of customary international law through the gradual accretion of state practice and *opinio juris*, as states consult and negotiate with one another as good neighbors to harmonize their national regulations in accordance with equitable principles.

Of course, even if mandatory cooperation were to become firmly embedded in international competition law, it could not completely level the playing field between states. Great powers will continue to wield disproportionate influence over the global economy regardless of whether international law considers regulatory cooperation optional or mandatory.[79] Nonetheless, mandatory cooperation is preferable to the current laissez-faire approach to extraterritorial regulation because it would give weaker states legal protections that they could use to counter great power domination. Mandatory cooperation would bring the interests of weaker states to the fore as legitimate considerations that powerful states must formally recognize and address (not simply ignore) in international negotiations. Although weaker states would lack the right to veto powerful states' preferred solutions, the other side of the coin is that powerful states could not lawfully impose their preferred solutions on weaker states unilaterally. Hence, if weaker states hold out for a more equitable deal, powerful states would have three choices under

[79] See Ryngaert, 'Jurisdiction in International Law', p. 204 ("Harmonization is not achieved nor does cooperation take place in a power-free environment."). Critics have accused the European Union and the United States of coercing less developed states to adopt national competition laws modeled on their own. See Dabbah, *International and Comparative Competition Law*, p. 3 (lamenting that "rules, practices and theories that are developed in certain parts of the world – mostly in the European Union (EU) and the USA – have come to be *forced down the throat* of countries in developing parts of the world, often with the aid of international organizations" (emphasis in original)).

international law: (1) they could offer to sweeten the deal; (2) they could declare a stalemate and impose (impermanent and reversible) provisional measures while continuing to pursue international dialogue; or (3) they could submit the dispute to a third-party. This limited menu of options would give weaker states leverage to counteract, however imperfectly, powerful states' asymmetrical bargaining position. Outside mandatory cooperation's domain, weaker states have no such protections. Thus, mandatory cooperation would likely enhance weaker states' capacity to protect their national interests, at least relative to the status quo.

Global Cooperation in the Digital Era

Mandatory cooperation faces significant headwinds in the digital era. The dominant market power of some global technology companies has prompted states to defend their "digital sovereignty."[80] For example, the European Union's Digital Markets Act (DMA) imposes strict requirements on large web platforms like Amazon, Facebook, and Google, which function as "gatekeepers" for the global electronic marketplace.[81] Former US Trade Representative Charlene Barshefsky has excoriated the DMA as a "rigged competition law" because it "seems designed to impose blanket prohibitions on the business models and conduct of US companies."[82] However, European leaders have rallied behind the Act, seeking to rein in Silicon Valley tech titans while grooming homegrown alternatives. "The battle we're fighting is one of sovereignty," French President Emmanuel Macron has proclaimed.[83]

Amidst this transatlantic tug-of-war over the digital economy, multinational technology companies have pleaded for greater regulatory cooperation. In April 2021, Google Vice President Karan Bhatia lamented that "the technology trade relationship between the US and Europe – once one of the closest in the world – is

[80] Frances G. Burwell and Kenneth Propp, 'The European Union and the Search for Digital Sovereignty: Building "Fortress Europe" or Preparing for a New World', Atlantic Council, June 2020.

[81] See Regulation of the European Parliament and of the Council on contestable and fair markets in the digital sector (Digital Markets Act), 2020 OJ (COM 2020) 842.

[82] Charlene Barshefsky, 'EU Digital Protectionism Risks Damaging Ties with the US', Financial Times, 2 August 2020. On April 23, 2022, the European Parliament announced that it had reached agreement with EU member states on the Digital Services Act.

[83] Ibid.; see also Anu Bradford, 'The Brussels Effect' (2012) 107 *Nw. U. L. Rev.* 1, 22 ("The EU is expected to defend its right to regulate its own market whenever competition in that market is affected.").

fraying."[84] Bhatia urged the White House to accept the European Union's invitation to participate in a new EU-US Trade and Technology Council (TTC):

> An expedited high-level trade dialogue on technology issues is critical to avoid unilateral approaches on pressing issues like data flows that are essential to commerce, regulation of digital platforms that we all use every day, and other essential components of a modern economy. A TTC could also prevent divergence on emerging areas like artificial intelligence and other advanced technologies and promote cooperation on third-country technology challenges.
>
> Of course, a TTC needs to be set up for success. When entering trade negotiations, each side typically avoids preemptive or unilateral actions that might foreclose meaningful alignment. In entering a TTC, both sides should commit to meaningful consultation before taking any further actions harming transatlantic tech trade. The US should not enact new privacy or technology trade control regulations without consulting with the EU; the EU should pursue bilateral consultation to ensure technology initiatives like the Digital Markets Act reflect the EU-US values-based alliance. Quickly forming a TTC can help drive a consistent and non-discriminatory approach on these challenging new areas of technology regulation.[85]

Bhatia's vision for an effective transatlantic partnership aligns closely with the requirements of mandatory cooperation. According to Bhatia's proposal, American and European regulators would renounce "unilateral approaches" that undermine the other's sovereign authority. Instead, they would jointly pursue cooperation through procedures that reflect due regard for their equal sovereignty. These procedures would include giving notice of potential investigations, exchanging relevant information, consulting regularly, treating foreign interests without discrimination, avoiding preemptive actions that could frustrate alignment, and pursuing international consensus in good faith. Robust cooperation between the European Union and the United States would benefit technology companies like Google by enabling them to organize their business around a more consistent and predictable set of regulatory ground rules.

There are some encouraging signs that regulators in Europe and the United States might be ready to embrace tighter regulatory cooperation for the digital economy. Two months after Bhatia's plea for transatlantic cooperation, the European Union and the United States formally

[84] Karan Bhatia, 'The U.S. and Europe Should Launch a Trade and Technology Council', Google: The Keyword, 9 April 2021.

[85] Ibid.

announced the establishment of a high-level TTC. Among the initiative's major objectives was the aspiration "to facilitate regulatory policy and enforcement cooperation and, where possible, convergence, . . . without prejudice to the regulatory autonomy of the United States and the European Union."[86] The parties also formed a US-EU Joint Technology Competition Policy Dialogue to "focus on approaches to competition policy and enforcement, and increased cooperation in the tech sector."[87] US regulators raised detailed objections to the DMA in private correspondence. They also negotiated face-to-face with their European counterparts, seeking amendments barring the DMA from discriminating unfairly against American companies.[88]

Time will tell whether these efforts will produce a tighter transatlantic consensus about how best to safeguard competition in the digital marketplace. Enhanced cooperation between the EU and the United States would only be a first step, of course. Taking mandatory cooperation seriously would also require deeper engagement with other states and regional organizations, including developing nations that have criticized the EU and the United States for engaging in "digital colonialism" through multinational corporations like Google.[89] For the time being, however, recent efforts to bridge the transatlantic divide between the EU and the United States offer grounds for cautious optimism that even states and regional organizations with divergent interests might be able to find common ground as they replace unilateralism with cooperation.

[86] US-EU Summit Statement, White House Briefing Room, 15 June 2021, para. 17.

[87] Ibid., para. 19; see also EU-US Joint Technology Competition Policy Dialogue, Inaugural Joint Statement Between the European Comm'n, the US Dep't of Justice Antitrust Division, and the US Fed. Trade Comm'n, 7 December 2021 (reaffirming the sides' intention and "mutual interest in cooperating on competition policy and enforcement overall and especially in technology sectors" through "coordination and knowledge and information exchange, . . . potentially contributing to greater alignment").

[88] Samuel Stolton, 'US Pushes to Change EU's Digital Gatekeeper Rules', Politico, 31 January 2022.

[89] See Nick Couldry and Ulises A. Meijas, *The Costs of Connection: How Data Is Colonizing Human Life and Appropriating It for Capitalism* (Redwood City: Stanford University Press, 2019), pp. 6–18 (arguing that data colonialism parallels traditional colonialism by involving the appropriation of resources (data) and the establishment of relations premised on foreign domination); Michael Kwet, 'Digital Colonialism: US Empire and the New Imperialism in the Global South' (2019) 60 *Race & Class* 3, 4 (describing digital colonialism as a "structural form of domination exercised through the centralized ownership and control of the three pillars of the digital ecosystem: software, hardware, and network connectivity").

12

Mandatory Dispute Resolution

"Nicaragua Shall Not Be the Patrimony of Imperialists"

In 1927, a guerilla force commanded by General Augusto Caesar Sandino began carrying out attacks on US Marines and American mining interests in Nicaragua.[1] Sandino's fame and popularity spread quickly throughout Latin America, fueled by his vigorous critique of American imperialism:

> I will not abandon my resistance until the . . . pirate invaders . . . assassins of weak peoples . . . are expelled from my country . . . I will make them realize that their crimes will cost them dear . . . There will be bloody combat . . . Nicaragua shall not be the patrimony of Imperialists. I will fight for my cause as long as my heart beats.[2]

Opposed to Sandino was Anastasio Somoza García, appointed as Nicaragua's Director of the National Guard at the urging of the United States. Somoza would go on to found a family dynasty that ruled Nicaragua with US support for forty-three years (1936–1979).[3] Commenting on "the special nature of the House of Somoza" the day the leftist *Frente Sandinista de Liberación Nacional* (FSLN) took Managua in 1979, the editors of the *New York Times* lamented that not only "have the Somozas owned a lordly share of the country's riches, but bribes and kickbacks have been their price of doing business."[4]

When the United States pulled its marines out of Nicaragua in 1933, negotiations commenced between the US-backed government and Sandino's guerillas. The peace process was upended, however, by an act of treachery that would become a culture-defining landmark of

[1] See Sergio Ramirez and Lyman Baker, 'The Kid from Niquinohomo' (1989) 16 *Latin Am. Perspectives* 48, 66–72.

[2] 'Nicaragua: Defy!', Time, 16 January 1928, https://web.archive.org/web/20101121012549/http:/www.time.com/time/magazine/article/0,9171,731362,00.html.

[3] Editorial, 'Somoza's Bitter Legacy', NY Times, 19 July 1979, A18.

[4] Ibid.

Nicaragua's history. On February 21, 1934, during a ceasefire and immediately following a round of peace talks, Somoza's National Guard detained Sandino, his brother, and two of his generals outside the Presidential Palace. They summarily executed Sandino and his associates the same day. Two years later, Somoza orchestrated a *coup d'état* that launched his family's forty-three-year dynastic fiefdom.

The National Guard remained loyal to the Somoza *ancien régime* long after the Sandinistas deposed Anastasio Somoza, the third Somoza despot. With US support and guidance, former members of the National Guard and other opponents of the Sandinistas created the *contra* force, a paramilitary organization based in Honduras that engaged in more than 1,300 terror attacks on civilians and civilian infrastructure in Nicaragua between 1979 and 1990.[5] In addition to supporting the *contras*, in 1983 and 1984 US operatives mined various Nicaraguan harbors and conducted attacks on shipping in Nicaraguan territorial waters.[6]

In a case of David-and-Goliath proportions, Nicaragua filed suit against the United States at the International Court of Justice (ICJ).[7] Nicaragua alleged that the United States breached its obligation under Article 2(4) of the UN Charter "to refrain from the threat or use of force against the territorial integrity or political independence of Nicaragua."[8] Nicaragua also alleged that the United States violated general and customary international law by engaging in or supporting a wide range of unlawful interventions, including armed attacks inside Nicaragua, the mining of harbors, aerial trespass, and efforts to coerce and intimidate the Government of Nicaragua.[9] On the merits, a majority of the ICJ found that the United States, "by training, arming, equipping, financing and supplying the *contra* forces or otherwise encouraging, supporting and aiding military and paramilitary activities in and against Nicaragua, has acted … in breach of its obligation under customary international

[5] Gary LaFree, Laura Dugan and Erin Miller, *Putting Terrorism in Context: Lessons from the Global Terrorism Database*, 1st ed. (New York: Routledge, 2015), p. 56 (noting that *contra* forces "carried out more than 1300 terrorist attacks").

[6] David Rogers, 'U.S. Role in Mining Nicaraguan Harbours Reportedly Is Larger than First Thought', Wall Street Journal, 6 April 1984; Case Concerning the Military and Paramilitary Activities in and against Nicaragua (Nicaragua/US), Merits, Judgment, 1986 ICJ Rep. 14 (27 June), para. 80 [hereinafter Nicaragua Merits Case].

[7] Case Concerning the Military and Paramilitary Activities in and against Nicaragua (Nicaragua/US), Application Instituting Proceedings, 1984 ICJ General List No. 70 [hereinafter Nicaragua Application].

[8] Ibid., para. 15.

[9] Nicaragua Application, paras. 20–25.

law not to intervene in the affairs of another state."[10] A majority likewise found the United States in breach of customary international law prohibiting the use of force against another state by virtue of mining and maritime operations directed against Nicaragua.[11] Separate majorities concluded that the United States had violated customary and treaty law for having conducted overflights and for having imposed a general trade embargo on Nicaragua in violation of a 1956 Treaty of Friendship, Commerce and Navigation between the two states.[12] The ICJ therefore ordered the United States "to cease and to refrain from all such acts as may constitute breaches of the foregoing [customary international law and treaty] obligations" and to pay Nicaragua reparations for the injury caused.[13] Adjusted for inflation, the original USD 12 billion reparation award would have been more than USD 31 billion in 2023.[14]

Several years before specific reparations were ordered, however, the United States disputed the ICJ's jurisdiction to hear the case.[15] The ensuing debate over jurisdiction is especially significant, as it vividly reveals the rival conceptions of international law that have dueled throughout this book; that is, the absolutist and voluntarist understanding, on the one hand, and the constitutional view that gives pride of place to sovereign equality and equitable principles, on the other.

This chapter draws on the *Nicaragua Jurisdiction Case* to make three arguments concerning the jurisdiction of international courts. The first is that the foundational principles of mandatory cooperation – the duty of states to resolve disputes peacefully, sovereign equality, and the duty of states to exercise sovereign powers equitably – entail that states have a duty to resort to arbitration or adjudication if good faith negotiation, mediation, or conciliation fail to resolve an impasse.[16] The second argument builds on the preceding one to explain why the role of consent

[10] Nicaragua Merits Case, para. 292.
[11] Ibid.
[12] Ibid.
[13] Ibid.
[14] Ben Norton, 'U.S. legally owes Nicaragua reparations, but still refuses to honor 1986 Int'l Court of Justice ruling', Geopolitical Economy, 28 June 2023.
[15] Case Concerning the Military and Paramilitary Activities in and against Nicaragua (Nicaragua/US), Jurisdiction and Admissibility, 1984 ICJ General List No. 70 [hereinafter Nicaragua Jurisdiction Case].
[16] For ease of exposition, in this chapter we will generally refer to "arbitration or adjudication" as simply adjudication, and intend it to refer to impartial third-party dispute resolution mechanisms available at international law where the decision-maker has authority to make a binding judgment and order a remedy after giving the parties a fair opportunity to be heard.

within the *Nicaragua Jurisdiction Case* was attenuated in favor of compulsory jurisdiction. The third argument defends the duty to seek adjudication as an equitable constraint on state sovereignty.

In the final section of the chapter, we enlist UK constitutionalism as a comparator to reply to realist objections to international adjudication based on the possibility of states withholding their consent to the jurisdiction of particular courts. We also address the United States' use of its Security Council veto to avoid the reparations ordered by the ICJ.[17] Article 94(1) of the UN Charter stipulates that "[e]ach Member of the United Nations undertakes to comply with the decision of the International Court of Justice in any case to which it is a party," while Article 94(2) provides recourse to the Security Council for states to enforce ICJ judgments.[18] Publicists noted quickly that the United States' use of its veto in this context was in sharp tension with the legal principle that prohibits parties from being judge and party of the same cause.[19] We concede that the veto held by the permanent five members of the Security Council (P5) strains international legal order, and this strain is especially pronounced when it is used to avoid a remedy flowing from an ICJ judgment. Nonetheless, we claim that this abuse of power does not denude a relevant ICJ judgment of either its legal status or its value as the international community's authoritative judicial condemnation of a violation of international law.

Between Authority and Power

Established to build on and replace the Permanent Court of International Justice (PCIJ) of the League of Nations, the ICJ was founded in 1945 as the judicial organ of the United Nations.[20] All Member States of the United Nations are parties to the Statute of the ICJ, which is annexed to

[17] When the Court ruled that it had jurisdiction and that the case was admissible, the United States refused to take part in the hearing on the merits and later used its veto in the UN Security Council to obstruct Nicaragua's attempts to obtain the remedy ordered by the ICJ. Keith Highet, 'Between a Rock and a Hard Place: The United States, The International Court, and the *Nicaragua* Case' (1987) 21 *Int'l Law.* 1083, 1092–1095.

[18] Article 94(2) stipulates that "[i]f any party to a case fails to perform the obligations incumbent upon it under a judgment rendered by the Court, the other party may have recourse to the Security Council, which may, if it deems necessary, make recommendations or decide upon measures to be taken to give effect to the judgment."

[19] See, e.g., Highet, 'Between a Rock and a Hard Place', p. 1094.

[20] UN Charter, art. 92.

the UN Charter.[21] The ICJ derives compulsory jurisdiction over legal disputes from unilateral declarations of states-parties made pursuant to Article 36 of its Statute. Article 36(2) provides:

> The states parties to the present Statute may at any time declare that they recognize as compulsory ipso facto and without special agreement, in relation to any other state accepting the same obligation, the jurisdiction of the Court in all legal disputes concerning:
>
> a. the interpretation of a treaty;
> b. any question of international law;
> c. the existence of any fact which, if established, would constitute a breach of an international obligation;
> d. the nature or extent of the reparation to be made for the breach of an international obligation.[22]

In addition, Article 36(5) provides:

> Declarations made under Article 36 of the Statute of the Permanent Court of International Justice and which are still in force shall be deemed, as between the parties to the present Statute, to be acceptances of the compulsory jurisdiction of the International Court of Justice for the period which they still have to run and in accordance with their terms.[23]

On August 26, 1946, the United States made a declaration, pursuant to Article 36(2), recognizing the jurisdiction of the Court subject to certain reservations, the most significant of which stated that the declaration would "remain in force for a period of five years and thereafter until the expiration of six months after notice may be given to terminate this declaration."[24] In other words, the United States accepted the ICJ's jurisdiction for five years, and thereafter indefinitely, but subject to withdrawal on six months' notice. On April 6, 1984, however, just three days before the Court received Nicaragua's application to commence proceedings, US Secretary of State George Shultz preemptively notified the UN Secretary-General that the 1946 declaration "shall not apply to disputes with any Central American State or arising out of or related to

[21] Ibid., arts. 92, 93.

[22] Statute of the ICJ, 18 April 1946, art. 36(2) [hereinafter ICJ Statute]. As discussed below, the ICJ may also acquire jurisdiction through a special agreement between two or more parties to bring a case to the ICJ, or through states agreeing within a treaty to submit disputes over the treaty's interpretation and application to the ICJ.

[23] Ibid., art. 36(5).

[24] Nicaragua Jurisdiction Case, para. 13.

events in Central America."[25] This narrowing of the ICJ's jurisdiction over the United States purported to "take effect immediately and . . . remain in force for two years."[26]

The 1984 notification would prove controversial, but before the Court could consider its possible legal effect, it had to consider whether both Nicaragua and the United States were otherwise subject to the Court's jurisdiction. Under Article 36(2), the ICJ can have compulsory jurisdiction over an international dispute only if a reciprocity condition is met: the parties concerned must be states "accepting the same obligation" to submit to the ICJ's jurisdiction.[27] So, for Nicaragua to rely on the US declaration of 1946, Nicaragua had to show that it too was subject to the Court's compulsory jurisdiction.

To this end, Nicaragua relied on Article 36(5), which allows a declaration accepting the PCIJ's jurisdiction to serve as a declaration accepting the ICJ's jurisdiction. Nicaragua cited a 1929 declaration from its authorized representative to the League of Nations, stating: "On behalf of the Republic of Nicaragua I recognize as compulsory unconditionally the jurisdiction of the Permanent Court of International Justice."[28] However, Nicaragua apparently never deposited its declaration with the Secretary-General of the League of Nations in Geneva, as required under the Statute of the PCIJ.[29]

This meant that Nicaragua had never become a party to the Statute of the PCIJ, and therefore had never been subject to the PCIJ's jurisdiction. Nonetheless, Nicaragua argued that its 1929 declaration sufficed to confer jurisdiction on the ICJ via Article 36(5). Recall that Article 36(5) stipulates that declarations accepting the jurisdiction of the PCIJ must be "still in force" to activate the ICJ's compulsory jurisdiction. Accordingly, Nicaragua had to argue that although its 1929 declaration ultimately failed to bring it under the jurisdiction of the PCIJ, the declaration nonetheless was "still in force" within the meaning of Article 36(5) so as to give the ICJ compulsory jurisdiction over Nicaragua.

While an eleven-judge majority of the Court sided with Nicaragua, the five judges who dissented on this point – Judges Jennings, Ago, Oda,

[25] Ibid.
[26] Ibid.
[27] ICJ Statute, art. 36(2).
[28] Nicaragua Jurisdiction Case, para. 15.
[29] Ibid. Unlike in the case of the United Nations and the ICJ, the League of Nations and the PCIJ were established separately, with the consequence that Members of the League of Nations were not automatically states parties to the Statute of the PCIJ.

Mosler, and Schwebel – arguably had the more persuasive doctrinal arguments. Four of the five held that the ICJ had other grounds for jurisdiction. Judge Schwebel, however, wrote a lengthy dissent, denying jurisdiction across the board and cogently laying bare the relative frailty of the majority's legal arguments. Judge Schwebel rightly pointed out that under international law the plain and ordinary meaning of "in force" denotes that a treaty or norm is binding on the parties to which it applies. Accordingly, following the plain and ordinary meaning, a declaration would "still be in force" only if the party that made the declaration is still bound by the declaration's terms.[30] As Nicaragua never deposited its 1929 declaration with the Secretary-General of the League of Nations, the declaration was plainly not "in force" in this conventional sense.

Nicaragua admitted that its failure to deposit its ratification meant that it was never a party to the Statute or Protocol of the PCIJ, and therefore was never bound by its 1929 declaration to submit to the PCIJ's jurisdiction. Nicaragua insisted, however, that because its declaration "had not expired," it remained "'in force.'"[31] The majority agreed that Nicaragua's declaration was still "in force" because "it was valid for an unlimited period" with "a certain potential effect which could be maintained indefinitely."[32] This "potential effect" was the declaration's potential to make Nicaragua a party to the Statute of the PCIJ upon ratification and delivery to the Secretary-General of the League of Nations. Importantly, this potential effect could have ended at any time had Nicaragua put a temporal limit on its declaration. At the expiry of such a hypothetical limit, the declaration would have been invalid and not "in force," whether expiration took place prior to or after the deposit of ratification. By separating a narrow understanding of validity from the question of whether the declaration bound Nicaragua to the Statute and Protocol of the PCIJ, the majority explained how in principle a non-deposited and nonbinding declaration could be "in force" within the meaning of Article 36(5), and thereby serve as a foundation for the ICJ's jurisdiction over Nicaragua.

The majority and minority writers also offered contrasting interpretations of the underlying purpose of Article 36(5). For Judge Schwebel, the core purpose of Article 36(5) was to allow the ICJ to assume the compulsory jurisdiction of the PCIJ as it existed at the time the ICJ

[30] Nicaragua Jurisdiction Case (Schwebel, J., dissenting op.), paras. 14–16.
[31] Ibid. para. 15.
[32] Nicaragua Jurisdiction Case, para. 27.

was established. Having never accepted the PCIJ's jurisdiction, Nicaragua fell outside the scope of Article 36(5), Judge Schwebel argued. In contrast, the majority held that the purpose of Article 36(5) was not limited to transferring compulsory jurisdiction from the PCIJ to the ICJ. According to the majority, the provision's wider object was to ensure continuing "progress" toward "the cause of compulsory jurisdiction."[33]

In support of their divergent views, the majority and dissent both cited the ICJ's judgment in the *Case Concerning the Aerial Incident of 27 July 1955 (Israel v. Bulgaria).*[34] In that case, Israel sought to establish the ICJ's jurisdiction over Bulgaria based on a ratified 1921 declaration that made Bulgaria a party to the Statute of the PCIJ. Bulgaria argued that Article 36(5) did not apply to its declaration, because Bulgaria did not become a UN member and a party to the ICJ's Statute until 1955, long after the PCIJ ceased to exist. The Court sided with Bulgaria, holding that a declaration in force vis-à-vis the defunct PCIJ could not be revived to apply to the ICJ. In the course of its judgment, however, the Court signaled that the purpose of Article 36(5) was to maintain to the extent possible seamless continuity between the PCIJ and its successor: "the clear intention which inspired Article 36, paragraph 5, was to continue in being something which was in existence, to preserve existing acceptances, to avoid that the creation of the [ICJ] should frustrate progress already achieved."[35] Reflecting on these findings from *Aerial Incident*, the Court in the *Nicaragua Jurisdiction Case* agreed unanimously that a core purpose of Article 36(5) was to ensure that the ICJ's creation would "not result in a step backwards in relation to the progress accomplished towards adopting a system of compulsory jurisdiction."[36]

Noting that Nicaragua was represented at the San Francisco Conference and signed and ratified the UN Charter, the majority argued that Nicaragua's 1929 declaration had become legally binding through Article 36(5). In support of this argument, the majority quoted *Aerial Incident*: "Consent to the transfer to the International Court of Justice of a declaration accepting the jurisdiction of the Permanent Court may be regarded as effectively given by a State which, having been represented at the San Francisco Conference, signed and ratified the Charter and

[33] Ibid., paras. 33, 35.

[34] Aerial Incident of 27 July 1955 (Israel v. Bulgaria), Preliminary Objections, Judgment, 1959 ICJ Rep. 127 (26 May) (hereinafter Aerial Incident).

[35] Nicaragua Jurisdiction Case, para. 32; Nicaragua Jurisdiction Case (dissenting op., Schwebel, J.), para. 29 (citing Aerial Incident, p. 145).

[36] Nicaragua Jurisdiction Case, para. 33.

thereby accepted the Statute in which Article 36, paragraph 5, appears."[37] According to the majority, Nicaragua's ratification of the Statute of the ICJ had "exactly the same effects as the ratification of the Protocol of the [PCIJ] would have had, that is to say, in the case of Nicaragua, the step from potential commitment to effective commitment."[38] By ratifying the Statute of the ICJ, Nicaragua "effectively" consented to convert its 1929 declaration into a legally binding acceptance of the ICJ's compulsory jurisdiction, the majority concluded.

Judge Schwebel offered a narrower interpretation of the *Aerial Incident* dictum concerning participants in the San Francisco Conference. He noted that the dictum followed these findings:

> Article 36, paragraph 5, considered in its application to States signatories of the Statute, effects a simple operation: it transforms *their acceptance of the compulsory jurisdiction of the Permanent Court into an acceptance of the compulsory jurisdiction of the International Court of Justice* . . . Article 36, paragraph 5, governed the transfer from one Court to the other of still-existing declarations; in so doing, *it maintained an existing obligation* while modifying its subject-matter.[39]

In short, Article 36(5) was concerned solely with maintaining states' preexisting commitments to accept compulsory jurisdiction, facilitating "the transfer to the new Court of the compulsory jurisdiction of the old," rather than extending the ICJ's jurisdiction to states like Nicaragua that had never formally embraced the PCIJ's jurisdiction.[40]

The divergent conclusions reached by the majority and Judge Schwebel reflect different visions of the role that compulsory jurisdiction plays within the international legal system. For Judge Schwebel, compulsory jurisdiction is an artifact of state consent and, as such, apt to be read down if a state fails to express its consent in clear conformity with formal requirements. In contrast, the majority envisions compulsory jurisdiction as an ideal of legality underlying the creation and practices of both the PCIJ and the ICJ. As such, for the majority compulsory jurisdiction serves as a constitutional principle that should guide interpretation of the enabling statutes of international courts, with ambiguities resolved in favor of compulsory jurisdiction, and with infringements on compulsory jurisdiction requiring express and unequivocal statutory language.

37 Ibid., at para. 35 (citing Aerial Incident, p. 142).
38 Ibid.
39 Nicaragua Jurisdiction Case (dissenting op., Schwebel, J.), para. 27 (citing Aerial Incident, pp. 137, 138) (emphasis added by Judge Schwebel).
40 Ibid. (citing Aerial Incident, pp. 142, 143) (emphasis added by Judge Schwebel).

This constitutional interpretive principle helps to explain why, for the majority, it was significant that the drafters of Article 36(5) declined to use the term "binding."[41] It also clarifies why the majority presumed that "the highly experienced drafters" of the Statute of the ICJ would have used "a very different formula from the one which they in fact adopted" if they had a "restrictive intention" with respect to Article 36(5) – especially given the drafters' "overall concern" to aim at "the maximum, and not some merely quasi optimum preservation" of compulsory jurisdiction.[42]

A similar difference in approach marks the majority and dissenting opinions' handling of Secretary Schultz's 1984 notification that purported to remove the United States from the ICJ's compulsory jurisdiction vis-à-vis Nicaragua. As noted, the United States' 1946 declaration permitted the United States to withdraw from the ICJ's compulsory jurisdiction only after six months' notice.[43] Having never given notice to terminate – in conformity with the six-month notice period or otherwise – the 1946 declaration remained in effect. Therefore, according to the declaration's plain terms, the United States remained subject to the ICJ's compulsory jurisdiction vis-à-vis other states "accepting the same obligation."[44] However, the 1984 notification purported to suspend for two years the effect of the 1946 declaration in relation to "disputes with any Central American State or arising out of or related to events in Central America."[45] If legally valid, the 1984 notification would have denied the ICJ jurisdiction to hear the case Nicaragua filed three days later.[46]

The majority affirmed the conventional understanding that declarations "even though they are unilateral acts, establish a series of bilateral engagements with other States accepting the same obligation of compulsory jurisdiction, in which the conditions, reservations and time-limit clauses are taken into consideration."[47] In applying this general principle to the facts before it, the majority acknowledged that the United States retained the right to modify or terminate the 1946 declaration. Nevertheless, the majority held that the United States "assumed an

41 Ibid., para. 30.
42 Ibid., para. 34 (citing Barcelona Traction, Light and Power Company, Limited (Belg. v. Spain) Judgment, Preliminary Objections, 1964 ICJ Rep. 6, 32 (24 July)).
43 Nicaragua Jurisdiction Case, para. 13.
44 ICJ Statute, art. 36(2).
45 Ibid.
46 Nicaragua Jurisdiction Case, para. 54 (citing Nottebohm Case, Preliminary Objection, Judgment, 1953 ICJ Rep. 111, 122 (18 November)).
47 Ibid., para. 60.

inescapable obligation towards other States" under the 1946 declaration "by stating formally and solemnly that any such change should take effect only after six months have elapsed as from the date of notice."[48]

Judge Schwebel's central argument for giving effect to the 1984 notification turned on the principle of reciprocity and the idea that the United States could not properly be held to a six-month time constraint that did not also apply to Nicaragua. Whereas the majority concluded that Nicaragua could terminate its declaration on such reasonable notice as good faith might allow, and that such notice would have to be greater than three days, Judge Schwebel asserted that Nicaragua had the right to terminate its declaration on immediate notice. He pointed out that states-parties were entitled to withdraw from the UN Charter on immediate notice, and that other states had withdrawn from indefinitely accepting the ICJ's jurisdiction without a period of reasonable notice.[49] For the dissenting judge, this raised the question of whether the United States should not also be entitled to modify or terminate its declaration on immediate notice, under a principle of reciprocity that is "closely tied to considerations of mutuality and of the sovereign equality of States before the law and before the Court."[50] Judge Schwebel thus relied on an argument of principle that the parties would not be treated as legal equals if Nicaragua were permitted to engage the Court while possessing an entitlement to immediate termination not enjoyed by the United States. In his view, the United States had a "reciprocal right" to modify or suspend its 1946 declaration on immediate notice, which it did with the 1984 notification, thereby leaving the ICJ without jurisdiction to consider Nicaragua's claims.[51] The majority, on the other hand, held that reciprocity "is concerned with the scope and substance of commitments entered into, including reservations, and not with formal conditions of their creation, duration or extinction."[52] Accordingly, for the majority, "reciprocity cannot be invoked in order to excuse departure from the terms of a State's own declaration."[53]

Once again, the majority treats compulsory jurisdiction as a preeminent constitutional ideal against which state declarations and principles such as reciprocity must be interpreted. The minority judge, by

48 Ibid., para. 61.
49 Ibid., paras. 100–106.
50 Ibid., para. 110.
51 Ibid., para. 115.
52 Ibid., para. 62.
53 Ibid.

contrast, adopts a more voluntarist understanding of compulsory jurisdiction. He privileges a conception of state sovereignty under which states have maximum leeway to accept or not the compulsory jurisdiction of the ICJ, including an entitlement to opt out of its jurisdiction just days before an adverse state files suit. For Judge Schwebel, the 1984 notification as well as considerations of reciprocity, mutuality, and sovereign equality must be read through a voluntarist lens. Nonetheless, despite the substantial differences separating the contending judgments, they also reflect shared presuppositions and points of reference. We briefly set these out now, since having the common ground in view lays some of the foundation for the arguments that follow regarding the mandatory nature of using peaceful means to resolve disputes at international law.

The common ground that unites the majority and dissent in the *Nicaragua Case* is their shared understanding that legal principles attenuate the requirement for state consent to the jurisdiction of international courts and tribunals. First, the judges all affirmed or presupposed that the parties' relations between themselves and to the Court were informed by principles of sovereign equality, mutuality, reciprocity, and formal legal equality. While they disputed the content and application of some of these principles, none suggested that legal principles could be supplanted by pleadings of self-interest or a notion of might makes right. By the same token, the judges all recognized that relevantly similar past judgments carried persuasive authority with respect to the case before them. They all acknowledged that fresh consent was not necessary for a state to be subject to the compulsory jurisdiction of the ICJ; prior consent to the PCIJ, via Article 36(5), was adequate. Similarly, they all acknowledged that consent signaled decades ago through declarations under Articles 36(2) or 36(5) did not need to be reasserted for the ICJ's compulsory jurisdiction to remain intact. They likewise agreed that, in principle, exercises of past state sovereignty could fetter future state sovereignty (e.g., notice periods established for terminating a declaration). This marked a departure from the principle of plenary authority that governs legislative lawmaking in most states, under which a present legislature cannot fetter or constrain the lawmaking power of a future legislature. The judges on both sides also accepted that once a state files an application to initiate a proceeding, parties to the proceeding cannot modify their declarations of acceptance to avoid the ICJ's jurisdiction.

Lastly, the judges agreed that both parties had an "obligation to seek a solution to their disputes by peaceful means in accordance with international law."[54] In the next section we deploy this and other foundational premises of mandatory cooperation to argue that if states in a dispute reach an irresoluble impasse, they have a general duty at international law to submit their dispute to adjudication. We argue that this duty is independent of treaty-specific duties to seek adjudication that are sometimes triggered if a dispute arising within a treaty framework proves intractable.[55] The duty therefore applies even when states have not specifically committed to international adjudication or arbitration by treaty or through unilateral declarations.

The Duty Seek Adjudication

As discussed in preceding chapters, states have a duty under Article 2(3) of the UN Charter to "settle their disputes by peaceful means."[56] Article 33(1) of the Charter makes the obligation concrete where "the continuance of [a dispute] is likely to endanger the maintenance of international peace and security."[57] In these circumstances, the Charter requires parties in conflict to "seek a solution by negotiation, enquiry, mediation, conciliation, arbitration, judicial settlement, resort to regional agencies or arrangements, or other peaceful means of their own choice."[58] Relatedly, the Charter prohibits states from resolving disputes by force or the threat of force unless they are acting in self-defense or authorized by the Security Council.[59] Citing with approval Article 33(1), the Court in the *Nicaragua Merits Case* added that the injunction to resolve disputes by peaceful means has the status of customary international law, with the implication that it legally binds all states.[60] If follows that states are under a legal obligation to use peaceful means to settle conflicts even if they have never formally consented to the norm, and indeed even if they oppose it. The duty to use peaceful means to resolve disputes is international law's doctrinal expression of one of mandatory cooperation's central prescriptions.

54 Nicaragua Merits Case, p. 149, para. 292.

55 E.g., UN Convention on the Law of the Sea art. 125(1), UN Doc. A/CONF. 62/122 (1982), Part XI, § 5 (obligating states parties to submit disputes to the Seabed Disputes Chamber).

56 UN Charter, art. 2(3).

57 Ibid., art. 33(1).

58 Ibid. In Chapter 1 we characterize these as procedural obligations, and throughout the book point to various contexts in which parties are found to owe each other a duty to consult and negotiate with one another in good faith.

59 UN Charter, arts. 2(4), 51; ch. VII.

60 Nicaragua Merits Case, p. 145, para. 290.

The *Nicaragua Case* also illuminates international law's embrace of sovereign equality as a deep-seated principle and organizing idea of mandatory cooperation. The first substantive principle articulated in the UN Charter is that the UN system "is based on the principle of the sovereign equality of all its Members."[61] From the standpoint of sovereign equality, differences between states in terms of their geographic size, population, wealth, or military strength are irrelevant. All states enjoy equal authority to govern within their territory and to represent their people internationally, and all states are to be treated as legal equals in their interactions with one another.[62] Mirroring and informing the content of the sovereign equality of states, the Charter likewise affirms that peoples enjoy equal rights and self-determination.[63] From these constitutional principles of international legal order – where sovereign equality is understood to entail rights to equal self-determination – it follows that no state is entitled to dictate terms to another state or its people. An imperial entitlement of this kind would imply that the subordinate state and its people would not be self-determining equals; by hypothesis, their international rights or internal governance would be subject to the will of one or more ascendant states.

The difficulty from the standpoint of international legality is not simply that, as a matter of fact, the strong would dominate the weak. The graver concern is that the strong would be *legally* empowered to dominate the weak, contrary to international law's understanding of sovereign equality as the legal equality of states that represent peoples equal in rights and self-determination. Recall from Chapter 1 Vattel's claim that "a small Republic is no less a sovereign State than the most powerful Kingdom."[64] Vattel's quip that "a dwarf" is as much a person as "a giant" offers an apt image of the contest between legal equals that in

[61] UN Charter, art. 2(1).

[62] UN General Assembly, 'Declaration on Principles of International Law concerning Friendly Relations and Co-operation among States in Accordance with the Charter of the United Nations', UN Doc. A/RES/25/2625 (24 October 1970) (affirming that all states are "judicially equal" and that each "enjoys the rights inherent in full sovereignty").

[63] UN Charter, art. 1(2); see also Declaration on the Occasion of the Fiftieth Anniversary of the United Nations ¶ 1, GA Res. 50/6, UN GAOR, 50th Sess., Supp. No. 49, UN Doc. A/50/49 (1995) (declaring that states "reaffirm the right of self-determination of all peoples, taking into account the particular situation of peoples under colonial or other forms of alien domination").

[64] Emmerich de Vattel, *The Law of Nations, Or The Principles Of Natural Law Applied to the Conduct and Affairs of Nations and Sovereigns* (Charles G. Fenwick trans., Dobbs Ferry, New York: Oceana Publications, 1964) (1758), Preliminaries, § 18.

1984 would see the "dwarf" Nicaragua challenge the "giant" United States under the aegis of sovereign equality.

A further animating principle of mandatory cooperation that supports a context-sensitive duty to seek adjudication is the obligation of states to exercise their sovereign powers equitably, which is to say, with "due regard" for the interests of other states and foreign nationals.[65] As discussed in previous chapters, due regard for foreign interests does not require putting them ahead of national interests, but it generally does require "reasonable, appropriate, optimal regard."[66] An exercise of sovereign power that fails to show due regard for the interests of other states or foreign nationals is akin to an abuse of right, where the right holder exercises a right in a way that causes needless or disproportionate harm to others.[67] And so, in the *Lake Lanoux Arbitration* that pitted upstream France against downstream Spain,[68] the Tribunal held that France, in its exercise of sovereign authority over waterways within its territory, "is under the obligation to take into consideration the various interests involved, to seek to give them every satisfaction compatible with the pursuit of its own interests, and to show that in this regard it is genuinely concerned to reconcile the interest of the other riparian State with its own."[69]

Bringing the threads together, core doctrines of customary international law prohibit the use of force to resolve disputes while also requiring states to use peaceful means to resolve them. Sovereign equality demands that states be regarded as legal equals authorized to represent peoples equal in rights and self-determination. For states and their peoples to enjoy sovereign equality so understood, other states cannot be entitled to dictate terms or otherwise use unilateral force against them, as international law provides. Instead, states must resolve disputes through peaceful means, as international law provides, and they must be prepared to exercise their sovereign powers equitably for the sake of a just resolution.

Ideally, states will settle their disputes though good faith negotiation, mediation, or conciliation. If rivalrous parties reach an intractable

[65] See, e.g., Chagos Marine Protected Area Arbitration (Mauritius/UK), Case No. 2011-03, Award, para. 534 (Perm. Ct. Arb. 2015).

[66] Jonathan B. Wiener, 'Disregard and Due Regard' (2021) 29 *NYU Envt'l L.J.* 437, 461.

[67] Robert Kolb, *Good Faith in International Law* (London: Bloomsbury Publishing, 2017), pp. 142–145 (discussing international "abuse of right" as including "manifest disproportion of interests" and "arbitrary action").

[68] See above Chapter 2.

[69] Lake Lanoux Arbitration (Fr. v. Sp.), 24 ILR 101, 139 (1957).

impasse, however, then the duty to use exclusively peaceful means to resolve disputes must be understood to include mandatory adjudication. To allow stronger parties in these circumstances to avoid adjudication altogether would infringe sovereign equality and raise serious questions about the legitimacy of the international legal order. Moreover, having the shadow of mandatory adjudication in the background of negotiations will tend to give the parties' negotiations salutary contact with legal standards and precedents, since both parties would know that if they fail to settle, a judge or arbitrator will decide the matter. This account of mandatory adjudication resonates with the views of two theorists who loom large in the literature on international dispute resolution: Thomas Hobbes and Immanuel Kant.

In *The Doctrine of Right*, Kant claims not only that individuals have a duty to leave the state of nature to enter a civil or rightful condition (i.e., a state, preferably a constitutional republic) but also that an individual in the state of nature "may impel the other by force to leave this state and enter into a rightful condition."[70] Kant's justification for the use of force in this context focuses on the lack of a judiciary in the state of nature. While admitting that the state of nature need not be a dystopia of relentless war, he insists that "it would still be a state *devoid of justice (status iustitia vacuus)*, in which, when rights are *in dispute (ius controversum)*, there would be no judge competent to render a verdict having rightful force."[71] In a civil condition, the judge's verdict has rightful force because the judge enjoys the standing of a public authority who is authorized to apply law to facts to resolve disputes. Private individuals in both the state of nature and civil society have no such standing. If they resort to force rather than legal institutions to settle disputes, they simply impose their will on others. So, for Kant, using force to bring someone into a civil condition is legitimate because the actor who seeks to remain outside the law, breaching their duty to enter a rightful condition, purports to reserve to themselves an entitlement to set unilaterally the terms of their relations with others.

Kant's uncompromising insistence on the necessity of legal order lends principled support for the ICJ's judgment in the *Nicaragua Jurisdiction Case*. If the ICJ did not exercise jurisdiction, the United States might

[70] Immanuel Kant, *The Metaphysics of Morals* (Mary Gregor trans., New York: Cambridge University Press, 1991) (1797), p. 124; see also Arthur Ripstein, *Force and Freedom: Kant's Legal and Political Philosophy* (Cambridge, MA: Harvard University Press, 2009), chs. 6 and 7.

[71] Ibid. p. 124 (emphasis in original).

continue to assert the prerogative to intervene in Nicaragua unilaterally, frustrating the establishment of a rightful condition between the two states. On a Kantian approach, therefore, the commanding necessity to establish legal order would arguably justify the majority's strained interpretation of the ICJ Statute, as well as its willingness to discount Nicaragua's failure to ratify its 1929 declaration and its rejection of the United States' eleventh-hour stratagem to evade the Court's compulsory jurisdiction.

Hobbes also gives adjudication an exalted place in his legal and political theory. Before setting out the state of nature and developing a solution in *Leviathan*, Hobbes offers an account of "right reason" (i.e., public reason or authoritative reason) that is itself a compressed version of the extended argument he will later give for a legal order designed to ensure peace. When there is a controversy, Hobbes says, "the parties must by their own accord set up for right reason the reason of some arbitrator or judge to whose sentence they will both stand, or their controversy must either come to blows or be undecided."[72] Hobbes subsequently insists that it is a "law of nature" (a legal principle knowable through reason) that parties in a dispute must "*submit their right to the judgment of an arbitrator*," and that a failure to do so results in them being "as far from peace as ever."[73] The arbitrator, in turn, must "*deal equally between them* ... The observance of this law ... is called EQUITY."[74] Hobbes likewise subscribes to the venerable principle *nemo iudex in causa sua*, "*no man is a fit arbitrator in his own cause.*"[75] For Kant, this principle is simply a presupposition of public adjudication; adjudication must be impartial to avoid collapsing into unilateralism. Hobbes, however, offers a complementary but different justification for *nemo iudex* and impartial adjudication generally.

Hobbes' rationale for adjudication is not that the strong will unjustly dominate the weak without it, but that equity allows each party equal benefit, and so "if one be admitted to be judge, the other is to be admitted also; and so the controversy, that is, the cause of war, remains, against the law of nature."[76] Taking Hobbes' argument in stages, his initial claim is that if one party were made judge, the other party would no longer enjoy

[72] Thomas Hobbes, *Leviathan with Selected Variants from the Latin Edition of 1668* (Edwin Curley ed., Canada: Hackett Publishing Co., 1994), p. 23.

[73] Ibid., p. 98 (emphasis in original).

[74] Ibid., p. 97 (emphasis in original).

[75] Ibid. (emphasis in original).

[76] Ibid.

equality before the law, in violation of the principle of equity. Formal equality could be restored by making both parties judges, but doing so would return them to the state of nature, where all are entitled to judge for themselves how best to pursue their self-preservation. Thus, for Hobbes, as for international law, the duty to seek adjudication is tied closely to the idea that the status of disputants as legal equals – equals under law in civil society and not the state of nature – depends on the availability of adjudication. Whereas for Kant adjudication makes equal freedom possible, for Hobbes adjudication makes legal equality possible. In international law, the principles of equal freedom and legal equality are the double helix of sovereign equality's DNA. Inextricably linked, they are both necessary and together sufficient to explain the equal independence of sovereign states made possible by an international legal order structured by mandatory cooperation, part of which includes the duty to seek adjudication in the event of an irresolvable impasse.

Jurisdiction as Equity

The duty to seek jurisdiction rests on relatively mundane legal premises: the prohibition of the use of force to resolve disputes, the duty to use peaceful means for this purpose, sovereign equality as equal independence and legal equality, and the duty to exercise sovereign powers equitably. Nonetheless, it remains the case that international law is conventionally understood to require states to consent to the jurisdiction of specific courts in order for those courts to have jurisdiction over them. In the *Nicaragua Jurisdiction Case*, for example, the two parties had signaled consent by unilateral declaration.[77] States may also come under the ICJ's jurisdiction by special agreement through which they jointly petition the Court to hear a specific matter. And states can include in treaties jurisdiction clauses that accept that Court's jurisdiction to resolve disputes over the interpretation and application of a treaty.[78] Today there are some 300 treaties with jurisdiction clauses.[79] The justification usually given for the consent requirement is

[77] See, e.g., Case Concerning East Timor (Portugal v. Australia), Judgment, 1995 ICJ Rep. 87, 101, para. 26 (30 June) (affirming that "one of the fundamental principles of its Statute is that it cannot decide a dispute between States without the consent of those States to its jurisdiction").

[78] UN Charter, art. 36(1).

[79] ICJ Frequently Asked Questions: www.icj-cij.org/frequently-asked-questions.

one that appears on the ICJ's website: "States are sovereign and free to choose how to resolve their disputes."[80]

Of course, states are not entirely "free to choose how to resolve their disputes." As we have seen, generally they cannot use force or the threat of force; instead, they must choose how to resolve disputes from the peaceful means available. Plainly, the ICJ does not contest the requirement that states must cooperate with one another in good faith and use peaceful means when they disagree. Still, giving sovereignty even this much latitude poses a puzzle: if states are entitled to stand on their sovereign rights to choose how to resolve their conflicts, and if this discretion allows them to insist on an alternative to adjudication, such as continued negotiation or nonbinding mediation, then in the event of an impasse is the alleged duty to seek adjudication really a duty at all?

A possible solution to the puzzle draws on mandatory cooperation's principle that sovereign rights must be exercised equitably, a principle that distinguishes sharply between sovereign rights, on the one hand, and the equitable requirement that states use their rights with due regard for other states and foreign nationals, on the other. Just as France in the *Lake Lanoux Arbitration* enjoyed territorial sovereignty over the waters within its territories but nonetheless had to exercise its sovereignty in a manner that took Spanish interests into account, if a genuine and intractable impasse arises in good faith negotiation, mediation, or conciliation, the parties to the controversy are subject to Hobbes' equitable injunction to submit their dispute to an impartial third party. Assuming the parties are not already subject to the jurisdiction of the ICJ, another international court, or an arbitral tribunal, their sovereignty entitles them to decide jointly on a convenient forum. But their sovereignty does not allow them to imperil sovereign equality by avoiding impartial adjudication altogether if best efforts otherwise fail to settle the matter.[81] The distinction between law and equity and its salience in international law can thus explain how states may

[80] Ibid.

[81] For an argument from similar premises in favor of international courts enjoying jurisdiction without prior state consent for disputes arising from nonvoluntary obligations (i.e., customary international law, general principles of law, and *jus cogens*), see Mathias Kumm, 'Towards an International Rule of Law: Why the Jurisdiction of International Courts Does Not in All Circumstances Depend on State Consent' (draft version on file with authors). Kumm's argument is compelling, but our method is to take on board as much of international law's self-understanding as possible, and for now it seems that, along with sovereign equality and mandatory cooperation, international law's self-understanding includes the view that states must consent to be subject to the jurisdiction of particular courts.

have sovereign rights to determine how to resolve their conflicts, but also be subject to an equitable requirement to exercise those rights in a way that gives due regard to other states and foreign nationals, with the implication that irresolvable impasses must go to impartial adjudication.

Admittedly, in cases such as the *Lake Lanoux Arbitration*, the equitable constraint on sovereign power operates at the object level of determining the appropriate primary rules, with a background institution already in place to resolve the dispute. With the puzzle under consideration – explaining how states can have the right to choose how to resolve disputes while being under a context-sensitive duty to seek adjudication – the assumption is that an adjudicative institution is not yet seized with jurisdiction, and that equity can explain and inform the duty of the parties to seek an impartial third party. Still, in both cases the core equitable justification is the same: under appropriate circumstances, legal rights must be exercised in accordance with equitable constraints to ensure they do not become vehicles of abuse and corrosive to the rationale for having the relevant rights in the first place. Concretely, the right of sovereign states to choose a convenient forum must be reconciled and coordinated with the duty to seek adjudication; from a legal point of view, the former cannot serve as pretext or device to avoid the latter.

A skeptic might consider the equitable requirement to seek adjudication too weak and amorphous to be of significant assistance to parties in real world disputes. The *Nicaragua Jurisdiction Case* shows, however, that where consent is in doubt or there are questions attending formalities required to communicate consent, judges who ultimately rule in favor of compulsory jurisdiction do so because they recognize the value of the constitutional and equitable grounds for compulsory jurisdiction. The debate between the majority and Judge Schwebel revealed that, in practice, a majority bench of the ICJ was prepared to defend the finest of distinctions (e.g., "valid" declarations versus "binding" declarations) to support the cause of compulsory jurisdiction inaugurated with the PCIJ and continued with the ICJ. Statutory text, relevant case law and contrary historical evidence were read down in order to sustain the case for jurisdiction. The principles in favor of jurisdiction thus provided resources for creative gap-filling and statutory interpretation. Plausibly, the majority were comfortable resting jurisdiction on somewhat fragile textual and jurisprudential grounds because they believed (i) the parties had a general duty to seek adjudication that the United States was trying to avoid, (ii) the parties had in substance consented to jurisdiction through unilateral declarations, and (iii) the ICJ was an appropriate venue for the matter's adjudication.

Opting Out and Legitimacy

Realist skeptics may yet question the value of international adjudication on the ground that states can opt out or refuse from the outset to accept the jurisdiction of adjudicative regimes. Skeptics might also observe that using the Security Council to enforce remedies ordered by the ICJ against the P5 may prove challenging given their possession of a veto. The *Nicaragua Jurisdiction Case* is again illuminating. Although the ICJ refused to accept the 1984 notification, the United States eventually did withdraw from the ICJ's compulsory jurisdiction in 1986. The withdrawal came shortly after the ICJ released its judgment in the *Nicaragua Jurisdiction Case*, though only after giving six months' notice as prescribed by the 1946 declaration.[82] And as mentioned in the introduction to this chapter, the United States used its veto on the Security Council to avoid paying the sizable awards ordered in favor of Nicaragua. These aspects of contemporary international legal order chafe at the constitutional aspiration of compulsory jurisdiction that motivated architects of the PCIJ and the ICJ. The possibility of states opting out and avoiding remedies also strains the international rule of law. Nonetheless, this institutional frailty does not show that international adjudication lacks legitimacy or fails to count as law.

In liberal democracies, the rule of law ordinarily implies that officials and private citizens alike are subject to the law, including the compulsory jurisdiction of municipal courts.[83] In commonwealth countries, however, Parliament and its Members (when acting in their official capacities) are not subject to significant swaths of the ordinary law. Under the doctrine of parliamentary privilege, Parliament and its Members are immune from suit in relation to activities considered necessary for Parliament to fulfill its constitutional tasks, such as control of "debates and proceedings

[82] Treaties and International Agreements Registered or Filed and Recorded with the Secretariat of the United Nations (19 September 1985 to 11 October 1985), 1408 UNTS 270.

[83] See, e.g., A.V. Dicey, *Introduction to the Study of the Law of the Constitution*, 8th ed. (London: Macmillan & Co., 1915), p. 189 (asserting as a tenet of the rule of law that "no man is above the law" and that "every official, from the Prime Minister down to a constable" is subject to "the ordinary law" and "the ordinary tribunals") [hereinafter Dicey, *Introduction*].

in Parliament" as guaranteed by the UK Bill of Rights of 1689.[84] Similarly, public officials who perform their duties in good faith typically enjoy immunity for harms that result from their conduct as officials.[85] In individual states as well as in international legal order, the judiciary lacks comprehensive jurisdiction, notwithstanding that compulsory jurisdiction is the default norm at the national level and usually applies irrespective of a subject's consent.

There is also an important sense in which the sovereign right of states to choose how to resolve their disputes parallels parliamentary sovereignty under the UK constitution. For constitutional theorist A. V. Dicey, the British unwritten constitution consisted of two closely connected legal principles: parliamentary sovereignty and the rule of law. Parliamentary sovereignty, according to Dicey, meant that Parliament has "the right to make or unmake any law whatever; and, further, that no person or body is recognised by the law of England as having a right to override or set aside the legislation of Parliament."[86] Parliament's lawmaking authority is therefore both plenary and supreme. As Mark Walters has argued, however, on Dicey's account Parliament's sovereignty is determined and conditioned by law in three ways: "first, law defines what Parliament is; second, the sovereignty enjoyed by Parliament is itself a legal power; and, third, the sovereignty of Parliament is legislative sovereignty only, i.e., it is not the power to do anything but only the power to make law through legislation."[87] These legal attributes of parliamentary sovereignty, Walters claims, condition how it can be exercised and make it possible for Dicey's second constitutional principle – the rule of law – to complete the United Kingdom's law-giving framework.[88]

Dicey believed that the rule of law required due process and formal legal equality, but perhaps more significantly still, it also required judges to interpret Parliament's legislation "in the spirit of legality" and consistent with "the general spirit of the common law."[89] Today, judges in

[84] See, e.g., Ontario (Speaker of the Legislative Assembly) v. Ontario (Human Rights Commission) (2001), 54 O.R. (3d) 595 at para. 23.

[85] See, e.g., Pierson v. Ray, 386 US 547 (1967) (establishing the doctrine of qualified immunity for police officers).

[86] Dicey, *Introduction*, p. 37.

[87] Mark D. Walters, *A.V. Dicey and the Common Law Constitutional Tradition: A Legal Turn of Mind* (Cambridge: Cambridge University Press, 2020), p. 165.

[88] Ibid., p. 281.

[89] Dicey, *Introduction*, p. 409.

commonwealth countries interpret statutes and review administrative action using a "principle of legality" that calls on them to interpret legislation, to the extent possible, in a manner consistent with human rights, common law values, and equitable principles.[90] Administrative action that encroaches on rights, values or principles without express statutory warrant may be declared invalid. It is a vexed question whether, ultimately, Parliament is entitled to use unambiguous language to infringe gratuitously legal principle *and* have that plain language applied by the courts.[91] Generally, however, "[p]arliamentary sovereignty means that Parliament can, if it chooses, legislate contrary to fundamental principles of human rights," though it must use especially clear language because "Parliament must squarely confront what it is doing and accept the political cost."[92]

The point for present purposes is that in the United Kingdom and commonwealth states without written constitutions, Parliament can effectively avoid judicial review by using express language. Much as states at international law can use their sovereign power to withhold or withdraw consent to avoid the jurisdiction of particular international courts, Parliaments can use their plenary lawmaking power to adopt express language to avoid judicial review of administrative action that infringes on human rights or common law values. In both cases, the use of plenary sovereign power can result in an evasion of accountability before judicial authorities that may strain the rule of law. Yet, in both cases too, judges can take up David Dyzenhaus' recommendation that they adopt the role of a "weatherman" who reports on the repugnancy to the rule of law of both a statute that offends principles of legality and a state policy that breaches the duty to seek adjudication.[93] And in both cases, a failure of

[90] See, e.g., R. v. Secretary of State for the Home Department, ex parte Simms [2000] 2 AC 115, 131 (HL) (affirming that "[f]undamental rights cannot be overridden by general or ambiguous words") [hereinafter Simms].

[91] See, e.g., T. R. S. Allan, *The Sovereignty of Law: Freedom, Constitution, and Common Law* (Oxford: Oxford University Press, 2013), pp. 141–142 (asserting that Dicey's hypothetical statute that calls for the murder of all blue-eyed babies may be "formally valid" but "in substance void" for its violation of the rule of law). David Dyzenhaus interprets Dicey to affirm that a statute that infringes the rule of law or legality may be valid but is nonetheless illegal precisely because it encroaches on the rule of law or legality: David Dyzenhaus, *Constitution of Law: Legality in a Time of Emergency* (Cambridge: Cambridge University Press, 2006), pp. 57–58 [hereinafter Dyzenhaus, *Constitution of Law*].

[92] *Simms*, n. 98, p. 131, *per* Lord Hoffmann.

[93] Dyzenhaus, *Constitution of Law*, p. 200.

legality may be recognized as such only because in other cases legality visibly succeeds. That Nicaragua won both the jurisdiction and merits cases showed that sovereign equality can serve as the basis for a system of adjudication in which the weak can successfully challenge the strong as legal equals.

One final comparison to British constitutionalism offers further grounds for doubting the force of the realist critique. The rule of law for Dicey consisted in judicial review of administrative action. The main institutional tools used by judges conducting review were the prerogative writs. The substance if not the form of these writs is still found in the remedies available in judicial review of administrative action today, which include: *certiorari* (quashing or setting aside administrative decisions), *mandamus* (ordering the performance of a public duty), *quo warranto* (requiring a demonstration of legal authority), *habeas corpus* (requiring the presentation of a detained person and justification of the detention), and prohibition (supervising the jurisdiction of ecclesiastical and administrative decision-makers).[94] The writs originated in the Middle Ages and were generally issued by the king or his delegates (e.g., the Court of King's Bench, the Privy Council, the Lord Chancellor) to address a complaint against an inferior tribunal or an administrative decision-maker. They embodied the king's prerogative power to supervise the diffuse institutions administering justice on the king's behalf.

Consider, for example, the writ of *certiorari.* The writ began in the thirteenth century as a written request issued by the king to obtain judicial records for examination. At the turn of the seventeenth century, *certiorari* was available from both Chancery and the Court of King's Bench. S. A. de Smith notes that the anonymous author of *A Treatise of the Maisters of the Chauncerie* identified *certiorari* as a "writ of grace."[95] When Francis Bacon became Lord Chancellor in 1618, he issued an order that writs of *certiorari, habeas corpus*, and prohibition (among others) should not be issued without his approval. His purpose, according to de Smith, was to maintain

[94] Edward Jenks, 'The Prerogative Writs in English Law' (1923) 32 YLJ 523; S. A. de Smith, 'The Prerogative Writs' (1951) 11 *Cambridge L.J.* 40; Paul A. Warchuk, *The Writ of Certiorari and Its Scope, 1600–1800: For the Orderly Administration of Justice* (Cambridge: submitted for the degree of Doctor of Philosophy, 2023). The sketch of the prerogative writs provided in the text is drawn from these sources.

[95] de Smith, 'The Prerogative Writs', p. 43 (citing *A Treatise of the Maisters of the Chauncerie* (written c. 1596–1603), reprinted in Hargrave's *Law Tracts* 292).

the principle "that writs closely associated with the rights of the Crown should not issue out of Chancery to the subject as of course."[96]

Within less than two decades, applications for *certiorari* were largely made to the Court of King's Bench. The Court began to use *certiorari* not only to examine the final orders and convictions of justices of the peace, but to quash them if warranted.[97] Before a claimant could ask the Court to examine or quash an order or conviction, however, they had to show sufficient cause to acquire the writ of *certiorari*. If successful, the claimant would deliver the writ to the clerk of the peace who held the relevant record, and the clerk would subsequently return the record to King's Bench for examination and disposition. The Court's examination was strictly limited to the written record. In some cases the record failed to include evidence that was readily available. The claimant could request that the clerk of the peace prepare a detailed factual record, but only with the consent of the local justices subject to the writ.

For purposes of comparison with international adjudication, there are three particularly important features of the seventeenth-century *certiorari* process: first, the availability of *certiorari* from Chancery by grace and not by right; second, the requirement to show cause to obtain the writ from the King's Bench; and third, the need to secure the consent of the challenged justices to have the record amended for examination. Together these features disclose a practice of judicial review conducted at the sufferance of the sovereign. In any given case, the affected individual could be denied from the outset the opportunity to have their record examined and an adverse decision quashed. The position of individuals vis-à-vis judicial review in the seventeenth century was thus in an important sense analogous to the position of weaker states seeking a forum for international adjudication. In both cases, the availability of a judicial forum depends on the consent of a public authority. While in the case of judicial review the relevant public authority is the subject's own judiciary and not another state, the prerogative writs were discretionary writs of grace that could be refused without notice or reasons. Whereas the majority in the *Nicaragua Jurisdiction Case* found that states must give reasonable notice to withdraw from the compulsory jurisdiction of the ICJ, seventeenth-century British courts were under no obligation to give notice or reasons for declining an application for a prerogative writ, since they were exercising the king's

[96] Ibid.

[97] *Berries Case* (1637), in Henry Rolle, *Un Abridgment des Plusieurs Cases et Resolutions del Common Ley* vol. 1 (London: printed for A. Crooke et al., 1668), pp. 734–744.

prerogative. The position of an individual seeking judicial review was in this way more precarious than Nicaragua's when it instituted proceedings at the ICJ against the United States.

Over time, the fragility of the individual's standing to apply for judicial review lessened as the practice became more established and customary. By the end of the nineteenth century, Dicey was able to identify judicial review as the central institution of the rule of law, and the rule of law as one of the two fundamental principles of the UK constitution. It is impossible to know whether the practice of international adjudication will follow a similar trajectory. The lesson we can glean from the history of the prerogative writs is that legal institutions do not necessarily spring into existence fully developed. They can take considerable time to catch up to their underlying presuppositions, and progress is unlikely to be linear. Nonetheless, relatively inchoate legal institutions such as international adjudication have value notwithstanding their deficiencies because they contribute to the transparency and accountability of public authorities. They also provide stable venues for dispute resolution and the salutary development of law as a culture of justification.[98]

Much the same can be said in reply to the objection that the Security Council veto of the P5 members makes a mockery of international adjudication. At the founding of the United Nations at the San Francisco Conference in 1945, the Big Five countries presented the veto power as a non-negotiable feature of the draft Charter.[99] Other states reluctantly accepted the P5's privileged position based on the pragmatic calculation that their own sovereign equality and national security could be better preserved in practice if they entrusted international peace and security to the Security Council's "legalized hegemony."[100] The motivation of the critique of the veto is that the P5 can always use it to avoid a judicial remedy, and on its face the veto is an affront to sovereign equality given that it is held by five states rather than all. We need not deny the inequality produced by the veto, however, to recognize that the ICJ offers an independent public forum in which claims of right may be assessed and settled. The United States' use of its veto did nothing to

98 See Etienne Mureinik, 'Emerging from Emergency: Human Rights in South Africa' (1994) 92 *Mich. L. Rev.* 1977, 1986.

99 Stephen C. Schlesinger, *Act of Creation: The Founding of the United Nations* (Cambridge, MA: Westview Press, 2003), p. 223 (recounting how the Big Five defeated an Australian amendment to alter the veto).

100 Gerry Simpson, *Great Powers and Outlaw States: Unequal Sovereigns in the International Legal Order* (Cambridge: Cambridge University Press, 2004), pp. 170–171.

diminish the ICJ's authoritative judgment in favor of Nicaragua: the veto blocked enforcement of the judgment but had no effect on its authority as a judicial statement on the international wrongs committed by the United States against Nicaragua. The United States' assiduous efforts to deny the ICJ's jurisdiction – efforts expended while knowing that an adverse judgment could never be enforced – suggest that the United States itself considered the ICJ's proceedings to be significant.

The veto available to the P5 is a particular instance of a wider concern in public law, which is executive compliance with judicial decisions. When Chief Justice Marshall decided in Worcester v. Georgia that Georgia laws purporting to seize Cherokee lands violated federal treaties,[101] President Jackson is famously said to have responded, "John Marshall has made his decision: *now let him enforce it!*"[102] President Jackson and Georgia simply ignored the decision. Courts generally have no direct enforcement mechanism against their executives, and when state interests and judicial orders do not align, they ultimately may have to rely on what Dyzenhaus refers to as "the compulsion of legality."[103] The compulsion of legality arises from the obligation of states "to justify all acts of state as having a legal warrant, the authority of law."[104] This compulsion thus follows from a commitment to the normativity of law, and entails "that jurists proceed as if law's claim to authority can be vindicated."[105] Whether states comply with international judicial decisions out of rational self-interest, a sense of duty, socialization or internalization of human rights norms, or a mix of motives, it bears underscoring that they comply with roughly 65 to 75 percent of the ICJ's decisions.[106] For most states subject to the ICJ's compulsory jurisdiction, the reasons for compliance tend to outweigh the reasons for defiance.

101 31 US (6 Pet.) 515 (1832).

102 Edwin A. Miles, 'After John Marshall's Decision: *Worcester v. Georgia* and the Nullification Crisis' (1973) 39 *J. S. Hist.* 519, 519 (emphasis in original).

103 David Dyzenhaus, 'The Compulsion of Legality', in Victor V. Ramraj (ed.), *Emergencies and the Limits of Legality* (Cambridge: Cambridge University Press, 2009), pp. 33, 34.

104 Ibid.

105 Ibid., p. 39. Some scholars have explored how a formal or objective compulsion of legality in international law contributes to a "socialization" or "acculturation" of states that is driven by international human rights law, increasing the cost of noncompliance with human rights norms, and thereby creating an internalized or subjective compulsion to comply. See, e.g., Ryan Goodman and Derek Jinks, *Socializing States: Promoting Human Rights through International Law* (Oxford: Oxford University Press, 2013).

106 Karen J. Alter, 'Agents or Trustees? International Courts in Their Political Context' (2008) 14 *Eur. J. Int'l Rel.* 33, 58.

Conclusion

Pitting a hegemonic power of the North against a small and developing state of the South, the *Nicaragua Jurisdiction Case* reveals the ICJ majority's steady commitment to compulsory jurisdiction and sovereign equality. The majority used these ideals as guiding principles to read down formalities usually required to indicate consent and to dismiss the United States' last-minute attempt to withdraw its acceptance of the ICJ's jurisdiction. While the United States was eventually able to avoid the remedy ordered, it could do so only by disregarding a judicial order and breaching its duty to the Court to comply. This breach of duty could neither avoid nor tarnish the ICJ's judgments on jurisdiction and the merits. A tiny country ruled as a dynastic fiefdom by three generations of corrupt despots took the United States to court for waging an illegal campaign of violence against it and won. While the rise of reactionary nationalism in recent years may make the aspiration of international legality seem utopian, the proliferation of international courts since the end of the Cold War and the emergence of a customary duty to resolve disputes through peaceful means offer an important counterweight.

Within mandatory cooperation's framework, the duty to seek adjudication when other peaceful means have been exhausted is explained as an implication of viewing sovereign equality as the legal equality of states tasked by international law to govern and represent peoples that are equal in rights and self-determination. In practice, sovereign equality means that no state can rightfully dominate or dictate terms to another. The duty to seek adjudication adopts the form of a constraint on sovereignty and takes its substance from equity; thus, it is an equitable constraint on exercises of sovereignty. Adjudication serves as an antidote to unilateralism and as a guarantee of legal equality. While international adjudication today cannot lay claim to the kind of universal compulsory jurisdiction enjoyed by its national counterparts, it compares favorably to judicial review of administrative action in its early days, when individuals had to rely on "writs of grace." In summary, as the institutional apex of mandatory cooperation, international adjudication enables states to resolve their disputes as equals under law, and through peaceful means oriented toward justice.

13

Conclusion

The New International Law

Having endured the turmoil and brutality of World War II, many international lawyers in the 1940s were eager to reform the international legal system for the benefit of future generations. Among the most prominent voices calling for international law's reconstruction was Alejandro Álvarez, the renowned Chilean jurist, scholar, and diplomat. For decades, Álvarez had campaigned to establish a "new international law" based on principles of international solidarity and cooperation.[1] Álvarez argued that the classical, absolutist conception of state sovereignty should be retired in favor of a new approach that better accounted for states' interdependence and common interests of the international community.[2] Addressing a gathering of Latin American lawyers in 1943, Álvarez attributed the war's horrors to Europe's antiquated, individualistic legal culture. Treating states as independent agents without any obligations to the greater good was a recipe for perennial conflict and misery, he claimed. To save humanity from future calamity, international law should instead embrace and promote solidarity – a sensibility "unknown in Europe," but "strongly developed in the nations of America and its rulers."[3]

[1] Alejandro Álvarez, *La codification du droit international* (Paris: Pedone, 1912), pp. 33, 127–128; Alejandro Álvarez, 'The New International Law' (1929) 15 *Tr. Grotius Soc.* 35; see generally Martti Koskenniemi, *The Gentle Civilizer of Nations: The Rise and Fall of International Law 1870–1960* (Cambridge: Cambridge University Press, 2001), pp. 302–305.

[2] Alejandro Álvarez, *Exposé de Motifs et Déclaration des grands principes du Droit International Moderne* (Paris: Internationales, 1936), p. 23.

[3] Liliana Obregón, 'Noted for Dissent: The International Life of Alejandro Álvarez' (2006) 19 LJIL 983, 1014 (quoting Álvarez). Tom Long and Carsten-Andreas Schulz have documented Latin American states' "republican internationalism" during the late-nineteenth and early twentieth centuries, including support for the constitutionalist

Following his election to the International Court of Justice (ICJ) in 1946, Álvarez sought to make his new international law a reality. In a series of separate opinions, Álvarez asserted that the legal reformation proposed in his scholarly writings was already well underway, and he argued that international courts like the ICJ should play a leading role in promoting its progressive realization.[4] The "strictly individualistic international law" of previous generations was "being more and more superseded by what may be termed the *law of social interdependence*."[5] This new law took as its point of departure the observation that

> States are increasingly interdependent: and that consequently they do not form a simple community, as formerly, but rather a veritable international and organized society. This society in nowise abolishes the independence and the sovereignty of the States, nor their legal equality (Article 2 paragraph 1, of the Charter); but it limits this sovereignty, and the rights which flow therefrom, in view of the general interests of this society.
>
> In accordance with the Preamble to the Charter, the new organization – and consequently, the new law which flows therefrom – must have the following ends in view: to maintain peace, to consider the general interest, to safeguard fundamental human rights, to promote co-operation between States, to bring their interests into harmony, to promote economic, social, intellectual and humanitarian progress. The old individualistic law had none of these purposes; it took account only of the interests of the individual [States] considered in isolation.[6]

model of sovereign equality under international law. See Tom Long and Carsten-Andreas Sculz, 'A Turn Against Empire: Benito Juárez's Liberal Rejoinder to the French Intervention in Mexico' (2024) *Am. Pol. Sci. Rev.* 1, 8–9; Tom Long and Carsten-Andreas Schulz, 'Republican Internationalism: The Nineteenth-Century Roots of Latin American Contributions to International Order' (2022) 35 *Cambridge Rev. Int'l Affs.* 639, 641, 649–650.

4 See, e.g., Conditions of Admission of a State to Membership in the United Nations (Article 4 of the Charter), Advisory Opinion, 1948 ICJ Rep. 57, 68–69 (28 May) (sep. op. Álvarez, J.) [hereinafter Membership Case]; Competence of the General Assembly for the Admission of a State to the United Nations, Advisory Opinion, 150 ICJ Rep. 5 (3 March) (sep. op. Álvarez, J., dissenting) [hereinafter Admission Case]; Corfu Channel (UK v. Alb.), Judgment, 1949 ICJ Rep. 4, 40–48 (9 April) (sep. op. Álvarez, J.); International Status of South-West Africa, Advisory Opinion, 1950 ICJ Rep. 128, 183–185 (11 July) (sep. op. Álvarez, J., dissenting); Effect of Awards of Compensation Made by the United Nations Administrative Tribunal, Advisory Opinion, 1954 ICJ Rep. 47, 68–70 (13 July) (sep. op. Álvarez, J., dissenting).

5 Membership Case, p. 68 (emphasis in the original).

6 Admission Case, pp. 13–14; see also Corfu Channel, p. 43 (arguing that international law no longer regarded "sovereignty as an absolute and individual right of every State, as used to be done under the old law founded on the individualist régime," but instead framed sovereignty as "an *institution*, . . . which has to be exercised in accordance with the new international law" (emphasis in the original)).

This new law of social interdependence "approaches nearer to the notion of equity," Álvarez argued.[7] Its equitable character was apparent in various characteristics:

> (a) it is concerned not only with the delimitation of the rights of States, but also with harmonizing them; (b) in every question it takes into account all its various aspects; (c) it takes the general interest fully into account; (d) it emphasizes the notion of the duties of States, not only towards each other but also towards the international society; (e) it condemns the abuse of right; [and] (f) it adjusts itself to the necessities of international life and evolves together with it.[8]

These features of the new international law could not be dismissed as mere *lex ferenda*, Álvarez argued, because states had incorporated them into the UN Charter and other international agreements. Nonetheless, Álvarez recognized that the new international law had yet to fully supplant the absolutist conception of state sovereignty.[9] Until this transition was complete, the international community could expect to encounter jarring collisions between the old order and the new. These clashes were the birth pangs of a new international legal system.

Throughout the nine years he served on the ICJ, Álvarez presented himself as a lone voice in the wilderness – a solitary prophet for the new international law.[10] And true to prophetic tradition, his visionary pronouncements often encountered a skeptical, if not openly hostile, reception. None of Álvarez's contemporaries on the ICJ joined his separate opinions or endorsed his account of the emerging law of social interdependence. Legal scholars sharply disputed some of the conclusions Álvarez derived from his account, including his controversial claims that the General Assembly could override a Security Council member's veto[11] and that the ICJ could exercise compulsory jurisdiction over states without their consent.[12] With the onset of the Cold War, his appeal to global solidarity appeared increasingly quixotic amidst rising geopolitical tensions, economic rivalries, and proxy wars that divided East from West

[7] Corfu Channel, p. 40.

[8] Ibid.

[9] Ibid.

[10] See Edvard Hambro, 'Les opinions individuelles et dissidentes des membres de la Cour Internationale de Justice' (1964) 34 *Nordisk Tidsskift Int'l Ret* 181, 192 (noting Álvarez's prophetic role).

[11] Admission Case, p. 20.

[12] See, e.g., Frederick Honig, 'The International Court of Justice 1947–1950' (1951) 14 *Zeitschrift für ausländisches öffentliches Recht und Völkerrecht* 497, 539–540 (casting doubt on Álvarez's position).

and North from South. Critics argued that Álvarez had "built a house of cards" by positing "the existence of a sentiment of solidarity" which did not, in fact, prevail among states.[13] Consequently, Álvarez's argument for a new international law went largely unheeded during his tenure on the ICJ, dismissed by contemporaries as an idiosyncratic, utopian project lacking a solid foundation in state practice and *opinio juris*.

Foundations of Mandatory Cooperation

Despite the limited reception of his approach while he served on the ICJ, history has shown Álvarez to be a jurist ahead of his time, astutely anticipating trends that would transform international law over the next several decades.[14] Álvarez predicted the emergence of a new set of equitable obligations – what we call *mandatory cooperation* – which safeguard sovereign equality in our increasingly interconnected and interdependent world. As this book has shown, mandatory cooperation now applies to a wide variety of domains, requiring states to engage with one another in a spirit of mutual respect and accommodation, while resolving their disputes peacefully through negotiation or international dispute resolution. States must refrain from abusing their sovereign rights, and they must collaborate in safeguarding common concerns of humanity. True to Álvarez's original vision, these obligations promote "economic, social, intellectual and humanitarian progress" for humanity's collective benefit.[15]

The ICJ has taken a leading role in promoting mandatory cooperation. In dozens of judgments and advisory opinions, the Court has declared that states must cooperate with one another to resolve disputes involving matters where their sovereign jurisdiction is uncertain, concurrent, or jointly shared, or where their sovereign rights are interdependent. As prior chapters have shown, ICJ jurisprudence now supports applying mandatory cooperation to the apportionment of international rivers, maritime delimitation, fishery conservation, and atrocity prevention, among many other subjects. Other international courts and tribunals have followed the ICJ's lead, holding that mandatory cooperation applies to disputes concerning pollution of the marine environment and conflicting legal entitlements under international trade agreements.

[13] William Samore, 'The New International Law of Alejandro Alvarez' (1958) 52 AJIL 41, 54.

[14] An excellent collection of essays on Álvarez's contributions to international legal theory was published in 2006 in Volume 19 of the *Leiden Journal of International Law*.

[15] Admission Case, pp. 13–14.

Meanwhile, national authorities have enshrined requirements to cooperate in dozens of landmark agreements, including the Antarctic Treaty, the UN Convention on the Law of the Sea, the Genocide Convention, the Outer Space Treaty, and the International Covenant on Economic, Social, and Cultural Rights. These treaties reflect the international community's growing recognition that cooperation is necessary to respect the principle of sovereign equality and fulfill states' responsibilities to safeguard common concerns of humanity. Thus, the international community has pivoted slowly but surely to codify by treaty the new international law Álvarez envisioned nearly a century ago.

Significantly, mandatory cooperation now rests on a more solid legal basis than Álvarez's early sociological account. Rather than assume national authorities share Álvarez's commitment to global solidarity, international courts and tribunals today base mandatory cooperation on the juridical principle of sovereign equality. Under this approach, cooperation is a *legal* requirement that applies to all states irrespective of whether they are motivated by concerns for cosmopolitan justice. Indeed, mandatory cooperation is necessary to safeguard states' sovereign equality precisely because without it stronger states could abuse their rights with impunity by imposing their will on weaker states. Ironically, mandatory cooperation has flourished over the past seventy years precisely because international courts and tribunals have embraced the legal-formalist approach to international law that Álvarez himself questioned.[16]

Mandatory cooperation likely would not have emerged when it did without the sustained intellectual leadership and advocacy of international lawyers like Álvarez from the Global South. Throughout the nineteenth century and into the early twentieth century, Latin American delegates to international conferences, such as Carlos Calvo of Argentina, Ruy Barbosa of Brazil, and José Tible Machado of Guatemala, laid the groundwork for mandatory cooperation by lobbying great powers of the Global North to recognize and respect the principle of sovereign equality.[17] During and after World War II, anticolonial nationalists in Africa, Asia, and Latin America

[16] See Koskenniemi, *Gentle Civilizer*, pp. 303–304 (discussing Álvarez's rejection of legal formalism in favor of social and political realism).

[17] See Robert A. Klein, *Sovereign Equality Among States: The History of an Idea* (Toronto: University of Toronto Press, 1974), pp. 52–62; Martha Finnemore and Michelle Jurkovich, 'Getting a Seat at the Table: The Origins of Universal Participation and Modern Multilateral Conferences' (2014) 20 *Glob. Governance* 361; Long and Schulz, 'Republican

campaigned successfully for the international community to accept sovereign equality and the right to self-determination as twin pillars of a new international legal order.[18]

These hard-won victories transformed the international legal system. The right to self-determination called for dismantling colonial rule, liberating formerly colonized peoples to pursue self-government within their own independent states. Sovereign equality, in turn, aimed to protect weaker and newly independent states from great power domination.[19] For anticolonial nationalists, sovereign equality's primary contribution was to affirm that newly independent states were entitled to freedom from foreign intervention.[20] But the principle also had broader applications, which came to light only gradually through the accumulated jurisprudence of international courts and tribunals. Taking sovereign equality seriously meant that great powers could no longer act unilaterally in domains where their sovereign rights were entwined with the rights of other states. Instead, the principle of sovereign equality mandated that great powers would have to cooperate with their less powerful neighbors to resolve many disputes through negotiation or third-party dispute resolution based on equitable principles. Like the right to self-determination, sovereign equality promoted global liberty – especially, but not exclusively, for formerly colonized peoples – by dismantling formal hierarchy and unequal membership in favor of a more egalitarian international legal order.[21] Without decades of concerted advocacy by international lawyers and diplomats from the Global South, it is doubtful whether this transformational realignment of the international legal system would have come about.

Internationalism', pp. 649–650; Carsten-Andreas Schulz, 'Accidental Activists: Latin American Status-Seeking at the Hague' (2017) 61 *Int'l Stud. Q.* 612.

[18] UN Charter arts. 1(2) and 2(1); Declaration on Principles of International Law concerning Friendly Relations and Cooperation among States in accordance with the Charter of the United Nations, GA Res. 2625, 25 UN GAOR Supp. No. 28, 121, UN Doc. A/8028 (1970).

[19] See Adom Getachew, *Worldmaking After Empire* (Princeton: Princeton University Press, 2019), p. 98 (observing that anticolonial nationalists embraced the principle of sovereign equality to "ensur[e] that the powerful states of the world would not dominate weaker and smaller members of international society.").

[20] See Declaration on the Granting of Independence to Colonial Countries and Peoples ¶ 7, GA Res. 1514(XV), UN Doc A/4684 (14 December 1960).

[21] Getachew, *Worldmaking After Empire*, p. 98.

Mandatory Cooperation's Unfinished Business

This does not mean that international law's reformation is complete. Far from it: mandatory cooperation remains a work in progress. In some domains, mandatory cooperation has achieved a high degree of international recognition through judicial and arbitral judgments and extensive codification in multilateral treaties, whereas in others it is only beginning to enter international legal discourse. An important objective of this book has been to trace and illuminate mandatory cooperation's development by specifying its legal basis while pointing to areas where the international community's commitment to sovereign equality has yet to bear fruit as mandatory cooperation.

The case studies in this book suggest that mandatory cooperation tends to develop in several stages:

(1) A state asks an international court or arbitral tribunal to resolve an international dispute concerning states' uncertain, concurrent, or jointly shared jurisdiction or conflicting sovereign rights.
(2) The international court or tribunal delivers a judgment affirming that the states concerned must harmonize their equal sovereignties by pursuing a negotiated solution in accordance with equitable principles.
(3) Taking cues from the international judgment, states incorporate mandatory cooperation into treaties for the relevant field.[22]
(4) States establish institutional frameworks, develop soft law instruments, and adopt domestic laws and policies to facilitate international cooperation in accordance with their obligations under international law.
(5) States cooperate to resolve disputes in the relevant field through consultation, information-sharing, negotiation, and third-party dispute resolution.

The further an international legal regime progresses along this path, the more mandatory cooperation becomes entrenched in positive law and state practice. As international judicial decisions, arbitral judgments, and treaties elucidate mandatory cooperation's requirements, the law's

[22] States sometimes accept legal obligations to cooperate by treaty without advance prompting from an international court or tribunal. However, when states agree to cooperate in this fashion, it remains open to debate whether they have done so because they recognize that international law already requires their cooperation. A judgment from an international court or tribunal affirming mandatory cooperation removes this ambiguity.

applications within a particular field become more legible to national authorities. Establishing institutional frameworks, soft law instruments, and domestic laws and policies facilitates state compliance, allowing mandatory cooperation to cross the threshold from formal law into the realm of practical implementation. Finally, the ongoing practice of consultation, information-sharing, negotiation, and third-party dispute resolution reconciles the legally equal sovereignties of stronger and weaker states.

Since international dispute resolution often serves as a catalyst for mandatory cooperation, it should come as no surprise that mandatory cooperation's requirements are most fully developed in fields of international law that frequently generate international arbitration and adjudication, such as the regimes governing rivers and oceans. In contrast, mandatory cooperation's development tends to lag in areas outside the jurisdiction of international courts and tribunals. Until states expand access to international dispute resolution, there will be no equivalent of the *Lake Lanoux Arbitration* or the *North Sea Continental Shelf Case* to clarify how mandatory cooperation applies to issues such as transnational cyberattacks or refugee burden-sharing. This dynamic has delayed mandatory cooperation's development in a wide variety of areas where sovereign equality calls for its immediate application.

Mandatory cooperation most clearly requires development in contexts involving threats of transboundary harm. International courts and tribunals have recognized that mandatory cooperation governs cross-border environmental harm,[23] and states have committed by treaty to cooperate with one another in preventing and suppressing transnational piracy and terrorist attacks.[24] However, these measures capture only a small fraction of transboundary harms. Infectious diseases, malware attacks, and financial contagion do not respect national borders. Atmospheric pollution in one state contributes to rising sea levels, deadly droughts, and catastrophic storms on the opposite side of the globe. Regulatory failures in a single national jurisdiction can endanger populations, economies, and ecosystems worldwide, eroding states' independence. Mandatory cooperation calls on states to work together to prevent, suppress, and

[23] See, e.g., Case Concerning Land Reclamation by Singapore in and Around the Straits of Johor (Malay./Sing.) (Provisional Measures), 8 October 2003, ITLOS_F3–F4_6–64, p. 10, paras. 76–78, 92; Certain Activities Carried Out by Nicaragua in the Border Area (Costa Rica v. Nicar.), 2015 ICJ Rep. 665, 706, para. 104 (16 December).

[24] See above Chapters 5–7.

mitigate these and other transboundary harms – even in contexts where they have not specifically consented to these requirements by treaty.[25]

By clarifying when, why, and how mandatory cooperation applies to international relations, the legal framework outlined in this book can assist national authorities to identify settings where international cooperation is mandatory without having to await direct guidance from international courts and tribunals. The criteria are reasonably straightforward: whenever interstate disputes involve matters that are subject to uncertain, concurrent, or jointly shared jurisdiction or conflicting sovereign rights, mandatory cooperation applies. States must consult with one another, share relevant information, and pursue either a negotiated solution or international dispute resolution in accordance with equitable principles. Conversely, mandatory cooperation does not apply when international law supplies a controlling rule of decision or assigns decision-making authority exclusively to one side.[26] All interstate disputes can be divided into one of these categories; either a dispute concerns a setting where states' rights are settled, independently controlling, and mutually exclusive (making mandatory cooperation inapplicable) or their rights are uncertain or interdependent (activating mandatory cooperation's equitable requirements).

Challenges Ahead

Whether mandatory cooperation can withstand the current antiglobalist backlash remains uncertain. Within the past decade, nationalist political parties in Europe, Latin America, and the United States have challenged the constitutional vision of international legal order enshrined in the UN Charter, joining authoritarian states that seek to establish an international regime akin to the pre–World War II Old World Order. Great powers like China, Russia, and the United States have chafed against the constraints of sovereign equality and mandatory cooperation, sometimes pursuing imperialist agendas at odds with other states' rights under international law. Mandatory cooperation places faith in states' sociability and their capacity to work together to address common concerns even when this may require compromises

[25] See above Chapters 9 and 11.

[26] For example, states are entitled under international law to veto foreign annexations of their territory. See Ingrid Brunk and Monica Hakimi, 'The Prohibition of Annexations and the Foundations of Modern International Law' (2024) 118 AJIL 417.

that impact their immediate self-interest.[27] Under the sway of nationalist political agendas, however, some states are resisting the constitutional model of sovereign equality by continuing to invoke the old absolutist model. Other states recognize international law's call for cooperation yet shirk their commitments. As a result, the emerging international law of mandatory cooperation remains vulnerable to national backsliding despite its firm foundation in international treaties, customary international law, and judicial decisions.

The international community's efforts to combat the COVID-19 pandemic illustrate some of the recurring challenges for mandatory cooperation. As early as 1931, Álvarez argued that international law required states to cooperate with one another to prevent the spread of infectious diseases for humanity's collective benefit.[28] After World War II, the international community established the World Health Organization (WHO) to coordinate its collective response to public health emergencies.[29] The WHO later embraced mandatory cooperation by issuing the International Health Regulations (Regulations), which require states to notify, consult, share information, and assist one another in addressing emerging public health emergencies, such as deadly epidemics.[30] However, these legal obligations failed to prevent COVID-19 from infecting over 150 million people and claiming over three million lives worldwide between 2020 and 2023.[31]

In 2023, an independent review panel commissioned by the WHO's Director-General delivered a landmark report evaluating the international community's response to the COVID-19 crisis.[32] The panel concluded that the pandemic's catastrophic impact on human health and the global economy were exacerbated by cooperation failures between the WHO and national authorities. The panel called for systemic

27 Scholars often associate this vision of state sociability with Hugo Grotius. See, e.g., Hedley Bull, 'The Importance of Grotius in the Study of International Relations', in Hedley Bull et al. (eds.), *Hugo Grotius in International Relations* (Oxford: Oxford University Press, 1992), pp. 65, 93; Hersch Lauterpacht, 'The Grotian Tradition in International Law' (1946) 23 BYBIL 1, 24–30.

28 Alejandro Álvarez, *Exposé des motifs et déclaration des grands principes du droit international moderne* (Washington, D.C.: Institut américain du droit international, 1931).

29 'History of the WHO', World Health Organization, www.who.int/about/history.

30 International Health Regulations, 3rd ed. (2005), arts. 6–8, 44, World Health Org. The Regulations govern 196 states parties. Ibid. p. 59.

31 The Independent Panel for Pandemic Preparation and Response, *Covid-19: Make It the Last Pandemic* (2023), p. 4 [hereinafter Independent Panel Report].

32 Ibid. p. 8.

change at the international level to prevent future pandemics. Specifically, the panel recommended that the international community develop a robust surveillance and global alert system for infectious diseases, establish a Global Health Threats Council to facilitate intergovernmental coordination, create an international platform for vaccine development and distribution, and codify these and other commitments in a new framework convention for pandemic response.[33] To prevent the next pandemic, states would have to commit to "a change of paradigm to a resilient, equitable and inclusive system for pandemic preparedness" based on robust regulatory cooperation.[34]

While the independent review panel was conducting its study, the WHO convened an intergovernmental negotiating body (INB) to prepare a framework treaty on pandemic preparedness and response.[35] The participants finalized a new Pandemic Agreement in May 2025.[36] The Pandemic Agreement recognizes that averting the next pandemic will require "the widest possible international and regional collaboration, cooperation and solidarity with all people and countries . . . in order to ensure an effective, coordinated, appropriate, comprehensive and equitable international response."[37] While the Pandemic Agreement affirms "the principle of the sovereignty of States in addressing public health matters,"[38] it also commits states to cooperate with one another "to sustainably strengthen the pandemic prevention, preparedness and response capacities of all Parties, particularly developing country Parties," through sharing research, facilitating technology transfer and access to vaccines, sharing scientific and legal expertise, financial assistance, and other means.[39]

A skeptic might question whether the new Pandemic Agreement will deliver better results than the WHO's Regulations. Without an enforcement mechanism to ensure that states notify, consult, and coordinate their responses to infectious diseases, what is to prevent states from

[33] Ibid. pp. 45–59.

[34] Ibid. p. 58.

[35] Press Release, *Governments Progress on Negotiations for a Pandemic Agreement to Boost Global Preparedness for Future Emergencies*, World Health Organization, 20 September 2024.

[36] *Pandemic Prevention, Preparedness and Response Agreement*, World Health Organization, 27 June 2025.

[37] WHO Pandemic Agreement, WHA78.1, 20 May 2025, Annx., pmbl., https://apps.who.int/gb/ebwha/pdf_files/WHA78/A78_R1-en.pdf.

[38] Ibid.

[39] Ibid. arts. 9–12, 17.

shirking their obligations to cooperate? Is it reasonable to expect affluent states to meet their commitments to transfer proprietary technology and provide financial assistance to less affluent states? Will less affluent states prioritize pandemic preparation and response over other national concerns, such as primary health care, education, and economic development? On a skeptical view, the Pandemic Agreement is vulnerable to the same critique as Álvarez's solidarity-driven account of the new international law: to the extent that its success depends upon states prioritizing community interests over their national self-interest, the Pandemic Agreement might be thought to rest on a utopian house of cards.

One weakness of this critique is that it assumes cooperating for pandemic response runs counter to states' rational self-interest. Not all international cooperation problems are zero-sum games. Global pandemic response is better understood as what game theorists call a "stag-hunt game."[40] Because participants in a stag-hunt game are each better off participating if others participate, they lack incentives to defect so long as others remain within the game. If there is one lesson that the COVID-19 pandemic has driven home, it is that every state has a commanding political, economic, and humanitarian interest in supporting the global pandemic response game. No one wants another deadly epidemic to spiral out of control. Even the most tough-minded political realist should appreciate that international cooperation to prevent and mitigate global pandemics serves every state's rational self-interest. It is reasonable to expect, therefore, that states can be persuaded to cooperate in fighting deadly epidemics if other states bear their fair share of the costs. Hence, the primary obstacle to achieving a more effective global regime for pandemic response is not convincing states that cooperation is worthwhile in the abstract but instead persuading them that specific international institutions, such as the WHO, are fit for service and equitably apportion the costs of cooperation among participating states.[41]

[40] Buğra Sarı, 'Problem of Cooperation in a Stag Hunt Game: Great Power Politics in the Covid-19 Pandemic', in Erman Akıllı and Burak Gunes (eds.), *World Politics in the Age of Uncertainty: The Covid-19 Pandemic*, Vol. 1 (London: Palgrave Macmillan, 2023), p. 33.

[41] As this book goes to press, US President Donald Trump has announced that the United States will withdraw from the WHO based on concerns about the organization's perceived ineffectiveness and the United States' high financial burden relative to China and other states. Exec. Order, 'Withdrawing the United States from the World Health Organization', The White House, 20 January 2025.

Some international disputes, however, are zero-sum games. For example, dwindling fresh water at the Rio Grande means that the more water Mexico or the United States draws away for its use, the less is available to the other. Similarly, in both the *North Pacific Fur Seals Case* and the Icelandic Cod Wars, states competed to harvest scarce resources, risking a tragedy of the commons. Each of the parties to these disputes would have preferred to claim exclusive jurisdiction, but international law at the time conferred concurrent rights over the relevant resources. Had the disputes involved one-off interactions, the logic of a one-shot prisoner's dilemma might have driven the states to defect from international cooperation. But international disputes are seldom one-shot interactions; they typically arise within ongoing, multifaceted relationships between states that are, in many respects, mutually interdependent. Accordingly, states often are best served by embracing mandatory cooperation for conservation and sustainable utilization. Through sustained engagement, states may cultivate the mutual trust necessary to facilitate conservation and sustainable utilization over the long haul.

Mandatory cooperation is less likely to thrive when defections are hard to detect and violations do not invite reciprocity or retaliation. Transnational cybercrime illustrates this challenge. As discussed in Chapter 5, international law obligates states to exercise due diligence to prevent and suppress harmful cyberattacks emanating from their territories. However, it can be difficult to pinpoint where such attacks originate, and even when this can be discerned, it is not always clear whether the originating state has exercised due diligence to prevent or suppress the harm. If the originating state benefits from such attacks, and if it does not expect to be the target of similar or more damaging attacks, it may have weak incentives to cooperate with transnational law enforcement.

Similar dynamics jeopardize international cooperation to address climate change. All states have an interest in avoiding the catastrophic environmental harm associated with climate change. However, given the high costs associated with transitioning away from a carbon-based economy, some states may prefer to freeride on other states' efforts to mitigate climate change. There is a serious risk, therefore, that states might pledge to reduce their carbon emissions to spur action from other states without keeping their own commitments.

Mandatory cooperation addresses these misaligned incentives. With the recent advisory opinions on climate change from the ICJ, the International Tribunal for the Law of the Sea, and the Inter-American

Court of Human Rights, there is now international jurisprudence affirming that states must contribute to the international campaign against climate change – even if they would prefer to freeride on others' efforts.[42] By affirming that international law *requires* cooperation, these advisory opinions raise the reputational costs of noncompliance. In theory, the advisory opinions' conclusions could also lay the groundwork for international sanctions or countermeasures against nonconforming states.[43] Absent robust information exchange and independent monitoring, however, defections from international cooperation may be difficult to identify and deter. The more defections occur and become normalized, the harder it will be to persuade conforming states to continue to make sacrifices for the greater good. For hard problems like climate change, mandatory cooperation's success or failure ultimately may depend on states accepting Álvarez's invitation to embrace a "spirit of solidarity" that transcends national self-interest.[44]

Another challenge to mandatory cooperation involves great powers imposing their will on less powerful states. As discussed in Chapter 1, when Russia invaded Ukraine in 2022, Vladimir Putin opportunistically invoked the absolutist model of sovereignty.[45] But Russia is hardly the only powerful state to infringe the principle of sovereign equality. The United States violated the principle when it conducted clandestine operations in Nicaragua and then refused to cooperate in related proceedings before the ICJ.[46] The United Kingdom disregarded Mauritius's equal sovereignty when it unilaterally established a marine protected area around the Chagos Archipelago in 2010.[47] And China continues to undermine its neighbors' sovereignty by uni-

[42] See Chapter 7.

[43] See Miles Jackson and Federica I. Paddeu, 'The Countermeasures of Others: When Can States Collaborate in the Taking of Countermeasures?' (2024) 118 AJIL 231 (discussing international collaboration in the taking of countermeasures, including the breach of *erga omnes* obligations).

[44] Alejandro Alvarez, *International Law and Related Subjects from the Point of View of the American Continent: A Report on Lectures Delivered in the Universities of the United States, 1916–1918, Under the Auspices of the Carnegie Endowment for International Peace, Including a Comparative Study of the Universities of Latin America and the United States* (Washington: Carnegie Institute for International Peace, 1992), p. 79.

[45] See Chapter 1.

[46] See Chapter 12.

[47] Chagos Marine Protected Area Arbitration (Mauritius/UK), Case No. 2011-03, Award, paras. 152, 534–536 (Perm. Ct. Arb. 2015).

laterally claiming sovereignty over the entire South China Sea in violation of its neighbors' rights to participate as equal partners in maritime delimitation.[48]

For great powers like China, Russia, the United Kingdom, and the United States, complying with mandatory cooperation means giving up some of their capacity to direct international affairs unilaterally. Hegemons do not cede such power easily. Even when they have accepted legal obligations to cooperate, they may at times backslide into unilateralism. When countries elevate leaders who romanticize the Old World Order in which might made right, international cooperation inevitably suffers.[49] For these reasons, it has taken the better part of a century for mandatory cooperation to rival and in some cases displace state unilateralism as the governing regime for settings where states' rights under international law are mutually intertwined.

The Chinese Vision

Given these dynamics, some may think it is naive to believe that great powers could accept mandatory cooperation as a general principle of international law. Yet, recent signals from Chinese President Xi Jinping offer a basis for tentative optimism. Since the 1950s, China has viewed international law through the prism of the late-Premier Zhou Enlai's "Five Principles of Peaceful Co-existence": mutual respect for territorial integrity and sovereignty, mutual nonaggression, mutual noninterference in internal affairs, equality and mutual benefit, and peaceful coexistence.[50] Within the past several years, however, Xi has updated the Five Principles by offering a fresh "Vision of Building a Community with a Shared Future for Mankind,"[51] presenting the principle of sovereign equality and the Chinese ideals of "harmony within diversity" and

[48] See Evan J. Criddle and Evan Fox-Decent, 'Mandatory Multilateralism' (2019) 113 AJIL 272, 314–317.

[49] See, e.g., President Donald Trump, 'The Inaugural Address', White House, 20 January 2025.

[50] China's Initiation of the Five Principles of Peaceful Co-existence, Ministry of Foreign Affairs, The People's Republic of China, www.mfa.gov.cn/eng/zy/wjls/3604_665547/202405/t20240531_11367542.html.

[51] *Carrying Forward the Five Principles of Peaceful Coexistence and Jointly Building a Community with a Shared Future for Mankind*, Address by H.E. Xi Jinping President of the People's Republic of China at the Conference Marking the 70th Anniversary of the Five Principles of Peaceful Coexistence, 28 June 2024 [hereinafter *Carrying Forward*].

"solidarity toward common progress" as foundational cornerstones for international order.[52]

In a June 2024 speech commemorating the seventieth anniversary of the Five Principles, Xi characterized the Vision as a principled framework for reconciling sovereign equality with the increasingly interdependent nature of sovereign rights and authority. According to Xi, the Five Principles acknowledge "the importance of mutuality and equality in handling state-to-state relations, thus highlighting the essence of international rule of law, i.e. the intercorrelation of rights, obligations and responsibilities of all countries."[53] Accordingly, Xi presented international cooperation as the key to harmonizing states' equal sovereignty in settings where states lack exclusive sovereign rights or authority over matters of international concern:

> The Vision captures the reality that all countries have a shared future and intertwined interests, and sets a new model of equality and coexistence for international relations . . .
>
> The Vision responds to the world's prevailing trend of peace, development, cooperation and win-win, and opens up new prospects for peace and progress.[54]

Although Xi did not use the term "mandatory cooperation," his proposed approach aligns closely with the conception of international law defended throughout this book. As Xi acknowledged, the principle of sovereign equality prohibits states from abusing their rights by imposing their will on one another. Instead, states must consult and negotiate in good faith with an eye to finding mutually acceptable solutions to their common concerns. Xi also recognized that states must cooperate to safeguard international peace through multilateral norms and institutions, not the unilateral use of force. In each of these respects, Xi's call for "a new type of international relations" founded on peaceful cooperation echoes what mandatory cooperation already requires of states.[55]

There is room, of course, to question the depth of China's commitment to mandatory cooperation, particularly given its controversial campaign to establish de facto sovereignty over the South China Sea. A cynic might read the Vision as part of a broader national strategy to

[52] *A Global Community of Shared Future: China's Proposals and Actions*, The State Council Information Office of the People's Republic of China, The Third Belt and Road Forum for International Cooperation, September 2023.

[53] *Carrying Forward.*

[54] Ibid.

[55] Ibid.

steer the international community toward a new generation of Chinese-sponsored international frameworks – including the Global Security Initiative, Global Development Initiative, Global Civilization Initiative, and Belt and Road Initiative – which would augment China's global influence and normalize autocratic government.[56] International partnerships that purport to be "win-win," such as China's various agreements to construct hydroelectric dams along the Mekong River, may operate in practice as tools for exploitation and domination, forging chains of economic dependency and imposing serious environmental harm.[57]

Be this as it may, the fact remains that China's Vision offers a principled restatement of both the constitutional model of sovereign equality and the associated requirements of mandatory cooperation. Contrary to conventional wisdom, China no longer envisions a minimalist international legal order focused solely on facilitating peaceful coexistence but instead supports a "new model" that accepts sovereign equality as a constitutional principle of international law and pursues intensifying cooperation to harmonize states' "intertwined interests."[58] With the public-facing rhetoric of a great power like China now emphasizing international cooperation as the path to realizing sovereign equality, there is hope that other great powers may eventually recognize and embrace mandatory cooperation as a general principle of international law.

How Good Neighbors Cooperate

In Robert Frost's classic poem, *Mending Wall*, the narrator presses his neighbor to explain why the two must meet each spring to repair breaches in a stone wall that divides their properties. The neighbor replies simply, "Good fences make good neighbors."[59] This principle also applies to international relations: by dividing Earth's territory among states and prohibiting foreign intervention, international law establishes jurisdictional boundaries that enable states to coexist as equal sovereigns.

But good fences are not enough to make good neighbors. In the interconnected world of the twenty-first century, states do not resemble reclusive landowners on independent estates. Rather, as Eyal Benvenisti has observed, state sovereignty today is "more analogous to owning

[56] See Michael Schuman, Jonathan Fulton and Tuvia Gering, 'How Beijing's Newest Global Initiatives Seek to Remake the World Order', Atlantic Council, 23 June 2023.

[57] See Chapter 2.

[58] *Carrying Forward*.

[59] Robert Frost, 'Mending Wall'.

a small apartment in one densely packed high-rise that is home to two hundred separate families."[60] The fate of each state is inextricably intertwined with every other state. One state's actions can easily impact another's rights, as when a state pollutes a transboundary river or emits ozone or methane into the atmosphere. States also interact with one another in common spaces outside the jurisdiction of any single state, such as the high seas and Antarctica. They depend upon each other to accommodate their exercise of sovereign rights, as when landlocked states seek access to blue water. And they rely upon one another to carry out their joint-stewardship responsibilities, including protecting international human rights, preserving world heritage sites, and conserving global biodiversity. "The sense of interdependency is heightened when we recognize the absence of any alternative to this shared home, of any exit from this global high-rise," Benvenisti remarks. Add to the mix existential threats like climate change and nuclear proliferation, and it becomes clear that the "privilege of bygone days of opting out, of retreating into splendid isolation, of adopting mercantilist policies or erecting iron curtains is no longer realistically available."[61] Accordingly, being a good neighbor in the twenty-first century requires far more than merely refraining from violating other states' territorial integrity and political independence; it demands that states cooperate with one another for their own and humanity's collective benefit.

Mandatory cooperation is how international law responds to these pressing concerns. As this book has shown, it is only by cooperating in accordance with equitable principles that states can reconcile their equal sovereignties in settings where their sovereign rights are interdependent. International cooperation is necessary, therefore, to respect the principle of sovereign equality under international law. But mandatory cooperation's value extends beyond legal-formalist concerns about sovereignty and the rule of law. As international lawyers and jurists from the Global South have long recognized, the principle of sovereign equality serves an important practical function in safeguarding weaker states from domination by great powers. Moreover, it is only through robust multilateral cooperation that states can respond effectively to the great existential threats of our time, such as global pandemics, nuclear proliferation, and climate change. Perhaps more than at any previous era in history,

[60] Eyal Benvenisti, 'Sovereigns as Trustees of Humanity: On the Accountability of States to Foreign Stakeholders' (2013) 107 AJIL 295, 295.
[61] Ibid.

"[h]umanity's welfare – and, indeed, humanity's very future – depend on solidarity and working together as a global family to achieve common goals."[62] While presently a patchwork quilt and a work in progress, mandatory cooperation makes possible the idea of humanity as a mutually supporting global family.

[62] UN Secretary-General António Guterres, *Our Common Agenda: Report of the Secretary General* (New York: United Nations, 2021), p. 3, available at https://www.un.org/en/content/common-agenda-report/assets/pdf/Common_Agenda_Report_English.pdf.

INDEX

Printed by Integrated Books International,
United States of America